BANK ROBBERY
FOR BEGINNERS

BANK ROBBERY
FOR BEGINNERS
A story of criminal stupidity and its VERY SERIOUS CONSEQUENCES

ANTHONY PRINCE

MACMILLAN
Pan Macmillan Australia

First published 2010 in Macmillan by Pan Macmillan Australia Pty Limited
1 Market Street, Sydney

National Library of Australia
Cataloguing-in-Publication data:

Bank robbery for beginners: a story of criminal
stupidity and its very serious consequences /
Anthony Prince.

ISBN: 9781405040471 (pbk.)

Bank robberies – United States.
Criminals – Australia.
Sentences (Criminal procedure) – United States.

Other Authors/Contributors:
Marx, Jack.

364.1552092

Typeset in Granjon 13.5/18.5 pt by Midland Typesetters, Australia
Printed in Australia by McPherson's Printing Group

Papers used by Pan Macmillan Australia Pty Ltd are natural, recyclable
products made from wood grown in sustainable forests. The
manufacturing processes conform to the environmental regulations of
the country of origin.

For Mum and Dad,
unconditional love always

ACKNOWLEDGEMENTS

The warmest of thank yous to my friend Jack Marx. Your passion helped bring this story to life and your patience ensured that I was able to get my message across.

And to the many people who loved and supported me through my darkest time – I know who you are, there are too many to name – my eternal thanks.

PROLOGUE

You can learn a lot about yourself the first time you point a gun at somebody's face. In that moment, I learned a few things about who I was and what I was going to be.

For starters, I learned that I was in deep shit and, this time, nobody was going to be able to bail me out. In that instant, I instinctively knew I was going to jail, probably for a long time, and that there was nothing I or anyone else could do about that.

The irritating thing is that, at the very same time, I learned that I wasn't such a bad dude after all. It took me pulling a gun on someone to learn that I actually had a heart. The look on the face of my victim was something I couldn't bear – that look of innocence draining to something like horror, and all because of me. As I looked into that face, I knew there was no way I was ever going to do anything like this again, that I was never going to be a career criminal, one of those bad motherfuckers from the movies who can pull a gun on someone and think nothing of it.

I was never going to be someone like Dave, for example, who is one of those people. Dave is hard, a career criminal and a seasoned street fighter. He used to deal marijuana, from plants that he grew hydroponically in sheds built especially for that purpose. One day some crackhead came to him and asked for something harder – some cocaine or heroin. Dave said he didn't deal in those kinds of drugs, only pot. The crackhead persisted – 'C'mon, man, just some coke or some meth . . .' – but Dave told him to get lost. When the crackhead didn't move, Dave gave him a push to help him on his way, and as he did Dave saw a wire fall out from underneath the crackhead's jacket. He was taping him for the Feds, setting him up. So Dave did what Dave does: dragged the crackhead inside his house and beat him half to death. He then picked him up and put him inside a 44-gallon drum, nailed a lid on it, drilled a hole in the bottom, stuck an oxyacetylene torch through the hole, turned it on and went for a beer. By the time he got back, the crackhead was nothing but a pile of ash in the bottom of a barrel.

I had to share a cell with Dave. That's the sort of person the world believed I was, thanks to that one day in the American winter of 2005, when I pointed a gun at some-body's face. I am now known to the world as Anthony Prince, bank robber, ex-jailbird. That wouldn't be so bad – it would even get me kudos in some places – but for the fact that I'm known as one of the stupidest bank robbers in history. 'Dumb and Dumber', the newspapers dubbed me and my partner in crime, Luke Carroll, though they never said which one was which. I don't think it really matters. On that day, we were each as dumb as the other.

This is the story of that stupid day, what happened there and all the things that happened next. I've thought a lot about whether I should be telling it – there are so many people with so many stories to tell that are worthier than mine, I know – but I've decided any story is worth telling as long as you tell the truth. You just never know what good might come from it.

When Luke and I were in America, there was this older guy who worked with us, a real character, but a bit of a lost cause. He lived alone and occasionally we'd go over to his house for a smoke with him. He had this huge TV and a recliner chair pushed up right against the wide screen. He'd just sit there with his little tobacco spittoon, his ashtray, a whole smoking station pushed against the world's largest TV. We'd make jokes with him about how he badly needed to clean up his act. Then, shortly after we'd gone to prison, he visited us – made a trip of several hours just to see us – and he said to us: 'Man, you guys getting arrested has just snapped me out of my stupor.' Apparently, he'd given up smoking, gone back to the gym, even gone and bought a proper lounge suite. It was weird – our stupidity and disaster had somehow transformed him into a new man. And it was permanent – he wrote to us often, and visited us a few times.

A great guy, who was somehow made even greater by some bizarre connection he'd drawn between his own life and our predicament.

So you really never know what the future will hold when you decide to do something completely stupid.

And writing this book is far from the most stupid thing I've ever done, as you will see.

Anthony Prince, 2010

1

I was never a bad kid, never aggressive or antisocial. I never bullied other children or tortured small animals. I was respectful towards people with disabilities and if I made jokes about them it was strictly in private. I responded well to authority, if I thought the authority was worthy of respect. I obeyed the rules of board games and ball games and never pretended to know something I didn't. I never punched anyone or vandalised anyone's stuff, and the few times I did make fun of some other kid I always felt bad about it later, even if I didn't admit it to anyone.

My biggest problem as a kid, I think, was that I didn't really understand what 'risk' was all about. I was always stacking it on my bike because I just wasn't afraid of what might happen – either that or the thrill of the moment always triumphed over the thought of what my actions might result in later. So I was forever breaking bones, dislocating shoulders, spilling blood and making a dick of myself, often in pursuit of showing off to someone or other. It's a personality flaw that would trip me up big-time when I grew older.

I was born on 19 June 1985 in Henderson, New Zealand, the only boy and the youngest of three children to Peter and Jennifer Prince. When I was a few days old, the family moved to Newcastle in New South Wales and then, when I was four, we moved to Rosebank, near Byron Bay. This was where I really grew up, on a 20-hectare rainforest property half an hour from the coast. Our nearest neighbour was over a kilometre away. We were, and are, a very close family.

This is important because stories like the one you're about to read aren't supposed to happen to good families. But they do. People in jail don't always come from broken homes on the wrong side of the tracks. Bad things happen to good people, and good people can do very bad things. I've learned that much.

My father is in finance and my mother is a nurse. They were and are logical and affectionate parents. Their idea of discipline is to talk things through, educate by example, and they encouraged me to always be straight up and talk about things. I was never punished as such – never belted or locked up or had my things thrown in the garbage. My mum and dad just gave me the facts, let me know how they felt about decisions I was making and hoped that I'd work out for myself what was right.

From the day I started school, I found I couldn't sit still and concentrate for any decent length of time. I was restless, hyperactive, disruptive in class and I lacked what teachers called 'focus', which is their way of saying I was bored shitless. My mind was always drifting out the window, wandering over hill and dale, imagining things that had nothing to do with what was going on in the classroom. I was only seven when I was diagnosed as having Attention Deficit Disorder, and for a brief while I even took Ritalin, a drug that dopes out hyper kids. But when Mum and Dad saw what it did to me, which was to basically turn me into a well-behaved zombie, they decided they liked the old ADD Anthony better, and I stopped taking the medication. I credit this with my ability to stay off drugs, if I have to.

The obvious outlet for my excess energy was to play sport, where hyperactive, risk-taking show-offs are always welcome. Dad had been an avid Rugby Union player in his day, and encouraged me to play, too. So I did well at that for a while, playing at representative level for my school and district. But, when I was about sixteen, I sustained some pretty severe knee injuries that were devastating to a teenage sporting career.

With education and sport taking a back seat, the only things left were surfing, girls and drugs. Fortunately, by this point, I lived in Byron Bay.

I suppose it's around this time that observers might have been tempted to say Anthony Prince was straying from the straight and narrow. I got drunk for the first time at fifteen – my sister had a sneaky house party when Mum and Dad were away – and I began smoking weed and hanging out with 'the wrong crowd'. In other words, I was a pretty ordinary teenager. My school grades suffered a bit, but I graduated, got my Higher School Certificate from Trinity Catholic College in Lismore in 2003, and even got the principal to write that I was 'well-liked', 'trustworthy', 'honest' and 'has shown considerable understanding of the need to take responsibility for his actions' – a claim that would be pretty hard to substantiate a few short years later.

I got a job selling mobile phone contracts for Optus, then went with Telstra when they offered me more cash. I was just marking time, blowing away the years until I felt I was ready for university, where the serious business of studying marketing and management would begin. That was the plan.

But life doesn't always go according to the plan, mostly because plans tend not to take into account the people you meet along the way. And it's always other people who change your mind about things. In that regard, there are two people I met during this time of my life who were to become important figures over the next few years.

One was Clare, the first romantic love of my life. I met her at high school when I was seventeen and she was sixteen. She was gorgeous, with incredible big blue eyes and the cutest lips that made me just want to squash them into mine. I don't know whether it was just young love, but there seemed such an intense connection between us – a feeling that we were meant to be together – and we fell in love very deeply and affectionately. For the next few years we were inseparable. I was sure we were going to be in love for the rest of our lives.

The other person of significance I met at this time was Luke Carroll, a local boy who had lived not too far from me all those years. I liked him instantly when I met him. He had a dark, almost emotionless sort of humour. He was very much a lone wolf – had never really had a girlfriend, had never been responsible for anyone. He was his own man, and he didn't feel the need to conform, even for the non-conformists. When he spoke, which wasn't often anyhow, he didn't think it necessary to look around and see what others thought of what he had to say. I always admired that about him, and I often caught myself wishing I could be a bit more like him. I was always very social, always wanting to be with friends, and seeking their approval, like most young people do. But Luke didn't seem to need any of that, and I admired him for it. I guess it's what they refer to as 'cool'. That was Luke all right. A dickhead, for sure, like me. But cool as fuck. We surfed together, hung out, smoked dope. We were trouble waiting to happen.

I remember being in trouble with the law only twice growing up. Once, when I was very young, I got busted stealing lollies from a local store. There was no prison sentence there, of course – just a lot of fingers wagging at me and harsh words spoken. The next time I was in trouble with the law was when I was in my teens, and lost my licence for a year. I went and bought this motorbike that wasn't registered and I was riding it on the road without a licence. Mum and Dad found out about it and went a little psycho at me, but that didn't stop me from riding it. Eventually, one night, I got pulled over and busted. I had to go to court and it was all pretty serious. Looking back, of course, it was nothing at all.

I suppose, since my teenage years, I've had this streak in me to buck authority. I don't consciously think to myself, here are some rules and I'm gonna break 'em, but I guess I don't respond well to knowing there's an imaginary fence and I'm forbidden to jump it. All I ever needed was a bit of encouragement and I was up for anything.

It all began because Luke's father owned a ski shop down in Jindabyne and had friends over in Colorado who owned a ski shop too. The crew in Colorado had extended a standing invitation: when Luke finished school he could come over – bring a mate if he wanted – and they'd organise work in their ski shop and accommodation for the tourist season. So Luke asked me if I'd like to go and of course I jumped at it. I didn't know how to ski, but I was a decent surfer and skateboarder, so I knew I'd pick it up quickly, and the thought of unleashing it in Colorado for a few months seemed good to me. I got right down to business, started saving money, sold my car, organised a three-month student visa and it was all happening. I even stopped smoking dope. Some things in life require heavy sacrifices.

It all happened very quickly and, today, I don't really remember saying goodbye to friends, which bothers me. My journey overseas wasn't supposed to be such a big deal – I was only meant to be going away for a few months, so I don't remember any significant farewells with any of my buddies. That's something that was to trouble me for many years, as I tried to conjure memories of my friends during the long days and nights alone.

Naturally, in the last few days before I left Australia, I saw a lot of Clare. We packed a lot of love into those days. The funny thing is, on that last morning I was a mess, crying my eyes out, while she remained quite stoic, holding it together. I remember packing up my room in the family house, because I was moving out, and somehow the act of doing both – moving out of home and saying goodbye to my girlfriend at the same time – was too much for me to handle emotionally. There was some sort of finality to it which, at the time, I couldn't place.

Mum and Dad were to drive me to Brisbane airport, so Clare and I said our goodbyes by the side of the car before we left. Again, I was all tears and snot, while she was dry-eyed and coping with it like a soldier. I guess someone has to cry during goodbyes.

Clare had decided to miss the scene at the airport, probably because she knew it would be too emotional and she'd crack. So the last I saw of her that day was as I waved to her out of the car window, weeping like a jerk. She was standing on the verandah, waving back, keeping it together.

As we drove up the highway and I tried to dry my eyes, I looked out of the window at the car next to us, and driving it was this young girl who was singing along to a song I couldn't hear. I read her lips and knew instantly that she was singing along to a Maroon 5 song that Clare completely adored called 'She Will Be Loved'. I'd personally never thought much of it until that moment. There's a line in that song – something about how goodbyes don't mean much after all – and suddenly I was very moved by it. Over the next few years, I would hear that song in my head many, many times. Occasionally, I would actually hear it playing on a radio somebody had, or the video would be on a prison TV, and I'd stop and really listen hard to it, fall into it, and I'd be able to imagine Clare so strongly that I could almost smell her.

At the airport, I remember Mum buying me a nice woollen jumper. I remember pulling it on and being struck by how comfortable it was – not just because it was woollen, but because it had come from my mum. I was aware at that moment of how tight and close my family was, and, while I was excited about travelling, I remember wondering how I was going to cope being so far away from my family for the first time.

My mum and dad were very supportive of me going overseas with Luke. They knew what we were like, and probably suspected that we were bound to get up to ordinary, harmless mischief, but they were basically encouraging, gave their best, wished me well, and urged me to simply be careful.

When I look back upon that little scene as if I'm viewing it from above – all those smiling, loving faces at the airport that morning – and remember that they would not be together again for the next half a decade, I'm overwhelmed by sympathy for them all. I'm also compelled to take my thumb and forefinger and flick that Anthony Prince dickhead in the ear.

I don't think I had any preconceptions about Colorado at all before I got there. Like a lot of people, I thought of America in stereotypes – I knew a bit about Los Angeles, New York and the deep south, and that was it. Colorado was just some place that appeared in a John Denver song. I think I would have been struggling to point out Colorado on a map of the USA.

Vail itself was beautiful in the sense that there was snow and the mountains were pretty dramatic, but what struck me was how crook it seemed close up; the snow melting and turning to dirty sludge by the side of the road, all that sort of thing. In a way, what I saw in Colorado was emblematic of how I felt about America overall – that it looks all very dazzling from a distance but is uglier the deeper you get into it. You get there with a voice in your head telling you that this is America, the place where all the important shit in the world goes down. The jewel of the western world. But then you can't help but notice how fucked it is as well. The people are fat, they're racist, they're driving these huge fuel-guzzling cars they don't need. They're beating their wives. They talk too much. Everything's about money. It didn't take me long to understand that America wasn't the Disneyland we are sold on the television. And I suppose along with that realisation came a contempt I started to have for America, a feeling of disrespect for the place and the people that was to show itself pretty strongly within the next couple of months.

Luke and I checked in with the people who were more or less sponsoring us there, Robin and Carol. They were a pretty interesting couple. She was an Australian who had gone over to America and married this guy, who was your typical Yank in a nutshell. He was all, 'Yeah, man!', with his hair swept back in this fluffy sort of coif – a trust fund baby whose parents were fucking loaded, and here he was at 45 years old, working in a ski shop and living in this massive log home, no kids, totally full of himself. He was one of those guys who walks into a room and thinks everyone else becomes a moon in his orbit. And why not? He had the gravity to pull it off, and he had that amazing American readiness to please and impress. His accent meant everything to him, and you knew he'd rather die than lose it.

That first night, we were up at their house before we went to our apartment. We were having dinner and drinking Heineken – a big American dinner with lots of chips and gravy and side dishes everywhere. There was this big hot tub, and at the end of dinner Robin said, 'Hey, man, you wanna get into the hot tub?' Luke and I thought it was a great idea, because it was so cold, so we jumped into the hot tub in our boardies and were having a great time, just sitting there drinking and loving it. Suddenly, Robin comes strolling out buck naked, his big American dong swinging in the night air of Colorado, and jumps straight in beside us. Luke and I couldn't say anything, but we each saw the look on the other's face, and we probably put more bubbles in the hot tub just trying to hold our laughter in. It's just that full-on American way – brash and forward – that will always trip Australians up.

But the truth is Robin and Carol got us jobs in the ski shop, organised our accommodation, helped us out with a lot of things, so I owe them for that. They even got us annual ski lift passes, which usually retail for about US$2000. They put in a lot of work. Once we were set up, of course, they cut away and let us run our own race – we saw them occasionally at work, but we were pretty much on our own.

Later, when the shit hit the fan, they became strangers who I doubt I'll ever see again.

Luke and I immediately snapped into life on our working holiday, getting the free bus into Vail Village each day and working at Pepi's, the ski store. We lived in one of a little row of duplex apartments. We were getting it cheap, and living like kings, really – two bedrooms, two bathrooms, lots of room for just two blokes. Most of the other people our age who we knew were sharing similar apartments with eight or nine other dudes. So we were doing pretty well. It was a good place to bring people you wanted to meet, and there were so many late nights where our little house was filled with travellers, local folk and American girls.

Considering we were there for three months, and that I was nineteen and a single Australian boy on a working holiday, I think I was a pretty good boyfriend to Clare. I got as much interest as I could in that town – not a lot, but enough to keep my ego from evaporating completely – and I basically behaved myself. It's a shame, really, considering where I was going to be spending the next four years. There was no lovin' where I was headed, that's for sure.

But my position at Pepi's gave me a unique inside track when it came to getting to know people. There was one little shorty I recall from Oklahoma, with black hair and dark eyes, who I met when she was renting ski gear from Pepi's. She came back to our place one night. Unfortunately, she was a church-going Catholic, who was always breaking out praising God, in our apartment of all places. I remember Luke asking her what she thought was going to happen when we died, and she was insistent that we were all going to heaven and that the Lord should be thanked for this in advance. At the time, we argued that what she needed to do was eat some mushrooms, smoke some weed and experience a little of what life's like without Jesus peering over your shoulder. Strangely enough, I developed a pretty good friendship with her, despite the fact we were polar opposites.

Another time, there was a girl, Kate, from Connecticut, who came into the store to get ski equipment, and I had to take down her name, her age, her shoe size, her address and phone number. I remember thinking how easy it was to become familiar with someone's intimate details.

Of course, the whole time we were there, technically speaking, Luke and I were breaking the law – we were going out every week drinking when, as far as American justice was concerned, we were underage. It was strangely offensive to have come from Australia, where we were entrusted to go out and drink like adults, to now find ourselves in a place where our normal behaviour was considered criminal, and it filled us with a weird sense of outrage. Later, I used this indignation to justify my actions when I started treating Americans like shit, when I shoplifted or stole from them. So I did a lot of that, excusing myself by believing I was engaged in some sort of international protest. We were good Aussie boys sticking the finger up at Uncle Sam for being such a tight-arse prude.

Looking back, what happened to us in Colorado was kind of like a small model of what our whole lives had been like to that point. Everything came too easily. We walked into good jobs, got our accommodation all sorted out for us, we were swamped with friends and chicks wanting to hang out, through no particular hard work or enterprise of our own.

It all happened for us, as if our lives were movies in which we were just actors, and some producer who we didn't even know was taking care of all the details.

It's funny how some little scenes stick in your memory for no good reason at first, then later acquire some sort of profound meaning. There was a club in Vail·called Eighty-One-Fifty, where touring acts would perform at night, and on one particular evening Public Enemy were playing there. I remember being right down the front, at the foot of the stage, off my head. Flavor Flav was leaning over the crowd, rapping, and that big clock that hangs around his neck was dangling in front of my face. So I reached up and started swinging it, hard. It'd swing back like a pendulum and I'd grab it and swing it back again. The security staff were watching me, glaring from the side of the stage, like wardens ready to pounce. But I just stared them down, kept grabbing the clock and swinging it back and forward. Tick, tock, tick, tock . . .

When I think of that little scene today, in light of what was about to happen, it creeps me out.

Vail is a bit like Byron Bay only with the mountains in place of the ocean. Its main trade is tourism, with the ski slopes being the primary attraction. There's one big highway running through Vail Valley, which is flanked by slopes with ski runs, lifts and resorts. Nobody would go there but holiday makers, so there's no local population that might fall into crime. It's just a high-class outdoor joint. There are fur coat stores on every corner, plush hotels; it's a very corporate playground. A crackhead in Vail would stick out a mile, and the cops would deal with him before he had a chance to get up to no good.

Luke and I were two of the very few teenagers in town, and conspicuous for that. The whole place is targeted to an older demographic, people with money who go there to ski. Who'd commit crime in a place like that? Nobody. Because, if you're there, you've already got enough money and you don't need anyone else's. Unless you're two guys from Australia who are going home soon without anything much to show for their time.

It was Luke who first noticed the weapon situation. I remember him commenting on how stupid it was that there were these BB pistols being sold in the supermarket, right next to the groceries. The laws in Colorado seemed a little loose with regard to a lot of things, as if they were still suffering a hangover from the days of the wild west. There is no need for a permit in the state of Colorado if you want to buy a rifle or a handgun, and you can have one in your home or carry one in your car if you want to. The only people who aren't permitted to have firearms are kids and convicted felons. We were kids, but we weren't convicted felons. Not yet.

There was a big store in Vail that was a supermarket on one side and a liquor store on the other, with a counter in the middle where you paid for your goods. Typically, there was one little Asian guy manning the register, facing one way or another at any given time. Luke and I would just go into the liquor store and lift huge bottles of cognac. I don't know how much booze we stole from that place – probably thousands of dollars' worth. We got into the habit of shoplifting in Vail, and we got away with it every time.

That store is really where it all started. I began shoplifting, an item at a time, and did it so easily that it pretty much became part of my daily routine. There was never any security in any store, so I'd just walk into a shop, see a snowboarding helmet or a jacket that I liked and walk out with it. It was that easy. It was all about confidence, really – just being sure enough of yourself that you didn't look sly or sneaky, to just brazenly walk out with whatever you had, as if you were stealing nothing at all. Every little theft made me bolder for the next.

Today, it's hard to reconcile this behaviour with the kid who grew up in Byron Bay. I think the only way I can explain it to myself is by recalling that weird sense of weightlessness that I felt the whole time I was in the USA. Australia is such a long way away – literally on the other side of the globe – that it's easy to convince yourself that your real life is half a world away, that you're living in some dream that won't really count on the ledger in the end. I've spoken to others who've travelled overseas and have been overcome by this strange feeling, too. Maybe it's peculiar to Australians, since we are so isolated from the rest of the world. I'm not trying to make excuses for myself – I was a little arsehole when I was in Vail, and I have to take responsibility for that – but it's too easy to say I just turned evil in Colorado. There has to be a reason for why I thought what I was doing was okay, and the only one that makes sense to me today is that I'd left my heart and mind in Australia, with my family, my girlfriend and the people I actually cared about. In America, I was a zombie, more or less. No soul.

We shoplifted the BB guns, of course, and, at nights, we were just carrying on like wannabe gangsters – filming ourselves talking like hard dudes, brandishing our weapons about. There's some footage we took of each other during those nights and, today, it's actually pretty hard to watch. In one reel, I'm filming Luke, saying: 'Okay, Sergeant Carroll, give me the breakdown on your weapon,' and he's like: 'This is a CO_2 ball-bearing pistol which I purchased from Walmart. What sort of a fucking country is this that you can purchase this shit from a supermarket?' And he's loading and unloading it, giving a demonstration as if he's an army commando. We're just kids. With toys. That's exactly what we were.

The fact is, you can buy these things from a shop, and they do look real and they can be used to fool people. You could probably even kill a person with one, if you held it against the right spot on their temple. They're pretty high-powered. And that's how we began to look at these devices – like real guns that were in our control. All I remember is us talking about how you could definitely stick someone up with these weapons. It was like a mutual brainwash – we gradually implanted in each other's head the truth that we could use these guns as tools to get us what we wanted. And what we wanted at that point in time was money.

You see, the whole trip for us was about money. It wasn't a holiday so much as a business opportunity. That's how we saw it. We were going to work for three months and come home with some money and experience. There were a couple of business ideas that we tried to get in on – like those shoes, Crocs, which were just coming out of Colorado at the time. We made contact with the guy who owned them and were talking to him about being his Australian distributors. Obviously, someone else had beaten us to it, and I doubt he would have taken us very seriously anyway, but that gives you an idea of the sort of mission this was supposed to have been for us. We felt strongly that something was going to happen in Colorado that would change our financial fortunes forever. As our time there began to come to an end and that thing hadn't materialised, I suppose we became disenchanted, or a little bit desperate. Going home in debt just didn't feel like part of the plan.

We first began talking about robbing the little Asian guy in the store. We were drinking his booze and smoking some weed, talking about how easy it would be. Then, somehow, the conversation drifted on to the bank. Why bother robbing a supermarket when we could just as easily do the bank? It seemed a natural progression of thinking. We weren't talking seriously, just blowing shit off into the night air.

That it was going no further than just conversation was what made it easy and safe to talk about.

I'd been inside the WestStar Bank in Vail plenty of times – often getting money changed for work, as well as doing my own banking, as I had an account there – and had noticed that there'd always been huge amounts of money just sitting around, next to counting machines and in bundles on desks. There was obviously a lot of money going through that town but, like I say, there wasn't a great deal of crime in Vail, so the bank had no security at all. It was just something I noticed as I was standing there in line. I'm pretty sure most people have thought things like this – you'll be standing in the line waiting for a teller, bored, so you start daydreaming, looking around. You're in a bank, so you're not going to start daydreaming about surfing – you're going to imagine that you're some dude in a heist movie, casing the joint, taking it down. That's all it was. There was no real planning going on, or any sort of mental investment happening. I'm not even sure it registered in my brain at the time. All I know is that, later, when Luke and I spoke about it, I recalled that the bank was an easy target.

It was just a crazy midnight conversation between two stoned friends. It wasn't supposed to be anything other than that. But, somehow, once we'd let that particular genie out of the bottle, it kept coming back to taunt and tempt us, and we never did work out how to make it go away.

*

One night, Luke and I were pretty twisted and were sitting at home waving our pistols around, as usual. The night got a bit crazy and Luke started shooting at things – trees, passing cars, windows across the way. Someone complained, and the next thing we knew the police were at our door. It turned out a window had been smashed. Seeing as neither myself nor Luke would own up to having been the culprit, we were both arrested, for 'Damage to Property and Firing a Weapon', which is actually a felony. We had our little day in court, and narrowly slipped out of getting convictions.

But this incident seemed to signal a break from our previous lives. From that night, the stakes went up a notch. Our thefts became more than just random shoplifting as our criminal behaviour became like a 'project' we were nurturing in our spare time. We began writing down the numbers of credit cards that were presented by customers in Pepi's where we worked. We set up a PayPal account into which we intended to transfer small amounts from those credit accounts. It would be a pretty slick little scam and, provided we didn't get too greedy with the amounts, the chances of us getting busted were slim. All we needed was a bank account that wasn't connected to either of us, and then we'd be able to pay the money from PayPal into that bank account.

There was a South African dude who was staying with us who found himself unwittingly wandering into our crosshairs. He was a decent sort of a guy. But at that point, Luke and I were so out of control that it didn't really matter to us whether people were good guys or not. It was like we were just desensitised to humanity. So, one night, about a week before he was due to go home, we went through his bag and pinched his passport, with a view to setting up that bank account with it sometime later. For the next few days the poor bastard was storming through the house in search of his passport, tearing his hair out, pleading with us to help him find it. We were just playing dumb ('Gee, man, I dunno . . . you must have left it on a bus or something . . .') and all the while we had it stashed.

When I look back on this, I don't like the person I see. I cringe when I think of that South African dude and the hell we put him through. The whole time while he was going crazy searching for his passport, I was feeling like the biggest cunt, and if it had just been me I probably would have 'fessed up and given the passport back to him. But I was different when I was with Luke, which is not to say that Luke was necessarily a bad influence – I'm sure he felt the same as I did. There's just something about being in a duo.

When there's two of you, some weird kind of loyalty kicks in – a commitment to the one you see as your partner in crime. I used to wonder why criminals would be so stupid as to involve another person in their secrets; why take the risk of trusting someone else when you can operate faster and more securely alone? I now know the answer. When you've got a partner, you're less willing to wimp out. You're less likely to care about other people, like you normally would, because your duty is to your partner. All the ordinary checks and balances that govern your behaviour as a human being – fear, compassion, sympathy – are superseded by your loyalty to your friend. And your partner's courage emboldens you, too.

In that department, Luke was a good partner to have in crime. He had this amazing ability to just shut down his emotions and switch off. I remember later in court, when our parents were reading statements to the judge, being a complete mess myself, crying as I heard my mum and dad speak. Then Luke's mum gets up with this most impassioned speech, weeping as she was begging the judge to please let her son come home. Her sadness made me cry all over again, and I wasn't the only one in the courtroom who was crying, either. But when I looked up to see how Luke was coping, he was just staring straight ahead, no emotion at all. I'm sure he was crying inside but, somehow, he was able to make it all go away. It was a gift that would probably get him through the next few years.

One day we found a wallet in the foyer of the hotel complex that housed the ski shop where we worked. It had about $150 in it, so we naturally pocketed that. But, more importantly, it had a credit card inside. Luke and I were sure we could do some serious damage with that card.

Later, during our lunch break, we went down to this computer store and I tried to buy a top-of-the-range iPod with it. They ran the card through the system and then said that the card had been declined. We feigned surprise and disbelief ('Declined? Gee, that's odd . . .') and made them run it back through a couple of times before leaving the store in 'confusion'. From that moment we were screwed.

A day later – a Friday – the cops came into Pepi's and spoke to me and Luke. They wanted to know if it was us on the security footage trying to use someone's stolen card. We denied it, of course, but they were playing pretty tough, saying that they were just waiting for the computer enhancements of the footage which would prove once and for all that it was us. I kept denying it. I felt they were bull-shitting about the computer program – that it was just some crap they'd seen on *CSI* – but I also felt it was only a matter of time before they closed in on us.

That night, Luke and I realised that our holiday as petty thieves was at an end. On Monday the police would surely come into the store and arrest us. We had to get out of town – perhaps out of the state, maybe even out of the entire USA. To Mexico, or maybe Amsterdam, which was a place we'd often spoken about. But what about this bank? Were we really going to leave town without exploiting that sure opportunity? We were just about out of savings, I already owed my parents a few grand, and I'd promised Clare I'd take her on a holiday to New Zealand when I returned. Going home now, wondering about what we might have pulled off, just didn't seem like an option.

It was then we began to talk very seriously about rolling the bank. Until then, it had been a little fantasy occasionally spoken out loud: I'd bring it up again, then Luke would drop it; Luke would bring it up and I would drop it. It was a crazy idea floating around in the sky, waiting for both of us to be stupid at once. Here was that moment. We were desperate and afraid, but still feeling strangely bulletproof. It was as if all we had needed was a reason for the plan to become necessary. Now we had that reason. That robbing the bank was the only thing to do really made sense to me on that night.

So we started planning it, seriously talking about how we were going to do it. I knew roughly the time that the tellers arrived to open the bank. If we got there early, before any other customers arrived, we could be in and out with a few grand before the streets would become too crowded.

It never seemed to occur to me that people might connect the two troublesome Australians, who'd shot out windows with BB guns and who'd tried to use a stolen credit card, with the two guys who'd rob the local bank. I suppose the thought of flying out of Vail, leaving behind all our troubles, was too strong. It seemed irresistible. Once again, that feeling of being in a fantasy when you're far from home was triumphing over everything else. Australia and our real lives seemed very far away. We were dreaming.

There was one moment when I suddenly recalled the trouble I'd been in before, with the unregistered motor-cycle and all the drama that had created back home. At the time, it had really freaked me out and had greatly disturbed my parents as well. In that moment when I remembered it, all the feelings of trauma and regret came back, and were very clear to me again. I seized the moment and told Luke that I wanted nothing more to do with this enterprise, that we were in enough trouble as it was and I didn't want to go any further. I explained to him that I'd been in trouble before and never wanted to go back there again. Luke thought about it for a while and then responded, to my surprise, that he had never been in any trouble so he guessed he'd just have to learn his lesson for himself. He would go ahead with the robbery, he said, whether I joined him or not.

Here was my opportunity to be tough, like Luke was always tough, to be my own man, to myself display those qualities that I so admired in my friend. All I had to do was stand firm, wish him luck, but say I'd made up my mind and that I was not having any further part in this scheme. It's the sort of thing Luke would have done – followed his own mind, regardless of what anyone else thought, or what anyone else intended to do. And I've thought a lot about those few moments, and the opportunity I might have given both of us to back out. I'm pretty sure Luke was just bluffing, that he wouldn't have gone through with it without me. I might have saved us both. But I blew it. Instead, I allowed myself to think that I owed it to my friend to stick by him, that I couldn't let him rob the bank without me.

It took me a very long time to get over the memory of the decision I made. The only way I cope with it today is by knowing I'll never be that pissweak again.

I also remember one stupid moment when we asked each other the classic question: 'What's the worst thing that could happen?' I remember one of us saying, 'Well, we could go to jail for twenty years,' and then both of us rolling around laughing at how absurd that sounded. That's how far gone we were – completely fucked in the head. Not only were we discounting the very real possibility that we'd be shot dead by police, but the idea of us in handcuffs and prison clothes seemed so idiotic it made us laugh.

I can still see us in my mind's eye today, laughing at the thought of going to jail. Laughing our heads off.

What a couple of Desmonds.

2

On Monday morning we got up and didn't say anything to each other. We just went about packing in a silence that told us we really were going ahead with this thing. It was a very strange feeling that morning, like we were being dragged towards a destiny that had already been arranged and about which we could do nothing. Up till now, all it would have taken was for one of us to have called 'bullshit', stand our ground, and the entire project would have ended right there. But not this day. Now, we acted on the weekend's decisions. There was no more talking to be done about it.

I was still very nervous about the police and that business with the credit card – I was probably more edgy about that than I was about what we were soon to do. The thought of it translated to a feeling of being pursued, as if the police were going to knock on our door any second. We had to move fast.

I rang Pepi's and my boss answered the phone. I told him there'd been an accident, that I'd dislocated my shoulder and had to go home to Australia for surgery. I remember him sounding a little surprised at the suddenness of it all. Looking back, he was probably deeply suspicious (as if they don't know how to deal with dislocated shoulders in American hospitals). Anyway, he wished me good luck, I hung up the phone and got back to packing.

The plan was that we'd wait outside the bank until we saw the tellers arrive. Luke would be around the back, in the car park, and would alert me when they were coming by calling me on a two-way radio set we had shop-lifted earlier. I'd wait until the tellers opened the door, enter as close behind them as possible, then Luke would join me.

I knew the tellers by sight, but I didn't yet know their names. There was a younger, petite, pretty girl who I would later learn was Jessica, and an older, larger lady called Kim. They knew me, too, as I was a regular customer, so disguising ourselves was very important.

We'd be wearing ski masks to hide our faces – seeing as Vail was a ski resort, two blokes walking around in ski masks would not appear to be immediately suspicious – and we'd have our hoods over our heads. We would talk as little as possible, but make sure we used American accents when we did. Once we had the tellers lying on the floor, I'd cover them and the door while Luke took the cash and stashed it in a large pillowcase.

Once we had the money, the idea was to leave the bank and be as invisible as possible until we could get out of town. We figured it was not so smart to go galloping across Vail straight to our apartment, where we'd have to pick up the rest of our possessions before clearing out – our footprints in the snow would lead police straight to us, if nothing else did. We decided what we'd do was hit the ski slopes, like regular dudes, take a chair lift to the top of a run and snowboard down with the money, then catch a taxi back to our apartment. It was like a perfect alibi – nobody would ever suspect that two guys who'd just robbed a bank would go snowboarding straight away. It didn't seem to occur to us that the reason nobody would suspect it was because it was fucking stupid.

As an extra little touch, just to throw the tellers off the scent, I took the name tag I wore at Pepi's and fixed it to my jacket. Using one of those label-making guns that I'd pinched from somewhere or other, I gave this bank robber a name: 'Valley Electrical Dave'. I thought searching for 'Dave' might keep at least one police officer busy while Luke and I made our getaway.

The night before, we'd sussed out the pathways at the back of the bank, just to make sure we were familiar with the route that would take us to the chair lifts, and had buried our boards in the snow that morning, so that we could retrieve them after the robbery. It seemed to us that our plan was pretty foolproof, barring some unforeseen catastrophe.

It was snowing heavily as we trudged in silence towards the WestStar Bank. There was powder snow icing everything, and there were surely sick days being taken all over Colorado as people did whatever they could to stay out of the deluge. This sort of weather suited our purpose, but it also invested the morning with a dreary foreboding.

Another bad omen was the realisation that I'd left my ski pass back at the apartment, a discovery I made when we arrived in Vail Village, not far from the bank. There was no time for me to go back to the apartment to get it, as we'd miss the opening of the bank, so I had to purchase a new pass from the ski office in the village. This was not just an inconvenience – by revealing myself to the guy in the ski office, who knew me, I was placing myself in Vail Village moments before the robbery. But it couldn't be helped. We needed that pass, so it was a risk we had to take.

When we arrived at the bank, we split up, Luke taking his place out in the car park at the back, with me standing discreetly between two trees just a few metres away from the entrance.

The plan began to go off the rails almost immediately. The two-way radios weren't working properly. I kept buzzing Luke – 'Are they here yet? Are they here yet?' – but when he replied I just couldn't hear him properly. I kept testing for a few minutes until, suddenly, Luke was by my side. He hadn't been able to hear me at all. So we gave up on the two-way radios and decided to stand next to each other in the trees and communicate that way. It seemed to be working pretty well.

It was the younger girl, Jessica, who arrived first. We had expected them to arrive together, so that was a bit of a shock. At that point, we realised things weren't going to go as we had planned – every little moment that differed from what we had imagined was going to fully freak us out. We both had the wind taken out of our sails, and I remember our nerve fading right there, as we said to each other: 'Nah, let's forget it . . . this isn't right . . .' We were just about to turn on our heels and go when the other girl arrived and entered the bank. She was carrying a box with what appeared to be a cake inside it.

For just a moment, our retreat from the robbery had the momentum – we were already derailed and were still going home, spooked by the reality of what we'd dreamed up. But then I remembered the police, the credit card, and the shit storm that was brewing right behind our backs, unless we left town that day. Suddenly, I just didn't want to know about what was behind us in Vail. There was only one way out, and it was through the WestStar Bank. For the first time since we'd spoken of it, I was hit with a surge of faith in this heist. And so I pulled my hood tight over my head and marched through the snow, the door of the bank coming towards me as if the building was moving and not me.

I entered the bank first. The two tellers were behind the counter chatting. The anticipated fear and adrenaline was vague – all I recall is wanting to get it over with as quickly as possible. I opened my mouth and out fell the words, 'This is a robbery!' I held up my pistol. I remember the two girls turning and looking at me, like they knew me. The older girl, Kim, stared at me with a peculiar smile on her face, like she understood this was a joke and she wanted me to stop mucking around.

Suddenly, Luke came storming in from behind me, doing the whole madman-robbing-a-bank thing – 'Shut the fuck up and give us all the money!' – and then the girls' faces changed. The change was so dramatic I'll never forget it. Kim's mouth fell open like a drawbridge and her eyes seemed to double in size. And Jessica – poor Jessica – began to shake and spontaneously burst into tears, her hand going up to her mouth as a look of total horror swept across her face. She looked into the barrel of my gun as if it were her last moment on earth.

This troubled me. I hadn't expected it, crazily enough. In my mind, I knew it was only a BB gun, so I hadn't really expected anyone else to be shitting themselves about it. It was only when I saw her cry that I realised she had no way of knowing that this wasn't a real gun and I wasn't a real arsehole. I actually had to stop myself from telling her it was only a BB gun, and that I was a friendly hippie from Byron Bay who'd never hurt anyone in his life. In a way I wish I had – it would have probably earned me a lighter sentence, and it would have been pretty funny.

Unfortunately, what was happening wasn't funny at all. I had snapped out of my fucked-up stupor the second I'd lifted my gun. It was as if the very act of entering the bank had burst a bubble – this was no longer a joke, it was happening, in real time. People were really being robbed at gunpoint, and I was the one doing it. I felt sick and frightened by my own shadow, suddenly and terribly. My legs went weak and I had a brick in my guts. I wanted to walk straight out of there immediately, back into the world that had treated me so well all my life.

Evidently, Luke wasn't feeling so bashful. He was staunch behind the counter, shouting in an accent so undisguised he sounded like a Tourism Australia advertisement. In one stupid moment, I opened my mouth to shout out to him: 'Luke! Lose the Australian accent!', but stopped myself just in time.

Luke screamed at Kim to get on the floor and lie down. She was standing in a little gap in the counter that tellers could walk through and, as Luke shouted his directions, he pushed her through it and towards the floor – not hard, but with what I'd call a forceful guiding motion. She had come to work with her backpack on, and with all the shouting and terror Kim must have been pretty weak in the legs. As Luke pushed her, she fell forward, onto her knees and hands on the floor.

These girls had probably thought about this possibility every day: When am I going to be held up? How will I react? Kim was doing well. I don't know whether it was because she was older and had probably been working there longer, but she was handling it. I remember seeing her just lying on the floor, her mind ticking over. She didn't look scared. It was almost as if she was listening, taking it all in, trying to work out who we were. I remember being troubled by her calmness.

Luke then turned to Jessica, who was wet with hysteria.

'Where's the fucking money?' he shouted.

I don't know what Jessica's answer was – she was so fucked up she could barely speak, and her words were coming out as gibberish. There was something about a key.

Then Kim raised her head from the floor and translated what she knew Jessica was trying to say; that she needed a key to the safe and didn't have one. Kim said there were keys in her bag, which was on the bench next to the teller's register.

I don't recall either Luke or I ever talking about vaults or safes when we were planning the robbery. We'd only been thinking of the tills. When Luke shouted out asking where the money was, we got a shock when they said it was in a safe, and that she'd need to open it with her key. It was not something we had expected. In our minds, the most successful scenario was us making off with about ten grand, scooped from the registers in a matter of seconds.

Nevertheless, Luke ordered Jessica to get the keys from Kim's bag, which she proceeded to do.

At this point I noticed Jessica was so hysterical she was almost incapable of doing anything – her hands were shaking and she was blinded by her own tears. I had to say something.

'We don't want to hurt you, lady,' I said, in my best American accent. 'We just want the money. If you stay calm and give us the money, we won't hurt you and we'll go.'

It didn't seem to work. She fumbled in the bag until she found the keys and made her way to the vault at the back of the bank. There, on her knees at the safe, she was having trouble with the lock, and then when she got the outside door of the safe open she couldn't remember the combination. She was sobbing the whole time, and Luke was behind her with the barrel of his gun against the back of her neck. That was not necessary. But I guess that was Luke keeping his mettle up.

And that's probably how you get the job done in that game. If you're going to rob a bank, I suppose you're better off doing it like a bank robber, and not like the friendly family dentist, which is what I was being, or at least what I wished I was. I could see that these girls didn't need any more fear and terror – that was sorted. This was real enough. What they needed was someone who was going to convince them they were going to get out of this alive.

One of the many thoughts that were messing with my head at this moment was the memory of my sisters. Jessica, the younger teller, reminded me so much of my own sister, who happens to be called Jessie as well. She was about the same age, and even looked a little similar. This thought had first occurred to me when I'd had my gun in Jessica's face, and had kept re-entering my consciousness throughout the robbery, like some mosquito that won't go away. It is unusual in the history of bank robbery, I'm sure, for the bandit to start thinking tender thoughts about his own sister as he's taking down the joint. But there was a lot about this heist that was unusual. It was too surreal even for the perpetrator.

I turned my back towards the action and began to walk towards the door, in part because, subconsciously, I wanted to put some distance between what was happening and me. As I did so, I noticed this guy peering through the window, his face up to the glass as if he were window-shopping. This was a new complication. I walked up to the door just as he arrived at it. I opened the door slightly, and told him he couldn't come in, that there were electrical problems and we were fixing them. I said this from behind a ski mask and with a gun in my hand. He just got this look on his face that said: 'Yeah, right!' and missioned off around the corner. This guy was going to be trouble.

I stood at the door for a moment, looking out into the streets of the village, which were covered in holiday snow. People were beginning to go about their business, as if nothing was happening. I so much wanted to be one of them, with a boring nine-to-five job, and the promise of a little bit of joy at the end of the day with a few drinks and a safe night's sleep. I knew these few minutes inside this bank had cut us off from that world for the foreseeable future. It was a very depressing thought to have poking through the raw panic I was feeling. I wasn't just a naughty boy anymore, or a young larrikin who needed a stern talking-to. I was a crook, a bad dude. I was going down.

I began to wonder what was happening – why it was all taking Luke so long – so I went back into the bank and the sight that greeted me there gave me a shock: there was Luke, dragging this huge, bulging bag with money piled all the way to the top. I thought: no way! I hadn't expected a haul like it. I suppose most hardened bank robbers would be overjoyed to see a sight like that, but all I can remember thinking was that this wasn't supposed to happen. I'd expected him to come out with the bottom half of the pillowcase full, but this looked like something you only see in the lottery advertisements, where some lucky bastard has a huge sack with dollars spewing out of the top. How the fuck were we going to discreetly move this across town? In that moment, I guess you could say I realised I never was going to be cut out for bank robberies. This one had obviously been stupidly successful, and all I could feel was ripped off by fate. We had to get the hell out of there.

As we prepared to exit the bank, I very nearly followed my old habit of courteously turning, thanking the tellers and wishing them a good day. I'm sure it would have been appreciated.

We stepped out of the bank and into the open air, the light of the morning hitting me in the eyes, as if I were a vampire. We belonged in the dark – we'd just robbed a bank, a heist in which every second had felt like an hour but, in actual fact, the whole thing had lasted no more than three minutes. There was nobody in the streets to see us, but it still felt like one of those dreams in which you've stepped outside without any clothes on. I was paranoid about any human movement, any pair of eyes that might spy us and see what we were doing. Had we just reverted to the old shoplifting mentality we'd have swaggered through town with a bulging sack and nobody would have paid us much mind. But there was too much panic in our hearts this time. All I could think about was the girls in the bank being on the phone to the cops right away. If we'd been decent criminals, playing for keeps, we'd have tied them up, locked the door on our way out, given ourselves a chance.

We scurried down a series of little cobblestone paths covered in snow. We said nothing to each other, but just dragged this great big bag of money together. We turned a corner and dashed down a lane flanked by hotels on one side – these old-school Dutch buildings with sloping roofs – and a construction site on the other, with a cyclone fence made of wire. It was like our chances were being displayed for us right there: on one side, affluence and comfort; on the other, hard labour, with wire fences to keep us inside. And there we were, hauling this big bag of money down the middle, not really knowing how it would all end.

That little journey, through those cobblestone streets and lanes covered in snow, will stay in my mind forever. It could only have lasted for a minute or so, but the thoughts that ran through my head seemed infinite. The adrenaline from the actual robbery was gone, replaced by something more like dread. We spoke no words at all to each other. Nothing. All I could hear was Luke's breathing mixed in with my own, and the sound of our feet trudging through the snow. We'd just robbed a bank, and now we were on the run with a ludicrous amount of money. But apart from that, nothing had gone right, and that's all I could think about. We'd hurt that woman, and made the other one so terrified it seemed she'd probably be traumatised for life. The guy who came to the door had probably alerted the police before we'd even left the bank. We'd fucked up our phoney American accents. It had all gone so wrong. And it was at that point, as we dashed through the lanes, that I realised we weren't going to get away with this. Our only chance would be to hide so that nobody in the world would ever find us. That was too big a thought to process at the time – we were still free and running, and there seemed no time to contemplate the reality that told me the whole game was over, that we were already going to prison and there was nothing we could do about it now. I just didn't have the capacity in my mind to deal with it. So we kept on running, fugitives of a justice system that probably already had our names. We were like mice on a wheel.

We cut through a break in the laneway between two hotels, to a small clearing dominated by a huge pine tree. And it was there that we stopped, squatted down in the snow and frantically started to transfer the money from the bag into a backpack we'd bought for that purpose. Notes were just spilling everywhere, falling like litter into the snow all around us. One of the zips on the backpack wasn't doing up; it was full to bursting. We couldn't fit so much as a matchbox in there.

The plan had been to take our jackets off, put new ones on, and then stash our jackets and the gun and everything else in the backpack and take it with us. But there was so much money it was impossible – there was no room for anything but cash. The robbery had been too successful. And we were in such a crazy hurry – my mind was screaming at me to move it, to get the fuck out of there. I was thinking like an escapee with the law right on my arse – there was no time to be careful. My mind was completely hostage to this shocking feeling that someone was going to come around the corner and hold a gun to the back of my head.

So that's how we left things, under that pine tree, money everywhere, clothes with name tags on them. From a mile away you could tell some bank robbers had just stopped to catch their breath and change clothes. It was ridiculous.

We left the clearing and pretty soon were at the foot of the mountain, where we'd planted our snowboards the previous day. We dug them out and continued to where there was a fork in the path meaning you had to choose which ski lift you wanted to go to: Avanti or Born Free. We went for Avanti, the one on the left, the closest. But when we got there, because it was such a good day for skiing, the line for the lift was huge – a great snaking queue of people all waiting to get their tickets scanned so they could be taken up the mountain.

We couldn't just stand there, in line, like ordinary idiots, with the police on our backs. We didn't want to go back down the path towards town, as we were sure the cops would be coming that way looking for us. We had to try for Born Free, in the hope that it would be less populated.

So we left the line of people and started trudging up the snow-covered hill, off the beaten track, where nobody was walking. We weaved through trees and angled up the slopes. There were skiers coming down straight at us, who must have been wondering why these idiots were crawling through the snow. Looking back, it was the craziest detour – all our efforts at staying under the radar, being invisible, melting into the crowd, were for nothing when we embarked on that conspicuous trek across the mountain. You could have picked us out from an aircraft.

We eventually got to Born Free, which, thankfully, was nowhere near as populated as Avanti had been. We joined the end of the small line and in a few short minutes we were in a chair on the lift.

It's at this point that Luke suddenly turned to me, slapped my hand and exclaimed, 'Yeah, brother!'

I was not so enthusiastic. I said, 'You serious? That was fucked! Nothing went to plan.' He seemed a bit perplexed, or maybe he was just in denial, bringing a wall down on his emotions once again, trying to convince himself and me that everything was cool, that we were going to make it. I'm afraid this was one time when the partnership wasn't going to embolden me. I had a knot in my stomach that wasn't going anywhere. We were fucked and I knew it. I was just running now because there was nothing else to do.

We reached the top of the run, snapped on our boards and began down the mountain, the single weirdest snowboard ride I'll ever take, weaving left and right with thousands of stolen American dollars strapped to my back, the slope of the mountain propelling us back to the very scene of the crime. Funnily enough, the sense of movement calmed me down – rushing down the mountain, I was relaxed for the first time that morning. Just walking was agony, and standing still was terrifying. I only felt safe when I was moving so quickly that nobody could put their hands on me. I could have stayed snowboarding down that slope forever.

We eventually got to the bottom of the mountain, where the slow panic of our predicament was waiting for us. We took our boards off and lurched through the snow to an area known as Lion's Head, at the extreme west of town. It was from here that we had to call a cab to take us back to our apartment in East Vail, so that we could gather all of our stuff and continue on to Denver, from where we intended to get a bus to Mexico. We called for the cab and were waiting by the road when we saw it: a police car, pulling up slowly on the other side of the street.

It is very difficult to describe the feeling of terror that gripped me when I saw this, and how hopeless that feeling was, knowing that I was an enemy of the state. Just a few hours earlier I had been a free citizen, and now, all of a sudden, I was a fugitive, a prisoner in the open air, the entire might of the government backing any attempt to hunt me down. If those cops were to draw their guns and shoot me, there would be no outrage – people would think it was justice, and they'd go on living as if nothing had happened. It was a very sad, lonely realisation that had not occurred to me before that moment.

We saw police officers get out of the vehicle and walk around, seemingly looking for someone. Was it us? We didn't feel like hanging around to find out. It was way too hot in Vail and we had to get out of there fast. So we hurried down through a nearby mall to another bus stop, where we intended to hail a taxi, but before a cab could come along the free tourist bus arrived, one that does a continuous loop of Vail. It was going in the opposite direction to where we needed to go, but we were sitting ducks standing on the edge of the road, with police crawling all over the joint, probably looking for us. It seemed sensible for us to climb aboard.

Once away from the highway, we got off the bus outside of one of the many shopping complexes in Vail. There we went into a store and bought regular clothes, so that we could dump the ones we were wearing, which still linked us to the crime. We both got fully changed, right there in the store, and then, outside, we dumped our clothes and boards in the snow, saw a taxi and hailed it. The driver was overjoyed when we asked him to take us to Denver, 150 kilometres away and a trip of nearly two hours. That's quite a fare.

Outside our apartment, we asked him to wait while we retrieved our bags, which we'd packed earlier that morning, before we were outlaws. It was a simple task of moving a few bags from A to B, but it seemed to be taking forever, an endless, repetitive back and forth motion. I just wasn't comfortable unless I was moving at a speed faster than a human could run.

We were halfway through the task when the sound of a siren began in the distance. Luke and I looked at each other and swallowed hard. This was it. We began frantically tossing our bags into the taxi, swearing and trembling, sweating buckets. Our panic was so palpable that the taxi driver asked us what was wrong, why we were freaking out.

'Look, man,' I said, 'we've got a flight to make in Denver and if we miss it we're screwed!'

He seemed to respond to that and began helping us. And all the time the police siren was getting louder and louder.

We jumped in the cab and it took off at the same moment as the wail of the siren appeared to be just around the corner. We'd had it, I thought – our faces were already on TV, someone had seen us back at our old apartment and called the cops, who would see the taxi with two dudes inside, know it was us and bang us up for 25 years, if they didn't blow our brains out. The sound of that siren was making me nearly pass out with alarm.

Then it stopped. As our cab turned onto the highway, I looked out the back window but couldn't see a police car. The cab driver said something about an accident – there, in front of us, was a crash on the highway, with emergency crews already arriving. The siren had belonged to an ambulance that was rushing to the scene.

But we only got to enjoy our relief for a few minutes before our hearts began pounding once more – ahead of us, on the highway, we saw police, waving down traffic, motioning for trucks to pull to the side of the road. It looked like a road block, with police searching vehicles – no doubt to find us. We were done for. But, to our surprise and relief, when we reached the police line they waved us through. According to the cab driver, it had just been routine bad weather duty, with police directing traffic as crews shovelled through the snow.

We were finally on the highway to Denver. We told the cab driver that we'd surely missed our flight, but wanted to go to a motel close by to Denver airport. He said he knew just the place.

All the surging adrenaline of the morning, mixed with the fact that we hadn't eaten, made us sleepy, I guess. I can think of no other reason why two lads who'd just pulled off their first bank heist would fall asleep in the back of a cab. To this day I can't help but laugh at the fact that police were searching for two bank robbers who were, at that very moment, sound asleep.

We awoke outside this typical American hotel, with its pristine garden out the front, as if a bit of landscaping was going to make our stay more comfortable. I remember thinking at that time how so much of America was made of these little lawns and gardens, manicured in precisely the same way. Take a wilderness that the poets and painters had described as being so different from anything else in the world, and they go and give it cosmetic surgery until it all looks like Legoland. That's America for you. It was a funny thought to have at that particular time, but I recall it affecting me strongly: one of those little moments of clarity that occasionally poked through the chaos, then disappeared just as quickly.

We paid the taxi driver and shuffled our bags into the foyer of the hotel. It was only when the cab had pulled away that we began talking about the driver. Neither Luke nor I trusted him – he was a suspicious mix of inquisitive and quiet – and we were uncomfortable knowing that he could lead the police to the very hotel where we were staying. We had no idea how long we were going to stay – if all went well, we'd just repack our bags and get on a bus to Mexico that very afternoon – but we were sure the police would already be looking for us, and very soon we'd be on the local news.

So we got the bright idea to go to the hotel across the road instead. That way, we figured, if they came looking for us, they'd at least have the wrong hotel. As if the police wouldn't bother searching the hotel across the way, too. I'm afraid that, from this vantage point in time, our thinking that day doesn't seem terribly sharp. It seems more like the behaviour of children who are playing some kind of game, convinced that the adults searching for them will cut them some slack just to give them a chance. Of course, this wasn't how we were feeling at the time – we were desperately frightened and paranoid. And that was about to get worse.

I signed into the hotel under the name Les Norton, the character from the Robert G. Barrett books. I can't really remember why I did that – the name just popped into my head. Most probably, it was because Les Norton is forever getting into some sort of trouble, and I'd never felt more in trouble than I did that afternoon.

When we got into our room, we finally got to open the backpack and see what we'd achieved. Great bricks of money, bound with ties from the Federal Reserve Bank of America, were piled on the bed, in bundles of every denomination. We did a rough count of it, and only then did we realise how much we had stolen – it was well over US$100,000. In our fantasy and our planning, we had expected $10,000, maybe $20,000. This was insane. For me, there was no euphoria at all, no feeling of having struck it rich or hit the jackpot. In fact, as we counted, my feelings of security were inversely proportionate to the total, which crept higher and higher as my mood sank. It just made things worse. I couldn't believe we had done this. We weren't just chicken-shit bank robbers who were going to get a slap on the wrist for a stupid misdemeanor. This was a major crime and I knew it. I would have given just about anything to have been back at work at Pepi's, with none of this having happened.

We agreed we had to get out of town as fast as we could. We didn't think we were being pursued by the local sheriff anymore, but most probably by the State Police and the FBI, the CIA and the fucking Men In Black. Getting a flight would be dangerous – they might have our details at every desk in the state, waiting for one of us to hand over our passport. A bus seemed the safest way.

I looked in the Yellow Pages and, to my joy, saw that there was a Greyhound bus terminal just down the street. So we repacked our bags, collected ourselves and made our way down there, in the hope that the buses would be regular enough to get us out of the USA by nightfall.

When we entered the terminal, the scene that greeted us was one of total chaos. There were people everywhere, mostly Hispanics or Mexicans babbling to each other in Spanish. The noise was incredible – dogs barking and birds squawking, all sorts of animals wandering around as if this were some kind of zoo. The whole scene was so weird I felt like we'd stumbled onto some post-apocalyptic movie set. Standing in line, I felt as safe as I had way back when I was on the snowboard, racing down the mountain slope in Vail. Nobody was ever going to find us in the middle of this madness.

When we reached the desk, we said we wanted to get a bus to Mexico. We were told that buses didn't go to the border, that they only went as far as Albuquerque in New Mexico. When we asked about the next bus to Albuquerque, they told us that one had just left about five minutes before, and the next one would be in seven hours. My heart sank. Our luck was beginning to run out.

We realised we'd probably have to get a plane, as risky as that was. The best thing we could do, we thought, was to at least stash the money, or part of it. A backpack absolutely full of dollars would undoubtedly arouse suspicion when it appeared on the airport x-ray. We had to thin the bundles out so that it didn't look so obviously like the takings of a huge bank heist.

Down the road from the bus terminal was a bank, so we went inside to inquire about the possibility of renting a safety deposit box into which we could put the money until some later time. We spoke to the manager, who was polite and helpful, presumably because he had no idea he was talking to two outlaws who'd just taken down another bank at gunpoint. However, when he asked us if we had an address in the United States and we told him we didn't, he said that regrettably he couldn't help us, as the law requires that anyone renting a safe deposit box must have residential status in the USA.

We decided to head to the nearest post office and try to mail some money home. We purchased cardboard mailing boxes and piled as much money as we could inside – around US$20,000 in two separate boxes, one mailed to my home address and another one to Luke's post office box in Byron Bay. How and when we were going to retrieve them, and what the people at home might think, were not questions that occurred to me. We didn't have time to consider things like that. At this point, we were in survival mode. Thinking ahead was a luxury I felt I couldn't afford.

We decided we had better try to launder some of the money by converting it into something compact and easy to sell – jewellery, watches, anything small and expensive. It was then that we hailed a taxi which would turn out to be an interesting ride. The taxi was driven by a man named Martinez, a big, dark, heavy-looking dude who looked to me like someone who, had he known what we were up to, would have been happy to come along for the ride. Or at least he looked like a dude who'd keep his mouth shut. We asked him if he could take us to some jewellery stores, and he was happy to oblige, driving us to one nearby and promising to wait while we shopped inside.

The idea was to convert as many of the small-denomination banknotes as possible, as they were taking up the most room for the least return. So I swaggered into this jewellery store declaring I was there to spend up big, and to prove it I dumped US$25,000 in five-dollar bills right there on the table – wads of notes bound tight with bands from the Federal Reserve Bank of America. One might assume that jewellery stores take receipt of ill-gotten gains on a regular basis, and that if they shied away from such money the bottom could well fall out of their business. In any event, without any questions I was ushered behind a nice little polished wooden fence that told me I was a Very Important Person. Then a security guard opened a gate that allowed us into this little room where high rollers go to sit while the monkeys in the store bring everything to them as if they're kings and queens.

I was asked what in particular I wanted to see, and so I demanded a showing of Rolex watches. A woman disappeared for a while and at last returned with a tray of some of the most magnificent watches I had ever seen. There was one that sparkled with conspicuous diamonds that caught my eye, primarily because I knew it would be worth more than the others. When the woman told me I would not receive terribly much change from my pile of $25,000, I replied that I didn't care, this was the watch I wanted, and when I saw something I liked I took it – all that sort of crap. The woman nodded, smiled and said she'd just go and fetch the certificate.

'What certificate?' I said, incredulous. 'What the fuck are you talking about?'

'It's just the certificate of authentication, sir,' she replied.

Now, I never knew that expensive pieces of jewellery like this came with authentication certificates. So my big spender act was suddenly shattered by my own naivety and confusion.

'Don't worry about the certificate,' I said. 'Just give me the watch and we're sweet!'

'But you're going to need the certificate of authentication if you wish to sell the watch or have it valued,' insisted the woman. 'It'll only take a minute.' And then she disappeared out the back of the store.

Totally paranoid, I turned to Luke in a complete panic. 'This is bullshit!' I whispered. 'There's no fucking certificate.

She's calling the cops. C'mon, Luke, let's get the fuck out of here.'

Luke tried to calm me down, but I wouldn't have a bar of it. I was convinced we were somehow being set up to be busted. I stood, grabbed all the money from the table and stormed out of the little room, barging through the little polished wooden fence and marching out onto the street, with Luke following behind me.

Later, in court, that woman from the jewellery store claimed that she had gone straight out the back and called the police as soon as we had entered the store. I wonder. She called the cops all right, but when? After the sale had fallen through? It's interesting how people think that if they didn't actually hold the gun, then they haven't robbed anyone. I think a lot of people are like that.

We climbed back into the cab outside, where Martinez had been dutifully waiting. As we drove around and spoke, I noticed Martinez was listening, though he wasn't saying a word. He was just silent, staring straight ahead.

We asked him to take us to another jewellery store, and he pulled up outside one a little further up the road. We got out and went inside, browsing casually over the cabinet. I spied this 18-carat gold ring encrusted with diamonds, and began imagining it on Clare's finger. It was only worth $2000, which didn't seem like much, but would be an awful lot to brag about back in Byron Bay. Of course, I was now straying completely from the entire point of the exercise – we were supposed to be laundering the money, exchanging as much of it as possible for goods we could carry. But my greed and need for approval was derailing the plan right there. I was on a shopping spree, I couldn't help myself.

By the time we left the store, I had my ring and Luke had purchased a $10,000 diamond – that's as much as he could spend without having to show his tax file and social security number. We paid for it all in $10 notes, the staff of the jewellery store being careful to photocopy every note. It was ludicrous, Luke pulling bricks of money out of his pocket, laying them on the counter and saying: 'Here . . . how much is that?' The woman would count it and say: 'There's $2000 there, so that's $8000 in total.' So Luke would pull another brick out of his pocket and split it in half: 'There . . . how much is that?' It was just so stupidly obvious that we had never handled this amount of money in our lives.

The whole jewellery store adventure was becoming too stressful, and we had the feeling we were merely leaving a trail of clues behind us, the Hansel and Gretel of bank robbers. We got back in the cab and asked Martinez to take us to the airport.

It occurred to me then that each time we had been into jewellery stores, we had left our bags, full of stolen money, in the back of Martinez's cab. Had he ever decided to take off with our bags he'd have been astonished at what he found. Today, I wonder how much he knew at that point. Interestingly, as he drove us to the airport, he began to talk about his daughter, how much he loved her and how he wished he was able to provide her a better life – a curious thing to talk about, considering who was in his cab, and what their problem was.

I honestly don't remember anymore why we did it, whether it was genuine altruism, fear of having too much money or a belief that Martinez was dropping us the hint that his silence had a price. Perhaps it was a combination of all of those things. Whatever the case, when we pulled up outside Denver International Airport and paid our fare, I dropped one of our backpacks onto the front seat of the cab, one that I knew contained around US$20,000.

'This is for you and your daughter,' I said. Martinez just nodded slowly, smiled a little, said thank you in a very sincere tone, then reached around and handed me his card, in case we ever needed a taxi. We bundled our bags out of his cab, waved goodbye and he drove away.

The thing is, we didn't really want the money anymore. It had become nothing more to us than a burden we longed to be rid of. Looking back, I think when the robbery was done, it was over – the joke was complete, our curiosity satisfied. We didn't want to know about the rest of it, even the money. Sure, we needed money to get on buses and planes and to pay for hotel rooms, but that's all. In the end, we robbed a bank because we'd asked each other if we could, and neither of us had wanted to admit that we couldn't, that there was one adventure we couldn't pull off. If there'd been some kind of deal offered to us, where we were to give back all the money we still had and work to pay back the rest, I would have taken it in a heartbeat. I can't speak for

Luke, but at that point, I suspect, he was beginning to feel the same.

It was dark when we entered the airport, around 6 pm. We inquired about flights to Mexico, but they told us there were no more until the morning.

We wandered around the airport concourse for a while, trying to think of what to do. Was there anywhere else we could fly to? Should we hang it and try to make a break for home? Maybe they still hadn't worked out the identities of the guys who'd robbed the WestStar Bank in Vail that morning – there didn't seem to be any sort of unusual police presence at the airport, and nobody seemed to be watching us.

But we were tired. In our minds, we'd been running since morning, and it had been, without a doubt, the biggest day of our lives. When we realised we really had no choice but to go back to the hotel room we'd paid for and sleep until morning, we were both overcome by a sudden exhaustion. A night in a comfortable bed seemed like a great idea after all.

Before we left the airport, I decided to call Clare from a public phone. I needed to hear her voice, just to have a little bit of love and sanity in a loveless day that was as mad as all hell. When she picked up and said hello, it was like being suddenly anchored in a storm – her voice was such a calming little relic from a comfortable world that I knew was already lost to me. She sensed that something was wrong from the sound of my voice. She kept asking me what was wrong, and the first few times I denied anything was troubling me at all. But after a while I began to break down. I couldn't tell her the truth, not yet. All I could say was that I'd done something foolish and that I wasn't sure what the result would be. She kept pumping me for details – 'What, Anthony? What is it you've done?' – but I couldn't tell her. I said we'd just wait and see, and that maybe I'd tell her once it had all blown over. I told her I loved her, that I'd speak to her soon, and then I hung up.

It would be the last time, for a long time, that I'd speak as a free man to anyone I loved.

We awoke at the crack of dawn after a fitful night's sleep, immediately switching on the television to check the news for bulletins about ourselves. There was nothing – no mugshots, no mention of any bank hold-up at all. Maybe this sort of thing happened so often in Colorado that they didn't even bother reporting it anymore. Maybe they didn't even bother reporting bank robberies to the police these days. Maybe bank heists were just a part of life here, to the point where everyone had just gotten used to them, bank robbers no more reviled by society than skateboarders or Jehovah's Witnesses.

With the dawn of a new day, and the promise of fleeing to Mexico, it suddenly felt like we might get away with this after all. If Jessica and Kim hadn't identified us – which

I thought was at least a possibility – then the police would take at least 24 hours to conduct inquiries and piece it all together. Even then there was no guarantee they were going to know it was us.

But, just to be sure, we had to fly out early. Before we left the hotel, we repacked our bags again, trying to spread the money around and make it less conspicuous. We stuffed as much as we could in our pockets, in our belts, in our backpacks, in our socks and down our pants. We still had way too much.

On our way to the airport in the cab we talked about it, in whispers to each other. As far as I was concerned, we had one bag full of money too many. We could spread the rest out between us but we were still about $20,000 too heavy, that extra bag of money being too obvious and hard to explain. We were sure it'd be picked up by the x-ray screening.

When we got to the airport, we were still trying to decide what to do with the extra bag of money. We'd become kind of obsessed with it, and so we knew it had to go. Why we were having such trouble forcing ourselves to get rid of it I'm not really too sure, although I suppose it's not every day that you throw out $20,000 – it goes against every instinct of someone who lives in a western capitalist country. In the end, we decided to take the bag to the bathroom, salvage as much money as we dared from it, then dump it in one of the garbage bins outside the airport.

While we were in the bathroom, stuffing notes into all remaining pockets and crevices, one of us got the bright idea to take photographs of ourselves with all the money, before we threw it away. It was kind of like the stupid bank robber's version of holiday snaps that prove you were there, only where other people took photos of themselves standing proudly by the Grand Canyon or The Big Banana, Luke and I would stand next to money. I suppose we were having such a hard time saying goodbye to all this cash that we just had to get photos of ourselves with it, though I'm not sure who we were ever going to show them to. It's not as if we were ever going to have slide nights with our grandkids – 'Oh, this is when me and Uncle Luke robbed a bank in Colorado . . .'

Anyway, we took those photos, right there in the airport bathroom. I took Luke's first. He held up the money, fanned out in his hands, and was smiling like some sort of fucked-up geisha. Then he took mine. I held a fan of twenties in one hand, an entire brick of notes in the other, my arms crossed over as a Mexican bandit might pose with his pistols. Then I tilted my head back, pursed my lips and blew a sloppy kiss at the camera. Even as I was posing for it, a little voice in my head was whispering a warning that this photo would one day come back to haunt me.

Today, when I look at that picture, I see a complete Desmond who has a few minutes to live. Because that Anthony Prince doesn't exist anymore – not really. He didn't even last the day. The transformation that was to take place destroyed the fuckwit in that photo completely, and life for me would never be the same again. Not that

I deserve any credit for that, because the change was forced upon me. Had it not been, I'd probably still be the loser that I was – greedy, obsessed with money, convinced that wealth and conspicuous evidence of that wealth was the only sort of worthwhile status.

The point is that the photo of me clowning around with the money was to become very widely distributed as proof of what a fool I was. And I can't argue with that: the guy in the photo is a top-shelf dickhead, no doubt about it. But just because I can say that about myself doesn't make the photo any less embarrassing. The fact that it was so widely broadcast as the definitive image of Anthony Prince still gives me a bit of a kick in the guts. (I certainly hope my publisher doesn't use that photo for the cover of this book, but I don't like my chances, somehow.)

We eventually emerged from the bathroom and found a bin outside the terminal concourse. Then we dumped the backpack, full to bursting with small denominations from a bank robbery, inside. Maybe some lucky drunk would hit the jackpot while fossicking for his breakfast. I hoped so.

We made our way to the ticketing office, all the while looking around for signs that cops were searching for us. There didn't seem to be any sort of police presence at all – just the usual airport security guards. My heart began to thump harder, not out of panic, but relief. Perhaps we really were going to get away with this after all.

We asked the girl behind the counter for two one-way tickets to Mexico City. She responded straight away that they didn't sell one-way tickets, only returns. For one stupid moment I thought this was a real bummer, until I reminded myself that Luke and I weren't exactly strapped for cash. We agreed to take return tickets, presented our passports and checked our luggage. She fiddled with the computer for a while, told us our flight was leaving in half an hour, issued us with our boarding passes and smilingly wished us a happy trip.

We cruised around for a while, got a bit of breakfast, shopped a little. Then we went to the airport post office and mailed more money home. We were sure we weren't being watched.

The next few hours live in my memory not like ordinary recollections do, but more like a series of impressions that are joined together by a big blur of time, the exact duration of which I don't think I'll ever know. My memory of that time is so hazy because it's made up mostly of shock and panic, and the sort of disbelief that makes the blood rush to your head until you pass out. People talk of time moving in slow motion when they're witnessing or experiencing incredibly frightening or shocking things, and I think it's because, when you're that alarmed, your senses become so highly tuned they take in too much information – every smell, every sight, every word becomes amplified – and, later, when your brain has slowed back down to its normal speed, you suffer sensory overload. It all becomes crowded and fuzzy. But I can still see it if I close my eyes and think hard enough.

I can see myself moving towards the customs scan, lines of people waiting at the security point. There's a black lady in a security uniform. She asks to see our passports. She ushers us over to the side, as if we've been chosen for the security check. There are people who have been through this line, putting their shoes back on – maybe this is routine. I'm not worried by this. There are no police I can see. Bags down. Shoes off. Belts off. She asks me to take my hoodie off. We are asked to walk through the metal detector. I walk through. My shoes are waiting there. I sit down to put them on. Luke is taking a little bit longer than me, but eventually sits down beside me to put his shoes on, too. I look up and see everyone else moving through the line easily – I think that this is the way my life always works. I'm always the one who gets pulled aside, checked, suspected. I must have an untrustworthy face.

Someone screams at me.

'Don't move! Put your hands up! Don't move! Don't move! Get on your knees! Put your hands behind your fucking head!'

I look up and see people running towards me – they're all in black. Some are in bulletproof vests. They've got guns drawn. Pointing them at me. This is it. This is what we've been running from. Oh, fuck. It's over. It's the beginning of something really bad.

I'm on my knees with my hands behind my head. I'm cuffed. They pull me up and walk me. I see onlookers, staring. It's humiliating. My pants are falling down, because

I've taken my belt off, and I can't stop them from going down. No good. We are taken around a corner and down a hallway. There's a big room with computers, faxes, printers, workstations, and photocopies of me and Luke on a pinboard. This whole room is all about us. We are moved through that room until we come to cells. Two of them. They put us inside. I hear voices saying: 'We got 'em. We got 'em.' There are faces peering in the window.

This is big. This is fucking big. Why didn't I know this? How did I not know it would be this big? I robbed a bank! Now, everybody will know. The cops are high-fiving each other, laughing, behaving like jocks. They're ripping through our stuff, pulling out the money, stacking it. I can hear it. They hate our guts. Why? I didn't do anything to them, did I?

A guy in a white shirt enters and reads me my rights. I have the right to remain silent. Anything I say can be used against me in a court of law. I have a right to an attorney. But they also tell me I am going to jail for life unless I play ball. It's life for armed robbery, they say. Hours pass. The man in the white shirt comes back in and asks me if I want something to eat. He gets me a burger from some place in the airport. Then the suits turn up. FBI.

I hear what I think is Luke vomiting in the room next door, or maybe pissing himself. The cops are laughing, telling him he's made a mess that he'll have to clean up. I want to cry but I can't. I'm too scared to cry. Too shocked.

I agree to confess to everything. I don't need an attorney. If I just do the right thing maybe I'll wake up from this shit.

3

We had shackles clamped on ankles and wrists, all attached by chains to a belt on the waist, and were escorted like this down to an armoured van that contained cages for us to be transported in. All of these little insults registered in my gut: the shackles; a cage, like one for an animal, but for me; a hand grabbing my arm without asking; someone talking to me but not using my name, just ordering me around – all of these moments were fresh and startling the first time. They were little outrages I would get used to eventually, but not yet.

They split Luke and me up and placed us in separate vans, with two guards for each of us. The guards were an unnecessary measure – even if I'd fallen out of the van I was so numb I don't think I could have run anywhere. For the whole journey, the guards didn't talk to me at all, just between themselves a little. They spoke in a language of words and letters and numerals – little codes that meant something to them but not me. It was just another reminder that I was now on the outside of life in the world, that I was not involved in ordinary discourse or the courtesies that attended them.

I don't know how long the trip in the van really lasted, but, for me, it felt like hours. In reality it could only have been minutes before we turned down a driveway toward a basement car park, a battery of gates and electronic doors opening for us to pass through and closing behind us, armed guards everywhere. We at last pulled into a single garage and, once the door had closed behind us, the guards wordlessly ushered me out of the van. I noticed an electronic dumb waiter opening, the guards putting weapons inside before it closed and motored to some place above. We were entering into a place of intense security. I was so scared I could hardly breathe.

I was walked through corridors of concrete and steel, as dank and dark as a wartime bunker, with unfriendly sounds echoing from distant places – a violent shout, a jangle of keys, a slamming lock, the electric drone of a door being opened, like the sound of a buzzer from some depressing game show. This was a nightmare.

I was led to a single cell, placed inside and locked in. It was small, cold, with a concrete bench and a steel toilet in the corner. A single payphone hung on the wall. I picked it up and listened, in the vain hope that there might be some sympathetic voice from the outside world on the other end, but there was no dial tone. The walls were absolutely covered with graffiti, scrawls and names and angry declarations. I'm not sure how long I sat in there, waiting, wondering what was to become of me. Eventually, a guard came, opened my cell and led me to another small area. I was told to completely remove my clothes. I was to be strip-searched.

Once naked, I was ordered to put my hands behind my head, squat and cough. I was then told to stand, and led to another cell where I waited while they thoroughly searched my clothes. They gave them back to me and told me to get dressed. I was then led to an elevator, taken up a few floors and then walked down another maze of sad concrete corridors, all of them painted the dreariest greys or khaki greens. It seemed that even a bit of colour on the walls or uniforms had been removed just in case an inmate were to get some small joy out of it.

I spied the common area to my right as I passed by – steel picnic tables, a little TV up in the corner of the ceiling, housed inside a cage of its own, the volume way too loud as some episode of Jerry Springer farted from the speaker. Even those on television were prisoners here. That this was a world of punishment was something the superintendent of Denver City Jail did not want us to ever forget.

As I passed by cells I saw inmates sleeping, reading books, or just lying there staring at nothing. Those sounds kept echoing. The shouts were the worst – the banging on the door and the obscenities as some inmate lost it. I wondered how long it would be until I would become like that. I didn't imagine it would take very long for me to go crazy in this cathouse.

Eventually I arrived outside of a cell. There was one inmate inside. The guards ordered him to place his hands through a slot in the lower part of the door. They hand-cuffed him and ordered that he move to the rear of the cell. Then they opened the door and ordered me inside, telling me to stand at the rear of the cell until the door was closed. I did as I was told. Only then were we ordered forward, one at a time, and told to place our hands through the slot to have our cuffs removed. At last I was 'free'.

The cell was tiny – 1.5 metres wide at best. My cellmate was a black dude, late thirties, though he looked about 50, weathered, haggard, with stale, matted hair. He had the look of a crackhead – a look I would get to know well over the next few years. There was a crook little window through which you could look if you wanted a miserable view of the car park below. This guy was standing there, constantly, looking down, prattling on about his sister and how she was coming to bust him out, or bring him something she had promised. After a while he asked me what I was in for, and I told him I robbed a bank. With a BB gun. He laughed a little. Then, more annoyingly, he began to tell me what I'd done wrong, and how, exactly, I should do it next time.

This was a depressing reality of prison with which I was to become very familiar – the endless procession of prisoners who believe they are the international experts on all things criminal. Everybody knew how to do a job right, how to dissect what you did and tell you where you went wrong, and how stupid you were. It never seemed to occur to any of these wankers that people in prison aren't exactly shining examples of how to make crime pay. There were many things of worth to be learned from some of the robust characters of the prison system, but how to commit crime and get away with it was clearly not any inmate's area of expertise.

Anyway, once he'd instructed me as to how to take down a bank in future, he climbed up onto his bench and began a fitful, scratching sleep. I lay down, too, on my 'bed' underneath, which was basically the floor, with a slim rubber mattress, stained and full of holes. The crackhead's bed was no more than 10 centimetres above my nose. I remember lying down, closing my eyes, but being completely unable to think of anything but what had happened since I was arrested.

Everything had happened so quickly since that moment, and almost none of it was voluntary – every move I'd made had been ordered, every word I'd spoken coaxed out of me, every thought I'd had was concerned with what I was supposed to do the very next second, or where I was going, or what the fuck was happening. I had been like some kind of remote-control human who had no real will of his own, and all the while I'd been numb with this dread that I didn't even have the luxury to dwell upon, a panic that I could only feel and suffer. Here, at last, was the first chance I'd had to actually think for a stretch, about what had gone down and what might happen. I'm usually pretty positive, able to see the silver lining without too much trouble. But, this time, I couldn't think of anything nice, any memory from my life that might have carried me away on my imagination. Nothing like that belonged in here with me. My thoughts were entirely negative. I don't think I've ever felt so lost and lonely and scared as I did that night.

I remember rolling over and seeing a pamphlet on the floor, which I reached out and opened. It was Christian literature. Inside was a gay story about a little boy who was bad until one day he decided to announce his faith in The Lord and life became peachy forevermore. I remember being particularly crushed by that pamphlet, and the thought that it might be the only sort of literature I was going to be allowed to read for the next few decades of my life. Prisons are breeding grounds for born-again Christians, lost souls looking for anything to grab onto, any visitor who might treat them kindly, or who might help them turn over a new leaf in the eyes of the parole board. I was terribly worried that this might happen to me. I made a mental note to fight any influences that might change me from the guy I was.

I didn't cry that night, or sleep much. I was too fucked up to do either. I really did think my life was over. My entire insides were buzzing with panic, intense depression and maddening regret. If only we'd waited for the bus instead. If only we'd paid the taxi driver to take us all the way to Mexico. If only I'd refused to take part in the robbery. If only

I'd gone home sooner. If only I'd declined Luke's offer to come and work with him in Vail. If only I wasn't so weak, hung up on money and appearances. I was an absolute mess of sorrow and self-pity, and there was nobody to turn to for comfort. Nobody. It was the time in my life when I'd most needed love, and love had never been further away, replaced by nothing but concrete and loathing.

In the morning we were marshalled into the common room for breakfast, which consisted of a slice of white bread with cold gravy on top (a meal known as 'Shit on a Shingle' in the informal language of the jail menu) and a tiny carton of milk. I can honestly say that was the lousiest breakfast I've ever had in my life. Thankfully, I never had to eat at Denver City Jail again. Not long after breakfast I was told to put my hands through the slot in the cell door so I could be cuffed and moved to Jefferson County Jail, just under an hour's drive away.

Another van with cages, more shackles, more electronic doors opening and closing, another journey of unknown distance, more strip-searches – this time, I was ordered to 'uncover any crevices' that might be used to conceal something. I was issued a yellow jumpsuit and sandals and was subjected to a brief psychological examination designed to determine my level of 'risk' as an inmate, and the corresponding level of security that would be required to keep me under the thumb. It's a tiny sort of insult when you discover you're classified as low security – you're not dangerous, not smart enough, or crazy enough, to attempt an escape. That proud part inside of every man feels like showing them how wrong their classification system was about you. At any rate, I was classified as a level 5 prisoner.

JeffCo, as the inmates called it, was a different sort of prison from Denver City Jail. It was modern, clean, more like a mental institution than a jail. The entire complex was cylindrical in shape, with different levels stacked on top of each other. Each circular level was divided into four pods, like slices of pizza – A, B, C and D – with eight bunks and eight lockers in each. On level 5 – the ground level – there were no bars, cages or armed guards, only white walls and stainless steel. The cells were stacked on two levels, at the thick end of the wedge, all facing a large day room with two TVs. There were no doors on the cells in level 5 – everything in the cells and the day area was visible from a central security office known as The Fish Bowl, from where the security staff could see everything that happened in every cell, in every pod, for 360 degrees. Inside the day room was a single officer at a desk, a big yellow line around him on the floor, a barrier over which no inmate could trespass. That one officer opened doors for meals and for inmates who needed to go to the medic or for other things.

The only escape was through a door that led to a small recreation yard covered in wire mesh that allowed in sunlight and moonlight and rain – the little paradise of the entire prison, that kept many an inmate sane over the years. Basketball, volleyball and ping-pong could be played in the rec area, and there were pull-up bars for daily workouts.

There'd be a count at ten in the morning, four in the afternoon and nine at night. You'd have to be in your cell at those times, and they'd make you stand beside your bed, so that you could be accounted for. That sounds reasonable, but it was actually bloody inconvenient and could ruin your day. You'd be on your bed having a nap or something and you'd hear an officer call out: 'Four o'clock, stand up!' Then, of course, he'd take his sweet time to get around to your cell. Sometimes, he'd call out only to stand in his office chatting with some buddy while we were all supposed to stand to attention and wait for him. Many a time I lay back down and drifted off to sleep, only to be awoken fifteen minutes later by the bastard standing at the door of my cell shouting at me. As soon as I'd stand up he'd have moved along to the next cell. That would usually be held against you as an infraction, and once you had a few of those against your name you'd be shunted up to medium security for a spell.

Aside from that, there's the very nature of having another man shouting at you to stand up. It's the most humiliating, angering thing. A lot of people might think that it's just part of the prison deal – that those who are judged as criminals deserve to be treated harshly and in a militaristic fashion. But you've got to understand that prison inmates are still men, proud ones at that. In fact, an overabundance of pride is probably what landed them in jail in the first place. Yet here they are being screamed at and ordered around by other men, many of whom are weaker and less intelligent than your average male. Take the uniform and the keys off many of them and they'd be lucky if they could survive in these places, and yet they're lording it over everyone. It's unnatural and it happens daily, morning, noon and night. It's one thing that I never got used to, and, today, the easiest way to make me hate you is to aggressively tell me what to do.

When you're a new inmate, the first person you meet in your pod is the elected representative inmate of the pod, whose job it is to meet each new inmate and show them around, read them the rules and generally tell them what time it is. Mine was a big black dude called 'D' (he was Dwayne – D for short). He was about six foot two, pretty staunch but dead mellow, with one of those lazy black American accents that are very hard to understand until you've become acclimatised to them. He dutifully but unenthusiastically ran me through the list of rules on the wall of our cell – make your bed at all times, clean up your own mess, lockdown at these times, count time at these times, and so on – and then went and sat back down to watch TV.

As my luck would have it, there were no more beds available in my cell, so I had to sleep in what was known as a 'boat', which was basically a portable plastic canoe that a mattress fitted into. All the other bunks on either side were occupied, with me to be cast adrift in the middle of the cell. I had no locker either, but only a sanitary bag that I'd been issued, with a little toothbrush, tiny tubes of soap and shampoo, a towel and that's it. These were my worldly possessions, which I would keep safe under my mattress.

I looked around the cell for a while, read the rules. I don't know what I expected – certainly not a welcoming party – but the way everyone was so disinterested in me was uncomfortable. They were all just sitting around with headsets on in the day room watching the TV, because that is how the sound was transmitted.

Eventually, a few guys wandered into the cell to read or take a nap, and one of them introduced himself, a hard little Hispanic fella they called Gavino. He asked how I was going and I said all right. Immediately, he looked at me quizzically and asked: 'What sorta accent's that, man?' I told him I was Australian. 'Australian?' he replied, turning to his mate. 'Ya hear that, bro? This dude's from Australia!' And then the questions started.

I've never been the sort of guy who's necessarily patriotic – being born in New Zealand probably puts a bit of a dampener on my inner Aussie flag-waver – but I can exclusively reveal that being Australian is a bit of a bonanza in the American prison system, where the population is overwhelmingly Hispanic, African American, or Anglo Yank. There's a sprinkling of Poms and a few Asians, but being

Australian is a bit of a novelty. People are still curious about Australia, and see it as an exotic place from some distant part of the world, which I guess it is. From the moment that Gavino reacted to my accent I realised that being Australian was going to help me in this place.

And from what I was seeing I was going to need all the help I could get. There were plenty of people about my age in the prison, but they were obviously a lot harder than me – they were raw and schizo, bad American kids, and I knew I didn't have that gene in me. I remember very early on seeing two of them, a black and a white guy, about my age but significantly chunkier than me, who obviously had a problem with each other. They went into the bathroom and fought – a really vicious fight – and the white guy wound up getting the black dude in a headlock which he wouldn't release. He had the black guy on his knees, choking, until he finally let him go.

'Fuck, man,' the black dude gasped. 'You tryin' to kill me, man?!'

'Next time I will, motherfucker!' the white guy barked, before storming out all heroically.

Later that night, the white dude was sitting in the day room watching TV. He must have felt pretty comfortable, as there weren't all that many blacks in Jefferson – it was mainly whites and Hispanics. Unfortunately for him, one of the blacks that Jefferson did have was D, and the black dude the white guy had nearly strangled to death had obviously gone to D with a complaint.

D marched straight up to this white guy, stood in front of him and leaned down so that his eyes were an inch away from the white guy's eyes.

'Yo, white boy!' he thundered. 'You go near my man again and I'll fucken crush your motherfucken head in my bare fucken hands!'

It went on and on, at full volume, right in this white dude's face. Everyone could see it, everyone could hear it, and it just didn't stop.

'You fucken listening to me, bitch? I'll fucken waste your ass, you little piece of shit!'

The interesting thing about this was that the officer in charge was sitting about 3 metres away. Like everyone else, he could see it and hear it – he knew exactly what was going on. But he did nothing. Later, I would learn that D had a special place in this prison. He was respected by the inmates because he was a bad motherfucker when he wanted to be, but he was also respected by the screws because D helped get things done. If there was too much noise in the day area, D would step out of his cell and shout 'Shut the fuck up!' and it'd save the screws the hassle of having to do it themselves. If there were dishes to be done, D would organise the work party. He made things flow, and the whole prison respected him for that. But, in those early days, before I knew anything about anything, the scene with D and that white dude in the day room shook me up a little bit. It was such a blatant display of potential violence and inmate power, and it had happened right under the nose of the authorities. I realised that nobody was safe in this prison, that anyone could do anything to anyone if they wanted. All they had to do was know the right people, and here I was at the very bottom of that pyramid. I knew nobody, and that scared the shit out of me.

I had been in JeffCo for two days when I was called down to the day room. It was the early evening, about 7 pm, and one of the counsellors had a cordless phone in his hand – a special call had been organised to come through the prison's telephone system. I knew straight away that it was my mum and dad. I took the phone out into the corridor just outside the pod, which was thankfully deserted. I got out the word 'Hello?' and, when I heard their voices, I dissolved. I sobbed that I was so sorry, and then wept pathetically for the entire call. All the fear and sorrow I'd been feeling since being arrested came flooding out. All I could hear was my own misery, punctuated by the sounds of their voices trying to reassure me – 'Don't worry, Anthony. It's okay. We'll get through this . . .'

We'll get through this. *We'll* get through this. That got me. They were telling me that I was not alone, that at no time should I feel they were not here with me, suffering this incarceration and working through the problem. It was what they'd always done – they had always stressed to me that, no matter what happened, they were always beside me. Here was the greatest test of their love and loyalty and they didn't falter for a second. That was impressive – so impressive that it made me sob more wretchedly than before. I was completely inconsolable, wiping great oceans of snot all over the sleeves of my prison jumpsuit. I was a mess.

In no time at all, it seemed, the guard had his head around the corner telling me that I had one more minute, so I tried to straighten up. Mum asked if I was safe. Dad asked if I needed anything. Not once did they ask what I'd done, why I'd done it, or admonish me for being a bad son. The totality of their energy was devoted to assuring me that they were here, that they were on my case, and that everything would be all right. They told me that they loved me, as I told them, and then the call was over.

I tried to dry my eyes so that the other inmates couldn't see. I shuffled back into my cell, lay down in the boat, turning over on my side and facing away from the others, several of whom were lying on their beds, reading, or talking to each other. Every time I felt a big wave of sobs welling up in me I had to push it back down, because I knew if it started it wouldn't be stopped until it had been a deluge. Hearing my parents' voices had been the strangest mixture of comfort and pain to a degree that I have never felt before or since. To hear the voices of the ones who had loved me for my entire life was a long-awaited bliss, but it was lonely, too, knowing they were so far away, so isolated from me. It carried the sadness that I imagine might come when someone listens to a recording of a friend or relative who has passed away.

The cosy familiarity was instantly curdled by the sorrow of knowing they were, for all practical purposes, lost to me.

But even more crushing than that was the shame. Until that moment, I hadn't faced up to the reality of what a fucking stupid thing I had done. Upon hearing the voices of my mother and father, trying so hard to be strong for me (when I know today they dissolved themselves when they hung up the phone), I realised how selfish it was to assume that I was the only one who would suffer as a result of my actions. My parents were in hell for me, as were my sisters, my grandparents, and all of their friends in countless little ways. And Clare – how was she going to handle this? It really came home to me then that your life is never really your own, that you share it with those around you, and are responsible to them, if you love them at all. It was a lesson I was to learn again and again in the little laboratory of society that is the prison system.

As I was to eventually discover, Dad had been on his way to work when he took the call from Luke's parents. It was about 9 am. They suggested Dad had better come over straight away. Luke and Anthony have robbed a bank, they said, and are in an American prison. Dad thought it was a joke. He thought Luke and I had come home early, and that we'd jump out from behind some door or curtain to surprise him. So he agreed to be there as soon as he could. Then, when Dad walked in and saw their faces, he knew there was no joke, and that we weren't coming home for a good while yet.

*

It didn't take me long to gravitate towards a few inmates who, for one reason or another, I found I liked. One was Gavino, who I'd met on my first day in JeffCo, and who turned out to be something of a leader in our pod – a 'pod master', as they referred to him. He was from New England in the north-eastern corner of the USA, was 29 years old, intelligent and awaiting trial for drug conspiracy. He had a kind face, but the inmates called him 'The Babyfaced Assassin' for a reason. He was quick and fearless. He was also deeply religious, and reflected his beliefs in how he acted each day. He could always be seen sharing his food with others or sitting down talking to someone who was feeling down for whatever reason. He was good to me and I came to trust him immediately. That might sound like a dangerous policy to adopt when in prison – to trust people so quickly. But reputations are the only possessions anyone really owns in prison, and the good ones tend to wear their reputations proudly. Bad characters don't get much of a chance to fake it for long in prison. If you snitch or steal from other inmates you'll get a name for it, and you can learn a lot about a person's reputation by the way other inmates behave towards them. There's no hiding from who you are in jail.

There was Anthony Cordova, otherwise known as 'Scrappy Doo', who was eighteen and celebrated his birthday one day after mine. He was being done for a minor drug charge and was probably going home sooner rather than later. And then there was Cesar Cortez, a Mexican guy who was super tough, bald, about five foot five, with a big black moustache, black eyes and his surname tattooed over his pecs in Old English lettering. He also had the X14 tattoo, the mark of a heavy Hispanic gang from LA. Cesar always had something funny to say. He was one of those guys who's so good with phrases and little quotes that they get absorbed into everyone's language. When he first met me he asked me my name. I'd already decided that I wasn't going to introduce myself as Anthony – the name had way too many syllables for the population of Jefferson County Jail – and to introduce myself as Prince was a shortcut to having my lights punched out for being up myself. So I introduced myself as Tony, a good prison name, I figured. Because of my accent, Cesar thought I'd said 'Tiny', then added 'Loc's' to the end (Loc's is abbreviated Spanish for 'crazy'). So Tiny Loc's I became. It felt good to be initiated in this way.

In fact, Cesar was the first to wise me up to how someone like me would get by in prison. His talent, aside from the obvious, was, ironically enough, designing greeting cards. With anything he could get his hands on – crayons, charcoal, ink, some piece of card – he'd draw a dove or these immaculate little love hearts, using toilet paper to buff and smear the colours so that the card looked arty and dead professional, and he'd sell them to inmates for food or other items. There was always a market for Cesar's cards because inmates were always writing letters back home, or sending little gifts on important dates. In those early days, I remember Cesar was always saying to me: 'Tiny Loc's, you gotta get your hustle on. This is my hustle, what's yours? You gotta work out what it is and get it on!' He was telling me that I had to think of something that would help me to survive more successfully than the prison system would allow. I didn't know what to think – at that point, I didn't believe I had any sort of talent that people might pay for. But it got my mind active about what I could do, what special thing Anthony Prince could bring to the community of Jefferson County Jail.

But the one who made the biggest impression on me, though not necessarily a positive one, was Pete, a white dude from my cell who was probably only about five foot eight, had long hair in a ponytail and a long, red beard. He was a bikie of some sort, a small nuggety dude in his mid-thirties. A few of us were talking one night when Pete and I began having an argument about nothing important. It began humorously enough, with him referring to the dumb crime that got me in there (always the first thing people would pick on when wanting to wind me up), and me responding with a few 'ginger' gags that got a few laughs from the crowd. Somehow, this spurred me on to keep pushing it – with all the cellmates there, it felt good to at last be a bit of a cheeky bastard, more of the smartarse I was back in Byron Bay. I felt comfortable being my old self again, so I started ripping into Pete, like I used to rip into my mates back home. I think the one that finally tore it was something about how if he didn't shut up I was going to grab that girly ponytail of his and use it as reins while I rode him like the slut he was, etc.

His mood changed immediately. The room fell quiet as he went off at me, telling me I'd crossed a line, angrily asking me if I wanted to go at it. Somehow, it diffused, but we went to bed with a problem that night. The foot of his bunk faced the foot of mine, conveniently, as my feet needed the extra space that was vacant at the bottom of his. But there was no vacancy that night. Several times before dawn, I was awoken by his feet kicking mine into the wall. I knew that this would somehow be coming to a head the following day.

It was about mid-morning when I was in the day room playing cards, keeping one eye on my cell, where I could see that Pete was working out, occasionally looking out the door at me, muttering something under his breath. Suddenly he appeared at my table, calling me a little bitch, frothing, as if he'd just injected something. I was just trying to calm him down, telling him to chill out, but then he slapped my face, which I knew was something you don't let slide in prison. He told me to follow him into the bathroom, where all the little brawls happened. I didn't want to, of course, but I had no choice. I had to do this. If I didn't, I knew I would never be able to hold my head up in this place.

Once in the bathroom, Pete started to slap me around a bit, throwing a few haymakers that didn't really connect. I defended myself pretty well considering it was my first fight in prison – didn't throw any punches that scored, but didn't really cop any either, apart from a glancing blow that swelled my lip a little. It was all over in a minute, with Pete satisfied that his dignity had been restored in the eyes of the other inmates, and me.

Later, everything having been sorted, I asked him what it had all been about. He kind of furrowed his brow, shook his head, smirked a little bit and remarked on how I had a cheeky mouth that I ought to keep on a leash. But after that morning he and I were cool.

I learned a lot out of that little incident. Most important of all was the lesson that I should never get too cocky in here. What worked among friends back in Byron Bay wasn't going to cut it in the American prison system. For a start, Americans are a little different from Australians, in that they don't respond well to being ridiculed, even in jest. With my friends back home, a lot of our time is spent savagely ripping into each other, and even strangers in Australia can absorb a fair amount of that sort of humour. But in America, the only place anyone can get away with it is on the sitcoms, where the characters aren't real and the insulting things they say to each other to make the audience laugh don't really hurt. Americans aren't good at criticism. Particularly men. And particularly men who are in prison.

But the other thing I learned – something just as important – was to never back down to a challenge. Even if you get the shit beaten out of you, that is worth more than the humiliation and loss of respect that will surely come from showing others that you are a coward. It was a very fine line to walk – it wasn't about shaping up to other dudes or picking fights with others so that you'd look tough. It was just about respect, being able to hold your head up, to show that you had the courage to face anything that was coming your way. There was an awesome feeling of satisfaction that came from being able to do this, and it was an exhibition to myself as much as to any of the other inmates. I was surprised to learn that I had this courage in me after all. It was a very good lesson for me to learn quickly, and I never forgot it.

A few weeks after that first phone call with my parents I was summoned by an officer for another – this time, they were allowing me to speak on the phone in the medic's office, just a bland little room where I could close the door and be alone with them for a while. I steeled myself to hold it together, to keep myself from crying again, lifted the phone to my ear and said hello. The moment I heard my mum and dad's voices, the tears started streaming down my face again. I tried talking through the tears, doing my best to disguise them, to pretend they weren't there. Then Mum and Dad put Jessie on the phone. Then my other sister, Kylie. I soldiered on with my voice wavering while the tears rolled down my cheeks, all the while looking up at this toilet roll that was sitting on a shelf just above the desk.

Then they put Clare on.

I don't remember much about the rest of that call. I remember Clare crying, saying she loved me, that she'd wait for me, and that when I thought of her while in this place I could be sure she was thinking of me, too. I remember thinking about how the hell she was going to cope with this. She was a schoolgirl, and the thought of her waking up, dressing in her uniform, talking briefly to her boyfriend in an American penitentiary and then going off to school seemed just too ridiculous to contemplate. I also remember that, when I hung up the phone at the end of the call, the toilet roll was about half as big as it had been at the start.

One thing my father had told me during that call was that he and Mum had been speaking to an attorney in Denver who was likely to come and visit me soon. Not long afterwards, I was in my cell one afternoon when I was told I had my first visitor. Normally, the visiting room is a row of booths with bulletproof glass and telephones for speaking. But prisoners can meet face-to-face, flesh-to-flesh with their lawyers, in another room entirely. It's the only bit of outside human contact most inmates in JeffCo get.

Waiting there for me was a man with big blue eyes, wire-rimmed glasses and a bow tie. He introduced himself as Rick Williamson, a public defence attorney, and handed me his card. I noticed that his card introduced him as 'Warren Williamson', not Rick.

'Well, Anthony,' he said, in his big, officious American voice, 'it looks like you've got yourself into a bit of a predicament.'

It instantly made me feel better seeing how casual and slightly amused he seemed about the whole thing. It might have been the first moment when I realised that this whole experience was going to be exactly what I made of it, nothing more and nothing less. I could hang my head like a caged dog and be miserable the whole time, going through hundreds of toilet rolls as I mopped up all my snot, or I could move through it like a ball bouncing down a set of stairs, surrendering to the fact that my immediate future was a little out of my control, but that was okay. The fact that someone else was seeing my 'predicament' as something more or less interesting made me see that it, in fact, was. What was happening to me was really fucking interesting.

I wasn't sure that Rick was going to represent me, and Rick wasn't either. He simply told me he'd been speaking to my parents and that he was keeping them counselled with regard to my situation. As the Assistant Federal Public Defender, Rick had the latitude to choose to attend to certain cases, and apparently mine had piqued his interest. He'd taken it upon himself to liaise with my parents, the prosecutor and my case officers, with a view to assigning my case to someone from within his own office. During their conversations, my father had apparently asked him to 'say hello to the Ant Man for me'. Rick's first question was to ask why they called me Ant Man. I looked down at the business card he had handed me.

'Well, why do they call you Rick?' I asked back.

He laughed. Then he laughed again. I don't think he ever answered my question. What he did do in that moment, though, is decide to take on my case personally, which is something for which I'm forever grateful. I suppose people like Rick meet some pretty hard and hopeless cases in the daily grind of their careers, and when they meet someone young and relatively normal they find it refreshing, and they make it their business to get such people out of the American prison system, where they hardly belong. Over the next six months, Rick was to become my best friend, the guy who knew best how to wriggle me out of my 'predicament'. He sent me documents on a daily basis, kept me abreast of where my life was going. He also organised something that would help get me through the days ahead.

He told me to call him every afternoon at about 4 pm, in his office in Denver. You could make collect calls from within the prison, and calling your lawyer was okay at any time. We'd shoot the breeze for a minute or two, talk briefly about how my case was going, then he'd ask who I wanted to speak to. Normally, it would be my mum and dad. So he'd call them on conference from his office. They'd answer the phone and I'd hear him always making the same lame joke – 'Oh, I've got this crazy kid calling my office who reckons he's your son . . .' – and then I'd get to speak to Mum and Dad, completely illegally, every day. It kept me sane just knowing it was there, that I could smash through these walls and reach out to anyone I wanted, at any time. Even Rick's lame jokes kind of lightened the load. What a satisfying job those guys must have, and occasionally terrible, too. That's the deal, I suppose.

In that first meeting, I also impressed upon Rick my desire to write a letter to Kim and Jessica, the tellers at the

WestStar bank in Vail. They had been on my mind since the robbery, especially Jessica, and that fear in her eyes. I knew that to write them a letter might be seen as a cynical attempt to show the authorities what a nice guy Anthony Prince really was, but the more I thought about that the more I realised it was a stupid reason to not say what I wanted to say. I felt strongly that if they only knew how sincerely sorry I was, and that they had never really been in any danger from me at all, they might have a better chance of getting over any residual trauma they might be suffering. Rick thought that letter would be a nice gesture, and that I should write while he made inquiries as to whether the two ladies were at all receptive to the idea, and the proper channels through which the letter should be sent.

I went straight back to my cell and wrote that letter, in my own hand, the very same day:

Dear Miss Vasquez and Miss Cole,

I am writing to express to you both how sorry I am and how deeply I regret putting both of you through the bank robbery in March. You both have absolutely no reason to forgive me, nor do I expect you to.

I have no idea how frightening it would have been for both of you. I knew I was only carrying a BB gun, but there was no way for the two of you to have known this. Not until the robbery was happening did I realise what a stupid and wrong idea it was for us to do it. I never intended to cause any harm to the two of you, or place you in a distressful situation. But, as I say, only when it was happening did I understand how frightening it must have been for both of you.

What heightens my sorrow for you both is that I have two sisters about your age, I suspect, back home in Australia. Their names are Kylie and Jessie. It would greatly upset me to learn that someone had forced them through what you both had to endure.

The act of greed and selfishness you witnessed and endured is not how I was brought up, I assure you.

Again, I do not expect your forgiveness, nor do I believe I deserve it. I only want you to know that I am genuinely sorry for what has happened. My only hope is that while I serve the next several years in an American prison for my foolishness that day, I will have learned a hard and important lesson.

Yours Sincerely,

Anthony Prince

One of Rick's first initiatives was to organise for a psychiatrist to come and see me in prison, to see if he could work out what, exactly, was happening in my head. He spent a good few hours interviewing me, asking all about my childhood, my upbringing – everything leading up to my present situation in Jefferson County Jail. Of particular interest to him seemed to be the fact that I'd been unable to focus in class, that I'd been diagnosed with ADD, and that

I'd always had trouble following orders. I told him all about the robbery and was frank with him about all the events and misdemeanors leading up to it. At the end of the session, he thanked me and promised to prepare a report and forward it on to Rick.

'Okay, great,' I replied.

'Well,' he responded, with a smile and a shake of the head, 'I wouldn't say "great", but we'll see what we can do.'

Then he left.

I was crushed. What did he mean by that? Why would a psychiatrist, employed by the defence, shake his head at what he had just found? Had I just spent two and a half hours providing the prosecution with the best evidence it had – proof that Anthony Prince was so fucked in the head he even freaked out his own psychiatrist?

I began to wonder about it myself, my character and personality. Maybe there was something seriously wrong with me. Had this robbery been so 'out of character' after all? Maybe I really *was* a dickhead. Or maybe part dickhead, a half of me I would never be rid of. Geminis are two-faced, if you believe that astrology hokum. Everyone who had ever loved me had only seen my angelic side, and couldn't understand how I could have done something like rob a bank. Maybe the answer to that great mystery was simple: that I wasn't just a kid from Byron Bay who'd done something incredibly stupid, but rather a stupid bank robber who'd fooled everyone for years into believing I was just a kid from Byron Bay. Perhaps my whole life had been heading towards this point, and in prison was where I belonged. Maybe I was psychotic and, like other psychotics, had no idea of how fucked in the head I was. I would find out, I thought, when I read the shrink's report.

I was spooked by this psychological bogeyman for days, and wandered around the prison like a ghost, worried about the contents of my head, which became more disordered and harder to fathom the more I worried. In the end, I decided that, whatever else might be going on in my brain, the thoughts my psychiatrist had put there were the things I liked the least. I determined to flush them out and forget it. There was no way his evaluation could be 100 per cent accurate, anyhow. He'd only spoken to me for a few hours. And I was, after all, considered so untrustworthy as to be locked within the walls of a prison. What sort of guy would believe a single word a jailbird said?

When that report finally came through, it made for interesting reading.

Anthony presented as a polite and personable individual. His speech and language were entirely normal. He easily offered eye contact.

So far, so good.

He initially manifested a somewhat superficial, cooperative friendliness.

What the . . .?

He is likely to be untrustworthy and unreliable, to persistently seek excitement and engage in self-dramatizing behavior . . . He probably fails to meet routine responsibilities . . .

Fuck off!

His communications may be characterized by caustic comments and callous outbursts . . .

FUCK OFF!

He may exhibit short-lived enthusiasm followed by disillusionment and resentment.

Although I'd been interested at the start, I decided I'd read quite enough of this bullshit, threw it aside and proceeded to brood on it for days.

It was about a month into my time in JeffCo when Mum and Dad finally came to visit. For me, it had been a pretty big month and a fucking steep learning curve. The frightened little boy who stumbled in here was considerably stronger and I'd acclimatised enough to my surroundings to feel at least partially comfortable. I was getting on with other inmates, getting used to the routine, starting to be at peace with where I was and feeling like I could hack this thing. Having visitors at all was the high point of every convict's day, but having my parents come all the way from Australia was a source of explosive joy for me. In the days before their visit I could think of little else, and on the day they finally came I was in a pretty buoyant mood. I was, in fact, so happy to see them I almost forgot where I was.

The moment I rounded the corner into the visitors' room and they saw me, dressed in my prison attire, my hair clipped short, shuffling along, they broke down. I suppose it was a shock, and I must have looked pathetic to them, their son imprisoned and unable to make physical contact. Mum just crumbled into sobs and Dad had big tears welling in his eyes, but I was so overjoyed to see them I never rose to meet their heartbreak. I was like: 'What's the matter? It's so fucking good to see you!', while they were both bawling their eyes out. In a way, I suppose it worked out well – had I dissolved into tears again, like I'd done on the phone, it would have broken their hearts even more. It was good for them to see I was handling it, that I wasn't so miserable after all.

It wasn't the easiest or most affectionate meeting I've had with my parents, that's for sure. There was only one phone and there was two of them, so one or the other had to sit out while the other spoke. Eventually, I noticed that there was nobody in the booth next door, so I reached around, grabbed that phone and told Dad to do the same. So I spoke into both phones while Dad poked his head around into the other booth. Not exactly a cosy family picture, but we had to take what we could get, and it worked for us.

We spoke about Rick and my case, and the prospect of me being out of prison sooner rather than later. The outlook at that point was a little grim. Mum and dad had heard from various sources that I might expect to receive twenty years, while another inmate had told me he thought I was likely to only get three. The truth, as far as we knew, lay somewhere between those two extremes.

It's very hard to describe the peculiar frustration of seeing the people you love on the other side of a sheet of glass, knowing they've come from the other side of the world and can get within an inch but cannot touch. I know it was weird for them, too, seeing their son, their baby, being kept from them by somebody else, a stranger who had nothing to do with any part of their usual world. From my perspective, though, as a little bit of theatre, the visit could not have been a more successful performance. All through the visit I'd had inmate friends poking their heads around the corner, smiling and waving at my parents, or slapping me on the back as they passed by to engage their own visitors at booths further down – it gave a very convincing impression of a happy, healthy, friendly prison community. At first, it was probably a little alarming for them to see me being so chummy with these over-tattooed dudes who were clearly career criminals, but, on the other hand, from the way we were communicating with each other it was clear to them that I wasn't alone, wasn't on the outer in here. And that was comforting for them.

They stayed for a few weeks, bunking down in hotels nearby, or camping in the national park when the weather was all right. They visited me every day, each visit becoming a little more cheerful and light-hearted than the last. It was weird seeing them, for the first time, as rather beautiful people. They're both in their fifties and, so I'd thought, fairly ordinary middle-aged people, but compared to the ugly, bald, toothless homies and crackheads of Jefferson County Jail, Jenny and Peter Prince looked like fucking supermodels. I made a note during that first visit of theirs to renew my relationship with my mum and dad when this ordeal was over, and to do my best to keep them looking as young as they did, rather than giving them grey hairs by robbing banks and so on.

But how long would this ordeal really last? It would take me another few months to find out for sure.

4

I was awoken at 3.30 am on 15 June 2005 to begin one of the longest days I was to experience in the United States: my plea hearing at the Federal Courthouse in downtown Denver, Colorado. I was taken down to a holding cell at Jefferson, where I waited with about twenty other prisoners until 7.30 am, when we were finally shackled and shuffled onto a transfer van completely sealed by metal cages. An uneventful and not particularly scenic journey into Denver ended after 30 minutes in front of the courthouse, where a guard with a mirror on the end of a pole made a slow inspection of the underside of the vehicle. A hydraulic steel gate then descended into the earth, and our van continued into the basement of the courthouse, from where we were led into holding cells made of stainless steel and concrete. Here we would wait until our hearings were called.

Hours passed. I tried to sleep, using a toilet roll as a pillow, but it was so very cold I had to keep getting up and doing some push-ups just to stop from shivering. At last, at 11.30 am, Rick showed up and met me in a small meeting room to discuss the day's proceedings and rehearse the things I had to say in front of the judge.

Through Rick, I had become aware of details of the prosecution's case, and discovering exactly what police had known about Luke and me had been interesting to say the least. The more I'd learned over the months, the clearer it had become that we hadn't had a chance on that day in March.

When police were called to the WestStar Bank in Vail, they arrived within minutes of Luke and me leaving. Kim and Jessica's descriptions of the bandits were tight, and, most significantly, they both reported that the robbers had accents that were either European or Australian. The attending policeman immediately thought of Luke and me, for he had already had dealings with us over the stolen credit card. We had left a healthy trail of footprints and dollars in the snow, along the winding cobblestone paths behind the bank, and it wasn't long before our little picnic spot under the pine tree was discovered, the abandoned jetsam of our robbery – the BB guns, our jackets and assorted banknotes – strewn around the clearing. As luck would have it, the female officer who had attended our little late-night window-shooting rampage weeks before was on the job that morning, and she recognised our weapon of choice – the Daisy Powerline

Air Pistol – immediately. Police went straight to Pepi's, where they not only learned that we'd suddenly departed that very morning, but noticed the name tags being worn by staff were identical to the one that had been worn by 'Valley Electrical Dave'. The guy at the Vail Ski Office confirmed that I'd been there to purchase a replacement ski pass just moments before the robbery. Another workmate recalled seeing myself and Luke waiting in line at the ski lift immediately after the robbery. Before we had even snapped our snowboards onto our feet that morning, police had faxed our mugshots to every point of exit in the state.

In fact, for all our dumb and dumber behaviour, the police in Vail didn't exactly prove to be The Untouchables that morning, either. They had been listening when Luke and I had called a taxi from Lion's Head at the bottom of Born Free, and the police officers who'd alighted from the car and sniffed around on the other side of the road had been looking for us. All they'd needed to do was look across the road and they would have seen us standing there with our backpacks bursting with money.

Considering the authorities knew our identities so quickly, it's amazing that Luke and I were able to get out of Vail at all, let alone stop off at our old apartment, smile our way past a traffic cop and sleep all the way to Denver. Had we only thought to pay that cab driver $20,000 to take us to Mexico, we'd have surely given authorities the slip (although, it has to be said, we'd probably still be stuck in Mexico, broke, unable to ever show our faces at an airport).

And what of Martinez, the taxi driver in Denver? Well, it turns out he was probably the most interesting character in this whole affair, and certainly the only winner.

Upon learning from me that we'd given a taxi driver a bag containing $20,000, police in Denver, using the business card Martinez had given us, tracked him down for an interview. Yes, he remembered picking Luke and me up, driving us around the city of Denver and dropping us at the airport. But when asked about the money, he replied: 'What money?' And that's the story he stuck to. When police checked his work record at the taxi company and found he'd mysteriously taken the Monday night off after leaving Luke and me at the airport, Martinez couldn't really explain why.

Martinez, it turned out, had been a sharper operator than his passengers that day. He kept no bank accounts, so police were unable to trace the money, and when the FBI looked into his profile, it became clear he was no greenhorn. He had a healthy list of offences dating back a decade, for drugs, firearms, obstructing police and miscellaneous mischief. He'd even done a few years in assorted prisons. There we'd been, convinced we were the scary felons in the back seat of this poor boob's taxi, when in actual fact he was the man and we were at his mercy. I can't help but laugh, though, when I think of how he might have reacted when he saw us on the news or read about us in the paper, and realised he'd had about $100,000 sitting on the back seat of his cab while Luke and I had been jerking around in the various jewellery stores. All he would have had to do was put his foot on the accelerator and nobody would have ever seen him again.

For a while, the FBI were threatening to strap Martinez to a polygraph, just to see if he was telling the truth. They had two reasons for doing this. Obviously, they suspected he was lying, but, worryingly, they also suspected we were. They thought it was possible that Luke and I had stashed the money somewhere else with a view to retrieving it later. I couldn't blame them for thinking this, as they knew we'd tried to rent a safety deposit box for that very purpose, but having that doubt there was not helping our case at all, so I was seriously hoping the lie detector would be employed. Unfortunately, forcing someone to take a polygraph test is not as easy as it sounds, even for the FBI. In the end, Luke and I were forced to pay back the $20,000, the only portion of the money that was deemed unrecoverable (the Feds had retrieved the boxes we'd sent home). I was sure that one day I'd get to take this up with Martinez personally, as he was bound to show up in any one of the prisons in which I resided over the next few years, but it never happened. To this day I wish him well, and hope the money went towards a better life for his daughter, if she existed at all. Somehow I doubt it, though.

There were some documents I'd seen that were either amusing or depressing, depending on how I was feeling whenever I recalled them. One was the firearms tracing information sheet from the Bureau of Alcohol, Tobacco and Firearms. Routinely, when a weapon is used in a crime, the police will send the weapon off to the ATF to have it thoroughly examined, identified on the national database and, if it can't be identified, recorded for future reference as being a weapon in circulation. Evidently, the police in Vail felt like doing things by the book, so they sent off the firearms from our robbery for the usual trace request. A very formal and scary-looking summary sheet had come back from the ATF, filled out with as much information as the examiner had managed to ascertain. It was pretty funny to look at – where other trace summaries would speak of such legends as the Glock 9mm or the 357 Magnum, ours wasn't quite so intimidating:

Manufacturer: Daisy
Model: Powerline 15 XT
Caliber: .177
Type: BB pistol
Anticipated disposition: Destroy

I was amused by the thought of the poor stooge who'd been forced to go through with the paperwork, and the solemn ceremony that might attend the destruction of a Daisy Powerline .177 calibre BB gun.

Another document of interest to me was the Vail Police Department's list of items recovered from the snow near our apartment in Vail. Like a little snapshot of a life I'd left behind, it more than adequately revealed my lack of caution as a criminal, and my lack of caution generally, with regard to the things I loved:

White zip tie
Motorola Talkabout T6500
Large, Silver Billabong jacket with 'Valley Electric Dave' name tag on left breast
Black/Orange Rosignol snowboard
Miscellaneous trash items
Photo of unknown white female . . .

But these were just distractions in what was a pretty serious situation. According to Rick, the prosecution was going for a heavy sentence of between 87 and 108 months – seven years minimum. That was considerably lighter than the 20 or 25 years some had spoken of, but it was more than I wanted to consider. Seven years. When you think of something you did seven years ago, you realise what a huge amount of life that really is. I'd still be in jail today.

Rick was convinced we could get the years down significantly, and the first way to go about that was to plead guilty to the indictment. Ironically enough, courts like guilty prisoners – or, at least, prisoners who plead guilty. It saves the court the time and hassle and money of a trial. The judge rewards those who spare the court the bother. And, realistically, there was no doubt I was guilty. As hilariously entertaining as our case might have been for a jury, it just wasn't necessary. Both Luke and I were pleading guilty. It was our first step to freedom.

After meeting with Rick, I went back to my holding cell for a lunch that was a banquet compared to what they serve in JeffCo – a roll with ham, cheese, lettuce and tomato, with a bag of chips and a cup of Coke. That might seem like a pretty shitty lunch to most people, but, for the incarcerated, it's a charming little bit of home.

I then lay down on my toilet roll again and slept until 3.45 pm, when I was finally called, cuffed and led into the courthouse. There was a healthy crowd of reporters and various onlookers in the gallery. I quickly scanned for Mum and Dad and spotted them. They looked weary-eyed – they'd no doubt been sitting there for as long as I had been downstairs.

The judge entered and we were all told to rise. I was made to swear an oath that everything I said would be the absolute truth. For the next twenty minutes the eyes of the crowd burned into the back of my head as I answered the judge's questions, mostly to do with whether I had read my plea and understood it. It was a very intimidating feeling – more intimidating, in fact, than anything I had encountered in prison. I remember wondering what it said about me that I was more scared of the court than I was of the prison. But I guess everyone who is yet to be sentenced by the court feels that way.

The judge set the date of 8 September for my sentencing and excused us. I had a few seconds to turn to my parents.

When I saw them, they looked so stressed and worried that for a moment I forgot I was the one in trouble. I mouthed the words 'I love you' and blew them a kiss before I was shuffled back into the bowels of the prison system. I just wanted them to feel I was okay, and not to worry about me, but I cried a little bit as I returned to the holding cell. I wanted this nightmare to end not just for me, but for them, the two people who were feeling everything I was feeling, but who were not allowing themselves to imagine the times when I was feeling safe and passably happy.

The next day, some newspapers reported my courtroom air kiss as if it were proof of my arrogance.

I celebrated my twentieth birthday in Jefferson County Jail. It also happened to be Father's Day in America, so the visit I shared with Mum and Dad was particularly affectionate that day – as affectionate as you can be through one-inch-thick glass. Cesar Cortez made me a very impressive birthday card, my name in Old English script with signatures and quotes from all of my cellmates. I never thought I'd receive something so precious from a prison.

Seeing that it was Scrappy Doo's birthday the next day, and that he was being released the day after that, the guys in the cell organised a 'spread', which is something that was done on special occasions. They took a garbage bag and filled it with about ten Maggi noodle soups, some pork rinds and some sausage that someone had pilfered from somewhere — anything that might add some flavour to the mix — then poured in some boiling water, threw a blanket over it and let it sit for a while. When it was ready, the boys all sat around with chips and dipped into the stew. It wasn't five-star dining by any means, but it was a nice change from the regular meals, and it always made for a really good social event where everyone, for once, seemed pretty happy.

A few days after this Dad had to go back home to Australia, to take care of his own business affairs, leaving Mum behind for a few weeks. Over those weeks I noticed how canny Mum was in developing a rapport with each of the deputies in the prison. She's very outwardly friendly anyway, so it was natural for her to be like this, but it seemed a bit funny to me at first that she was being so friendly with the very people who were making my days and nights so tough – particularly a certain Deputy Schwartz, a real hard nut, who seemed to take a shine to Mum. It took a little while for the significance of it all to sink in.

Mum eventually went home, too, but not before many long visits that often went half an hour longer than they were legally supposed to. Time and again Mum would keep sitting there as the clock ticked passed the use-by date, a deputy occasionally popping his head around the corner, smiling and moving along. Many times, Mum and I just sat and looked at each other, in silence – something we knew we weren't going to be able to do again until she and Dad returned for my sentencing in September. Phones were for talking, but faces were for looking into. That's how I saw it.

About three months into my time at JeffCo, I had relaxed enough with prison life to fall back into my restive habit of pushing boundaries, cutting corners, taking the lazy route rather than doing the hard yards. Because the prison environment is so controlled and so regulated, this translated into notable transgressions, which felt to me at the time like little more than normal behaviour – forgetting to make my bed, keeping pieces of food in my locker and forgetting about it, little things. But they make a big deal out of those. I remember once I climbed out of bed and just wandered into the day room where I sat down to watch TV while I was waking up. The next thing I knew, one of the screws had taken my mattress, blankets and everything, dragged it up onto the second tier and was throwing it all down onto the day room, sheets and blankets floating down while the other inmates roared laughing: 'Ah, ha ha . . . Australia!' Just the simple act of forgetting to make your bed became a major incident.

There was a screw called Rose, a little dude with a tight military haircut and a major case of Short Man Syndrome. Naturally, he didn't seem to like me very much, what with me being six foot two. He's the sort of guy you'd imagine would really get off on at last being in control of an entire building of tall guys. He was an obsessive compulsive, wanted everything spick and span, the bed sheets turned over at 45-degree angles, and would have you on your belly under your bed polishing some tiny, unseen corner. I suppose I have to admit that he ran it well – he was, as far the system was concerned, an excellent screw – and every inmate did what he said because they knew if they didn't they'd be off to The Hole. But there was a demeaning, controlling side to him that was quite obnoxious in its own way. He had pockets always filled with little candies which he'd hand out to inmates when they did something good, as if they were dogs and he was flipping them treats. I'm not sure if this was an intentional insult or just thick, but some prisoners took great offence to it.

I used to spend quite a bit of time observing screws and imagining what types of kids they'd been – it was a good solitary mind game that helped pass the time. But, without fail, the kid I'd see in my mind would always turn out to be the same: a little bit smaller than the other kids, a little bit nerdy, either bullied or subtly dominated by other kids. That's why they'd want to be cops or screws, so that, at last, they could dominate others.

Rose was a pedant, but he wasn't a bastard. He'd write down all your infractions, mark them dutifully on your file in the computer, using the correct terminology and the right spacing, but he wouldn't necessarily act on them. The letter of the law was that a certain number of infractions scored an inmate some time in The Hole, which, in JeffCo, translated as a spell upstairs in the higher security section. Rose was at least cool enough to see that lots of little infractions didn't add up to much – either that or he was too obsessive about order to notice when infractions were piling up.

One day, Rose went away for a week, and this other screw took his place, a fat bastard with no sense of humour at all. He went through my file and noticed that I had eight infractions, ranging from such things as having an egg in my locker to failing to make my bed. He appeared in the doorway of my cell and told me to pack my things, because I was going to The Hole. When I asked him why, he told me that I had eight infractions, and that having four infractions was enough to warrant being sent to The Hole.

'But I haven't done anything wrong,' I said. 'Not today.'

'I don't care,' he replied. 'Get your arse upstairs.' (Or your 'ass', as the Americans refer to it.)

So that was it. I was headed to The Hole, for how long I had no idea. What pissed me off the most is that he only let me take five of the fifteen books that Mum and Dad had given me or sent since I'd been inside. In medium security, five is the total number of books one is allowed to have. This guy was going to play by the rules, all the way down to the wire.

Medium security was quite a departure from the luxury of minimum. There was only a limited time allowed in the day room, which was very small and had only one TV. There was no recreation area, and only one shower, with privacy provided by a half-size door over which everyone could see from the hallway. Each cell was about 3 metres by

1.8 metres, with one bunk, a bench and a toilet right there. Despite there being only one bed, it was two-to-a-cell, so I had to sleep on a mattress on the floor. As if this all wasn't tough enough, I was moved to a cell with some prick who snored so much that sleeping was practically impossible. This was going to be hard – the minimum stay in The Hole was 30 days. I braced myself for a hard stretch.

But, on my third morning in medium, I was woken and told to pack my things – I was going back to my old pod in low. Apparently, Mum had found out I'd been moved, and had jumped on the phone to her old mate, Deputy Schwartz, who immediately gave the okay for me to be returned to my old pod. A little bit of motherly courtesy evidently moves mountains in an American prison.

The demand for presentation of paperwork was a fairly regular routine whenever a new inmate entered a cell he had to share with others. His cellmates would want to know about the guy they were going to be living with, and your court documents, which every prisoner has access to, didn't lie. Anyone refusing to hand over paperwork was 'strongly encouraged' to find another cell, and anyone whose paperwork revealed something unsavoury – a bit of rolling over to the authorities, or some cruelty to kids – would be either shown the door or ostracised unless he could adequately explain himself.

In August, an incident occurred in our pod involving a new guy who was being harassed over his apparent reluctance to produce his paperwork. The guy went to the authorities and snitched – which probably gives you some idea of what might have been in his paperwork – but baulked at naming who, exactly, his harassers had been. Faced with a dilemma, the deputy in charge came up with the bright idea of moving every single one of us out of the pod, except for the guy who'd snitched.

This was a major drag, as it meant I had to get to know a whole new pod of prisoners and a whole new cell of buddies. More annoyingly, I'd begun my own 'store' back in my old pod, which had been doing quite well. Once a week, all prisoners would be allowed to buy food from the commissary shop, so, using money Mum had placed in my account, I'd stock up on items and save them in my locker – apples, eggs, Maggi soups – so that I could sell them to other prisoners during the week, when everyone was a little short between commissary days. Naturally, they wouldn't be able to pay with money, so instead they'd pay with the promise of more stuff – someone desperate enough for a Maggi soup would buy one for the promise of two when the commissary shop was open again. I'd racked up quite a book of promises from prisoners within my pod, and now that I'd been shifted the entire business had been gutted. I suppose that's the risk of operating a credit business in such an unstable environment as a prison.

One good thing that came out of being moved is that I got to meet Deputy Anthony S. Memory, a screw for whom

I was to develop a great deal of respect. He was from the UK originally – big, brash and a little bit rough. He was one of the few screws who wouldn't hesitate at getting physical with prisoners if he felt it was needed, but he was fair and brave and there wasn't too much bullshit about him, so he had the respect of the other prisoners. He was also a champion ping-pong player, and was always up for a challenge on the table if any prisoner wanted to try his luck. He was a good bloke. I think a lot of the prisoners saw him as almost a prisoner himself – he was a Pom, a fish out of water a long way from home, and so he was like everyone else in here. He obviously hated the bad side of the job, but enjoyed a camaraderie with the prisoners as well as the other screws.

But it was here, in this pod, on the eve of my sentencing, that I began to feel myself sometimes sinking to rock bottom. I'd be sitting at the card table thinking about my situation, or listening through the headphones to music that would take me back to nights I'd had in Byron Bay, drinking and hanging out with friends. Or I'd be looking at the few photos I had of Clare, who'd seem to become more beautiful each time I looked at her, and I'd recall how soft she felt and how long it had been since I'd felt anything so tender. Then I'd remember that it would be years before I would feel that tenderness again. Maybe a decade. Maybe never. Then I'd sink so low that there seemed no way out of the pit.

I realised in those times how important it was to have something to look forward to. It couldn't simply be my eventual release, which was completely out of my control. It had to be something that I could work towards on a daily basis, something that would make it worth getting out of bed in the mornings. I could start studying, I thought – Mum had mentioned the possibility of doing a course by correspondence – but that seemed a long way off. I had to think of something that didn't require anything or anyone else. The answer was right under my nose, literally. A moustache.

No, I'm only kidding. The answer, which was under my nose, was my own body. Ever since I'd been an adolescent, I'd been self-conscious about my physique – I was always such a skinny runt of a teenager, and only my height saved me from being seen as a total wimp. Now, here I was in prison, with a whole lot of heavy dudes and nothing but time to burn. It was obvious: I could start working out, use this time inside to build myself up. I began to focus on how good I'd feel when I got out and stepped into the real world with a prison-pumped body. The prospect got me very excited, and I began doing push-ups, sit-ups and pull-ups on the bar in the rec area. I noticed little improvements in myself almost immediately.

But I also noticed I was becoming a little more aggressive with each noticeable improvement. I think the sheer physicality of working out must have raised my testosterone level a bit. Of course, I was anxious about a lot of things – my pending sentencing; my psych report, which was still bugging me – and it seemed all it needed was for my blood to be up and I'd start wanting to release all of that tension onto the head of some motherfucker, of which there were many. I began getting cheeky with others again, or starting trouble over stupid things. I would constantly have to remind myself of how shitty life was in medium security, or how damaging a bad record in here could be when it came to my sentencing.

I was right on the edge one morning in early September when news came through that some southern states had been decimated by Hurricane Katrina. The TV showed areas of New Orleans that had been completely submerged, and other houses had water up to their ceilings, the occupants having lost everything. There was talk of looting, of thousands of people being suddenly homeless, whole families forced to seek refuge in football stadiums where people were being bashed and raped. It was a very weird feeling to be watching something from the outside that looked worse than what was happening in here, to realise that we were safe when free people on the outside were not. And that weird feeling made me feel good. It made me realise that things weren't so bad, that life could be worse for me than to be in prison, clothed and fed, knowing that the people I loved were safe, knowing that I had buddies in here to talk to or play cards with. I was being a prat by getting angry at my situation, which, when I thought about it, had always been completely within my control. It was me who put me here, not anybody else, and it was me who was going to get me out.

I can say today that it took Hurricane Katrina to calm the storm that had been brewing in my own head.

Mum, Dad and Clare arrived just a few days before my sentencing hearing. Seeing Mum and Dad was terrific as usual, although the odd grey hairs I spotted on both of them troubled me a little, as I knew I was the cause. But seeing Clare was a strange and conflicting experience. She was beautiful, as always, perhaps a little more so than I had remembered. I'd spent so much time gazing at the handful of photos I had of her that I'd reduced her to a one-dimensional figure – just a portrait, and seeing her in the flesh reminded me of little things I'd forgotten, about the way she moved or held her mouth. I wanted so much to smash through the glass and be with her. But the glass wasn't all that was separating us.

This whole experience, the distance, and the passing of time had ripped us apart. Once upon a time, we'd been joined at the hip, but now so much had taken place without the other – every silence between us was like a little universe that wasn't being spoken about. We spoke a lot about us, our relationship and where we wanted it to go once this whole thing was behind us, and it was nice to hear her speaking that way so sincerely. But it seemed the more she spoke of her devotion to me, the more I felt like a dragging anchor around her waist, holding her back from living a young life.

I shared this with her and expressed my (half-hearted) desire that she live her life to the full and not worry about being faithful to me. She responded that, quite simply, nobody made her feel like I did. It was my little imperfections, she said, that made me perfect in her eyes. Dressed in prison clothes with a phone to my ear as I awaited sentencing for robbing a bank with a BB gun, I must have seemed especially perfect to her right at that very moment.

Subsequent visits after that first day saw these gnawing feelings of mine thawing a little, and I eventually began to open up to Clare, to stop thinking like a loser and just behave as if everything was – well, not fine, but just a temporary obstacle that didn't have to poison our love for each other. In the days and nights in prison, I'd often be tempted by the beautiful women on the TV – the Spanish Channel in particular – and I'd begun to fall into a pattern of thinking about those random girls during my closed-eyed fantasies. But the minute I saw Clare again they were all obliterated from my memory bank, each daily sighting of Clare furnishing my mind with more images to 'play' with. It's funny how being unable to touch can really make you appreciate a partner (I'd recommend one of those booths of glass with telephones for any married couple with troubles).

One night, after Clare had visited, I had a dream that seemed to last forever. In it, Clare and I were meeting in a house I didn't recognise, a place that was abandoned but for people occasionally coming and going. I wandered through the house for a while and, when I went to re-enter the room where I'd left Clare, she was with some stranger. From my vantage point I could see them together, touching, intimately. Then I saw that Clare was naked. I turned and bolted through the house, smashing windows and punching walls in a rage. Eventually, I returned to the room and began unleashing my fury on this strange dude, punching the shit out of him as he begged for mercy. What was strange about this dream is that my own violence woke me up more than once, but whenever I went back to sleep the dream was waiting there for me – Clare, still nude, and the dude still waiting for another bashing, which I was happy to give him. By the time I woke up in the morning I was emotionally exhausted.

I spent most of the day in a terrible mood, wondering what this dream was supposed to mean. Did some higher power – some bad director of dreams – want to show me what life would be like without Clare? Why? How was I supposed to use that information in prison? It was only going to torment me, and it did. For the first time in our entire relationship, I began to think about how horrible it would feel to be without her in my future, and to know that she was with someone else. Like all obsessive thoughts in prison, once that one got a hold of me it held on and drilled in like a fucking tattoo. I could barely concentrate on anything else, and I became so abrupt with everyone that I began getting on my cellmates' nerves.

I began to rationalise that this dream must have been a warning – something I was doing was endangering my relationship with Clare. It couldn't be letter-writing, I thought, because I wrote her more letters than I wrote anyone, and I called her as often as was humanly possible. In the end, I decided it must have been my infidelity – something or someone was telling me that I wasn't being as faithful as I could be. Of course, there were no girls in my prison, so there was no opportunity to be unfaithful, but that didn't mean I was doing the best I could do. I decided, right then and there, to say 'no' to the girls on TV, and the ones who occasionally did the rounds of the pod, in the porno magazines. I would be faithful to Clare in the only way I could – by refraining from thinking about anyone but her.

The next day, I got Rick to patch me through to Clare's parents, who I spoke to on the phone. I reassured them that their beautiful daughter wasn't wasting time on some no-hoper who didn't completely respect her and love her with all his heart.

Deputy Memory woke me at 3 am, told me my big day had arrived and that I'd better get up and at 'em. To wake myself, I went out into the recreation yard for a stroll in the cold air. The sky above was so black, every star so clearly visible I felt I could almost see the edges of each one. And, in the middle of them all, a crescent moon – the first moon I had seen since I'd been in this place. I began to think about the usual stuff – the vastness of things, the smallness of me – until it became a pretty deep moment. I just stood still, my head tilted back, and fell into the sky.

'Oh, Lord,' I found myself praying, 'if you're really up there, like . . . for fuck's sake, give me a break.'

I was so deeply into that universe that I scarcely even noticed when Deputy Memory appeared beside me. He had a razor in his hand, for me to shave with, but he said nothing for a moment, because he could see I was thinking. We just stood there for a while, not looking at each other, just looking up. Then Memory did the most amazing thing. He put his hand on my shoulder, squeezed it a little, in a way that told me we were both strong, and reassured me that everything was going to be okay.

'Just remember, Prince,' he said, 'no matter what happens today, remember that this is only a temporary experience.'

It was, in its own way, an extraordinary thing to say. It was true – everything we go through is only temporary. One day, my experience in prison would end, just as surely as my life would end one day, too. As impossible as it seemed at that moment, me standing there with him would be a memory that was left on the other side of the world, long ago. All of this stuff – the bunks and the lockers and the pods and the cellmates and the screws – would all be like some life lived by some other dude and written down in a book. For just a moment, I got a really strong feeling about that, and it moved me inside to get on with my day.

I showered, shaved, dressed and went down to wait for the bus that would take me to the court. When I returned

I would know how long this temporary experience had
left to run.

Once at the courthouse, I met with Rick, who went through
the expected proceedings of the day one more time. He had
gone to a lot of trouble for me. A few days earlier, he
had organised for my mum and dad to meet with the
man who would be prosecuting me, the Denver District
Attorney, David Conner. For the loved ones of an accused
person to meet with the DA is not unheard of, as it can be
useful for spouses or parents who want to understand the
State's case. However, Rick also thought it would be useful
for me, because if David Conner saw that I came from a
good family, he might be persuaded to go a bit easier on me.
There were limits, of course, to how much he could do – as
the District Attorney, he had a responsibility to the American
public to execute his duty. But, as Rick explained to me, the
DA was a human being, and if he could be convinced that
a prisoner was a decent kid from a decent family, why not
convince him of that?

As it turned out, David Conner also happened to be an
avid Rugby Union fan, a fact of which Rick had always
been aware. Apparently, upon meeting my mum and dad,
Conner had gone through the motions, declaring that the
crime I had committed was very serious, and spelling out
to them exactly why the prosecution was going for such a

stiff sentence. Then Rick somehow managed to let it slip that Dad had played Rugby Union at an international level. The rest of the meeting dissolved into an extended conversation about Rugby Union, the primary reason for the lunch seemingly forgotten.

As Rick had said, you have to use everything you've got.

When I entered the courtroom my heart started racing so hard I was sure other people could hear it. Luke entered the court at the same time as me, and we gave each other a quick look, a short smile. We had so much to say to each other, but there was no time today. I quickly scanned the audience (that's what it felt like – a live studio audience) and spotted my mum and dad, Clare, Luke's folks, and a host of reporters and curious onlookers. I also saw Kim and Jessica, the bank tellers.

Judge Figa entered the courtroom and a voice said sternly: 'All rise.' The sound of everyone obeying the order was somehow frightening – here was this man in a flowing cape, entering the room like Darth Vader, with everyone in awe of him, and my future was in his hands. Weird.

The prosecutor, David Conner, began the proceedings with a muscular monologue delivered in his Texan drawl about how this had been a 'sophisticated crime' and that the people of America demanded our incarceration for at least eight or nine years. He seemed to be stuttering an awful lot for a man determined to lock me up and throw away the key, and, as his condemnation of me as a criminal became louder and louder, I began to wonder how this man could possibly have looked my parents in the eye knowing that this was what he intended to do. Almost immediately upon me thinking that, Conner stopped, quite suddenly, announced to the judge that he had some other business he had to attend to, and asked to be excused. He would leave his assistant, he said, to represent the prosecution for the rest of the day.

Rick then took the floor and began his argument on my behalf. With the help of Mum and Dad, Rick had amassed an impressive dossier of character references, from my high school principal and other teachers, family friends and business associates of my parents, even the odd MP. He made much of my good record, my evident remorse for the crime, and the fact that the entire episode had been ridiculously 'out of character'. But, and there can be no getting around it, the real core of Rick's argument was that I was basically little more than a dill. In contrast to how the prosecutor had painted things, Rick's telling of the robbery at the WestStar Bank made it sound like more of a slapstick comedy sketch than a crime, with Luke and me as two bumbling idiots who were never in danger of getting away with it. He had a lot to work with – the BB guns, the walkie-talkies that didn't work, the 'getaway' down the mountain on snowboards, the jewellery store splurges, the taxi cab 'tip' . . . somehow, Rick made it sound like some stupid B movie in which Luke and I were the real victims. He pleaded for the court's sympathy for the two boys who'd been mocked and ridiculed in newspapers all over the world, saying that 'coverage has been unflattering in the extreme'.

As evidence of this, Rick presented to the court various newspaper articles and headlines: the original 'Dumb and Dumber' article from the *Daily Telegraph*, which catalogued me and Luke in 'the hall of fame for stupidity'; 'Me and My Stupid Mate', with a photo of me, from the *Sydney Morning Herald*; and an article that called us the 'dumbest armed robbers in the annals of US criminal history', which ran alongside a poster for the movie *Dumb and Dumber* only with pictures of our heads stuck over those of the actors.

'Far from being portrayed as daring criminals or folk heroes,' argued Rick, 'like Butch Cassidy and the Sundance Kid, or, in Australia, Ned Kelly, Anthony and Luke have been excoriated in public – humiliated, belittled, and mocked; the modern media equivalent of being put in the stocks and pelted with refuse by the public.'

Rick even went so far as to find some study or other that proved a teenager's mind was basically malformed. Which was all excellent for the sake of my case, but it's a strange feeling to be sitting in a court, listening to some guy argue that you are 'incredibly stupid', all the while knowing that guy is supposed to be on your side.

It then came time for statements from our parents. Luke's mother was first. From the moment she stood, it was clear she was fighting a losing battle against her emotions. She soldiered on, pleading with the judge to see Luke as she did – as a loving son who had, in his own way, been traumatised by this whole experience. Luke's mum had always been nice to me, and in the many years I'd known her I had never seen her cry. Seeing her so devastated, tears streaming down her cheeks as she told of her love for Luke, just dissolved my will to stay in control, and I felt I was on the verge of crying, too.

Then my father stood and read a very deep, compassionate story of me growing up, and what I really meant to him. His words broke that last bit of composure I had left, and I began to sob. Rick handed me his handkerchief, which I then proceeded to fill as Mum stood and drilled a little further than even Dad had. I was quietly impressed that they had managed to get through their speeches without breaking down and making it difficult for the judge to understand them.

Then it was my turn, and I stepped to the podium, the piece of paper trembling in my hand:

I'm very nervous, Your Honour, so I wrote down some things I wanted to say. I thank my mother and father, Jennifer and Peter Prince, and my girlfriend Clare Taylor for being in court today. All of them have travelled from far away to be here for me. Thanks, too, to Ms Hind of the Australian Consulate for her help and for being here today. I also see there are some people here from Pepi's Sports, where I used to work in Vail, and Mrs Dunlap, the mother of one of my old cellmates. I thank all of them for being here as well.

At this point you would have been forgiven for thinking I was accepting an Oscar, rather than pleading for a lenient jail sentence. I decided I'd better move it along.

Your Honour, it is important for me to tell you today how sorry I am for my actions.

I then had a little note to myself that read: 'face tellers', as I wanted to directly address Jessica and Kim. I had been terrified that I was going to read this instruction out aloud, and had carefully rehearsed reading the speech, taking my time to pause at this point and think about what I was doing. The end result of all the nerves, rehearsing and caution was that, when I came to the words 'face tellers', I stopped dead, paused, then slowly and deliberately swivelled on the spot, like some clunky old robot from the 1950s, until I faced the two women whom I'd somehow managed to terrorise six months before.

I want to apologise to Ms Cole and Ms Vasquez for what I put them through. It was wrong. I am ashamed at my behaviour and very sorry at having frightened them so badly. I do not deserve their forgiveness, but I still must tell them I am sorry.

Though my delivery might have been a little shaky, I was actually quite sincere on that point, and I made sure I glanced up to look both Jessica and Kim in the eyes as

I said it. I remember them both looking somewhat defiant, as I guess they deserved to do. But I also remember Jessica nodding her head slightly at one point, and seeing what I thought was a vague twinkling of sympathy in her eye. That made me feel good. Perhaps the day would come when she would be able to forgive me. I hoped so.

I apologise to everyone in Vail, particularly those at Pepi's Sports. This was no way to repay them for their kindness. I apologise to the police, the FBI and the prosecutors, for all the trouble they have been put through because of me.

This was bullshit, of course. Why would I apologise to the police who'd laughed at Luke and me when we were sick with fear, or the prosecutors who were doing their best to lock me away for a decade of my life? But if I'd told the truth – that I wished they'd all get hit by a fucking bus on their way out of the courthouse – I would have copped a few more years than I wanted. On with the show . . .

I'm sorry for the embarrassment I've caused my home country.

Face Clare.

Clare, I apologise to you. I am grateful that you are still standing by me, but am sorry for the pain I have caused you. I am sorry you have had to spend your birthday visiting me in a foreign jail.

Face Mum and Dad. Fuck, man, don't cry.

And I want my mum and dad, who have been so wonderful to me my whole life, and are here for me now, to know how ashamed I am for what I did.

My voice was trembling and I could feel the dam ready to burst, but I somehow kept my finger in it.

You raised me to behave better than this. I am sorry for the heartache I have caused you, and for the trouble I have brought to your lives. It gives me hope to know that you still love me and are here for me even though I have let you down so badly. If there is another thing I am sorry for, I am sorry that it took something like this to wake me up, to make me value what I had, like the people in my life who love me and who I love. The things I took for granted, like my friendships, nature, but especially my freedom.

And now I turned to face the judge. How weird it was to look into the eyes of a bloke – just a bloke – who had the power to either set me free or fuck my life wholesale.

Your Honour, during these last six months in jail I have learned more about life and society than I have in the past six years. I have realised how sheltered from the dark and evil side of life I have been by growing up in a quiet country town and having such a loving, protective family. I feel I've never had to experience this dark side, so I couldn't fully appreciate how lucky I was to live in such a non-violent, carefree environment.

Make sad puppy eyes at His Honour.

My time in jail has opened my eyes, and mind, to how dark and scary life can really be. I now have a much clearer view of the wrong side of life and how lucky I am to have been blessed my whole life. I know I will never cross into this side of life again. Many people would like to know how I could do something like this. I wish I had an answer, for my sake as well as theirs. What I did was greedy and selfish, but I'm still not sure why I did it. Even the day I was arrested I could not believe what I'd done. How could I have let myself? I can say I blame no one but myself. I knew better. I was raised better.

And now, cue the orchestra for the big, melodramatic finish.

On March 21 of this year I was meant to be going home to be with the people who I care about the most, to a country I love, to a job I enjoy, to turn twenty and to get on with my life. Instead, because of what I did, I spent my twentieth birthday in jail and I will see more birthdays behind bars. I think of this every morning when I wake up not at home in Byron Bay but on a bunk in a jail cell. I think of this when I have to talk to my mum and dad and my girlfriend, Clare, through a piece of glass on a jail telephone, without being able to feel their touch. I know I must be punished. But I want you to know, Your Honour, that I am afraid of being alone, far from my country and the people I love. I am very afraid of prison and what it will be like. But I promise this to everyone who has stood with me, and to Ms Cole and Ms Vasquez too: whatever prison I am sent to, for however long, I will do my best to show that I have learned from all of this. So that when I'm allowed to go home one day, I can work hard to make up for the years I have lost, to make up for what I did, and to show those who love me that I deserve their love. Thank you, sir.

It was a performance, no doubt about it. But it was performed with conviction, because I meant it. I really did. While I wished I could walk straight out of that courtroom and into the arms of the ones I loved, I knew it wasn't going to happen because it wasn't the right thing. I deserved to be locked up for a while, and I knew it. There was something seriously wrong with me to have done the things I had done in Vail, both on the day of the bank robbery and on the days before. I had needed all of this – the prisons, the courts, the judge, the prosecutor, even the rotten press – to drive it home to me that I seriously needed to change myself for the better, to become more of a man about things, more of a captain of my own life. In my heart, I felt like that change had already occurred, as I'd made so many deals with the world about how I was never again going to be the person who allowed himself to be in this mess. But, deep down, I knew it was going to be a longer process than that. At the time, I was at peace with the fact that I might well get seven, maybe eight years, hopefully not nine. I was hoping for six.

When the judge announced that he had come to his conclusion, I felt as if my heart was going to swell up and close over my throat till I passed out. Then I heard his words: he declared that my punishment would be 54 months in prison, six of which I had already served. Four years. Luke got five.

As they led me away I turned and winked at my parents, and I couldn't have given a fuck about what the press might make of that.

After the sentencing, Rick met me downstairs and was surprisingly disappointed – he had thought I'd get closer to three years. I found myself in the weird position of feeling as if I should be consoling him, as it seemed at first that he was taking it as a point of professional pride. It took me a little while to work out that he actually did feel for me – he'd worked hard on this case because he thought I deserved to be free. We'd become so close I was sure he felt as troubled by my situation as my own father. It felt good to reassure him that I was delighted with the result, as I was.

I mean, we robbed a bank, Luke and I, and we got away with a lot of money. We were on the run for a day, and they don't like bank robbers who get away, even for that short amount of time – they like to show people that being on the run from the law is a bad place to be. We hurt the tellers, emotionally and, apparently, physically. We actually had zip ties in our bags, which was only half an idea in our heads, but indicated to the police that we were prepared to tie the tellers up. It was no small thing. What we did was flat-out bad.

As I went through prison, the discrepancy between my crime and my sentence became something of a liability. Dudes would ask me what I was in for, and I'd tell them I robbed a bank. They'd ask how much I got, and I'd tell them 130 grand. Next they'd be demanding to see my paperwork. They'd want to know why I got such a light sentence for what is really a heavy-duty crime. Some would be convinced I snitched or turned rat. But that was a problem for further down the track.

Interestingly, Rick believed that the prosecutor's departure from the court was significant. Attorneys don't just excuse themselves from the court like that, Rick said, in the middle of a sentencing. What could possibly be more important to a prosecutor than a major case he was prosecuting? This was a clear sign, Rick claimed, that the prosecutor's heart had not been in it, otherwise he would have stayed around to see the case through to the end. Why he left we can only speculate. But then, as Rick reminded me, he did love his Rugby Union.

5

It was only a couple of days after the sentencing that I was awoken early one morning and told to pack my stuff. I was being shipped out to a Federal prison where, presumably, I would spend the next few years. There was no time for goodbyes with the people I'd met in JeffCo – they all knew how abrupt these things can be, so the ones who cared had already said their goodbyes and exchanged details with me.

Together, Luke and I were shackled, placed in a van and driven to a place called Divide, about two hours south of Denver. Waiting for us there was a small jail called Teller County. Only when we arrived there were we told that this was not our destination, but only a stopover on our way somewhere else. How long we were to stay here we didn't know.

Teller County Jail was a small, low-key facility housing about 200 inmates, both male and female (not mixed, of course). There were two people to each cell, which had a decent toilet and a door that actually closed. There were small luxuries here: long pencils to write with, rather than the stumpy little offcuts I was used to; toothbrushes that were new and clean; a better variety of food to eat. These little things began to become reliable signs of the quality of the establishment you were staying in, just as the brand of coffee satchels or the contents of the mini-bar are give-aways as to the quality of a hotel room. I learned to rate American jails and prisons the same way.

The downsides were that the day room was much smaller and you had to request to be taken outside to the rec yard, but that wasn't such a big deal. Teller County Jail was okay by me because I could easily just stay in my own cell if I needed some time away from the Yanks (they're hard work, day after day). Mostly, though, what was good about Teller was that Luke and I shared a cell, so we got to really talk for the first time since being arrested.

It took us a little while to start talking at all about that morning in March, what we'd done and what it had meant to both of us since. It was very strange talking with Luke about it – the whole event seemed to have happened in a different universe altogether. Even though only six months had elapsed, our lives were now so different it was hard to recognise the boys in our memories. It was a relief to hear Luke declare that he wished the whole thing had never

Photo day for Year 12 seniors, mid 2003. I combed my hair out in my best attempt at an afro.

My eighteenth birthday, 2003, with Kylie, Clare and Jessie.

Clare and I playing with the camera in 2003. She would always blink when the flash went off.

At Vail, January 2005.

Cool hand Luke, mucking around with our weapon of choice, the Daisy Powerline 15XT .177 calibre BB pistol, about a month before the robbery.

The scene of the crime: WestStar Bank, Vail, Colorado.

I enter the inner door of the bank...

Luke enters behind me...

Despite the bad picture quality, the anguish on Jessica's face is evident as I point my gun at her. I hate this picture more than any other.

The loot.

The infamous photo.

The moment of truth at Denver International Airport, captured by security cameras.

A picture of me taken by police just minutes after my arrest. It's rare to have the worst moment of your life caught on film, and the fear, regret and hopelessness is all over my face.

The Jefferson County Detention Facility, known as JeffCo.

Rick and Mum in Rick's office. This is how he always looked – always smiling, always the bowtie.

Not looking too enthused, at Youngstown,
Ohio on 1 May 2006.

Shannon, striking a pose with which the
inmates of Youngstown were to become
intimately familiar. By the time I was
released in 2009, this photo had become so
dog-eared I had to cut the corners off.

Me and my brother Dejesus, from Dominican Republic, Youngstown, March 2007. Even the guitarists on the walls of the prison seemed to pay attention to what Dejesus had to say.

With Afghani mate, Abdul Satar, in Youngstown, June 2007. Though he was serving ten years for drug conspiracy, I suspect Abdul might never have touched a drug in his life, but was unfortunate enough to be from Afghanistan at a time when it didn't pay to be so.

Me and my Trinitario brother, Joaquin, in Youngstown, June 2007. Idyllic backdrops like this one appeared on the walls of every prison I visited, presumably so as to fool our loved ones back home into believing we were in paradise.

Pouring my heart out to my sister Kylie in November 2007. Unlike at JeffCo, contact visits were common in Youngstown, but they were earned and the slightest infraction could rob you of them.

Me and Dad squaring off at Christmas in Ohio, 2007. It's the closest he's ever come to headbutting me.

Best mates.

Me and the notorious Hew
Griffiths, the Aussie done for
copyright infringement, in
Youngstown, January 2008.
Despite the benign nature of
Hew's crime, the fellas in my block
nicknamed him 'serial killer'. This
picture explains why.

My workout team in Youngstown,
January 2008. Gabriel 'G', Abdul
and Vu (Vietnamese-Canadian,
ten years for guns and drugs).
Small yet powerful in his ways, Vu
was a leader on the inside, uniting
a divided Asian population into a
force to be reckoned with.

My Mexican buddy, Gabriel, or 'G', in Youngstown, January 2008. A devout Jehovah's Witness, G was extremely kind and generous ... until pushed. I still communicate with him on Facebook.

Me and Jamaican homeboy, '45', in Youngstown, January 2008. He taught me that, before anything else, I was a man. He also had it bad for Shannon.

Me and Mum during one of her many visits, this time in Youngstown in March 2008. With travel and accommodation, it would cost a visitor from Australia an average of ten grand to see me in the US. For me, it was always priceless.

Allenwood medium.

Me and some of the Dirty White Boys, August 2008. Left to right, back row: Scott (two years for drugs), Billy (five years for drugs), Justin (six years for guns and drugs), Bones (30 years for armed robbery), me. Front row: Greg, Jeff (fifteen years for a long list of offences), and Bubba (twelve years for guns, drugs and assault).

Me and Dirty White Boy Justin, aka 'Lucky', in Allenwood, August 2008. He had a brewery behind a fake wall in the back of his locker, and needed gloves and a mask when mixing his 'white lightning', which he reckoned was '100 per cent proof'. It got all the boys dead maggot, I know that for sure.

Mum.

Siblings together again: Kylie, Jessie, me and the kids.

happened. I don't know why that surprised me, or what I'd expected him to believe. I suppose I'd harboured a suspicion that he might regret the robbery hadn't gone according to plan, or that we hadn't escaped to Mexico. But Luke had been dwelling on the same scenarios as me, and had come to the same conclusion: if we'd made it to Mexico, we'd have been imprisoned in that country until we turned ourselves in. As far as Luke was concerned, the only thing that was worthwhile about the robbery was that it had made him realise how good his life had been before, and how his own desire for something 'better' had been more or less pointless. Being in jail had made him realise that he'd actually been pretty happy with what he'd had after all.

Seeing each other again, and talking to each other, reminded us of the friendship we'd almost forgotten. At one point, Luke made a comment about how I was probably the only friend he'd had to whom he'd been able to open up about things. This was nice to hear, but sad, too, as I thought it was probably the most revealing thing Luke had ever said to me.

I was beginning to see Luke in quite a different light. He'd changed, of course, as I had – six months in this pressure cooker would change anyone. But, more importantly, the way I viewed him had changed. Gone was the friend I would have followed anywhere, and who I'd admired for my own childish reasons. As my admiration of him disappeared it was replaced by something more sympathetic – just an understanding of him as someone who had a lot of good qualities, but who, like me, could fuck up in the biggest way possible. I realised I was actually beginning to like him more this way, and that I liked myself more, too.

We were only in Teller County for a few weeks before Rick visited me, all the way from Denver. He came with good news: the next day, he said, Luke and I were to be shipped out to our Federal prison, at Allenwood, Pennsylvania, on the other side of the country. He explained to me that the Allenwood Federal Correctional Complex (FCC) consisted of three facilities: FCI low (low security Federal Correctional Institution); FCI medium; and USP max (high security United States Penitentiary). I would be sent to FCI low and would stay there unless I misbehaved. Rick also revealed to me that this would probably be the last time he and I would see each other.

Of all the people I had come to know over the last bad few months of my life, it was Rick who had been the most precious. It was his hard work that had secured for me a lower sentence, and he who had given me the most hope when I was down, with all the little 'escapes' from prison he had devised for me. It really hit home at that moment that he hadn't been an attorney so much as a friend – he had personally taken me on as a client because he liked me, and had worked hard to keep me safe and happy because he liked me. In many ways he had become the link between me and my mum and dad, like the American Ambassador for the Prince family, and I was going to miss having him so close. He had also been, for six months, the only person from outside of a prison with whom I had enjoyed any physical contact at all. Our meetings would always end with Rick giving me a big, fatherly hug, and on that day in September 2005, there was real emotion in it.

Rick urged me to call him regularly, and I did so for the remainder of my time in the United States, but I have not seen him since that day. Outside of my family, I do not know of anyone to whom I owe so much.

Federal Marshals came in the early morning, shackled me, Luke and a few other inmates, bundled us into a van and drove for a short while before unloading us at a very weird, secluded airstrip in what seemed to be the middle of nowhere. Our van parked and waited. Nearby, I could see rows of buses packed with prisoners from some other Denver prison. There we sat, in eerie silence, until at last the sound of an aircraft arriving broke the creepy stillness of an empty desert.

The plane was just like any passenger aircraft, only painted totally white, with absolutely no markings whatsoever. This was obviously our ride, its attempt to remain inconspicuous making it look like the most remarkable aircraft in the sky. A squad of police cars rolled into view and unloaded about two dozen cops, all armed with 12-gauge shotguns and sidearms, wearing bulletproof vests and war faces. Two police cars continually circled the aircraft like Indians circling wagons, and, in the sky, two helicopters buzzed back and forward. They weren't mucking around – the only thing missing was the dramatic soundtrack music. I have to admit to being kind of flattered by the intense activity my presence appeared to cause. Only presidents, astronauts, rock stars and prisoners get to experience this sort of welcome at an airport.

Still shackled, we were searched, had our names hollered at us a few times, then were finally stacked onto the plane. The cops then took their seats and the plane took off, bound for where we weren't told. It was sort of amusing trying to imagine the types of monsters that all this security and secrecy was designed to discourage. What sort of idiotic evil genius would try to hijack a plane full of criminals? The cops seemed to understand this, too – once on the plane, they were having a good day out, chatting and laughing loudly with each other. The prisoners didn't speak. We had nothing much to talk about.

After a short flight we landed somewhere in Montana, another lonely airstrip. More prisoners climbed aboard and then we were off again. After a while in the air, the view began to change – the parched landscapes of Colorado and Montana gave way to lush green mountains and valleys, with little rivers darting around in between. It was only then I realised that, for the first time in my life, I'd missed an entire summer. Only four to go, more or less, and then I'd be able to actually experience one again.

We landed somewhere to pick up more prisoners. Someone told me it was Seattle. For some reason we were going west, in the opposite direction to Pennsylvania. We took off again, banked and flew back towards the east. By the time we landed in Oklahoma, a planeload of very irritated prisoners had been in transit for twelve hours – a tough haul even for first class commercial passengers, let alone those who have to wear handcuffs. And, after all of that, we'd only travelled as far as one state to the east of Colorado. About the best thing I could say of the journey was that the airfare was at the right price.

The accents in Oklahoma were different from those I'd become used to in Colorado – less whine, less twang, and not as high-pitched; a mellower drawl that was more pleasing to the ear. It was the sound of good-ole' country folk. Unfortunately, there was nothing else about Oklahoma that recommended itself to the travelling prisoner.

Grady County Jail was not unlike JeffCo, only where Jefferson had been sterile and clean, Grady was filthy. The clothes, towels and sheets they provided were stained and smelled like they hadn't been washed in weeks. The phones didn't work, the taps worked when they felt like it, the common TV got reception on one channel only and the food was only edible because if you didn't eat it you would die. The rec area consisted of a basketball court with a flat basketball sitting miserably on the concrete. The quality of the prison seemed to be reflected in the mood of the inmates, which was sullen and sour. That first night, I tried to sleep with no pillow and under a flea-bitten blanket about the size of a beach towel.

I woke in the morning to find that Luke had wound up being in the same pod as me. We didn't know how long we were being stationed here before leaving for Allenwood – maybe this was how it was going to be for the next few months, a slow trip across the United States with a day's stopover at a time in all the worst jails between here and Pennsylvania. At least Luke and I could try to stick together and survive by whingeing to each other about it. I remember playing chess with Luke one morning, with chess pieces moulded from toilet papier-mâché on a chessboard consisting of misshapen squares of ink smeared on the surface of a picnic table. While sitting there thinking about my next move, I had one of those sudden moments of clarity, remembering the grand plans we had for Mexico, and all the things we were going to do after our great money-making project in Colorado. What I saw before me made me laugh to myself. Things never quite work out as you dream them, do they?

Luke kept me sane in Grady County. He didn't try to, he just did. Having someone there from my old life reminded me of what Deputy Memory had told me – that this experience was temporary. Luke also reminded me of

Byron Bay and, sometimes, after talking to him about home, all I'd have to do was go and lie down, close my eyes and I could see it all. Sometimes, Luke and I just sat there and said nothing to each other at all, and it was nice to be in the company of someone who didn't need to talk. Old friends are like that. So I could probably even say that Luke kept me alive in Grady County. The food sure didn't.

Strangely, once I bothered to speak to a few of the other inmates in Grady County Jail, I found them to be so nice it was peculiar to find them in a prison. There was one black guy doing fifteen years for selling someone a few grams of crack, and a softly spoken Mexican who was doing ten years for possessing 15 kilograms of coke. So many seemed like decent folk who wouldn't hurt a fly. I remember one morning having my breakfast delivered (our food was delivered to our cells – there was no dining area), and the inmate worker delivering it was a fat old man who was sweating from having trudged up the stairs.

'Thanks, bro,' I said, feeling sorry for the old farmer.

'No worries,' he replied. 'By the way, the name's Tom.'

I told him I was Tony, from Australia.

'Well,' he sighed, in his Oklahoma drawl, 'I sure am glad to know you, Tony.' Then he shuffled out of my cell and on his way.

What the fuck was that nice old man doing here? And where were his kids, his brothers and sisters? What became of his mum and dad? Did they ever know he was here? Did he ever have a wife, or a sweetheart?

Clare. She kept popping into my thoughts in Grady County, and I often tried to banish her from my mind, as she was too good to be hauled into this shithole. In fact, she was too good for any of this, too sweet and special to be the girlfriend of a guy in this horrible little jail. I began to wonder whether she might be thinking so too. Each time I'd speak to her on the phone, she'd tell me of some night out she'd had with friends, and I'd wonder about all the dirty bastards out there who were free to try to put their hands on her. I'd listen for sounds of guilt or regret in her voice, and I'd later replay her words in my mind, examining every breath for a sign. A few days of this and then I'd banish her from my mind again. She was too pretty and precious for this place. One day, we'd be together again, for the rest of our lives.

On our twelfth day in Grady County Jail we were woken at dawn and told to move out. There had been rumours going around that we were headed to some joint in Georgia for a while. Who knew what sort of dungeon awaited us there?

We were shackled again, driven to the airport again, stacked on a plane like cattle again. We flew for hours until we began circling a city surrounded by rivers, lakes and green forests, the colours almost blinding after so many months in the grey world of prison. I asked a guard if he knew what state we were in. To my surprise, he told me it was Pennsylvania. At last. I'd never looked forward to a prison so much in my life.

We landed at a massive industrial airport complex in Harrisburg. I could see from the window other prison aircraft with no markings, buses lined up everywhere, armed guards moving prisoners from planes to vans, from vans to buses, from vans to planes. There was so much movement all around it was like it was being choreographed for some kind of James Bond film.

One of the lasting memories I have of the American prison system is the sight of guys sitting around with completely dorky glasses on – big, thick-rimmed, nerdy frames with lenses that magnify the eyes to about five times their normal size. This was common because prisoners would often need glasses but couldn't afford to pay for proper lenses for themselves, so the prison system would provide them with these crook, old, brown, dirt-cheap, one-size-fits-all pair of magnifiers that looked like 3D glasses, or those novelty ones you might buy in a joke shop. I always found it really sad that anyone who wanted to make something of themselves in prison by doing some reading or studying would be rewarded with the humiliation of being made to look like a geek.

I remember being ordered from the plane and onto a bus, where I sat next to this really hardcore white dude with one such pair of glasses – which made him look like a goggle-eyed freak. He was a lot shorter than me but covered in tatts, with long dirty fingernails, a real seedy-looking character.

He began telling me how he'd been arrested for having an automatic weapon. I was just sitting there listening to him when I was suddenly struck by another one of those weird feelings of clarity – just one moment out of many where I sort of viewed myself from the outside and above, like I was looking down on the two of us talking, then further up, so I was looking down on the bus, then down on the airport filled with buses and planes and criminals. What I saw was myself as this tiny little fucking country boy, being overwhelmed at every stage, way out of his depth. That's exactly what I was, I suppose.

After a fairly long journey on the bus, I was alarmed to see us pulling into Lewisburg, a United States Penitentiary – 'The Big House', as I'd heard it referred to by prisoners in the past. This place had a reputation, and I was worried that I had somehow been accidentally sent to a maximum security prison. Thankfully, I was told we would not be entering the main area of the prison, but rather a holding area, where we would be staying for the night en route to Allenwood. This was good news – from the outside, Lewisburg was very intimidating, the entire complex enclosed by a 30-feet-high brick wall that seemed to exist not only so criminals couldn't get out, but so that good people couldn't see in.

Inside, we were strip-searched and fed for the first time in about twelve hours – the all-American peanut butter and jelly sandwiches. After the sewage cuisine at Grady County, I felt I'd never tasted anything so delicious in my life. And after an entire day's travelling, I was exhausted, and slept deeply that night, but for only a short time.

At dawn, we were on our way again, and, about 30 minutes later, our bus arrived at the Federal Correctional Complex of Allenwood, Pennsylvania. It was a massive, multi-million-dollar compound set over 300 hectares of property. The three levels – low, medium and max – were spread out over a huge area, separated by lawns.

I was quite impressed, to be honest. I'd spent so much time in shitty, filthy little prisons since JeffCo, which was a sterile madhouse in its own way, and here I was looking at a proper prison, where inmates were mowing lawns or maintaining the rec yards. It was just obvious from my first sight of it that this was no halfway house, but more of a little city where prisoners were meant to stay for a good while. I remember thinking to myself: I reckon I could live here for a time. Then I remembered that's exactly what I was going to be doing.

At this point, Luke and I were separated, and I didn't really know when we'd see each other again. Separations like this happened without fanfare in here, and it's something that was always hard to get used to. You'd feel like complaining to the guards: 'Hey, buddy, can't I just say goodbye to my friends?', until you'd remember where you were, and that in the eyes of the world your friendships – your *happiness* – didn't matter. There was always a depressing and helpless feeling of sorrow that followed those moments.

I was strip-searched, dressed out, seen by a doctor, a psychiatrist and a case manager. I was then led into my dormitory, where the cells were not so much cells as divided living quarters — the walls were about six feet high, the ceilings another four feet above. Sitting up on my bunk on the top, I could look out across the whole dormitory. It seemed pretty cosy — nice thick blankets, a good layout, clean and tidy. It was clear the other cellmates took good care of their living space. I wondered what sort of guys would be so anal about their cell. My question was answered after a few minutes when they showed up to greet me.

Dave and Johnny appeared to be around the same age, but I later learned Dave was 43 and Johnny 31. They were two white boys of Italian background, both bits of work, with the same homicidal intensity in their eyes.

Dave was an absolute machine. He was six foot tall and incredibly well built, fit and lean. He'd gone to Thailand when he was seventeen and studied Muay Thai, a particularly hard martial art of which he was now a master. He'd tell me stories about the fights he'd been in and I believed all of them. He belittled everyone in the weight room — he'd stack every weight in the room onto the bar and just shrug it off. He was also a tattoo artist, which meant he was pretty sought-after in the prison system.

He'd lived in some of the toughest Federal penitentiaries for a decade and a half, and was due to be released the following year. From an inmate's point of view, he was the model prisoner – hard, blunt, would blow you off in a second, but straight up and honest with others. From the moment I met him I realised we were going to get along, which was very fortunate for me, in more ways than one.

Johnny was a bit less social, a quieter, mellower sort of intensity, but the same look in his eye that said you only fucked with him at your peril. He was three years into a seventeen-year sentence for manufacturing methamphetamine – he'd been caught with not so much as a gram of meth, but with enough ephedrine, an essential ingredient in meth, for the cops to predict how much meth-amphetamine he *would have* been able to manufacture. He must have had a lot. At this point in time, the way Johnny saw it, he didn't have much to lose. That made him a little more frightening than Dave, even though he was less impressive and intimidating.

Immediately, Dave and Johnny demanded to see my paperwork. I gave it to them and, once they saw that I wasn't a rat or a screw's pet, they accepted me. From the start, it seemed, Dave realised I was young, not used to the prison system and could do with some guidance. He was very considerate of me and that was good, but it had its downside.

I remember when I wanted to buy a new pair of shoes from the commissary, Dave was very strict about which pair he thought I should get. Against his wishes, I bought a pair of the Nike High Tops. When he saw them, he went ballistic. 'You got the brother shoes!' he fumed. 'What the fuck are you doing? I told you to get these ones and you got the brother shoes!' I told him I got them because I wanted to play basketball, but he just wouldn't accept it. As far as he was concerned, I'd betrayed the white race by buying the shoes that black guys wore.

I was coming to understand this sort of behaviour perfectly well. It wasn't just Dave who suffered from it, but a lot of guys who, like him, had been in prison a long time. As I've said before, being locked in a prison, with so many of your choices removed, can make it so that you start to obsess about little things, so that they take the place of the big things that matter. This was one of those things for Dave. In his own way, he was a stickler for the rules. He believed the blacks and the whites had little flags of their own – in their clothing, in their movements, the way they spoke . . . everything – and he believed they shouldn't be mixed. I have a hard time believing that he would have been racist when outside the prison – having travelled extensively in Asia, and studied martial arts, how could he be? But races gather together tightly in prison, to the point where you can almost generalise about them. And prison amplifies everything that is inside – like a big pressure cooker, it raises the temperatures of all the little thoughts and prejudices that take place within both the prison walls and the minds of the inmates.

Anyway, I knew that Dave liked to see the universe in its correct order, and that meant that I was to forever be the young buck who didn't know anything about anything, while he was the Original Gangster and I must respect that.

This hierarchy was fine with me – it wasn't as if I was ever going to challenge his authority – but it meant that any argument between Dave and me would always have to end with me being wrong and Dave being right. Like I say, if that was going to keep Dave happy, I was okay with it. It was probably mostly correct anyway.

I remember the night he told me about the murder that had landed him in prison all those years ago. I was sitting on the top bunk (the new guy always has to have the top bunk, as it's just a little more inconvenient to climb in and out of), with my legs swinging off like some little kid, asking him to tell me about the murder, as if I were asking Daddy to read me a story. So he told me about the drugs, the guy wearing the wire, the 44-gallon drum and the oxyacetylene torch. As he spoke, my legs slowed down and eventually stopped dead. Dave wasn't a prankster, or a tough guy looking for respect. He was the real deal. If he wanted you out of the picture, you were history. I think, by the time I met him, he only had a year or so left to serve. But you got the impression he would have thought nothing of adding a few more years to his sentence, if it meant sorting a problem out to his satisfaction. I was happy to be his cellmate. All I had to do was behave, which is what I was in here for anyhow.

The gangs of Allenwood were my introduction to the deeply segregated society of the American Federal prison system.

There were black gangs, white gangs and Hispanic gangs. But under those broad umbrellas there were Christians and Muslims, Crips and Bloods, Latin Kings, MS-13, Native Americans, Aryan Nation, Aryan Brotherhood, Mexican Mafia, Nortenos, Surenos, Nuestra Familia, the KKK and the Dirty White Boys. There were so many different and often opposing factions and tributaries and almost none of them got along. It was warfare all the time, with no boundaries. Imagine if every nation in the world had its borders removed and its population scattered, but we all remained at war with each other. That's what it's like in prison.

There were about 1200 inmates in the Allenwood prison system, and about 400 of them were Muslim. They were the predominant religion, and they were black, white, Hispanic and Asian, but predominantly African American. You could spot them from across the yard, huge black guys with big beards and marks on their foreheads from hitting their heads on the floor during prayer. Some white guy got smashed once for asking some dude if he was 'a nigger or a head-banger or what?'

But it was the Hispanic gangs that were really scary. In them, you could see a real life or death struggle going on. They didn't back down and they were frightened of nobody, because, while they might be the minority in some prisons, their numbers are vast in the whole US prison system. You'd see them walking past each other – a new inmate passing an old-timer – and throwing their sets up, the hand signals that identified the gang they were in. From one prison to another, they communicated perfectly well. You could do something to an MS-13 member in JeffCo and think you'd gotten away with it, but, months later, in Allenwood or Lewisburg, you'd cop a knife in the back of the neck and everyone would find out why.

Of course, people talk of gangs in prison as if it's all to do with thugs gathering to beat the shit out of each other, but what was fascinating to me about the gangs was how well structured they were. Typically, there would be the head of the gang and his deputy, who was ready to rise up at any time; a head of security, whose job would often be to make sure there was a weapon concealed in every room and yard of the prison, and that all members were aware of them; a head of finance, who handled everything from the gang's rackets in the prison to the bills they owed attorneys; a head of orientation, in charge of showing new recruits the ropes. They were structured like companies, because they were companies, in the true sense. But where most companies in society exist mostly to make profits for their shareholders, the company in prison exists solely to save the lives of its members.

I was to learn a lot more about gangs in prison, later on down the track. But, back then, in Allenwood, I was just fascinated. I suppose I knew that it was inevitable I'd have to choose a flag to march under. It went against everything I'd been brought up to believe, about accepting people for who they are, refusing to go with the mob, thinking for yourself and standing up against bullies – all of that stuff. But I hadn't been brought up in preparation for a young life lived in an American penitentiary. The rules were different in here. I'd have to be prepared to unlearn a few things, and hope I could relearn them when I got out.

The dilemma for every prisoner is to work out what to do with all your time. Because time is all you've got. In prison, nobody gets to buy their own clothes, show off their wealth or indulge in expensive hobbies. All you've got to think about is what you're going to do. It's when you don't have anything to do that you start to go crazy, or get into trouble for concentrating too much on your reputation, or how others see you. That can be a very dangerous pastime. People take how you feel about them very personally. Outside, someone might not like you for the clothes you wear, the car you drive or the girl they wished they went out with themselves. In prison, if someone doesn't like you, it's you they don't like, nothing else.

There was, of course, the strange world of prison commerce to get involved in, which interested me a great deal. In the Federal prison system, stamps were the staple currency, and the 'Storemen' – inmates who ran their own 'stores', selling food and hustling other odds and ends – were the ones who controlled the economy. If you wanted to buy some stamps, you bought them from the Storemen, who sold them to you for, say, 30 cents each, rather than the commissary shop, which sold them for 50 cents each. This was how the Storemen kept their economy running smoothly, by shutting out the legitimate economy and keeping their own inviolate. All it took was for a Storeman to make an initial outlay for stamps he knew he was going to sell at a lesser price. Like a futures trader, or anyone starting a business, he had to take a significant gamble to get the ball rolling. But it was a gamble sure to pay off in the end, as long as there were inmates who had money on the outside that needed to be changed into prison currency.

For example, if I got my mum or dad to put US$100 into a Storeman's account, the Storeman would give me, in return, $130 worth of stamps. It's a good deal for the Storeman, because the stamps he sold me will enter the market and probably come back to him in the end as I buy food or other items from him. For me, who's got more money outside than I'll ever have inside prison, it's a good deal, too, because I can now purchase items within the prison. In effect, each prison has its own exchange rate, which ebbs and flows depending on particular circumstances and politics.

This is how it works in every Federal prison in the United States. In the smaller jails, the economy is less structured – a couple of Maggi soups will pass as currency. But, in the Federal joints, it's hardcore, and all the rules of supply and demand economics apply. There were bookies, bankers, loan sharks, gambling rackets – this whole universe of commerce going on at a subterranean level. The screws knew it was going on, but there was very little they could do about it. The only way they could bust the economy was to find someone's book, some Storeman's record of accounts with regard to what he was owed and by whom. But the Storemen were generally clever enough to have devised their own coded accounting systems that couldn't be cracked by anyone.

In fact, the ingenuity of prisoners in general was to be a real eye-opener for me. It just proved there was practically nothing that could be done to stop a determined human being from doing what he wanted to do. Prisoners created the most sophisticated things – bongs, alcohol stills, syringes and radio sets – out of nothing. There was one guy I remember who had an entire miniature alcohol still in the back of his locker, hidden by a false wall which the screws had repeatedly failed to notice. The insides of other inmates' lockers told of all sorts of industry, with little multi-layered shelves made of wood or cardboard, or shrines to movie stars or pin-up girls who looked like they'd been designed and constructed by advertising agencies. All around was evidence of the old saying about necessity being the mother of invention, and of how pathetically hopeless it is for governments to try to control human nature. That drugs were so freely available in prison, of all places, was testament enough to the complete failure of the 'war on drugs'. If they can't keep contraband out of a prison, the most secure society a government can construct, what hope is there for keeping any banned substance or behaviour out of the free community? It seemed to me an irony that a Federal prison was perhaps the best evidence for the case against law and order.

Of course, I'd already tried to become a Storeman, with that ill-fated venture in JeffCo, and I tried a few more times during my career in the US prison system, but I was never very good at it. Somehow, I'd always wind up eating all the food. I was just so very hungry, all the time.

In any case, I hadn't come to prison to become good at being a prisoner. I decided to concentrate on the things that I'd like to get out of my prison experience, to think of it like an extreme learning institution. Four years was about how long it took to study something at university. Why couldn't I apply this time to improving myself, rather than just punishing myself? I already knew I was going to grow up a lot – I could already feel myself maturing and becoming more of a man about things – but I didn't want to graduate from the American prison system a better criminal (which wouldn't be too hard anyway, considering my crime). I wanted to make the time work for me, so that when I was returned to society I was more capable than when I'd been removed from it.

My mum had encouraged me to study long distance, to do the business and marketing degree I had always planned to do. She had sent me lots of information about studying with Australian colleges and universities by remote correspondence, so I began to throw myself into studying for a Special Tertiary Admissions Test (STAT). But I had to do more than that – the library facilities at Allenwood were limited, and I wasn't keen on becoming one of those geeky bookworms who sat around the prison like gnomes. The answer was pretty obvious when I looked at what impressed me about my cellmates.

I'd already seen in JeffCo what a daily workout could do for my physique and outlook. One thing that Allenwood had was a very decent gymnasium, with a full-size basketball court and a weight room with benches, free weights, bike machines and treadmills – everything that you'd find in a solid commercial gymnasium on the outside. I had no idea where to start, but it was clear that Dave and Johnny treated exercise like it was some sort of religion. They were constantly in the gym and, when not, could always be found talking to each other about different techniques. I decided I was going to lean on my cellmates to get together a program for me. But the plan hit a snag before it could even get off the ground.

One morning, Dave and Johnny decided to work on tattoos for each other. Tattooing was illegal in the prison, of course, but Dave was a pro at this. He'd fashion a tattoo gun out of rubbish – the tube from a pen, a guitar string as the needle, a toothbrush, an electric motor from a beard trimmer, with ink made from oil mixed with the soot that came from burned paper or plastic, some tape and a battery charger. Once again, a bit of prison ingenuity to boggle the mind.

Dave wasn't so stupid as to rely on me alone to act as lookout, so he employed the help of some other inmates, too, who were familiar with the drill. The problem is that all of us standing around the door of the cell made for a suspicious sight – what the fuck were all these guys finding so interesting in a doorway? The guards became suspicious, and, without us even realising, had exited through a side doorway and, holding their keys so as to keep them from jangling, crept into our hallway from behind us. Before we knew it they were there, right beside us. I tried to stand in the road but the officer just shoved me out of his path, bursting into the cell to catch Dave and Johnny red-handed.

It was a very uncomfortable moment – we were meant to be the lookouts and there we were, filing into the cell behind the screws, as if we were stragglers in their party. We just stood there with nothing to say as the screws told Dave and Johnny they were going to The Hole.

Dave, being Dave, argued with them – 'C'mon, man, you know I've been in here for fifteen fucken years, don't pull this shit.' The screws argued back – that rules were rules and all that – but they argued; the screws actually argued. That was what was different about Dave. If I'd argued back, the screws would have told me to shut the fuck up and do as I was told. But, with Dave, they argued their case, doing their best to make him understand where they were coming from. Even the screws knew not to tell Dave to fuck off. They respected him that much.

I knew there was going to be trouble when Dave and Johnny got out. In the meantime, it was nice to have a cell all to myself, where I could read, sleep, or think about Clare, long into the night and on into the day. The bliss wouldn't last very long.

As the end of 2005 approached, I felt I was entering a pretty good time at Allenwood FCI. I had completed my STAT for university, had been working as an electrician a few days a week (fixing household switches, cords, etc.), was solidly into an exercise program and, most importantly of all, was off the hook with Dave and Johnny, who had only spent a week in The Hole and weren't anywhere near as upset with me as they were with the others. In fact, Johnny had agreed to take on the role as my personal trainer, and once again I'd quickly noticed changes in my mood and motivation, and the way my body was starting to feel. Lifting iron was becoming addictive, and the protein shake I'd have afterwards, made of egg white powder, peanut butter and hot chocolate mix, was better than most of the meals I'd 'enjoyed' in Jefferson, Teller or Grady counties.

I suppose when you start feeling good is when you're in danger of getting cocky – that's how it's always been for me. As soon as I become too familiar with someone or my surroundings, I begin to develop a bit of a swagger in both my behaviour and my mentality. It's a lesson I'd learned very early on in JeffCo – to keep a cork in my inner smartarse – but JeffCo was now a long way away, and I'd always been good at forgetting my lessons.

It was just a few days before Christmas. Snow was falling outside and there was that expectant yuletide feeling, even in prison. Perhaps I was a little emotionally jarred by this, thinking of my family at home, and Clare, and how this would be my first Christmas without them. Whatever caused it, I got mouthy with my case manager, who was up my arse about something that today I can't even recall. Basically, whatever had started it, I was guilty of not obeying a direct order from my case manager, who was tearing me one for it. I responded that I thought he was 'a joke'.

'Would you think I was a joke if I sent you to The Hole?' he said.

At this point, all I had to do was suck it up and keep my mouth closed – I had already gotten away with calling him a joke, and I am frankly surprised he didn't march me to The Hole for that alone. But Anthony was now among Johnny and Dave, the hard, respected crew of the unit. What I forgot was that I was still a newbie, and I couldn't expect to bathe in the respect Dave had earned over the years.

I turned to the case manager, snarled and said, as cool as fuck: 'You do what you gotta do.'

What a Desmond. I'd just earned myself a one-way ticket to The Hole, a few days before Christmas. Next to a certain banking transaction I'd attempted to carry out earlier that year, it was quite possibly the most stupid thing I had done in 2005.

Every prison has its own version of The Hole, also known as The Box or The Cage. In low security, The Hole is often nothing more than an unwelcome promotion to medium security, as it was in JeffCo. But in Allenwood, The Hole referred to the Special Housing Unit, a wing of the compound especially set aside for inmates who were believed to be in need of a period of attitude adjustment. All rights were removed, all social prison activities wiped from the daily itinerary. The wardens, known by other inmates as 'the All Right Crew', would bang on your door in the middle of the night, ask: 'You all right?', then move along before you could answer. Just another way to remind you that you were in the punishment wing.

All there was to do in The Hole was think, and thinking tended to make me depressed. I started by thinking about Clare, how beautiful she was, and how lucky I was. Slowly but surely, this train of thought metamorphosed into how unfortunate she was to have shacked up with a dickhead like me – a guy in prison for robbing a bank with a BB gun. What a catch for a girl who could have whoever she wanted. Down, down my mood spiralled, until finally I took out a pencil and paper and wrote her a letter soaked in self-pity, in which I basically encouraged her to move on, to leave me behind like a mortally wounded soldier. She was too lovely to be held back by me, a man who barely deserved her. I professed my love to her, of course, but insisted I only wanted her to live life to the full, that it was unfair of me to expect her to remain obligated to a lover who wasn't there. It was a supreme document of self-sacrifice, and I fully expected her to reject it, to respond that she loved me, wanted nobody else, etc. But I felt very noble writing it. (Curiously, Clare would later tell me the envelope arrived, opened, with no letter inside it – it's probably pinned to the wall in some sorting room at US Post, the staff stopping every now and then to read it and snigger just one more time.)

I began to think hard on who I was, why I was here, and what was to become of me. This sank me further into depression as I concentrated on the negative things: my need to impress others; my restlessness and lack of discipline; my desire to retaliate when annoyed, only to feel guilty about it later. I saw myself as having two distinct sides that didn't get along with each other. I was like a dog that was loyal and affectionate, but, when running with the pack, a very different dog. It would be all right if I was one or the other – either a needy arsehole or a sympathetic pushover. But being both of them didn't work, particularly in prison. When with Dave and Johnny, it was easy to let my bad side take over and go with the flow, to refuse to mix with 'niggers' or gays just to impress my friends. Then, later, my conscience would not let me forget what I'd done, and I'd be tormented by it. The way I'd been brought up was not allowing me to get away with the daily moral compromises of prison life.

These are the thoughts that swirled through my head in The Hole, and sent me deeper as the hours went by. I wrote them down – all these negative thoughts I was having about myself – and tried to convince myself that being aware of them was a positive thing. But then I'd read them and start to hate myself for not acting on them sooner.

When in a mood like this, it always helps to have someone else to focus the hatred upon. How fortunate I was, then, to have been placed in a cell with Joke Boy, as I dubbed him. A fat little pig of a middle-aged man who made my skin creep, he thought he was a fucking genius, and was always walking about in his boxer shorts, exposing a back so matted with hair it had knots in it. He was all 'Let me tell you something, son' and 'You listen to me, boy', as if he were some kind of sage, but he was actually just a filthy fat wanker, who never missed an opportunity to suck up to the wardens, making jokes with them that only he would laugh at. He was one of those dogs you knew would think nothing of ratting you out, if only to get a pat on the head from his superiors.

One day, while strutting around in his shorts, the hairy little midget declared: 'You know, I'm not terribly out of shape for a 54-year-old.' My response was simply: 'Yeah, whatever.' It was all I could think of, and I didn't want to waste too much energy on the fucker.

I decided to focus my rage on Joke Boy, venting my anger in the most inventive ways. I began by farting a lot, silently, which would have troubled him, seeing as he was on the bottom bunk (of course). At nights, he'd sleep with a blindfold on, and a cup of juice on the floor beside him. From my vantage point above, I'd have spitting contests with my 'other side' (the bad one), a bullseye being the middle of the cup. Once or twice, I even dropped nasal blockages, whispering 'bombs away!' as I released my payload. Then I'd lie there and wait for the sound of his hand fumbling for his cup, then that magnificent slurping sound. Not very mature, but it passed the time.

Joke Boy made me realise how cool my own parents were by comparison, being around the same age as him. Their humour, love and complete lack of back hair became more impressive the more I dwelt on it. I thought about the freedom they had always given me, and how I had taken that freedom for granted. Look how I had repaid them. I wondered if others might judge my parents by my behaviour. That made me angry. As I lined up another payload to bomb into Joke Boy's cup, I determined to make sure that I would always take responsibility for my own actions, that I would let people know my parents had in no way influenced my bad behaviour, and that I would forcefully debate anyone who insisted it was otherwise.

I spent Christmas in The Hole. Then New Year, which felt like no new year at all. Joke Boy got shifted, only to be replaced by a balding, bespectacled 45-year-old who suffered panic attacks. He'd been sent to prison for the crime of giving away 80 of his prescribed OxyContin tablets. He got three years for that. No wonder he was in such a panic. What a crazy fucking world.

I began to go a bit stir-crazy myself, thinking too much on ridiculous thoughts. I remember hatching a grand plan in my mind for how Clare and I would make money when I returned home. I decided we would shack up in a bedroom for a month, the both of us exercising until we were in peak physical condition. Then I'd borrow a camera from my sister, Jessie, who was a photographer, and who could teach me the right way to take photos. Then I would buy ten rolls of film and take shots of Clare in suggestive positions. We would then build up a portfolio, which we'd send to magazines and TV stations and websites. We'd make a fortune from Clare's modelling, and we'd both be so happy and proud of each other. This particular dream rocked me to sleep many nights. I never really got past the photo shoot part.

At last, and just before I lost my mind, I was released from The Hole and back into the compound. The year 2006 was nine days old. The snow had melted and the weather was crisp. It was so nice to get some fresh air again, and to see the sky looking so blue.

After getting settled back into my cell I went to see my case manager, the one who had sent me to The Hole in the first place. During my time in The Hole, I had come to the conclusion that the privilege of being in low security came with the catch of having to kiss a fair amount of arse. I'd determined to front the man and deliver my most heartfelt apology for my behaviour and the things I'd said.

With a poker face, the man accepted my apology, agreeing with me that I'd acted badly. I promised him that it would never happen again. No it wouldn't, he said, because I was to be transferred to another prison.

I couldn't believe it. After all the aircraft, buses and settling in, I was being shipped out of Allenwood for someplace else. Naturally assuming I was being sent to a medium security facility, I asked whether I was being transferred because of what had happened between himself and me. He said that it wasn't the case, that I was simply being moved as part of the Immigrant Hearing Program. Apparently, the fact that I was now an illegal immigrant, due to be deported upon my release anyhow, qualified me to spend the rest of my prison time in an illegal immigrant facility.

This was bad news. I'd settled in to Allenwood, just as I'd settled in to JeffCo before it. Now I was being uprooted again, for a prison filled with Hispanics, Jamaicans, Dominicans and Asians, where I'd have a much harder time fitting in. There had been talk that the Australian Government might come to an agreement with the USA regarding me being transferred to complete my prison time in Australia, but the chances of that were slim. I did not like the thought of spending the next few years in an institution populated by inmates who probably wouldn't even speak my language. Dave didn't exactly lighten my spirits about it. He said I'd hate the immigration facility, which he believed would feature no weight room or library.

For the first time since this whole saga had begun, I became so despondent that I briefly considered taking the old 'easy way out'. But I thought I'd better give it a miss, as I'd probably fuck that up as well.

6

Not long ago, I saw a program on TV that speculated about what the world would be like if humans suddenly disappeared from the planet, and all the buildings and infrastructure were left to corrupt by themselves. I happen to know exactly what it will be like, because I've been there. It's a place called Youngstown, Ohio.

Youngstown was once a vibrant city, a big smelter for US Steel, but the people of Youngstown didn't bother to diversify, so when the steel industry went south after World War II, the town fell apart. Today, it's the weirdest, broken ghost city, with big civic buildings that once meant something now abandoned and crawling with vines, and grand old derelict houses that look like horror movie sets. Bruce Springsteen once sang a song called 'Youngstown', about a city that worked and worked to get America through the wars, only to be forgotten once the wars were won. That's Youngstown – a forgotten place. And this shithole was to be my home for the next two and a half years.

Not that I would be catching many of the sights during my stay. My accommodation was the Northeast Ohio Correctional Facility, one of the few buildings in Youngstown that was actually well populated.

I was transported from Allenwood to Youngstown with the usual circus – shackles, buses, armed guards. My first impression of the prison was not good, as it appeared to be very locked down, even more so than Allenwood, with several fences wrapped in razor wire. Once inside, it was the usual routine; open your mouth, turn around, spread 'em and cough, lift your sack . . . they didn't even have to tell me what to do anymore, or when to do it, as I'd done it so many times I knew it all off by heart.

What I noticed immediately was the difference in the attitude of the screws. They seemed a lot more down-to-earth and respectful than those at Allenwood, or even JeffCo – making eye contact, telling jokes, smiling a little here and there. It made a big difference. Only later would I learn that the reason for this was that Youngstown was a privately owned prison, so who they employed was entirely up to them. Since this was Youngstown, the broken-down city with no jobs and no opportunity, the staff of Northeast Ohio Correctional Facility was made up of people who otherwise might work in McDonald's, if only the town had been prosperous enough to have one.

The other thing I noticed immediately was that some of the staff were women – about 50 per cent of them, in fact – and some of them weren't bad looking. This was a refreshing change, but it was odd, too. How could it possibly be a good idea to throw women into this madhouse?

And it was a madhouse – almost two thousand prisoners, most of them Latin American, nothing but black hair and moustaches roaming around speaking Spanish. On that first day I saw one other white guy. The whole scene reminded me of that bus depot in Denver, with the animals and people all in together like an assorted zoo.

They gave me a bag of prison-issue clothes that also had a little radio set inside it, as if it were a show bag and the radio was the little prize, and showed me to my cell. It was a cell for two, a small steel table jutting out of the concrete wall across from the beds, a toilet at the back, a small window with a view of the sky and the rec area. I took the bottom bunk – figured it was about time I started asserting myself. I'd been a prisoner of the United States penal system for almost a year. I'd been in fights, served time in The Hole, made friends and enemies. I wasn't a newbie anymore.

The layout inside the units was not unlike that at JeffCo – ten cells on top, ten cells on the bottom, looking out over a day room with a few chairs and tables, four TVs, two microwave ovens, a couple of ironing boards. It was the same boring, functional view that was cut and pasted from one prison to the next, state after state.

I settled in pretty quickly at Youngstown, immediately acclimatising to the slackness of the place. It was low security, so the hours were loose – some nights I'd stay up late, listening to the radio, to some club channel that played the sort of songs we used to listen to back home while cruising around. It was easy for me to just close my eyes and drift back, imagining anything and everything. By now, my imagination had become very malleable, and I could make people come and go and do all sorts of things without too much trouble. Once upon a time, it had been hard for me to imagine people doing things they wouldn't normally do. But prison had forced me to become a stronger captain of my mind's eye, and I was able to direct the old population of Byron Bay to do whatever I wished. It was like I had this private soap opera waiting for me whenever I wanted to lie down, relax and pick up from where I left off. It passed the time.

But it didn't take long for the novelty of Youngstown to wear off, and the drudgery of a prisoner's existence to return. Trying to stay positive in these environments is actually exhausting, and all you need to do is lose focus for a day and the reality of your situation is waiting there for you. The noise that echoes from the dreary concrete walls, the filthy kitchen and showers, the constant haze from the fluorescent lights, always on, never going dark, the cameras on the walls watching everything, everywhere. Three times a day I was reminded of how little my pride and self-worth mattered, when a man would come in – just another man – and demand that I stand from my bed for him. It's very hard to describe the humiliation that this breeds in you, day after day, month after month. To be ordered, all day, to do this or not do that.

'Walk on the right side of the line, convict.'

Having to follow such orders, every day, and having these people talk down to you at every turn is enough to drive you insane. I think the only reason I survived it in the end was because I was so young, and being spoken to like a child – by teachers and elders – was an experience that wasn't buried so deep in my memory. I have no idea how the older prisoners dealt with it. I don't imagine I'd have been able to stand it if I'd been a mature man.

Of course, you mature pretty quickly in prison – a lot of the younger kids in Youngstown were covered in tattoos and looked so hard it was as if they'd been in prison since birth. I remember seeing one kid, who could have been no more than seventeen or eighteen, with a syringe tattooed on his arm, and it was faded enough to look as if it had been there for half his life. And the stuff they talked about was incredible. I recall pretending to be interested while this little Latino told me about the time he pistol-whipped his 'bitch' because she'd answered back to him. They spoke of guns and violence like me and my mates back home talked of chicks and getting drunk. I have never felt such a sheltered little virgin as I did when in conversation at the Youngstown prison rec yard.

There was one fellow who had changed his name to Mephistopheles Fetus-Grubber (presumably, he found his previous name embarrassing). He was the most obvious crackhead you could ever hope to see – skin and bones, a gaunt face that could advertise The Ghost Train, acne scars pathetically hidden behind immature tufts of facial hair, boils and sores filled with all sorts of chemicals and covered with Gothic tatts. I think he might have had one full tooth in his entire head – in the middle of the bottom gum – the rest being rotted black stumps protruding like broken fence posts from diseased, bleeding gums. You had to be very careful not to make him laugh, otherwise he'd open his mouth and you'd be sick.

But Mephistopheles Fetus-Grubber could draw. He was a fucking artist. Give him a $3 bag of coffee, a short pencil and a scrap of paper and he'd draw whatever you wanted and it would blow your mind. It was crazy to see such awesome talent festering away inside a prison, inside his body. I looked him up on the internet a little while back, and found someone who claimed he was out of jail and married, but that his wife wanted him to change his name back to what it had been before she met him.

Women.

The female screws in Youngstown were a peculiar lot. You'd have to wonder about a woman who chose to work as a screw in a prison full of men. Some of them clearly were here to find a mate, probably because they knew the only useful men in Youngstown could be found in the prison, rather than outside where everything was broken and waiting for a man who could be bothered to get off his arse and fix it. There was one female screw, a Puerto Rican with the features of a piglet. She'd be forever stopping guys as they came out of the mess area after dinner, so that she could feel them up under the guise of searching for stolen food (as if anyone would steal that shit). A part of me actually liked it (a big part) when she'd fully caress my chest and stomach, and I'm sure that's what she had in mind. In prison, you had to take what you could get. I'm sure everybody jacked off over that Puerto Rican piglet, and we all felt regretful about it in the morning.

There was another screw called Renee, who was also pretty crook to look at, but she had blonde hair and blue eyes so we all tended to look past her haggard, crusty features. One night I was listening to the radio, to a local station that was broadcasting live from some local nightclub. The DJ was wandering through the crowd talking to people, when he suddenly asked: 'And who have we here?', and the unmistakable voice of our screw comes out of the speakers.

'Hi, I'm Renee, and I'm getting really drunk . . . tee hee hee hee hee . . .'

The next day we all ripped her a new arse for it, which didn't go down too well, seeing as she was so hungover. A few months after that, Renee was going around telling people she was pregnant. Then, one day, she just stopped, until it became clear she wasn't pregnant anymore. Another life abandoned in Youngstown.

There were all sorts of rumours, of course, about which screws put out, for how much and to whom. There was one old cougar who was rumoured to be an ex-stripper, who was available to any inmate who could produce $300. It got me to wondering about some of them, and whether they might be prospects. There was one female officer who always seemed so psyched, who'd always be coming into my cell under the guise of 'checking' it, then she'd hang around and chat, like she had nowhere else to be. I always put this down to my accent – a girl from Youngstown, Ohio had probably only ever seen or heard an Australian on TV – but I couldn't help but wonder what my chances would be if I jumped her. She certainly seemed to be open to it. But then, that's the mistake every guy makes, to think that friendly women are lusting after them.

Plus, my heart still belonged to Clare, who was writing to me often and appearing nightly in my thoughts. It was important for me to stay true to her, in the little ways I could while in prison. Still, I couldn't help but notice whenever secretary Rodriguez stared at me for ages, or that secretary Adams had the most incredible arse that I was sure you'd be able to stand a beer on, if ever I could get her to a barbecue.

Naturally, there was another type of lovin' an inmate could engage in, if he had the inclination, and if there's one question I've been asked more than any other since returning from the prison world, it's whether the folklore about prisoners being forced into homosexuality is true. I wish I could say it's a big myth, but it isn't. Shit happens.

I'd encountered gay inmates back in JeffCo. There'd been this one dude who I got along with, who one day had told me about how his missus had called the cops on him and dobbed him in – something to do with crack. One day he showed me his charge sheet, and I noticed that his partner's name was Victor. This confused me, so I asked him about it. He told me, very matter-of-factly, that he was gay.

Now, this didn't trouble me, because my mum and dad had been very careful to bring me up believing in treating all people equally, no matter what their race or sexual persuasion. So I continued being friendly with him – playing cards, basketball with him, generally hanging out. Then one day he gave me a Bible, for reasons I didn't understand, until he looked me square in the eye and insisted I read a certain page, as there was a passage there I might be very interested in. When I went to that page, there was a note from him telling me that he thought I was really hot, that he really wanted to get up to something, and that if I was staying up late that night, he'd like to meet me, sneak off somewhere and get it on.

Later when I saw him (not 'later' later, just . . . a little later), I said to him: 'What are you tripping on, dude? I'm just not into that.'

He was cool with it. We got along after that.

But that was back in JeffCo. Youngstown was different. It was dirtier, crazier. The yard was always filled with little

Hispanic gay guys who would just walk past staring, voicelessly flirting. Apparently (so somebody told me) white guys with blue or green eyes were pretty sought after by certain folk in Latin America. It was very unnerving at first.

When I got to know some of them a little better, they became a lot more forward and vocal about it. They'd shimmy up to me and try to get it on: 'Hey, Australia, all I want to do is suck your dick, man . . .'

I learned pretty quickly to dismiss it – politely in private, more aggressively in public – and to just explain that I didn't care what they did but that I was not into it. They generally respected that. I never had anyone try to force me to do anything. Once again, I was lucky that I was connected with the right people, but whether you became bait for someone also had a lot to do with how heavily you stuck up for yourself. If people saw that you were a stand-up dude, that you were fairly strong and prepared to defend yourself, they wouldn't bother making you a target for that sort of thing. A lot of that came simply from your walk, or the way you held your gaze, something I'd learned from Dave and Johnny in Allenwood; the emotionless stare and swagger of the confident prisoner. I picked that up and perfected it very quickly, to the point where a lot of inmates I met were surprised that I hadn't been in prison for years and years.

It was the younger, weaker, more frightened kids who'd wind up being targeted, especially white kids preyed upon by blacks. Sometimes they'd be lucky enough to go to the right people for help – the Dirty White Boys or the Aryan gangs would be concerned enough for them to warn everyone away. But it did happen. I remember one little crazy kid in Youngstown called Oscar. He managed to smuggle in drugs of some sort and slipped them to his cellmate in a drink. In the morning, his cellmate woke up and complained about a sore arse. There was a big investigation about it – the cell was blocked off with crime scene tape (a very strange sight – a prison cell surrounded by police tape telling people to 'keep out'). Apparently, Oscar had been infected with HIV. I don't know what happened with that investigation, or the poor cellmate. I can only hope he wasn't in there for parking fines.

The most striking contact I made in all my time at Youngstown – for me, the most significant person I met while in the USA – was a man called Dejesus (pronounced DAY-HAY-SOOSE). Dejesus was Dominican, but had lived in the USA for many years. He was 35, bald, just under six foot tall, with dark tanned skin, big Hispanic lips and dark brown eyes. He was a little overweight, I suppose, but he wore it well. The thing that was impressive about this dark and dangerous fellow was that he had so much heart in him. If anyone talked to him the wrong way, he never did his block, but rather calmly corrected them, straight up. I always admired that about him. He'd been through so much shit while he'd been in prison. His mum had died of cancer, his wife had left him and had tried to take all of his money. He was a survivor.

Dejesus grew up in a violent neighbourhood in the Dominican Republic, on a street where knife fighting was as common as street basketball or beach cricket might be in other places. When he was just in his teens he smuggled himself into the USA on a boat, selling cocaine on the streets of New York just to get by. He became good at it, and eventually took command of 'The Company', as he called it, and came to control almost an entire block in Brooklyn, NYC – flats and houses from which he sold crack and coke, or which were utilised as lookouts, safe houses, dummy safe houses or accounting centres. It was all so fucking professional and it basically pulled him and his family from the gutter. He was doing five years in Youngstown after one of his employees had snitched on him.

Dejesus was the man who finally got through to me about being a clown in prison. Though I'd learned to control my mouth well enough, I was still very jokey with everyone, and still believed it was better to be knockabout with people rather than walking around in a sombre mood all the time. But Dejesus set me straight on that score. I remember him taking me to task on it one day.

'So you like joking around with everyone, Prince?' he said. 'Well, maybe some people don't like to be joked with. Maybe I just got off the phone to my wife, who's been telling me how she's taking this or that from me, or fucking somebody else. You think I want to see Prince walking towards me with a big smile on his face, making some joke? Maybe I'm likely to crack and take it out on you, understand?'

I took the hint.

Dejesus was a great believer in reputation in prison. He was always promoting the idea of standing up to those who spoke down to you or didn't treat you with respect. He taught me how to be a good prisoner, basically, more so than any of the screws. He broke it all down for me – made the stupid behaviour make sense. He became like a bit of a father figure, I suppose. We cooked together and worked out together. Sometimes, Dejesus would ask me to read to him from books written in English, which he couldn't read. I got to read some interesting books this way, most notably Robert Green's *The 48 Laws of Power*, a book that seemed to have been written exclusively for men in prison. As I read it to Dejesus, I couldn't help but notice how many of the laws applied to Dejesus himself, as he already possessed most of the characteristics that were illustrated in the book.

As it turned out, Dejesus was the Youngstown 2IC of the Trinitario, a prison gang with a pretty solid reputation. The Trinitario (the Trinity or Special One) had its beginnings in a single incident in the infamous Rikers Island Prison in 1988. The founder was Julio Mariñez, aka Caballon, who, frustrated with the dominance of black and Hispanic gangs such as The Bloods and the Latin Kings, staged an impromptu, one-man mutiny while waiting to use the telephones that were being 'reserved' by other inmates. By the time he was finished, there was one gang member dead and several others wounded, the only injury to Caballon being twenty years added to his sentence, which he served at Sing Sing Prison (until he was himself murdered in 2009). The Trinitario was born that afternoon.

Although it was initially intended to be a brotherhood for Dominicans, the Trinitario began to evolve into a mongrel organisation, like the gang you have when you don't have a gang. Puerto Ricans, Cubans, Asians and Europeans were welcome in the Trinitario, the only prerequisite being a desire to look after your brother, whatever colour he may be. The gang was now huge within the American prison system, particularly in the heavy New York facilities such as Attica, Rikers Island and Sing Sing. They aligned themselves with no other gangs, although they were on better terms with some than others. In a way, the Trinitario was a home for the homeless, a nation for those who were lost to their own. Their slogan was *'Dios, Patria y Libertad'*, or 'God, Fatherland and Liberty'. They greeted each other by throwing up their sets and saying: *'Patria'*. Their brotherhood was their adopted nationality.

Dejesus was very cautious about introducing me to the Trinitario, but he always told me I was welcome to meet with the others, if ever I wished to explore the idea of being a part of it. It seemed to me like something worth considering – of all the gangs I had encountered in the prison system, this one seemed to have a heart and a conscience. Aside from the white supremacist gangs, the Trinitario was also the only one for which I was physically or morally qualified.

In the meantime, my friendship with Dejesus directly led to me finally getting my 'hustle on', as Cesar Cortez had encouraged me to do back in JeffCo. Because Dejesus was very much 'the man' in our sector of the prison, he was forever writing letters to the prison officials and various consulates, complaining about conditions in the prison or requesting certain things. He had always lamented the fact that, due to his lack of ability with written English, he'd been forced to write such letters in Spanish, when he knew full well that the authorities to whom he was sending them would be more likely to take notice of a letter in English. With my arrival in the prison, Dejesus at last had a translator who could take his dictation and correct his English.

When news got around the prison that there was an Australian guy – a friend of Dejesus – who could write in fluent English, the offers came pouring in. I was suddenly the go-to guy for anyone who needed anything written in the preferred language of the USA, and there is never a shortage of such people in an American immigration prison. For the next two years, I made a tidy profit by selling my written English skills, often to poor little Latino dudes who needed to apply for one thing or another, or plead with some authority in a standard of English that didn't expose them as illegal aliens.

One day, a big black dude called Tyrone came to me and asked if I was the one who could write an English letter.

When I replied that I was, he very gruffly asked if I could translate a 'letter to ma bitch'.

'Sure I can,' I said, and we went away to get a pencil and paper. But, when we sat down to write it, it became clear Tyrone didn't really know what he wanted to say.

'Juz write,' he shrugged and mumbled kind of nervously, '. . . hey, babe . . . y'know, like . . . wassup?'

I realised he needed a bit of encouragement.

'You want to tell her,' I ventured, 'that, you've been thinking about her lately? That you miss her, like, y'know . . . like the flower misses rain?'

'Yeah,' he smiled and nodded, 'all dat kinda shit.'

So began my career as the Cyrano de Bergerac of Youngstown Prison, writing love letters to American sweethearts from blacks, Hispanics, Mexicans and anyone who needed to impress a girl with his poetic grasp of the English language. It became something I really enjoyed doing, and I had a little fun slipping corny clichés and all sorts of inappropriate filth into some of them, if I thought the sender deserved it. But mostly I liked it because it revealed the soft sides behind all of those tough exteriors, all the tattooed tough cunts who'd suddenly be exposed as huge pillows underneath. It sort of proved to me that behind every hard motherfucker – every racist, every murderer, every crackhead and every criminal fraud – is a baby who just wants to be loved.

Today, I'm one of the few guys on the planet who can boast that he's sent pornographic love letters to the wives and girlfriends of some of America's most dangerous gangsters, and has not only lived to tell about it, but is a little bit richer from the experience.

In January 2007, nearly two years into my sentence, my mum and dad came to visit again, and brought with them my sister, Jessie. The first day, as always, was toughest – there seemed so much to say that saying anything at all seemed too trivial for words. What was happening between us all was so big that to ignore it seemed ridiculous, and yet nobody wanted to get too close to the truth of the situation: that this was awful and unreal, this separation that was being forced upon us. Just thinking on it – how some bunch of Americans who had nothing to do with the Prince family could dictate that we weren't allowed to be together – could turn you into an eternal anarchist. I always had to keep reminding myself that I had committed an armed robbery, but the incident felt so long ago it was as if they were punishing a different guy.

And, by now, I already was a different guy. I'd grown so much in prison, both physically and mentally. I was pushing stacks on the weight bench and reading more than I had in my life. I was studying for university, learning how to fight in the most intense training arena there was, and growing into an independent man with the guidance of people who don't accept anything less. I began to wonder how people back home would judge me when I got back, against the weedy little clown that had left for Colorado years before. I remember feeling proud of myself when I thought of that, and realising that prison was actually doing the job it was intended to do. For the most fleeting moment, I felt glad that I was where I was. Then I thought of Clare and I remembered that I was so far from anywhere.

Just how isolated I was from the rest of the world was brought home to me one day in the strangest of ways. While enjoying a visit with Mum and Dad, I noticed this elderly woman who was visiting another inmate. She appeared to be one of the charity visitors – people from some church or other who came quite frequently to visit prisoners who had no family or friends, or who simply wished for a visit from anyone. While talking to an inmate, this old woman asked if he wanted some food from the chicken machine, a stand-up dispenser that contained heated chicken wings one could buy for $2 a basket. The inmate said yes and the old woman stood and made her way to the machine. While she was there, I saw her quite clearly fumble the basket and drop the chicken wings all over the filthy floor at her feet, on which prisoners and screws walked with their boots that had been in the piss and the spit and the jizz of the prison. It would have taken her exactly $2 and the slightest effort to bin the dirty chicken wings and purchase a clean basket, but, being out of sight of the inmate, she just bent down, picked them all up off the floor, put them back in the basket and took them over to her prisoner, smiling as if nothing had happened.

Now, that mightn't seem like such a momentous incident, but, to me, it spoke volumes about where I was. Here was an old Christian woman who wouldn't hurt a fly, whose heart was so totally in the right place she was giving up her time to visit a stranger. Had she been at home, or anywhere on the outside, she wouldn't have dreamed of serving someone food that had just been pegged onto a dirty floor – or even a clean floor, for that matter. But in here, things were different. Here, the population were second-rate citizens, not even worthy of common respect in the eyes of society's most forgiving people. We were the lowest of the low, just above dogs, but way below those who weren't scum of the earth.

On the last visit before my family went home, after a month of visits every day, I found it hard to keep it together. I didn't want to dwell on the fact they were leaving and tried to steer the conversation onto happy things, but everybody seemed so miserable. I suppose when we'd had my sentencing coming up, we'd all had something to look forward to, as anxious as that wait might have been. Now, the only thing we had to look forward to was me getting out in two years' time. Two years seemed such a long time – so much had happened in the two years since I'd been arrested. My sister Kylie had given birth to a son, and I hadn't even been there to congratulate her, or welcome little Harry into the world. Our family had actually changed shape. It broke my heart to think on it.

But I managed to keep my spirits up, at least for show, until they left. To make them believe that life was okay for me was paramount. But, after they had left the building, and I was headed back to my unit, I caught a glimpse of them from a prison window – they were standing at the gate, holding each other, as if having collapsed into a sad embrace. I went back to my cell and cried as hard as I had on those first nights in JeffCo, before I'd begun to toughen up and grow. I suppose there was something almost like relief knowing that the little boy in me was still there, and the thought of that made me cry even more.

Something I always found very sad was the sight – and I saw it often – of inmates trying to snog their wives or girlfriends when, clearly, the passion was running one way only. You'd see them in the visiting room hanging out, staring into eyes that were darting everywhere else, inmates desperately trying to get some lovin' from a woman who was clearly over it, or probably rooting someone else. You could see the worried look in each prisoner's eye as he tried to see if his girl was still there for him. In that situation, a man will deliberately miss all the hints in the world.

It was after witnessing one of these sorry spectacles that I decided one day to phone Clare. It began as a nice call – breezy, loving enough – until she began to tell me about plans she had to go to Brisbane for a rock concert that coming weekend. There was a group that she was particularly keen on, a band whose members were all young guys with sleeves of tattoos and those big stretch earrings that never close over. Clare told me she found this style very becoming, and said that a man with good looks and these accessories was the type who really turned her on. There was something, she said, about unpredictability and recklessness that was attractive.

When I hung up the phone I wanted to go and put my fist through some living thing. Here I was, half a world away and in prison, while Clare was suddenly getting horny for guys who reeked of a little bit of manufactured 'bad'. I felt like the Man in the Iron Mask, locked away in a dungeon while some puny fraud was going to have his way with my betrothed.

Of course, I hadn't been entirely faithful myself. My locker was littered with pictures of girls – pages ripped from contraband magazines, or photocopies that had done the rounds of the prison. But they were only temporary diversions, eventually to be removed by female screws who didn't like sharing the limelight with pictures of Playmates and supermodels. What I couldn't deny was that I was having a long-distance flirtation with a real girl called Shannon.

Shannon and I had been boy-and-girlfriend during the puppy-love phase in Year 6 and Year 7. We melodramatically dropped each other like young lovers do and then drifted apart, but, upon hearing I was in prison in America, Shannon had begun to write to me. It turned out she had become an exotic dancer up in Queensland, so naturally

I insisted on seeing photographs of how she looked these days. To my delight, she began to send some, and then some more, always a little more provocative than the last. Her letters, too, were becoming more risqué, and I was only too happy to respond appropriately. I began to fantasise about her a bit, and I even once dreamed we were getting it on. Did this qualify as an affair? It was about as much as I could do from in here. The only actual 'sex' I'd had for two years was with myself – or, more correctly, with my 'fife'.

A 'fife' (pronounced 'fee-fee') was a cross between a fuck and a wifey, or a fake wife. The 'fife' was all the rage in Youngstown prison. There were two types: the first was just a latex glove blown up, with one of the fingers turned inside-out and coated with oil or soapy water until 'wet'; the second type – and my personal favourite – consisted of three latex gloves, two of which were stuffed inside the third glove before being filled with warm water to bursting, oil or soapy water coating the inside gloves until the 'fife' was 'wet' and begging for it. Every night, in every cell in Youngstown prison, a 'fife' was being fucked to within an inch of her life.

Naturally, with so little privacy in prison, a man had to overcome any bashfulness he might have about being busted wanking by his fellow man. Everyone expected everyone else to be as discreet as they possibly could, but modesty wasn't always possible, so awkward disposals of sexual frustration were generally tolerated. This tended to make everyone loosen up a little, though some were better at it than others. The Latin American men, in particular, seemed more comfortable around each other than the Australian men of my memory ever were.

One day, Dejesus asked me to follow him into his cell, where he said he'd show me something that he was sure would leave me very impressed. Once we were alone, it was with a rising feeling of dread that I saw that Dejesus was pulling out his knob. I was just getting ready to read my little hererosexual speech to Dejesus when he told me to relax, that he wasn't that way inclined, either, but simply wished to show me what he'd done to his dick: there, on the upper side, just near the head, were a couple of strange lumps, clearly foreign bodies under the skin. It was then that I learned about 'the operation', something that would change me forever.

According to Dejesus, and many others who could vouch for his words, 'the operation' was a process by which a small ball-bearing or two were placed under the skin of the penis. It was said to drive women wild, massaging the 'G-spot' by the means of an extra lump on the penis, and several guys who'd had it done had been on the outside and could testify to its orgasmic power. It didn't take me long to become convinced, and I soon found myself booking an 'appointment' with a Dominican dude who was said to be the best when it came to 'the operation'.

I paid a Mexican dude four books of stamps to fashion me a barbell, cut from a plastic domino, which he shaved with a razor until it was sculptured into two small spheres joined together. I then buffed and polished it up, over and over on concrete and stone, until it was as smooth as could be. On the day of surgery, my 'doctor' took a razor boiled in water and, while lookouts kept watch at the door of the bathroom, made a small incision just below the head on my tool. I was surprised at how little that hurt, but my joy didn't last very long. My doctor then put on some rubber gloves (which, presumably, had not recently been somebody's 'fife'), took a toothbrush handle that had been sharpened like a double-edged blade and proceeded to drive it under the skin of my penis, plunging deep towards the base in order to separate the skin from the muscle, so that the spheres could be inserted between. There are no words I know in the English language that can adequately convey the excruciating pain of this moment.

Once the skin and muscle had been pulled apart, the spheres were pushed into place, antiseptic cream was smeared on the wound and it was bound. The operation was declared a success, although I understood there was no way of knowing for sure until I got back to Byron Bay. In about two weeks, the wound had healed, and I was ready to go. For days, I lay on my bunk in my cell, trying to dream up ways that I might subtly spread the word about my cock to the girls of Byron Bay and beyond, who'd come stampeding to my place in the middle of the night, just to find out what all the fuss was about. In the meantime, this thing was really fucking annoying, but, like most things out of my control, I learned to live with it.

I only hoped that Clare would like having this weird thing inside her. I did it, sincerely, with her in mind.

When taking a shower in Youngstown, sandals would have to be worn at all times, due to the various fungal infections that raged through the prison. I remember seeing one dude whose feet were completely red, blistered and peeling, like they belonged on a corpse. There'd be piss and blood and jizz and everything in the shower, and it just wasn't worth the risk. The problem with the sandals was that they were not designed to assist you where fluent movement was concerned, and the bathroom was the typical place for trouble. It was worthwhile convincing someone – by paying them if you had to – to keep a lookout at the doorway while you showered, because that's when you were at your most vulnerable.

The violence in prison was something that, by now, I had become quite used to. It was a daily event, usually seasoned by the day's first game of 'prisonball', which was basically basketball but without the usual courtesy. It was all elbows in ribs and faces, very rough and hardcore, and it often set the tone for the rest of the day – a couple of dudes would develop a problem with each other on the court, and it would fester until they decided to sort it out at the end of the day or sooner. But prisonball was also a good way to get your body primed for whatever the day might bring. It's amazing how quickly you can get used to the idea of heavy human contact, if you force yourself to feel it regularly enough. Before I'd entered the prison system, the idea of someone punching me was terrifying, but not anymore. In here, it was almost a form of shaking hands.

Most of the fights I got into were started over something stupid – someone changing the channel of the TV while I was watching it, or making noise while I was trying to sleep. Sometimes I heard that someone who owed me money was being transferred, and I'd have to go and collect my debt, but I can scarcely separate one fight from another, or remember what caused them most of the time. Everyone was just so ready to jump at all times, you didn't have to do very much to encourage them. At JeffCo, I didn't know what I was doing, and, as I said, I'd never been in a fight. But in Youngstown, I'd gotten used to the fear of it and didn't shy away from it anymore, so it was potentially on every day. I'd realise, usually with plenty of warning, that myself and someone else were going to go at it, then we'd simply bump shoulders in the rec yard and it would be on. Most were just scuffles, little punch-ups with no real damage done. But sometimes it got more serious than that.

I had just spent a short stint in The Hole for reasons I can no longer recall, and when I got out I found that I had been moved to another unit entirely. My previous unit had been a mongrel bag, made up of Asians, Dominicans, Colombians, Cubans – a little United Nations of which I had membership. But my new unit was predominantly Mexicans, and they troubled me.

The Mexicans were dominant in Youngstown prison; MS-13 was probably the most feared of the gangs. Made up mostly of Mexicans and Central Americans, MS-13 members were ruthless and couldn't be trusted. Dejesus had always told me that if the Trinitario had a common enemy it was undoubtedly MS-13, for the fact that they bullied everyone and were allied with nobody. At this point, I seemed to be able to adapt and get along with black Americans, Hispanics and white supremacists, but I felt no connection with the Mexicans of MS-13. They represented the point where the old Prince charm ran out of influence.

On the morning that I was released from The Hole, I found a laundry bucket on wheels that appeared to be full of dirty laundry, so I emptied these clothes out on the floor and proceeded to wheel the bucket back towards The Hole in order to collect my clothing and bring it back to the unit. Within moments, I was surrounded by hostile Mexicans, barking at me in their own tongue. I was being shoved from the side and the back by hands I couldn't see. Eventually, one of them who spoke English asked me what the fuck I'd been doing. I replied that I was just borrowing the laundry bucket, and would put the dirty clothes back when I was finished with it. The Mexican told me that the clothes I'd thrown on the ground had been clean. I apologised once, twice, but that's all. When it became clear they weren't going to accept my apology I stopped giving it, and told them to fuck off and grow up. I copped a prolonged slapping and shoving that didn't hurt so much as scare me, though I worked my arse off not to show it.

It was fortunate that I didn't back down so easily, even if I had been shitting myself. A little while later, Dejesus heard a rumour about a white guy that the Mexicans planned to hit within a few days. He naturally assumed it was me, and so did I. This was fucking scary. When the Mexicans decided to stitch you up, you were history and there was nowhere to hide. I couldn't believe the fucking Alamo was being re-enacted because of a misunderstanding over laundered undies. Of all the stupid things I'd done, been busted for or gotten away with, it was emptying a laundry basket that was going to finally spell the death of me.

Eventually, Dejesus asked one of the ranking Mexicans what it was all about. He confirmed that there was a hit going down on a white dude, that two Mexican inmates had been assigned the job, that the target wasn't a member of the Trinitario and that it was none of Dejesus's business. Dejesus argued that, if the white guy was me, then it certainly was his business.

'Oh, no, homie,' laughed the Mexican dude. 'It's not Australia. If it was, we'd send more than two boys to do that job.'

It was with a strange mixture of emotions that I received this news from Dejesus. On the one hand, I was proud that I was at last commanding a bit of regard. My workouts were finally shaping me into a bit of an intimidating specimen, and my practising of the rules I'd been taught – first by Dave and now by Dejesus — was holding up to scrutiny. I was getting respect, not from some pimple-faced skate punk who lived with his mum and dad, but from a hardened Mexican prison gang.

But the incident also served to remind me of how vulnerable I really was. Had it not been for Dejesus I would have spent the next few weeks in a state of complete terror. And what if the hit had been for me? Who the fuck did I have to turn to? Going to the screws would have been fatal to what credibility I had with other inmates. I remember feeling deeply alone at that time, defenceless and very exposed.

This feeling was compounded by the knowledge that Dejesus would soon be going home. Though I was immensely happy for him that he was finally getting out of this shithole, I knew I was going to miss his presence in Youngstown. For a year he'd been my brother, and I'd learned more from him than I had from any teacher. Losing him was going to be tough, and might expose me, too, to dangers that would otherwise have kept their distance. But if Dejesus had taught me anything at all, it was the importance of standing up, being independent, solving your own problems as best you can and having confidence in your own power as a man.

It was in early 2007 that Dejesus finally left. His parting words of wisdom had to do with the need to form alliances with people I could trust.

Not long after Dejesus left, the head of the Trinitario approached me and asked whether I'd be interested in joining the brotherhood. I was a little surprised, as I wasn't entirely sure that I qualified. He told me that he thought I did, that I came with Dejesus's blessing and that he had assigned a few members to watch me over the preceding weeks, just to see what sort of race I ran and whether I was worthy. The Trinitario wasn't just for Dominicans, he told me, but for anyone who 'wants to do your time, not let it do you'.

It shouldn't be too hard for people to imagine why being part of a huge brotherhood like this had become attractive to me. The feeling of brotherhood I'd felt with Dejesus was being promised to me many times over. The knowledge that I would belong, to almost one hundred brothers who would stand beside me through thick and thin, was immediately irresistible.

I was given a list of rules, a code of conduct of sorts – no 'faggots', no snitching, no stealing from a brother – just a set of commandments to live by within the prison system. However, it was all in Spanish. Together, I and one of the other members took it upon ourselves to translate it into English for the first time. While sitting there in a back room of this shitty little prison library, typing on what seemed like a nineteenth-century typewriter, I was aware of the fact that I was a witness to something of a landmark moment for the Trinitario – the translation of its 'sacred text' into English. I was also the first Australian to be accepted into the brotherhood in Youngstown. I felt I was making history.

The basic premise of the Trinitario was that each member was to know he could rely on his brother for anything at any time. There was no doubt that each member would do his duty for his brother. The sacred hymn of the Trinitario was known as 'The Key'. It was five sentences long and it rhymed, when spoken in Spanish. If you ever met someone who threw up their set to indicate they were Trinitario, you would say: *'Dame la llave'* ('Give me The Key'), and that person would either recite it or be exposed as a fraud. Every Trinitario knew The Key. You had plenty of quiet time to rehearse it. It had to do with the story of the three brothers, Juan Pablo Duarte, Francisco Del Rosario Sanchez and Ramon Matias Mella, who, in 1884, agreed to form the secret society, the Trinitaria Identity, to help make the Dominican Republic independent from the Spanish, French, English and American forces that wrestled for control of the territory. It was in the spirit of this independence movement that the Trinitario had been formed.

I could recite the whole poem here, but I have no real reason to betray the Trinitario from my vantage point in Byron Bay. They were good to me. The process of joining and being accepted by 'the Committee' was a long one, but eventually I made it through and was formally initiated into the Trinitario on 23 June 2007, at a big banquet held in the rec area. From then on, I felt an enormous sense of belonging while in Young-stown. We didn't just gather together when there was trouble, but for good times, too – huge feasts we'd have in the rec yard, like a great extended family. Today, even from this distance, I still feel like a part of me belongs to the Trinitario.

*

A peculiar incident occurred in July, during a visit to a surgery in downtown Youngstown. Inmates could, if armed with a valid reason and the correct prescription from a prison doctor, be taken outside of the prison to visit a medical professional. For some time I'd been writing letters to the authorities requesting orthotic shoe implants to help support the weak arches in my feet, and when I got the Australian consulate on board with my request the prison officials suddenly sprang into action. Being shackled and driven by two policemen through the streets of Youngstown was quite a treat, although, even considering where I was coming from, I kept thinking: 'Nice place to visit, but I wouldn't want to live here.'

Eventually we got to the surgery and I was marched in shackles through a back door, so as not to alarm the law-abiding patients. A nice Indian doctor took my foot impressions in some special type of foam, and asked what sort of height I wanted to be lifted to. I replied that my height was not a problem, that I didn't want lifts but orthotics for my arches. The doctor responded that my prescription asked only for lifts, not orthotics. Several attempts to call the prison doctor proved unsuccessful, and so we had no alternative but to return to the prison and try to fix this another day.

It was a leisurely drive back to the prison, the cops taking the time to show me the streets and stop at traffic lights so that I could get a good look at the talent in town, which wasn't much chop at any rate. But I appreciated the drive, and the way the police seemed so relaxed, joking with me and smoking cigarettes, even offering me one, which I politely declined.

When we eventually arrived back at the prison, the cops were shuffling me out of the car when, suddenly, the shackles began unravelling, running through their loops like the chain of an anchor that has been thrown overboard. Within seconds, I was standing there with my arms and legs free, a pile of chains at my feet, the two policemen looking like they'd seen a ghost. Apparently, the screw who'd shackled me had failed to connect the chain at a critical point and the whole thing had just fallen away. Hilariously, to save them embarrassment, I wound up carrying my own shackles into the prison, pretending they were firmly attached and that I hadn't spent the last hour or so in the back of a police car with my hands and legs free, and a big pile of chains that could knock out a cop with one blow to the head and strangle the other before he knew what was happening. Imagine if I'd been a serial killer in prison for multiple murder. Those two cops would have been history.

This episode was symbolic of what a slack little prison Youngstown really was. Most of the time, the authorities seemed less interested in punishment or rehabilitation than simply turning over another day and another dollar. Since this prison was privately owned, there were all sorts of conspiracy theories about how it was screwing us out of money, the most common being the 'dinner conspiracy', which actually carried a bit of weight. The food in Youngstown was so relentlessly terrible that inmates regularly skipped meals in favour of using the commissary shop, which, naturally, was suspiciously well stocked with a wide variety of food and drink. It made sense for the prison to ensure that our mandatory meals were so shithouse we'd be forced to purchase extra food from them. Those who didn't – who neither ate the terrible dinners or purchased food from the commissary – would inevitably get sick, and so a visit to the prison medical unit was in order. Wouldn't you know it, the medical unit was privately owned, too. One way or another, the standard of food was going to have an inverse effect on the prison's profit margin.

I had cause to raise these very issues in my university course, when I chose Corrections Corporation of America, the very company that operated the prison that housed me, as a case study in my business studies syllabus. My unique insight into the workings of the company gave me an inside edge the other students didn't have (that year, I also received a distinction in 'Ethics Studies', interestingly enough).

The most immediately noticeable outcome of the food situation was that a good piece of food was a very precious commodity. As I've already said, prison tends to exaggerate all the little intricacies and irritations of daily life that would pass by unnoticed on the outside, and food was often central to that sort of neurosis. For example, two Dominican friends of mine were cooking together one night and, as was the custom, were being very strict about putting the exact same quantity of ingredients into the feast. But, when it came time to eat, one of them willingly shared his own portion with another inmate, who had contributed nothing. This should have been fair enough – so long as it was his own portion he was sharing, the other dude shouldn't have cared, but he did. For some reason, he felt offended that his efforts had gone into feeding another party he had not himself invited. This led to a feud between the two Dominican brothers that lasted several weeks.

Dejesus had farewelled his brothers in prison from under a similar cloud. A goodbye feast had been organised for him, with a few of us chipping in, although I paid for most of it. When Dejesus saw that all sorts of clowns had been invited to join in the feast, he took his plate of food and very dramatically threw it in the bin. He was quite passionate about the fact that he felt intimate with very few people, and the idea that even his friends were paying to feed some freeloaders made him crazy.

Another night, I recall the prison surprised us all by announcing there was chicken for dinner – a significant change from the unmentionable slop they usually served. The sight of grown men behaving like children over these tiny little chicken breasts was quite a spectacle, and none made more of a spectacle of himself than me. Somehow, the memory of how I'd used to discard whole chickens after a barbecue back home made me chicken crazy on this particular night, and, when I approached an Indian guy I knew to be a vegetarian, with a view to asking him for his chicken, he responded that he'd been so hungry that he had abandoned his vegetarian stance and eaten it. I'm sorry to say I went ballistic. I'd done so much for this guy – written his love letters, sold him food of my own – and he knew I was always up for buying his chicken from him, yet he'd selfishly eaten his chicken when he knew very well I'd come looking for it. It took me many days to get over this outrage.

I could see why Dejesus had always refused to smuggle chicken out of the chow hall.

'I used to be the CEO of my company,' he'd say, 'drive a Mercedes and wear expensive jewels. I ain't gonna descend to the level of having to traffic a piece of motherfucken chicken!'

And he was right. Dejesus was always right. Spend enough time in prison and your head really starts to go. You begin to obsess over little things, foolish things, things that never mattered when you were on the outside, and will never matter again once you've returned. I began to wonder whether my mind was going, and whether I'd ever recover it. Looking back, I think I did a pretty good job at keeping it together, mostly through working out and staying focused on the things I cared about: Clare, my family, my friends back home, and the wonderful day when I'd be free again.

But there is evidence that I fell off the rails sometimes, and became someone I no longer recognise. An entry in my little journal, dated 1 July 2007, provides the reader with a frightening glimpse of how deeply into the abyss I would occasionally descend:

I've just spent a good six hours on my arse in front of the tele, but for a great occasion. They televised Princess Diana's 46th birthday celebration. Prince Harry and Prince William had organised it and had artists from all genres and all countries performing for free. What an awesome event, so saddening for me to see what was lost. This world needs more people like her. She was such an amazing woman. I remember being so drawn to her, even when I was a child. The little video clips of her life, and the reminders of the many people with various disabilities and diseases that she personally touched, were so humbling. I can't stop thinking about how sad I felt, I could've cried – such a waste of a beautiful human. Why oh why did she die? It wouldn't be surprising to learn of some scheme behind her death – she was doing so much good for the world, no doubt this was becoming uncomfortable for some. She is dearly missed. Rest in peace, Lady Diana.

7

I'm not necessarily a superstitious guy, but when I heard that a Mexican inmate who practised Santeria (an occult-like Caribbean religion) was reading cards for $5 a throw on certain days of the week, I decided to book an appointment to see what my future might hold. The seer, a short, dark gent with gold and silver teeth, told me in his broken English to cut the cards into three even piles that represented the past, the present and the future.

He began with the past pile, revealing right from the start that I used to drink too much, which was untrue (together, however, we worked out that this must have been a metaphor for my weed consumption). The cards also showed that there was a young, pretty woman who missed me very much and was waiting for me to return (a pretty good guess). He told me that I used to have money before

I came to jail, but did no longer, and he revealed that there was another person who had gone to prison at the same time as me (a 'prediction' that would probably apply to 95 per cent of the inmate population). He then mentioned that there was another woman in the United States who loved me very much.

In the present, he saw that there was someone who wanted to see my blood. This wasn't a bad guess either, seeing that I'd had to commit a crime to be where I was.

Then came the future pile. The cards showed that Clare would be there for me when I returned, which was good news. However, they also said that I shouldn't be concerned about packing up and leaving Australia. This was a little unnerving. My parents and I had recently become aware that there might be trouble when I was released from prison, as, having been born in New Zealand, I had never formally become an Australian citizen. For one reason or another, I had never bothered to get an Australian passport. Now that I was a prisoner in an American immigration prison, and was soon to be deported, my status as a legal citizen was about to become a real issue in Australia. The Australian Government could just as easily say they didn't want to make a convicted bank robber one of their own. In other words, I might never be going home.

Today, it seems silly that it took a Mexican occultist in an Ohio prison to finally make me realise how much I wanted to be Australian. I knew that once I got out of prison I would never be allowed into the United States again, and I was more than cool with that. But the idea of being thrown out of Australia too was just devastating, and it stayed in my mind like some witch's curse for the rest of my days in America.

But cards that told the future were not the only cards in Youngstown prison. During the days in summer, the rec yard was like an outdoor casino, with all sorts of hustling and grinding going on, a lot of it centred around card tables. They played a variety of games, mostly poker, blackjack, spades and a few Latin American games that I never really understood. It was something else to watch all these crims and gangsters sitting around guarding their chips, which could be worth anything from $20 to $3000. I remember the head of the Trinitario sitting out there playing once, with a revolving roster of soldiers taking turns to guard his back and watch over his shoulder. (He ended up winning $300 in about an hour, which was excellent money in Youngstown, prison or not.)

Typically, the 'house' consisted of this one old Cuban dude who would roam around looking over the shoulders of the players as he collected his few chips from the 'pot'. He was a bad-tempered little cunt, and if anyone had forgotten to pay their chip to the house he would make a real scene, violently screaming at them so that everyone saw who the cheat was. At the same time, he really got off on the idea of being 'the man' at the local casino, and he'd go through with the pantomime of keeping his high-rolling customers happy by fetching them free sodas and cookies at regular intervals throughout the day. It was quite bizarre to see how little trappings of the outside world would make their way into prison. The only thing missing was a floor show.

As with every illegal casino, there were the occasional busts, and, just like the busts in the outside world, there were ways to avoid being caught in the net. Most busts would consist of a whole lot of screws storming the rec area and making everyone stand up against the fence. One by one they'd be taken away, questioned and then locked up in The Hole. But some who'd obviously been busted would appear back among the population sooner than others.

The truth is that most of the the screws in Youngstown were as corrupt as the prisoners. I knew one Colombian inmate who was running rackets on the street, was seriously cashed up and was well known to have one screw deep in his pocket. He was getting the guard to import all sorts of stuff for him: cigarettes (which he'd buy on the street for $4, and sell for anything up to $100 inside), workout pills, MP3s, gold chains and all sorts of trinkets. The screw became nervous about how much he was bringing in, and the risk attached to it. But the Colombian, who was paying the screw well, subtly reminded him of the barrel he had him over – all the inmate had to do was confess to what he'd been doing and who with, and the screw would find himself not only out of a job, but probably inside a prison himself. And you can imagine how delighted some prisoners would be when they viewed the paperwork of a former screw. So the Colombian's little scheme continued.

One corrections officer got busted once trafficking weed and blow into the prison, and the ensuing investigation swallowed about three other screws and a handful of inmates. All contraband went to ground for a couple of days, before everything returned to business as usual, and new screws with dollar signs in their eyes replaced the old ones.

I suppose you would have to be a certain type to want to hang with prisoners every day, even if you were supposedly on the other side of the fence. The job seemed to make a lot of them as crazy as the prisoners.

One day I had one of the screws enter my cell unannounced, as most did. However, he immediately tripped me out by closing the door behind him. This was not what screws were meant to do – doors to cells were meant to be open at all times – so I knew something weird was about to go down. He just stood there for a moment, staring intensely, as if he'd seen some sort of phantom. Then, when he spoke, it was quiet and deliberate, his eyes burning into mine. He had seen the light in me, he said. Yes. There was no mistake. Apparently, he'd seen me treating some other inmate with kindness in the rec yard and, as he'd watched, the light of The Lord had shone like a halo from my body. He believed it was time I familiarised myself with the Bible, and directed me towards a particular passage that he thought might be of interest to me. Of course, I'd been down this road with the Bible before and, when I'd consulted the passage in question, it had turned out to be an invitation to a root, so I wasn't enthusiastic about having a look this time, in my cell with this big black screw who had closed the door behind him. However, before I could give him the drill about my arse being strictly one-way traffic, he simply shook my hand and left.

When I eventually read the passage he had recommended I didn't really understand a word of it. But the whole incident spooked me for a little while, and over the next week or so I would lie in my cell with my eyes closed and ask God to give me a sign of some sort – some kind of definitive evidence that he was there. Breaking me out of prison would have been a good place to start. But it never happened. God was to remain a stranger. Looking around, it didn't seem to me that he was too powerful anyway.

The month of August, 2007 was a real dark one in Youngstown prison. It began with a Jamaican mate of mine dying from lymphoma. He'd just had some pains in his side and had gone to the hospital to have them checked out. Weeks later he appeared in the prison again, having lost a lot of weight and looking a little weak. I thought he'd simply spent some time in The Hole, which will do that to you. But he continued to work out every morning, eat his meals, make his bed, follow the rules. Then he was gone. It shook me up badly. How the fuck was someone meant to carry on knowing that he would die in this place, that the last precious days of his life would be spent as a captive?

It made me very anxious for home, more anxious than I'd been since March 2005. I wrote a lot of letters, to Mum and Dad, to Clare, to my grandparents and friends. It suddenly felt to me like I didn't have any time to waste.

No sooner had this mood entered my consciousness than I found out a Muslim guy in my unit had lost his three daughters in a car accident. We all saw it on the television news – his wife had been driving a brand new vehicle and had somehow steered the thing off a fucking cliff. She was in intensive care but the daughters had all perished. Of course, it had to happen to one of the nicest guys in the unit, who had a permanent mark on his head from the damage he'd do while praying, yet always had a smile for everyone as he passed them on his way, screws and inmates alike. The poor guy didn't come out of his cell for days. When he did, he seemed the same person, sadder, but serene, that same smile, and he continued with his worship, just as before. How could somebody keep their faith after such a devastating blow like that? I didn't know whether it was impressive or just crazy. If it had been me – if Clare and Mum and Dad had all been featured on a television news report that told of how they'd all drowned in the surf at Byron Bay, I wouldn't have been having any conversations with God that didn't involve a shitload of expletives.

Day after day, the rudeness of prison was being displayed to me, the inhumane idea of removing people from the ones they love. I know, I know – we were criminals and didn't deserve to be treated softly. But that man's children didn't deserve to die without their father there to comfort them in their last moments, or even save them, as he might have done. And what was he in here for? Probably drugs. Or probably just the simple fact that, like me, he hadn't sorted out his passport correctly. There were hundreds of horror stories in this place about people who'd lived their whole lives in the USA, having been brought here when they were children or babies, only to be taken from their families and friends once they were adults because they were discovered to be, technically, illegal aliens. The idea of locking up criminals seems fair to most people, until someone you love is considered a criminal for not doing their paperwork, or for taking a drug that makes them feel like they're in love. What a fucking weird world.

I was bouncing these thoughts around in my head one night when, at about 1 am, a screw burst into my cell and told me to get up and follow him. I didn't know what it was about, and I couldn't think of anything I'd done that was particularly bad, but I began to sweat nevertheless (being a prisoner tends to give one a permanently guilty conscience). He walked me down the hall and through a security door to one of the staff toilets. Then he took out a cup and told me to urinate in it, right there in front of his eyes. I knew I had nothing to worry about if this was a drugs test, but I was definitely worried about this particular screw, who spoke with a lisp and moved with certain feminine tendencies.

I asked him for a little privacy, please, but he insisted he had to watch me piss into the cup, just to make sure there was no funny business. This entire exercise was just so the creep could have a good look at my fucking penis. So I gave the arsehole quite a show, whipped out my modified tool and pissed into the cup. He was so transfixed that the idiot didn't even notice when I whizzed all over the outside of the cup, just so that I could contaminate his fingers. I hope he went and ate a doughnut straight away.

This place was filled with so much sadness and hate, but there was brotherhood, love and mateship, too, almost none of which came from the screws, or the people who were meant to be the 'good' men in here. A good screw was an exception to the rule. The rest were so into violating and humiliating their fellow man it was a crime that they weren't themselves locked inside.

One morning I was resting in my cell when one of my buddies informed me that another Australian had just come into the prison. I immediately assumed it was Luke and, after a little bit of detective work, found out which unit he'd been placed in. But when I went there to see him, the guy who was pointed out to me was not Luke at all. I decided to introduce myself anyway.

'Hey, Australia!' I shouted at him from the unit doorway. He looked at me very warily, and it took a good bit of beckoning before he began to approach me. I held the door open for him but, when he reached the doorway, he would step no further. I kept ushering him out, but he just stood there, all five foot five of him, bespectacled and nervous, looking me up and down as if I were the Mafia hit he had been dreading his whole life. Eventually, I convinced him that I wasn't there to hurt him, but simply to introduce myself to a fellow Australian.

It turned out this little dude was none other than Hew Griffiths, the ringleader of DrinkOrDie, the notorious confederation of internet hackers who'd been busted committing copyright fraud. Though I wasn't wise to the facts of his case until I returned to Australia, Hew was apparently big news at the time, for the fact that he was the first Australian to be extradited to the USA for conspiracy to commit copyright infringement. It was all pretty dodgy – the very idea of an Australian citizen being dragged over to be tried in America, before what was hardly a 'jury of his peers'. At the time, the Howard Government was sucking up to the Bush administration, and had rolled over completely when the Americans had demanded that Hew's arse belonged to them, despite the fact he'd never set foot on American soil in his life. According to Hew, DrinkOrDie had been nothing more than a loose collection of geeks who got their kicks from cracking the codes of software programs and sharing them over the internet. That he could wind up in an American prison seemed insane. Australians had held protest rallies in support of David Hicks, but nobody in Australia had given a fuck about Hew, who'd never left his home in Gosford.

That first night, Hew and I went for a long walk around the yard. We talked a lot about what had happened to him – he'd already served a couple of years in Silverwater prison in Sydney, where he claimed to have had a pretty rough time. He didn't seem cut out for prison – he was nervous, fidgety, and wasn't too healthy. He had dandruff, dry skin and teeth that looked like they needed a bit of attention. But he seemed honest enough, and I couldn't help but feel sorry for him.

Eventually, the conversation turned to me, how much time I'd done, how much I had left and, naturally, what I was in for. When I told him, his eyes widened.

'Dumb and Dumber?' he exclaimed.

Oh, brother.

Hew turned and basically ran straight into the perimeter fence, pissing himself laughing.

'No way!' he laughed. 'Arghh . . . fuck!'

Apparently, my reputation had preceded me. Hew couldn't believe he'd wound up in the same prison as one of the legendary dickhead bandits from Australia, who were famous, he said, throughout Australian prisons. It was a strange sort of feeling to know I was notorious for my dumb crime. Still, Hew's reaction was kind of nice. When we went back inside, I gave him a little care package from my locker – food, coffee, a few magazines. I knew what it was like to be in his position, new to a prison, alone, and wondering if anyone would ever give a fuck.

It made me realise, too, how long I'd been in the American prison system. That I could feel sorry for someone else was a good sign that I didn't feel sorry for myself anymore. I'd negotiated my way around this nightmare, had acclimatised to it and really wasn't doing too badly. Having someone from home who was a bit of a virgin in this place made me feel a bit better about my own predicament, and doing what I could to help him out seemed a pretty good way to pass the time. I approached the unit manager and got Hew moved into my pod, and my cell, where he remained for the next few months.

He wasn't the easiest cellmate to tolerate – he snored like a giant, was untidy and had a tendency to piss on the toilet seat, or leave dirty footprints on the table as he'd stand on it on his way to the top bunk. Sometimes, I'd hold a tin of talcum power under his nostrils while he slept, seeing how much of the stuff he could ingest before he'd wake (he never did). But talking to him was easy, because he was Australian. One really needs to be away from Australians for a long time to realise that they do share a common way of thinking that is quite different from other nationalities. Hew was strange, but it was a very Australian sort of strange. I remember, just a few weeks before he was released, he lamented that he couldn't stay for a few more months, as he was enjoying the results of the workouts we were doing. That was crazy, but it was a very Hew thing to say.

In the end, Hew Griffiths did pretty well. He wasn't really 'alone' in prison. He'd get letters all the time from sympathisers, people who didn't even know him, who'd send him cheques for a few hundred dollars just to let him know they thought what had happened to him was unfair. I remember Hew replied to one such letter, mentioning to the writer that he was sharing a cell with me. The guy wrote back telling Hew to ask me: 'What were they thinking?' He also asked Hew to ask me if I intended to write about my experience. I hope this book answers both of those questions.

One night I was working out in the gym, going strong doing reps and dips and basically pumping myself up as hard as I could. My brother, Abdul, from Afghanistan, was playing prisonball, and after a while I noticed the game was getting heated. When I finished my workout I decided to hang around and watch. It's lucky I did. This Chinese motherfucker, built like a bodybuilding model, started getting all crazy, throwing elbows and knees, playing as rough as he could. At one point, Abdul stopped the game.

'Hey I'm not looking for any trouble,' Abdul said, 'so please don't play dirty like that, okay?'

It was typical of Abdul – he didn't tough people out, but was always reasonable. Unfortunately, the dumber inmates often interpreted this as a sign that Abdul was a pushover. Big mistake. The Chinese dude kept playing hard and, when Abdul came from behind to steal the ball, threw a sharp elbow back that caught Abdul in the chest. Abdul cocked his arm and waited for the Chinese guy to turn and face him before clocking him right on the cheek. The

Chinese guy misfired a haymaker of his own as he staggered backwards. Before he could regain his balance, I ran out onto the court and stood beside my brother. I could see the wheels turning in the Chinese guy's brain: should I stay or should I go? After a moment, he just started screaming abuse as he turned and walked away. He was pretty insulting, and I had to stop Abdul from going after him to break his neck.

It was my first stand-up moment since joining the Trinitario, and I was pretty pleased with how it went. At no time did I feel any fear, just an understanding of what my duty was, and the fact I'd done my duty was noted. It was also good to see how opposition melted at the sight of just the slightest show of brotherhood. But there were to be greater displays in the weeks that followed.

The rec yard featured nine steel picnic tables that each seated four people. It was pretty much a 'first in, best dressed' situation, but the unwritten law was that the tables were divided more or less equally according to the numbers of each nationality in the prison; three for the Mexicans, two each for the Dominicans and the Jamaicans, and one each for the Colombians and the Chinos. On this particular day, the Mexicans, in what appeared to be a premeditated move, decided to occupy all of them – just a big show of power, nothing more.

I was in the library studying when I got the word that my assistance was required urgently outside. I tied my boots tight, put my razor blade in my mouth (as we always did when trouble was going down) and made my way out there as quickly as I could. The sight that greeted me in the yard was awesome – there must have been 600 dudes milling around, Dominicans, Jamaicans and Colombians together, all poised for one hell of a fight. In their hands were shanks and shivs, pens, blades, locks in socks – the tension was heavy. My brothers were all lined up against the fence, and as I joined them they shook my hand and smacked my back. It was a very powerful, overwhelming feeling, and I felt as if I was part of an army that couldn't be stopped by anything.

For a few minutes it seemed that World War Three was about to explode in Youngstown, but, somehow, a meeting of all the heads was organised in the middle of the arena. It was good to see our Trinitario guy going about his business – he definitely dominated the proceedings, the fiery little fucker, telling the Mexican guy where to get off. He told them we'd all packed our things in readiness to be trans-ferred after the bloodbath, if the Mexicans wanted it that way. The Jamaican dude made this really powerful speech about how his people were small in number, but had come from the hardest prisons in the country and would fight to the death without flinching. For a moment it really did seem to me like this was where it was all going to end, and I was surprised to find it was all right by me. The atmosphere was electric.

Amazingly, it all wound up peacefully – the Mexicans, impressed by the unexpected show of unified resistance, backed off completely, and they never really did recover their credibility after that day. The Trinitario came off looking quite victorious, and it was good to be on the winning side. But, for me, the most interesting figure in the whole affair had been that Jamaican dude who'd made the impressive speech. I made it my business to seek him out in the rec yard the next day, and to speak to him, just to see what his story was.

He turned out to be Richard Morrison, aka 'Storyteller', from the infamous Jamaican 'Shower Posse', who'd really made news in the 1980s and 1990s. Though officially regarded as a violent gang, the Shower Posse was unofficially employed by elements associated with the Jamaican Government as a counter-revolutionary paramilitary force, their job to 'destabilise' the socialist opposition, which usually involved assassination and murder. Though cagey about his exact role in the violence, Richard was frank about his participation in the trafficking of drugs and arms between Jamaica, Colombia and the United States. A qualified pilot, Richard claimed to have flown millions of dollars' worth of money and guns between Miami, Bogota and Kingston. During the early 1980s, the US Government had seemingly turned a blind eye to the operations of the Shower Posse – in fact, the way Richard told it, the CIA had all but assisted with the flow of arms, since the US had sought the help of the Jamaican Government in overthrowing the Communist revolution in nearby Grenada. But, once Grenada was successfully invaded and the old regime restored, the Jamaican hoodlums were no longer useful, and the US began making efforts to extradite Richard and his boss, the appropriately named Lester Coke, on charges of murder and drug trafficking.

America caught up with Richard in 1991, when he was 40, and he was sentenced to 24 years for trafficking cocaine. He got a better deal than his boss – while on remand in a Jamaican prison awaiting extradition to the USA, Lester Coke died in a mysterious fire that swept through his prison cell on 23 February 1991. His intimate knowledge of the Shower Posse's involvement with the Jamaican Government and the CIA died with him.

Richard was now in his mid-fifties, black as night and built like a grizzly bear.

He showed me a lot of his paperwork and various newspaper articles he'd kept, which proved his story to be true. He also treated me to a photographic history of the life he'd lived before being arrested, and it's fair to say it was the greatest argument against the old cliché that crime doesn't pay. There was Richard in a Ferrari, Richard in a Porsche, a Bentley, a Rolls Royce, a BMW, and always with gorgeous women in the passenger seats. He had property all over Florida and Jamaica, boats, airplanes, helicopters, all the toys of every drug lord's dreams. He'd been in prison for seventeen years but he swore every single moment was worth it. And why wouldn't it be? In prison, Richard was a lord, and everyone got out of his way.

Richard Storyteller Morrison was no visa jumper, street hustler or harmless internet hacker. He was the real deal. Walking back to my cell that night, I thought about how the stupid little thing Luke and I had done in Vail, Colorado had landed me in a prison next to a guy who'd helped to bring down a government. And I couldn't stop laughing at the thought of how ridiculous that seemed.

When Hew left, I got a new cellmate who actually made me miss Hew's snoring. The new guy had this annoying habit of snorting every couple of minutes – sucking an enormous amount of air and snot up through his nostrils and then swallowing it, the sound of it all sliding down his throat making me want to be sick every time. One night, when it was particularly shitting me, I called out to him to shut the fuck up, which he did. After about half an hour of silence I began to feel guilty, so I asked him what was wrong with him, why he had to make that terrible sound. He just pretended he was asleep and hadn't heard me. Little things like that tell people in prison that you're gutless. I made up my mind about him in that moment – I knew he was weak.

Reputation, reputation, reputation. That's all we had. All the cars, clothes, fancy titles and investment properties were left on the outside. In here, all you had was your reputation, which meant that every little thing you did and said counted on the ledger. More than the walls or the screws or the rules, the relentless obsession with reputation is what contrib-uted most to one's 'rehabilitation'. It made you think about yourself and who you were, how you appeared to others. In society, you can use material things to trick people into thinking you're something you're not, and you can even fool yourself with such shit. But, in prison, there's no hiding. You have to consider your naked self, every day. If what you see isn't good, it'll get to you, like endless bad reviews.

I could tell that I'd done a lot of growing during my years inside. Before going to prison, I never would have dreamed of telling a complete stranger to stop snorting snot down the back of his throat while I was trying to sleep. Now I was that man. I could look another man in the face and say: 'You're pissing me off. Watch yourself.' It felt good to be a stronger person.

My snotty cellmate was more like the person I had once been. He'd rather lie or pretend than face a confrontation. That seems like the easy way out at first, but it makes you a fake, and it forces you to eat shit when you don't have to. Consequently, my cellmate had problems. When he slept, his head would twitch from side to side, as if he were shaking something out of his brain. He'd twitch like he'd touched a live wire. Others noticed how sullen and uptight he seemed, and how he was certain one day to explode. I remember one dude predicting that he would one day walk into a McDonald's restaurant and massacre a whole lot of diners, and I remember thinking he was probably right.

This Dominican mate of mine, Andy, used to get up in the dead of night and threaten his cellmate with a padlock and chain, screaming: 'I'm going to kill you!' before shuffling back into bed. The next morning he'd remember nothing. Even sleeping in prison was a dangerous activity.

But, for me, the most interesting characters to observe in prison – though not necessarily the most likable – were those who'd had some kind of backup on the outside that was no longer with them. It was fascinating to see how they'd be forced to cope as lone wolves for the first time in a long time. For example, there was Tony, an Italian who claimed to be 'connected' and, since he was serving nearly twenty years for involvement in organised crime, he probably was. But for reasons unknown to me it seemed he'd been deserted in prison. He had no friends, no connections in here. He was a mobster without a mob.

Thanks to a motorcycle accident that had resulted in his losing a portion of bone in one leg, Tony walked with a limp so pronounced it looked like he was constantly picking cotton. But this disability didn't shrink his massive ego, which he liked to put on show all over the prison. He had 100 different faces – called you either 'my boy' or 'my man', depending on how superior he felt in your company – and reckoned he was a genius at reading people and manipulating them. Unfortunately for him, everyone saw right through him and thought he was nothing more than a wannabe Mafia tool. His penchant for asking people for a spoonful of their lunch or dinner actually resulted in the prison population naming a type of behaviour after him: if you'd been slightly ripped off by someone who hadn't deserved their winnings, you'd been 'Tonied'.

It's interesting how little weight the Mafia seemed to have among the prison population in Youngstown. Out on the street, the Mafia was the sophisticated end of criminality, but, in here, among the rats of the penal system, the Cosa Nostra didn't count for shit. Against the deathwish gangsters like the the Latin Kings and MS-13, and the blunt thuggery of the white supremacists, the traditional Mafia seemed like some sort of old-fashioned, well-mannered relic. This dynamic changed in the Federal prisons, where the laws of the street infiltrated the system. But in Youngstown, someone like Tony was very much on his own.

Nobody knew this better than Tony himself, which is why, when he learned about the Trinitario, he began to make noises about becoming initiated himself. The poor dickhead thought that just because he was a big knob in the Mafia that the Trinitario would bend over backwards to have him join their ranks. When the head heard about this he exploded – he was fully aware of Tony's fake character and wanted nothing to do with it. But when those lower in the hierarchy found out that the head had made a decision without consulting them, they cracked the shits and demanded that a decision be made at a meeting and through the proper channels. So a meeting was held in which Tony was given due consideration, the unanimous verdict being that Tony was shit and the Trinitario would have nothing to do with him. So much for due process.

One of the beauties of the Trinitario was its ability to fly under the radar. Where other prison gangs were very high profile, and therefore vulnerable to the scrutiny of the authorities, the Trinitario didn't advertise itself unless it was threatened. It was possible to exist in the prison at Youngstown and not even be aware of the Trinitario at all. It was like a snake in the grass – if you stood on it, then you would know.

I remember once walking through the rec yard and throwing up my set at a brother as he went by. A little later, I was approached by this heavy Jamaican dude who was known as 45, for reasons I can only guess. He was a hard soldier – braids, big jacket, saggy pants, and he walked with a slight limp that somehow made his street swagger seem more threatening. He walked right up to me, furrowed his brow, and looked out of the corner of his eye.

'You a Blood, mon?' he asked.

'What?'

'Ya mon, I see you reppin' da Bloods. Is that what you are, B?'

'Nah, man. I ain't no blood. I'm Trinitario.'

'Den why you be signin' like dat, mon?'

I explained to him that my sign was quite different from the Bloods sign, although I had to show him up close before he could see the difference. I found out later that he had been a Blood for a long time, since his first stint in State prison fifteen years before. He'd heard of the Trinitario, but knew very little about it. I told him what I knew of the relationship between Bloods and Trinitario – that I'd heard in some prisons they ran together, including this one, thanks to the fact that the Mexicans were the common enemy. He seemed to appreciate that. Turns out he was the only Blood in Youngstown.

He went on to tell me that he'd since turned his back on the gangster life – 'hung up my flag', as he put it – though old habits died hard, and he always had one eye open for his old allies. I told him I felt good in the Trinitario, that I loved the aspect of brotherhood, of being part of a huge family that rolled together in such a hostile place.

'But you a man before you anything else,' he said. 'Remember dat.'

In November, Dad and Kylie visited me, and we took full advantage of the fact that contact visits were allowed. Actually touching people who I loved was an amazing feeling. Kylie even brought little Harry along, whose blond hair, blue eyes and soft white skin seemed out of place among the filth of Youngstown. Cuddling him was beautiful, but I couldn't get rid of this awful feeling that I was contaminating the little guy. This prison was no place for him.

Of course, the wonder of visits like this was always tempered by the harsh conditions: hard plastic stadium-style seats positioned just far enough away to prevent 'prolonged touching'; cameras on every wall and in every corner; keys jangling; doors slamming; screws monitoring every move and barking at us when we touched too much or when

Harry got happy and started running around, or if my pants fell too low off my hip when I lifted Harry up for a cuddle, or if I stood too close to the vending machine as I was trying to see what food was in there. The screws never let a moment go by when they could remind us all that they were in charge. Stupid fucks. And then, when the visits were over, being stripped again, made to squat and cough, and pull your dick and balls aside, for a long time if the screw was gay and wanted to conduct a thorough inspection.

But that first visit from Dad and Kylie was notable in its own way. It was the day when I learned that Mum and Dad had decided to separate. At first I thought they were simply taking a break, and I made it clear that I was all for it. But then Dad explained that the house was on the market, lawyers were involved and assets were being split. It was the end of their marriage, and it had been ending while I had been languishing in a prison on the other side of the world.

This was a fucking blow. I couldn't believe the family that had accompanied me my whole life was collapsing. The bubble in which I'd lived was now burst. Everything that had made me who I was had come from the togetherness of these two people. Now that was ending. Fuck. And then came the thought about how much I myself might have had to do with it.

Dad insisted it wasn't the case – that he and Mum had just grown apart – but nobody was going to be able to convince me that my situation had not put a strain on things. There are plenty of kids from divorced marriages who know how it feels to ask that question: How much of this is my fault? Most of them would be told that to ask themselves that question is silly, but, in my case, it's not silly at all. My parents had sold all their investments and shares simply to keep coming to see me over here, and the worry I'd given them every day for years could not have been helpful. To this day I don't feel comfortable about it. To me, my mum and dad's marriage is just another casualty of a stupid decision I made one day in 2005, back when I thought nothing I did could ever rob me of my charming little life.

The next few weeks were angry ones for me, and the prison around me seemed to follow suit. Fights started breaking out everywhere, as if the world was inviting me to vent my confusion and rage by joining in.

The first occurred in the medical unit, where I was waiting patiently for a nurse to assist me. A female screw and a middle-aged male counsellor were walking a Mexican inmate into the office, when the inmate saw someone he knew waiting near me and stopped to talk. The counsellor immediately stepped between them, waving the Mexican on and demanding that there be no talking between prisoners – just another one of the unnecessary humiliations that these clowns like to inflict on you from time to time. The Mexican responded by throwing his elbow into the chest of the counsellor, who staggered backwards before charging the

Mexican, getting him in a headlock and trying to wrestle him to the ground. A nurse got bowled over in the scuffle. Staff were screaming, the fighters were grunting and I was sitting there laughing, because I just didn't know what else to do.

The call went out for a 'code red' — an officer down. Within seconds, the little room was full of screws, all tumbling over each other like bumbling police in an old slapstick silent movie.

The incompetence of the staff seemed to feature whenever there was this sort of trouble. A few days later, an inmate with a 15-centimetre stump where his arm used to be got into a fight with one of the screws. Even though he had nothing more than a stump, he knew how to use it, and threw a great punch that landed right on the screw's jaw. The screw was a big fat dude and didn't have too much trouble subduing the inmate, pressing him face first against the wall. But then the comedy started when the screw pulled out his handcuffs. It took him a few moments to realise that the cuffs were basically useless and that he'd have to improvise, so he snapped a cuff on to the good arm and began scratching his head while he searched for something to lock in the other one. He got the bright idea to fix it to the inmate's leg, but he soon learned it wouldn't reach that far. And all the while the inmate himself was just standing there silently, enjoying the amusement along with the rest of us, who were all pissing ourselves laughing.

Another time it wasn't so funny. A warden in another unit was doing the rounds and must have encountered a prisoner on a bad night. Whatever was said between the two ended with the prisoner pulling a blade from a disposable razor and slashing the screw in the mouth. This was a favourite cut as far as inmates were concerned – the old 'Joker' slice, with the blade running from the corner of the mouth to as close to the earlobe as possible. In every prison and jail I'd been in so far I'd seen someone with this tell-tale marking, usually made with a double-blade razor, so a thin strip of skin would be completely removed, making the scar more pronounced. The prisoner who did it to the warden must have had his reasons, but he would have paid a heavy price. I remember hearing of a punishment where inmates were put in a single cell and handcuffed to a table, crucifixion style. They'd have to sing out to the guards when they wanted to piss, at which point the screw would only release one ankle, allowing the prisoner just enough freedom to turn and piss into a pan, so as not to drench himself completely. This was one of the few concessions given to anyone who found themselves in that particular predicament.

It was in times of despair that I thought of Clare most. When things were going okay for me in prison, I didn't dwell on her as much. But when I got down, like I was now, I thought about her constantly. This time, I realised it had been some time since I'd heard from her at all. I decided to give her a call. The sound of her voice, I thought, would cheer me up.

It was a few weeks before Christmas in 2007. It was early in the evening. When she answered, she didn't sound particularly happy to hear from me – nothing serious, just a little bored, or perhaps not as excited as I'd hoped she'd be. She kept pressing the buttons on the telephone by accident, making the call disconnect. I decided to give up and try the next morning.

When I did, she answered sounding pretty much the same, only this time she said her sister and a friend were with her. She seemed distracted, continually breaking our conversation to speak to the other people in the room about inconsequential things. I found it hard not to become irritated – it seemed she'd forgotten how difficult it was for me to make calls, and how precious this time was as a result. Her demeanour was like I was calling her from the next room, and she'd simply see me in a little while anyhow. The distance between us was suddenly a giant chasm.

I hung up the phone and spent the next few days thinking on Clare and me, and I realised some things that hadn't occurred to me while I'd been working out how to live in Youngstown. I realised that I hadn't received a letter from her in months, and that the only times we'd communicated anymore was when I'd gone to the trouble of calling her. She had missed my last birthday completely, which was a first, but birthdays tend not to mean much to you when you're in prison, so I had let that slide. I took out the last batch of photos she'd sent me and looked at them. In one where she was holding her hand near her face I noticed that the gold and diamond ring I had given her was no longer there. My heart began to sink as I experienced a feeling I hadn't felt since I'd been an adolescent – that pain in the guts you get when you're chasing a girl and you realise she's just not into you. My heart was breaking. Over Clare. This is what it had felt like in the horrible dreams I'd had when I'd first come to prison. I'd been so caught up in the business of being a prisoner, a brother of the Trinitario, a good cellmate, a stand-up dude, I had completely neglected to notice that Clare and I were drifting apart.

In a way, she had remained the same in my mind, so my feelings for her were intact. But how could she feel the same way? I'd changed so much, in ways she couldn't even know. I began to feel terrified at the thought of losing her, particularly to someone else, perhaps even someone I knew.

There are many ways to fix a troubled relationship, though I realised few of them were available to me, being in prison. Whatever I did, it had to come from within – I had to be almost Buddhist about this, working on calming myself down before my thoughts drove me crazy. I just had to relax, do the right thing and hope that it all would just fall into place and everything would eventually work out. If I really loved her, I thought, I owed her that much. The best way to do this was to focus on myself and take my mind off Clare. And the best way to take my mind off Clare was to give Shannon a call.

Shannon had continued sending me letters and photos, each just a little more provocative than the last. I'd been replying in kind (no photos, just racy letters) in an effort to continually pump up the temperature. Unbeknownst to her, Shannon had become quite popular in Youngstown prison. Keeping suggestive photos of women away from the other inmates was a difficult business, particularly after you were spotted with a photo in one hand and your 'fife' in the other. The other prisoners couldn't believe I was getting photos like this from someone who wasn't even my girl, and any delivery of mail to my cell would be followed by a steady stream of prisoners who'd swagger in casually as if they'd been just passing by, only to eventually inquire as to whether I'd received anything new from Shannon.

When Shannon answered the phone, she made me feel like a rock star calling a fan. She was excited and breathless – turning it on a little for me, for sure, but it was greatly appreciated. I asked if she'd received my latest smutty letter, and she said she had. She had even shown it to a friend of hers, who had liked what I'd written as well. In fact, they had both decided to pose together for some photos that I would surely be receiving soon, depending on the speed of the mail.

She told me she got butterflies in her stomach whenever she saw a letter from me in the mailbox. She said I need never worry about her, because she knew where I was and knew what I wanted. This was more like it.

When I hung up the phone I went and lay down in my cell for a while. After that was all successfully concluded, I felt bad. I felt I'd betrayed Clare and abused Shannon, who was a good solid pal for knowing what I needed and not having a problem with giving it. In prison, all the chocolates and Bibles from all the Christian charities in the world don't come near the value of a photo of a pretty girl, or a letter telling you you're the man of her dreams, even if she doesn't really mean it. There's plenty of God and self-evaluation in prison, but there's no romance, that's for sure.

Keeping myself from falling into a deep depression was hard. I'd often be walking around when suddenly I'd be hit with the reality of where I was, how far from my childhood I was, and the things I loved. The destinations in prison were so limited, and even those in my imagination became stale after I'd overused them. That's when I'd begin to focus on my surroundings and I'd be reminded that I was living an imprisoned life. A little voice in my head would whisper: 'There's no way out', and I'd know it was true. In times like that, anything exciting and new was like a life preserver to a drowning man. Those letters from Shannon, and the photos of a girl smiling out at a man locked up far away, were the greatest distractions in a world from which I desperately needed to be distracted. I consoled myself and assuaged my guilt with the thought that, if ever a man had a reason to be unfaithful – regardless of what I deserved – it was me.

I don't remember exactly how it came to be officially understood, but it was in April of 2008 that the inmates decided they'd had enough. For too long we'd been putting up with an increasing level of bullshit from the screws and prison authorities regarding anything and everything, from lousy food to the enforcing of little rules that seemed to be being made up as each new day came along.

A good example occurred during a visit from my mother some months earlier. A prisoner normally would have to wait until informed that he had a visitor before he made his way to the visit area, but since Mum had been coming at 10 am every day for a week, and was due to arrive at the same time on that day too, I figured I might as well forget about being called and go down to the visit room anyway. When I got there, a screw asked what I was doing, and I replied that if he cared to look in the visit room he would see my mother. He looked, came back and said she wasn't there, and ordered me to return to my cell. I was about to do so, when I saw, out of the corner of my eye, my mum. She'd been there all along, and there's no way the screw could have missed her. When I angrily pointed this out to him, he had me frog-marched to The Hole for five days for disregarding an order. Typical heartless power-trip bullshit for no other reason but that he could.

There'd been a bit of a revolving door when it came to head wardens at Youngstown, and with each changing of the guard came a whole lot of fresh regulations as the new guy tried to put his stamp on the place. In the months leading up to April, we'd had all plastic knives and forks removed, along with all rubber gloves, which, for obvious reasons, annoyed us greatly. The prices in the commissary shop suddenly shot up, and vegetables were no longer available. Hour-long stand-up counts began occurring at night, when once they'd lasted no more than ten minutes. Some days, the rec yard would remain mysteriously closed, for reasons nobody could work out. Screws had been confiscating everything – nail clippers, beard trimmers, scissors and sewing kits, even though they sold them from the fucking commissary.

It all led to a general feeling that if we didn't buck they'd ride us into the dirt.

So the inmates went on strike, which took the form of all of us refusing to come out of our cells for anything. It began small but pretty quickly everyone got the gist of what was going on. The first the wardens knew of it was when nobody turned up for breakfast. They rode that for a whole day figuring eventually we'd break and give in to our hunger, but it's easy to starve yourself when the food is shit, and you've got your own in your locker anyway.

On the second day the screws began bringing trays of food around to our cells, but we told them through closed doors to fuck off. Later, they began forcing us back to the rear of our cell, and placing the food in the middle of the floor. The place become a cacophony of voices shouting out orders not to eat the shit. One inmate was stuffing the food through the crack under his door, until it was piling up like rubbish outside. When they yelled at him to clean it up, he yelled back. This non-violent protest was slowly becoming violent. When my cellmate needed his regular medication from the the medical office and they opened my cell door, I seized the opportunity to hurl the tray of food out into the common area. The joint went wild, banging on doors, slamming chairs and shouting obscenities.

It didn't take long for the authorities to panic, and their response was predictable enough, I guess: a SWAT team, dressed in full combat gear, with gas masks, helmets, shields, batons and tear gas at the ready. In they marched in single file, all the way to my cell door. What the fuck?

The captain yelled at me to get on my knees facing the rear wall, hands behind head, legs crossed over. I did as they asked. The door popped open and in they charged, someone squashing me into the wall with his shield pressed hard against my back. They cuffed me, stood me up and marched me out of my cell. The whole place was going insane, but it didn't exactly help my case.

'Yeah, fuck 'em, Prince. You tell 'em to go fuck 'emselves, Prince!'

I was led down the walk of shame to The Hole, all the while with a screw holding a video camera in my face, just waiting to record me saying or doing something out of line that could be used against me later. As I passed the dingy cells I spied Trinitario brothers who'd been down in The Hole for months. Man, this was not good.

For the next three months I was in The Hole at Youngstown – 23-and-a-half hours a day locked down, with 30 minutes from 5 am where I was 'allowed' to stand in an outdoor dog box and freeze. It was a terrible time – the worst of all my time in America. I sank lower emotionally than I'd ever been as each blank day dragged into the next, and each night saw the same lights in the eyes and the same shouts telling me to stand and be counted. There was nothing to do but think.

My cellmate was an Indian guy who stood by the door every day praying to be let out. He freaked out when they delivered him his 'wanted for investigation' paperwork – I was the one who had to chill him out. And my paperwork told of a 'high category' charge.

It was during those first few days in The Hole that I realised I'd only had nine months to go – nine months until I was free to return home, or at least free to leave. All I'd had to do was keep my head down and brass it out, but somehow nine months had seemed like such a long time to wait quietly when I'd been in low security. I began to wonder what my part in this stupid riot would cost me. Would I be here for another year or more? Would this event finally cost me my Australian citizenship?

Once again, I found myself in a state of deep remorse over something that I had done in the heat of the battle. Once again, I had become caught up in the moment, rather than thinking properly about the consequences for myself. The sound of those voices crying out my name when the SWAT team had marched me from my cell was the only reward I was going to get for my latest act of foolishness, and it would potentially cost me so much. I began to wonder if I hadn't learned a fucking thing in four years.

At the back of the cell were two 'windows' in the concrete – two long, skinny slits about an inch wide each, through which I could see a patch of grass enclosed by a concrete wall. During the day, correctional officers would stroll by and peep in, as if we were animals in a zoo. I began to look forward to them doing this, as it broke the monotony. I'd make bets with myself about how long it would take for another to walk by, then another bet about whether he'd look in or not, and another about which screw he would be. This went on forever, punctuated by meals, the only other break in the blandness of The Hole.

Out of sheer cabin fever, I began fighting with my new cellmate. He was this greasy little Mexican lad who, after a workout in the cell, would stand over the toilet and wash his balls in the water, which was disgusting to even have to listen to. He was a little older than me and he called me 'son'. So I'd challenge him to get up off his bed and find out which one of us was the child to the man. The bickering went on and on until a guard would walk past the two slits and I'd rush to see whether I'd been right this time. Once I got bored with that game, I'd wait until one of them was walking past my door and, as they'd come close, I'd kick it, hard, the clang of the steel always making them jump out of their skins.

The sleep deprivation added to the crazy thoughts and depression. To sleep one had to ignore one's surroundings: the constant hum of the air vents that ebbed and throbbed and made me feel I was hearing voices whispering; the sound of the water pipes rattling in the walls; a prisoner going mad like me, flushing his toilet twenty times over; keys jangling, doors slamming; people yelling out to each other in the middle of the night. Sometimes I thought it would never end.

The first inkling I had that I would soon be released was when I was woken in the middle of the night and asked to give a drug test sample. This, I thought, was a sign that the charge against me wasn't holding up – they needed something else to put me away. That was my reading of it.

It was in the first week of August that a screw informed me of the fact that there was some good news and some bad news. The good news was that I was being released from The Hole. The bad news was that I was being sent back to Allenwood, where I would serve the remainder of my sentence. Only this time, I was going to medium security.

My ordeal was a long way from over yet.

8

I am told to pack my things and be ready by 11 pm. I ask if I can make a phone call to my parents to let them know where I am going. The request is denied – I am a definite security risk, they say.

We wait in a holding tank downstairs until a bus arrives at 5 am. We are shackled, stacked on the bus and moved out. I thought I'd be a bit sentimental about leaving Youngstown, but I'm not. I realise that I don't want to see any of these places again, or even think about them, if I can avoid it. My body and soul have taken everything they need from this place. My brain doesn't need to store any memories from here.

It's a long, windy, uncomfortable five-hour drive to Harrisburg, Pennsylvania Airport. Once we arrive there, we are barred and shackled and moved to an old school bus with hard plastic seats. Half my arse is hanging off the side because of the fat bastard next to me. No point in complaining. At the back of the bus is a cage in which sits a lone US Marshal, aviator's glasses hiding his gaze and a loaded shotgun across his chest.

For the next few hours we ride in this tub, every head in front of me bobbing from the bad road and shitty suspension. I keep myself amused by watching prisoners falling asleep, their heads sagging onto the shoulder of the guy next to them before they snap bolt upright and apologise. Heads smack windows as we go over a bump, or bang together like coconuts, or slide down the window until disappearing. One guy in an aisle seat drifts lower and lower, his head sinking down, his body twisting and slipping off the seat until he is completely in the aisle. What strange entertainment. I try to stay awake for as long as I can. Once the sun comes up it's a little easier. But then the sun creeps higher and it becomes warm, and I begin to get tired. By the time we get to the airport it's midday, and I've been awake for 24 hours, surviving on nothing but the spectacle and a baloney sandwich they'd fed me for breakfast.

There are six more buses lined up at the airport, watched over by sentries all armed to the teeth – assault rifles, pistols and bulletproof vests. I am moved to another bus that will take me direct to Allenwood Medium Security Prison, and straight away I feel the difference in the screws. They're not fat, soft pricks like those in Youngstown, but are solid, tall and unsmiling. They stare you down. They're

all business. At least the seats are cushioned. I get one
to myself.

More buses arrive. Inmates file from planes and other vans,
dispersing to planes and other buses. Then begins the freak
show. All sorts of fuckers start piling on to my bus. It would
be funny if they weren't so menacing, and if I didn't know
I was going to be in the same pen as them. It's beginning to
dawn on me that I have been in low security for all my time
in prison. For all my feelings of having acclimatised to the
prison system, turns out I don't know shit. My education is
just about to start, and that scares the fuck out of me.

Big black fellows, arms like tree trunks and necks the
same. Braids, tatts and all hollering at each other – 'Yo,
brother. What's good?' – as if they're out on a school picnic.
They're not afraid of anything.

'Look at these motherfucken pink bitches,' shouts one.
'Fag-ass COs. Suck you, cracker!'

The black half of the bus laughs. They're openly cursing
the guards and encouraging one another to string together
increasingly vulgar insults.

'Pink bitch, what kinda honky fag shit you playing on
the radio? Some kinda inbred redneck shit taught you by yo
slut momma?'

The corrections officer doesn't look, doesn't answer back,
but just turns up the volume knob on the radio that plays
Hank Williams or whatever it is.

Then come the white boys – skinheads, white supremacists. They file on much more quietly and seriously, but no

less threateningly. There are no insults directed at their pink complexions, and they make no threats to the COs, most probably because they're white, too.

A bunch of about ten swagger on and occupy the remaining seats, avoiding any that already seat blacks. This seems a comfortable arrangement for everyone. They haven't said a word or looked sideways at anyone but it's obvious they feel superior in every way to the other passengers on this bus. I can't help but be impressed by their bold means of disclosure – shaved heads and tatts that boast of their prejudices from arms and faces and necks. Simple swastikas, elaborate crosses, guns or the letters 'SS' emblazoned on their necks. There is one hulking fellow who looks like Gene Simmons from KISS, eyeliner tatts on upper and lower lids, a dagger on his temple and a big SAC on his neck, which I later learn stands for 'Soldiers of Aryan Culture'. This dude doesn't seem to care one bit that the sight of him might breed vicious thoughts in the minds of these awesome black monsters that are already aboard the bus.

These fuckers are hard, and this is only medium. Heaven fucking help me.

Upon arrival at Allenwood I was given the usual examination, plus all my tatts and scars were recorded for future identification. Sometimes, apparently, prisoners can be so badly beaten or burned that the only means of recognition might be a tiny piece of skin, and whatever was written on it.

I suppose I'd been spoiled by my treatment in the other prisons, in JeffCo and Youngstown especially. I'd forgotten how hard prisons can get, and that I'd only experienced low security anyhow. This place was an entirely different game. You could see it on every hostile face.

Nobody – not the screws, not the inmates, not the medical staff or the counsellors – gave a fuck about where I was from or what I was doing. I'd received a bit of respect through the other prisons thanks to everyone's fascination with my nationality, my accent, my little story and personality. Here that wasn't worth a breath of air. Nobody cared. Even in Education, where I tried to impress the counsellor with details of the course I'd been doing, there was no enthusiasm for my life or future whatsoever. It was like a law had been passed whereby nobody was to give a damn about anyone else. It was so crushing and daunting to feel as if I was a newbie all over again, right back at the start, just like that first night back in Denver years ago. I used to think of that time while I was in Youngstown, and thank God that I'd moved on and grown stronger. Now here I was, back there again. It was a nightmare within a nightmare, like those bad dreams where you dream you've woken up, only to find that you haven't at all.

The compound itself was large, bigger than Allenwood Low, with a massive rec yard housing two baseball fields, a basketball court, a soccer field and a lot of grass. It was all very new and well kept. Layers of razor wire flanked the compound and bars appeared in windows of every size. The extra level of security was evident in everything and everyone, through the structure of the prison, the attitude of the COs and, of course, the inmates. There was a tension within them all, a reservedness, a lack of trust that was palpable. Medium security catered for prisoners whose cases featured a certain level of violence, and I felt very much like a pretender in those first days, like a wartime journalist who'd been given the wrong set of instructions and found himself at the front line with a gun in his hand. There were a lot of younger prisoners who seemed to still have something to prove to the world, and representatives from every gang you could name. This was a real prison. This was what Hollywood had always tried to replicate in their hardest, baddest depictions of the penal system. This was what I had always imagined when I'd thought of prison as a child, and what I had feared the most.

The entire prison was severely segregated, and I got a taste of that severity very quickly. I was shown to a six-man cell that I was forced to share with four black guys and one white. Normally, this wouldn't happen. In prison, if you were a man of any substance or backing, you would find your way to a cell with your own race. But I was nobody here – not yet. Like most new prisoners, I had to dwell in this racial purgatory for a while, shunned by the blacks who I was forced to bunk with, and shunned by the whites because I was bunking with the blacks.

The black dudes were heavy, unsmiling and somehow managed to convey their complete contempt for me without saying a word or making eye contact. After dumping my stuff, I stepped outside my cell and waited to be approached. That's how it happened in Youngstown – some white guys would see you and come and snap you up. But it didn't happen. I figured the fact that I was Australian mightn't qualify me as white in the eyes of the Americans here.

When it came time for chow, I entered the chow hall feeling as if I was on my own. The only person so far who had approached me at all was a black guy called Alvin who seemed somewhat mentally challenged – he had a tuft of hair on the top of his head and wire holding his teeth in place. Later I learned that this guy was as gay as they come, which is why I was the only one talking to him. It was this guy who shadowed me into the chow hall for my first public meal.

I sat down at an empty table. Alvin then sat down beside me, and only then did he decide to explain the seating arrangements and how things went down. Over in the distance were the white tables. On the other side were the black tables. The table we had chosen, directly behind the 'stand-up white' table, was a table reserved for rats, gay bitches and child molesters. I was told the other prisoners liked to let newbies choose their own tables, just to see what their stories were. I had probably been identified as a 'lover' – a white boy who loves blacks. Such people are disliked equally by whites and blacks, I was told.

So ended my first day in Allenwood Medium, a day when I couldn't have made a worse impression if I'd tried. That night, I climbed onto my (upper) bunk, said nothing to anyone, closed my eyes and dreamed I was back in Youngstown, which suddenly seemed like a school camp from some long-ago time deep within my schoolday memories.

It didn't take too long for it to be established that I wasn't the rookie I'd appeared on that first day in Allenwood. An opportunity arose for me to make up numbers in a football team, which happened to almost exclusively include members of a group known as the Dirty White Boys.

The Dirty White Boys stood out among the white gangs. Their name made them sound like they were a joke, but that couldn't have been further from the truth. They were full-on, hardcore white supremacists, and they never tried to hide it. They used to walk around in the rec area with their shirts off, playing basketball, or just hanging out, with iron crosses and SS symbols all over their skin like warpaint. I remember there was one guy who had a giant iron eagle on his back, with a huge swastika hanging off the eagle's talons. They were blatant about it, where a lot of other white supremacist gangs preferred to be a little more discreet. Everyone knew what the Dirty White Boys were about. If a black guy was to go up and ask a Dirty White Boy if he was racist, he'd do his best to explain to the guy how it worked: that he wasn't racist, he just believed that the white race was superior to every other race and that's all there was to it (no offence). I sort of admired that about them – the way they were quite happy to talk with anyone at any time. They just weren't very ethical. But then, according to legend, neither was I.

The Dirty White Boys were a little like how a white supremacist group might be depicted in a Hollywood movie. The shot-caller was Bubba, a 29-year-old blue-eyed skinhead of pure German descent. He was six foot one with a solid build and a stance that permanently thrust his jaw outwards, as if he were inviting someone to hit it. The entire purpose of his personality seemed to be to intimidate. He had a big iron cross tattooed on his arm, a Dirty White Boys tatt and the state of Texas on his pecs, and, on his stomach, the words *'Odium dum metuont'* – 'they may hate but they will fear', apparently. Justin was of Irish descent, with bright blue eyes and a reddish tinge to his beard – another skinhead in for guns and cocaine conspiracy. Billy was your typical Nazi redneck with a bald head, a spartan goatee and a body covered in lightning bolts, skulls and assorted words in Germanic text. Despite being the youngest, Bubba was undoubtedly the leader, and the others sucked up to him heavily, to the point where I often found myself feeling sorry for them. It also did not escape my attention how often they joked about each other being gay, mincing around, slapping one another's arses, as if the big joke was that they couldn't possibly ever be gay themselves. One of the younger ones, a guy called Bones, was especially amused by this sort of horseplay. I'd be surprised if he hadn't crossed over by now.

I fell in with the Dirty White Boys because I felt I had no other choice. There was no Trinitario in here that I could see, and running alone just didn't seem wise – exactly how unwise would be made clear to me just a few weeks later.

By now I had moved to a two-man cell which I shared with a white guy called Mike, a relatively harmless dude who didn't seem to want to run with anyone. One night, I was approached by a bunch of black Washington DC dudes who were hard and nasty fuckers. Their motto seemed to be 'What goes down in prison stays in prison' – in other words, being gay in prison didn't mean you were actually gay. They hunted in a pack, and clearly looked for lone wolves or lost white souls. Apparently, Mike had made them all hot and bothered by strolling past their cell from the showers each night, his long hair dripping behind him as he'd towel himself off along the way. They offered me $100 to turn a blind eye when they came calling. All I had to do was turn my back to the wall, or leave the cell if that's what I wanted to do. I refused, but they kept harassing me about it, claiming there'd be trouble if I didn't acquiesce.

It was definitely in the interests of my self-preservation to take the money and let it happen. But I just couldn't bear the idea of sinking Mike like that. I knew I'd suffer horrible guilt about it, probably for the rest of my life. So I summoned every bit of wisdom and courage that I'd learned from Dejesus, from Dave, from Storyteller Morrison, from 45 and the Trinitario, and decided to stand my ground.

There was no way, I said, that I'd do as they asked. They were asking me to aid in the rape of a brother. I couldn't do that, and they shouldn't respect anyone who could do that. And if they didn't take no for an answer, I assured them I'd have no choice but to take it up with both their brothers and the Dirty White Boys, to whom I had a duty to report something like this. To my relief, my bluff worked and the DC rapists moved elsewhere. From that moment I turned a corner in Allenwood. It was vain and stupid of me to think I could survive in Allenwood alone.

I determined to hang with the Dirty White Boys, not just for the sake of my own arse, but because that's simply the way I had to gravitate, towards my own race. That was how it went down in prison – being an enthusiast of 'multiculturalism' was just not an option. But I also reminded myself of what 45 had said, about being a man first, and how I was not to forget it.

After a few weeks of running with my new tattooed, hardcore, pea-brained career criminal, white supremacist friends, things were looking all right. I had proved myself in the showdown with the black wannabe rapists, which I made sure I described in dramatic detail to Bubba and the others, who were all very impressed. All I had to do was lie low for a few months, watch my mouth, and I was home free.

One morning in the rec yard, I spied a face in the crowd that I recognised from Ohio. It took a moment for the significance to sink in, but, when it did, I got that old anxious brick in my guts again. He was a brother from the Trinitario. I recalled how he had just gone missing one day from Youngstown, and now here he was, in Allenwood. I was in serious trouble.

Though not a member of the Dirty White Boys, I had definitely been taken in by the white clique as one of their own – they had given me food, shoes, radios, coffee, and had generally accepted that I was a stand-up dude who could be relied upon if things got bitter. To now turn around and tell them that I had been previously running with a Dominican gang – something I had conveniently forgotten to reveal – would not have gone down well at all, and to tell my Trinitario brothers that I had abandoned them for a white supremacist group would have been worse. I'd be a traitor to the brotherhood, and for what reason? From their point of view, it would look like all I was trying to do was protect my tiny white arse so that I could go home to my middle-class life in Australia. That sounded to me like a bashing offence at the very least. If the Dirty White Boys and the Trinitario exchanged notes, it would be easy to see how they could come to the conclusion that I'd been playing them both. In that event, a bashing would be a let-off.

When my Trinitario brother finally noticed me it was all handshakes and smiles, my gaze shifting nervously around the yard as I welcomed my Dominican friend. We said a quick hello and promised to catch up later. I should have told him to keep his mouth shut about me until I could speak with him, but I didn't. And neither did he. Apparently, he went straight to the head of the Trinitario in Allenwood and happily announced my arrival in the prison. Since the Trinitario was so under-represented in Allenwood, the head was delighted to hear I was there, and immediately began making plans for my grand return to the brotherhood.

I had a very sleepless night that night. It was like an extreme version of a husband being out with his mistress at a party and spotting his wife across a crowded room. I entertained stupid ideas about keeping them both apart, or about hiding myself from my brother, but that was impossible. I had to nip this in the bud before it got way out of hand.

The next day I scoured the rec area in search of my Trinitario brother, finally found him and pulled him aside.

'Listen, man,' I explained nervously. 'I know that we're brothers, and I'm proud of that. But, you see, I've got these white boys now and, y'know . . . I'm kinda' kicking with them. I'm here for you in any way, but . . . you know how it is, right?'

It wasn't the most eloquent speech, but, to my surprise, he immediately understood.

'Whoa, man!' he exclaimed. 'Why didn't you say something, bro? I mean, if that's the way you want to play it, Prince, cool. The problem is, I've now got to explain this to the head, and he ain't gonna be pleased.'

We spent a few minutes trying to devise a way to shimmy myself out of this situation, but, in the end, we agreed being honest was the only thing that could possibly work.

He returned to the head and, on my behalf, mounted a very sympathetic case for my defence. I was going home soon, he argued, to Australia, a long way from the world where the Trinitario roamed. I had ridden with honour in Ohio, he said, recalling the times I'd stood up with my brothers. He suggested to the head that the correct thing to do was to grant me an honourable discharge.

And that's what happened. Quietly, and with no fanfare, I was informed that I was no longer a brother in the Trinitario. It was a relief, but I was also very sad about it. The Trinitario had been good for me in Youngstown and, truth be told, I felt more of a bond with those brothers than I would ever feel with these racist arseholes. Once again, it seemed, I'd miraculously escaped the fate that I felt I'd probably deserved.

I made it a point to vocally reject the white supremacist ideology of the Dirty White Boys in the gentlest way that I could. Each time they tried to force a piece of dogma or right-wing literature onto me – the repetitive conspiracy theories about Jews taking over the world, the dodgy pamphlets of crackpot science that 'proved' the black man was no different from the ape – I explained that I simply couldn't see past the way in which I'd been indoctrinated from birth, which was to accept all races and religions, to tolerate them as equals. Winding back that sort of upbringing was a job that would require a lot of time, and I didn't have that much. I was going home soon. All I could do was promise them I'd stand beside them if shit went down, because that's what friends do, and the black guys considered me no friend of theirs. The Dirty White Boys seemed to accept this as the best from me they were going to get.

As I became more familiar with Allenwood Medium, it began to resemble more of a mental asylum than a prison. Some of the characters made an especially strong impression.

There was Wiggles. He was a five foot five black dude, and I was sure he must have had implants in his face, his cheekbones being so ridiculously pronounced. He obviously plucked his eyebrows, pulled his hair back in corn rows, and was always wearing lip gloss. He either shaved every minute or had lost all his facial hair, and he must have been taking estrogen or something, judging by the crook little breasts that jutted out from under his shirt. He also wore tight little pedal-pusher pants, and, from what I could see through them, appeared to have some sort of arse implant – cushions implanted in his buttocks to make them more ripe and inviting, I guess. When he walked, his big phoney butt would wiggle, hence his name.

At first, it seemed to me incredible that someone like Wiggles could possibly survive in a medium security prison. I was soon to learn how he did.

One day I was doing some cleaning and went to the broom closet to get a mop. When I opened the door, there was the leader of the Bloods, right in front of me, pounding into the arse of someone who was bent over a chair – someone who, unless I was very much mistaken, was Wiggles. I just stood with the door open for a nanosecond – in shock, I suppose – then closed the door as if nothing had happened and decided to try for a mop a little later.

Wiggles, I was to subsequently discover, was notorious as the boy who belonged to the leader of the Bloods, the most hardcore clique in Allenwood – about 100 strong, with a frightening reputation. The leader of the Bloods could pretty much do what he wanted and, evidently, one of the things he wanted to do was fuck Wiggles in the arse. So that's what he did, regularly, and everyone knew it. Wiggles was his bitch. So nobody messed with Wiggles, because, if they did, they'd have the leader of the Bloods on them, and there were no prizes for guessing what he liked to do with his victims once he had them begging for mercy.

But Wiggles wasn't just a one-man man. Reportedly, it was $50 (or about 130 stamps) to fuck Wiggles in the arse, and $20 for head. That's what they said, though I have to admit I never checked this out for sure.

There were others like Wiggles – a big black dude with fake breasts, a Mexican queer who worked in the barber shop and was as camp as a drag queen, but was strong and crazy and ferocious in a fight. It had never occurred to me that there could possibly be gang-bangers who were gay. I never thought it was possible, but it was rife in prisons. Today, when I see those little wannabe gang-bangers on the Australian streets, I can't help but wonder whether they're aware of what their heroes might be up to overseas.

The idea of getting with another dude never entered my mind, I have to say, but there were plenty of inmates who said that it would, if I was to stay in prison long enough. I couldn't wait to get out.

And then, of course, there was Clare. For four years I had dreamed about her, thought about her, touched her in my sleep. Though I'd flirted with Shannon and fucked with my 'fife', it had always been Clare who had been in my heart. The years had seen us drift into a slack groove of sporadic letters and occasional calls, but I still felt that we were strong enough to just pick up from when we left off. It wouldn't be long now. I could almost taste her.

Then one afternoon I had a call with my father that changed the colour of all of those memories. I was just a few months from coming home, and I thought I'd heard all the bad news that I could possibly hear while in prison. During the course of our conversation, I asked Dad if he'd heard anything from Clare, as I hadn't heard from her in a while. He took a deep breath and revealed that he'd heard on the grapevine she was seeing someone else.

Looking back, this was something I'd known deep down for perhaps a year or more, but the reality of it was so unbearable I'd chosen not to confront it. All the signs had been there – the forgotten birthdays, the letters slowing down to a trickle, the fraught conversations on the phone – to the point where only a complete idiot in denial wouldn't have worked it out for himself. But I suppose I was clinging on to the idea of Clare. She was, as far as I was concerned, the last relic of the life I'd lost all those years ago. I had changed. My friendship with Luke had changed. My parents were no longer together. All the warmth of my cosy life as I remembered it from before this whole nightmare had begun was no more. In my heart, I'd held on to Clare as the one constant dream to which I felt bound to return.

So I called her and asked her myself if the rumour was true, and she told me it was. She'd been seeing some turkey for a couple of months. More than that, even. He was nobody I knew, nobody I'd care to know. It didn't matter. When I got out, she said, I was going to have to get used to the fact that this was the way it was going to be.

I got a bit mad, of course. She'd been lying to me for a while, and she admitted it. But she said she'd only done that because she was worried about what I might have done to myself in prison, if I'd taken the news badly. It's understandable. Had she written to me that she had a new man in her bed every night of the week, I'm not sure how I would have taken the news in The Hole at Youngstown, Ohio. To protect me from the bad news was fair enough, and it was Clare all over. She didn't have the heart to hurt me, and that's what I always loved about her. She was nervous and sweet.

Clare was my first love, and the last casualty of my crime. She left me pretty much because of it. She stuck by me for a long time – came and visited me in prison twice, with her own money. But after the first year I think it began to drag on her. I still felt a bit ripped off about it all. That's just the man in me, I suppose. The cunt. Every guy's the same. There's nothing that can be done about it.

For the next few days I moped around, crying at intervals, raging at others. I didn't care about my reputation, or my freedom, or my self-respect. I was heartbroken for the first time in my life and in the worst possible place a man could be heartbroken. Other inmates tried to console me – even the toughest of them were surprisingly sympathetic. This was a drill with which every long-term inmate of a prison was familiar. She'll always go this way, they said. You've got to get over it. There's nothing you can do.

I obsessed over the fact that I'd always asked her if she was seeing someone else. 'Are you seeing any other guys? Y'know . . . I know that you probably want to. A hot girl like you. I know you get hit on all the time. It's okay, just tell me about it.' And she was always: 'No, Anthony . . . I see some guys sometimes but none of them compares to you.' It was my imperfections, she said. And what does a guy in prison for a stupid bank robbery say to that? It was just what I wanted to hear. It kept me feeling secure. So for all that time in prison I kept dreaming about her, and thinking of the day when I'd get out and we could be together again. When that dream vanished, all the others followed. I snapped at the screws and tried to pick fights. I suppose I briefly lost my will to live, or to look after myself at all.

In a way, the only thing that kept me sane was my university studies, which forced me to concentrate, though it was often difficult (try studying quantitative analysis in a medium security prison). But my studies suffered too as I became more reckless by the day.

It was probably fortunate that a screw took offence at my behaviour one afternoon and slapped me into The Hole, out of harm's way. It would be the scene of what was arguably my most memorable moment in the American prison system.

The Hole in Allenwood Medium was more like a hole than any of the others had been. It was just a cell for one, with a metal toilet and, next to the toilet, an air vent. This vent would be common to the cells next door and those stacked above, for how many floors I wasn't sure. But prisoners in different cells would talk to each other through these vents. At nights you could hear them whispering, someone's voice travelling from a few floors up to the intended receiver way below. In the day, they'd just rabbit on, sometimes having rapping competitions, which were interesting, until the novelty wore off.

One morning, these two Spanish dudes were talking to each other for what seemed like hours. I was trying to sleep, but they just wouldn't shut up, their voices barking out of my vent as if it was an intercom speaker. I began shouting into my vent, and at them: 'Shut up! *Callate! Cierra la boca!*'

But they just shouted obscenities back at me in Spanish, and English too. It took me a while to think of it, but at last an ingenious plan was hatched in my head, a way to win this little war once and for all.

After breakfast and lunch, I held onto my bowels and concentrated on cooking up the most monstrous amount of gas, which, in the end, seemed like several hours in the making. Once the gestation period was complete, I carefully parked my arse at the air vent, relaxed, made a sign of the cross and let that mother blow.

'Brrrrrrrrraaaaaaapppppppphhhhhhh!'

There was a long silence from our wing of the prison as the echo from the fart rang like the sound of some enormous gong being struck in an empty stairwell, and I rolled around on the floor in hysterics. I couldn't remember the last time anything I'd planned and executed had gone so well.

The Spanish dudes started muttering:

'*Que?*'

'*Te pedo?*'

'Aha . . . aha ha ha ha ha . . .'

'Ah . . . ha ha ha . . .'

Eventually, the entire Hole was pissing itself laughing in about five different languages.

Prison in America is a terrible place to be. There is nothing romantic about it, nothing to love. Everyone there is miserable, their lives having all gone horribly wrong. If you could make 30 of the poor bastards laugh at the same time, you had achieved something that was, in its own way, very special.

It felt good to be the bringer of so much joy to the American prison system.

I met a guy of American Indian and Mexican heritage, in his mid-thirties, tall, strong-looking, weathered. He claimed to have been in prison for most of his adult life. It was hard to reconcile this man with that past, because he seemed to me like a thoroughly decent guy who laughed easily and didn't seem too hung up about anything. But, later, someone told me he was something of a legend in the prison system. He'd worked his way down from super-max to a penitentiary, then to medium in the space of about twelve years. He had originally been sentenced for a drug offence all those years ago, but, very early on in his sentence, had become involved in a beef that was brewing between his own people and some blacks. A man with a short fuse, he decided to squash the beef by severing the head of one of the black guys and tossing it into the yard for everyone to see.

A chill went up my spine when I heard this. Here was a guy who, like me, had done something that had only taken a moment out of his life, and yet it would define him forever. I can say from personal experience that this man was a very decent human being, but the conventional wisdom is that it's impossible for a good person to do something so bad.

I began to wonder whether this whole notion of 'rehabilitation' had any worth at all. Is it necessarily bad people who do bad things? Do you fix them by putting them with other bad people? Had I learned a thing about myself since I'd been here, or was my remorse for my crime no greater than it had been when I'd pointed that BB gun at the teller's face? I knew my remorse was pretty strong then. The last four years seemed to have been such a waste.

As the new year of 2009 clicked over I began to feel swamped by the strangest panic. For four years I'd been pushing ahead, thinking forward, trying to stay focused on that day in the future when I would finally be free of this nightmare. Now that day was approaching fast, and all I could think about was what had happened, all the time I'd lost and things I'd missed, the life I would never see again. I had imagined my unhappiness would be inversely proportionate to the time I had left to spend in prison, but it seemed to be working the other way. It was like I'd woken only minutes before the end of an exam, tormented that I'd missed something, and that I only had second to find what it was.

A cellmate told me that my friends would be scared of me when I returned, but I knew it would probably be the other way around.

I spent my last few weeks in Allenwood drifting as if in a bit of a trance. I remember the little Hispanic dude who smeared shit on the doorknob of the warden's office, and I remember laughing the next day when the warden walked in wearing one white glove (somebody suggested that maybe that's what had happened to Michael Jackson). I remember being woken by a fight in my cell, two guys going at it like monsters, blood everywhere, spattered on the floor and the beds, the fight ending when one pleaded that the other was killing him. 'I'm dyin',' the voice of this big tough guy cried. 'You don' wanna do this . . . I'm dyin'!' And I remember lying there freaking about it, how one man could frighten another so badly. I remembered that I'd made someone feel like that once, in a bank in Colorado on a winter's day, back when I was just a stupid kid from Byron Bay who thought shoplifting alcohol was a bad thing to do.

Only days before I was released from prison, I met a young white dude who had just entered Allenwood for the beginning of a seven-year sentence. His most immediately noticeable feature was a missing right hand, severed from the wrist. Apparently, he'd constructed a home-made fire-cracker – a big one – and when he'd picked it up and crossed his living room some static or dodgy wiring had caused the thing to go off in his arms, blowing his hand clean out of the room. He had tiny blue dots all over his face – explosive burn marks that would never heal – and he was constantly asking me to repeat myself, as if he had a few wires loose of his own. Once he'd recovered in hospital, he was sentenced, under anti-terrorism laws, to seven years in prison for making and detonating an improvised explosive device.

One final reminder of the heartbreaking consequences that are born of one foolish moment.

I honestly don't remember much about leaving Allenwood prison. What I do know is that it was early on the morning of 19 February 2009, that there were more flights, more buses, a few days in an immigration joint, and a ride through New York where I wasn't welcome. It seemed America and I could not part ways quick enough, so the whole time is a blur. It was only once I was on the plane home, escorted by agents from the Department of Immigration, that my life seemed to come back into focus.

As the American coastline drifted away behind me, I couldn't shake the feeling that I was getting away with something – that, once again, I was slipping out of trouble. Sure, I'd gone to prison and paid for my crime, but I'd done it with a lot of support, from inside and outside, to the point where I was able to move through prison pretty smoothly, just doing my thing. I didn't lose anything of myself in America – nothing that was worth keeping, anyhow. I was left with a lingering guilt about the fact that I hadn't suffered enough myself. I felt like I should have been bashed half to death, or had my throat cut from ear to ear. I should have been punished harder for what I did to the two bank tellers and my family and friends.

But, somewhere over the Pacific Ocean, such thoughts gave way to more pressing matters. While using the toilets,

I was suddenly reminded of my 'operation', and, for the first time since I'd had it done, I wondered what the fuck I'd been thinking.

I landed in Sydney, then took off immediately for Wellington, New Zealand. The only way I was able to enter Australia again was through the country of my birth. My immigration details had been fast-tracked through and sorted in the nick of time. I was soon to be living in Australia, an Australian citizen, for the first time in my life.

I'm not sure how to convey the way I felt upon seeing Mum and Dad, waiting there for me as I emerged at last from confinement into the airport concourse at Wellington. I don't think those sorts of feelings can be conveyed adequately in words. It was like there were just a million different shades of brilliant, white-hot love and relief. We staggered out of the airport holding each other as if we feared someone was going to burst out of nowhere and take me away again. It felt strange trying to get used to the feeling of being allowed to go anywhere I wanted to go – left or right, fast or slow. I could hold my mum and nobody could say: 'That's enough.'

There was also a weird feeling of dread as we passed through the gates and doors at the airport. The last time I had been free – the very last moment when I'd been able to do as I pleased – was on a cold morning in 2005, in a building very much the same as this. I'd been tying my shoes when my world had ended. I never even got to do my laces up.

I had dreamed of going to bars, or restaurants, or spending my first night out under the stars, but suddenly all I felt like doing was going home to Mum and Dad's hotel room. I didn't want to be around other people – I'd been around nothing but people for years. All I wanted to do was be alone with them, where nobody else could bother us.

We drank Hennessy that night and I got drunk for the first time in nearly half a decade. Even without it, I marvelled at the little luxuries of the world: the softness of the bed; the quilt covers; the curtains; the carpet; the instant coffee satchels that a few days before had been currency for me. These little joys were waiting for me everywhere over the next few incredible days and weeks, in the sound of wind in the tops of trees or girls giggling on their way home from a party someplace – things we treat as the backgrounds to our lives, but which become precious when they're taken away.

The first bacon and eggs, the first beer, the first surf, the first steak, the first sex – and on the living room floor, right next to her parents' bedroom (it was amazing, and surprisingly comfortable). There was no end to the wonderful things with which I could reacquaint myself, the very same things I'd lost in the snow as I'd tried to get rich on the dumbest day of my life.

EPILOGUE

I'd been back home in Byron Bay for only a few months when a woman contacted me via Facebook. It was Jessica Cole Gunther, the teller from the WestStar Bank in Colorado, at whose face I'd pointed my gun on that day. She just wanted to let me know that she forgave me for what I did to her back in 2005, that she hoped I was well and that she prayed for me.

To say I got pretty emotional when I read this would be an understatement. With that short note, the book was closed for me on the stupidest thing that I'd ever done. I'm still in touch with her today. It's a nice thing to have come from it all.

My story is probably unusual for the fact that I'm one of those rare creatures of the penal system: someone for whom prison actually worked. I went into an American jail as a puny specimen, physically and emotionally. I emerged undamaged, a little bit wiser and a whole lot stronger for the experience. Without wishing to promote a crime wave, I'd recommend a stretch in prison for any young clown who thinks he's better than he really is – not just because it wakes you up, but because having the things you love removed from your grasp gives you a whole new perspective on your world. And, when you get it all back, you also get the greatest time of your life. It worked for me.

I continue the studies that I began in prison, and what the future holds for me is anyone's guess. But I know I changed a lot in America, a fact of which I am regularly reminded.

In Byron Bay, some time ago, this guitarist from a local hardcore band had an issue with me regarding his girl-friend (for some reason), and sent me a text message, of all things, telling me to stay away from her or he and I would go at it. He actually wrote: 'And if I can't do the job (which I admit I probably can't) I'll get my Bra Boy mates to do it for me.' I mean, what sort of a man sends a text message threatening to beat up someone with someone else? How much more cowardly can a threat be? And he was in a hardcore band, for fuck's sake! Prison might not be a perfect society – it's really the most imperfect, broken, twisted and unfair society there can be – but at least it teaches you to be a man and be responsible for yourself. If I'm proud of anything to do with this whole experience of mine, it's that I learned, at long last, to take responsibility for myself, and I learned that the hard way. The Anthony Prince who relied on others to lead the way, or to bail him out of his own troubles, never got out of Denver.

I've seen Clare a few times since I've been back – never in private, just her and me, but around friends or in a crowd. We've moved along, after all that. The truth is Clare did all right. She did more than all right – she was a champ. At the very least she deserves to have me declare that to everyone.

One of the first things I did when I got back to Australia was to go and visit Shannon, just to thank her for all the photos and the letters that got me through the maudlin times. We took a couple of photos together, and I sent them to my friends overseas. I love imagining the stir those photos caused when the mail was delivered in Youngstown, Ohio.

As for Luke Carroll, he was released from prison six months after me.

We still see each other every now and then, though we've both changed a lot, and our friendship, too. I can say I respect Luke today more than I ever did. We know what we're sorry for, and what we went through, together and apart. They called us 'Dumb and Dumber', and maybe they were right. But, today, we're blessed with the wisdom that can only be shared by two dudes who have massively, catastrophically fucked up.

And we never have really spoken in detail about what went down back in Vail, Colorado in the winter of 2005. There's nothing much to say, really.

But every now and then, when we see each other, we'll exchange a glance that lasts for just a second, a weary sort of look that seems to say: 'C'mon . . . what's the worst that can happen?'

ALSO AVAILABLE FROM PAN MACMILLAN

Rusty Young
Marching Powder

Rusty Young was backpacking in South America when he heard about Thomas McFadden, a convicted English drug trafficker who ran tours inside Bolivia's notorious San Pedro prison. Intrigued, the twenty-something Australian law graduate travelled to La Paz and joined one of Thomas's illegal tours. What followed took both men by surprise: they formed a strong and instant friendship and then became partners in an attempt to record Thomas's experiences in the jail. Rusty bribed the guards to allow him to stay and for the next three months he lived inside the prison, sharing a cell with Thomas and recording one of the strangest and most compelling prison stories of all time.

Marching Powder is a shocking, sometimes darkly comic account of life in San Pedro. In this bizarre prison, inmates are expected to buy their cells from real estate agents. Others run shops and restaurants, and hundreds of women and children live with imprisoned family members. It is a place where corrupt politicians and drug lords live in luxury apartments while the poorest prisoners are subjected to squalor and deprivation. Violence and crime are never far away, and sections of San Pedro that echo with the sound of children by day house some of Bolivia's busiest cocaine laboratories by night. In San Pedro, cocaine makes life bearable – even the prison cat is addicted to crack.

Yet amid the corruption, brutality and the daily struggle for survival, *Marching Powder* is also the tale of an unlikely friendship, forged in the oddest of circumstances, between a drug smuggler and a lawyer. It is the story of one of the strangest places on earth, where horror is leavened by humour and where cruelty lives side by side with compassion.

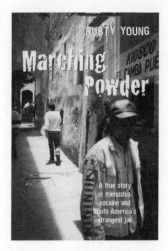

Kathryn Bonella
Hotel Kerobokan

Welcome to Hotel Kerobokan, the ironic nickname for Kerobokan Jail, Bali's most notorious prison. It is a dark and bizarre underworld of sex, drugs, violence and squalor, which has been home to a procession of the infamous and the tragic: the Bali bombers, Gold Coast beautician Schapelle Corby and the Bali Nine, among many others.

In Hotel Kerobokan's filthy and disease-ridden cells, a United Nations of prisoners – Australians, Americans, Germans, Brazilians, French, English, Scottish, Mexicans, Italians, Balinese and others – live crushed together in misery. Petty thieves and small-time drug users share cells with killers, rapists and gangsters. Hardened drug traffickers sleep alongside unlucky tourists, who've seen their holiday turn from paradise to hell over one ecstasy tablet.

Hotel Kerobokan is the shocking inside story of the jail and its inmates, revealing the wild 'sex nights' organised by corrupt guards for prisoners who have the money to pay, the rampant drug use, the suicides and the killings and the days out at the beach. It takes you behind the grim walls and exposes the jail's role in supplying high-grade drugs to tourists and dealers on the outside, the gang that rules the jail with terror, the corruption that means anything and everything is for sale, and the squalor and misery endured by prisoners in stinking, overcrowded conditions.

Written by Kathryn Bonella, the co-author of Schapelle Corby's best-selling autobiography, and backed up by hundreds of interviews with prisoners past and present, the truth about Hotel Kerobokan explodes off the page.

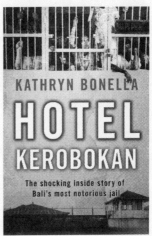

Warren Fellows
The Damage Done

In 1978 Warren Fellows, Paul Hayward and William Sinclair were convicted of heroin trafficking between Thailand and Australia. They were sentenced to life imprisonment in Bangkok's notorious Bang Kwang men's prison, the Bangkok Hilton.

It was the beginning of twelve years of hell for Warren Fellows. He has never spoken of those years to anyone. Until now.

The Damage Done takes you behind the bars of a Bangkok prison. A place where sewer rats and cockroaches are the only nutritious food, where autocratic prison guards giggle as they deliver pulverising blows and where the worst punishment by far is the *khun deo* – solitary confinement, Thai style.

Brutally honest and repentant of his initial crime, Warren talks about the decade of his life he lost in leg irons. *The Damage Done* is a brave and compelling book that poses harrowing questions on the nature of justice.

'This is not a book for the fainthearted. The reader will be repulsed yet magnetised by the contents of Fellows' book'
HERALD SUN

'… a solid story of pure misery that addresses you directly, like a man pouring out his heart in your living room'
SUNDAY AGE

HUNKY DORY

(WHO KNEW?)

Laurence Myers

The best I can remember from twenty years at the heart of '60s and '70s rock and pop

B&B
Books

First published in 2019 by B&B Books

Copyright © Laurence Myers 2019

The moral right of Laurence Myers to be identified as the author of this work has been asserted in accordance with the Copyright, Designs and Patents Act 1988.

ISBN 978-1-912892-29-7

Also available as an ebook
ISBN 978-1-912892-28-0

Jacket photography: Getty Images
Front cover images of Mick Jagger and Marianne Faithfull
copyright Gered Mankowitz

Typeset by Tom Cabot/ketchup
Cover design by Simon Levy
Project management by whitefox
Printed and bound by Clays

Hunky-dory

[Huhng-kee-daw-ree]

adj. informal

Fine: going well

Oxford English Dictionary

For

(in order of appearance)

Marsha,

James, Peter, Beth

CONTENT

CONTENTS

INTRODUCTION

O nce upon a time, a long time ago, a young ex-student of the London School of Economics sat at my desk in my Regent Street office. He was a nice young man, skinny with long hair and a distinctively large mouth. He was a singer with a band; I was his accountant and he was interested in pensions.

'After all, Laurence, I'm not going to be singing rock'n'roll when I'm sixty,' he said in his south London accent.

'No, you're not,' I agreed. How we laughed at the thought … Nearly sixty years on, my client – Mr Jagger – is not only still singing rock'n'roll, he is still fronting the greatest rock'n'roll band in the world – and he certainly does not live off a pension.

Six years after that meeting, another skinny young man with long hair, also a singer, sat opposite me at a different desk. I was no longer an accountant. I was managing artists. I thought that he was extremely talented but one thing slightly troubled me. Although his wife was by his side, he was clearly flirting with androgyny. It was the received wisdom of the times that it was mostly teenage girls who bought records, so their pin-ups should be handsome in an alpha-male way. After I agreed to take him on, I asked the young David Bowie his views on this.

'Don't you worry about that, Laurence,' he said, 'I know what I'm doing.' And he did …

A music-business journalist once asked me: 'What was it like to be at the heart of the British music industry in the fantastic sixties and seventies?' I truthfully answered, 'Who knew?' At the time, although the people I was dealing with on a day-to-day basis were exciting and interesting, I had no idea that – years later – many of them would be of historic interest and that much of the music I was then involved with would still be relevant more than fifty years later.

They say that, in life, timing is everything and 1964 was the perfect time for me to get involved with the music business. The rock/pop business had burst into the public psyche with a four-to-the-floor drumbeat thumping out the rhythm of a youth revolution. In America young men were burning their draft cards as a protest against the ongoing war in Vietnam. Youth in the UK were rebelling against the general mess that they were going to inherit from the post-war generation – the established class system that pigeon-holed the populace according to their accents and anything else that would upset their parents – especially their taste in music.

Unlike today, when a kid can make a record in his bedroom, records had to be made in expensive recording studios. Record sales, along with the rest of the economy, were booming. The major record companies had a total lock on the recording industry and took advantage of the artists who were providing the music that reflected the desires of the youth of the day – which were, largely, sex and dancing. The contraceptive pill had been introduced in 1961, encouraging the sixties to swing.

'Let's spend the night together,' suggested the Rolling Stones, and many did.

There was a real need for young business brains that would protect the artist against the rapacious practices of the record companies. Whom, you may ask, was amongst the first to fill this need? Twenty-eight-year-old me! How, you may ask, did I begin? Well, here's how – although if, like me, you sometimes skip the early years chapters in biographies, go straight to chapter six. I won't be offended.

1. THE FORTIES – THE WAR YEARS

I was born in London in 1936 within the sound of the Bow bells. This means that technically I am a cockney, but I spurned my birthright as soon as I could toddle, already hating the idea of having to learn to walk with shoulders rolling, thumbs in my braces, doing 'The Lambeth Walk' and shouting 'Oi!' Besides, I didn't think that when I grew up I'd want to wear suits that were covered in pearl buttons. Little did I know that through the eras of teddy boys, flower power, glam rock, new romantic and punk, I'd flirt with far worse.

I was three years old when what my generation call 'The War' broke out. It was *The* War because, like the misnamed 'The War to End All Wars' twenty-odd years before it, there was only one war that made the papers. I recently read that currently there are people trying to kill each other in something like three hundred 'conflicts' – as little wars are called – around the world. There is also, of course, the global war against terrorism. Will we ever learn? It seems, sadly, not.

War can be fun … if you are a child and protected from its true tragedy by your parents. For my contemporaries and me it

was an ever-changing adventure. Too many changes of schools
to take education seriously, and no expectancy to do well. Lots of
disruptions from air-raid warnings, fire drills, gas mask practice
and, of course, many bomb sites to play on. All wonderful stuff
but, to this day, if I ever hear a siren that has been programmed
to sound like a wartime air-raid warning, my stomach turns.

Like most kids during the war years, I went to a variety of
schools. Between 1940 and 1945 I attended a convent in Hitchin,
Hertfordshire, a boarding school in High Wycombe, a school in
Soho for refugee kids from Malta and a school for future gangsters in East Ham. There were other schools that I was sent to
for just a few days, as I was shunted around the country so that
Hitler could not find out where I was.

My father's parents came from Russia and my mother's
parents came from Poland and they were both very influenced
by the *Fiddler On The Roof* experiences of their recent heritage,
when Jews were thrown out of countries just for being Jews. This
was a generation that generally instilled in their children a need
to have their own businesses because:

A)   You could not get rich working for someone else. Being
rich was perceived as the best insulation from anti-Semitism.

B)   It was feared that anti-Semitism would inhibit the
advancement of Jews working in the general marketplace.

This was not as paranoid as you might think. In the 1930s,
National Socialism was politically and physically active against
the Jews in Germany, and Mosley's fascists were gaining trac-
tion in the UK. The 'ruling classes' may not have been overtly
anti-Semitic, but the cooks in the stately homes of England had
no need to learn how to make chicken soup or kosher salt beef

for expected Jewish guests, unless the guest was a Rothschild, which supports A) above.

In 1939 when the war started, my parents were operating a small hairdressing salon on the Barking Road, East Ham. During the war my mother Alice, a wonderful woman whom I adored and respected, battled on to operate the salon during my father Gerry's absence in the army. Our home was above the shop – a proud Jewish tradition that meant she could work all hours to make ends meet: an even prouder Jewish tradition.

I loved my father but found it hard to respect him. He was something of a Willy Loman figure, the titular character of Miller's *Death of a Salesman*, who relied on being liked to get him through life, happily allowing my mother to be the strength of the family. He was adorable and one of the funniest men I have ever known. He used to send me letters from 'your Daddy at the Front'. The 'Front' being the beach-front, Cleethorpes, the seaside town where he was safely stationed away from the London Blitz being endured by his wife and child.

According to my father, on one occasion when his platoon was strung out along the coastal terrain during one of the many invasion scares, he dropped his rifle, which fired a round. Anxious not to frighten his fellow soldiers, he shouted out: 'Don't worry, it's me, Gerry!' By the time the message was passed along to the ninth lookout, it had Chinese-whispered into a panicky: 'It's Gerry,' which was of course one of the slangy names for Germans. The alarm was raised, barracks were mobilised, Winston Churchill probably scrambled into his siren suit, and my father was lucky to only be punished with guard duty for a month.

Towards the end of the war, having feigned madness to avoid being posted abroad to Singapore where bullets were being exchanged in anger, he was committed to an army mental hospital in Bristol. Here there were three categories of inmates: the poor unfortunate, genuinely ill; the malingerers like Dad trying to get out of the army; and the army spies planted to try to distinguish one from the other.

Family legend has it that he conducted an orchestra that had no instruments and that he fired the second violin for playing the wrong note. There's a bad-taste sitcom in that story somewhere. In later years I asked my father how he, as a Jew, could not possibly wish to fight fascism, something that I was secretly ashamed of. He told me that the anti-Semitism in the British army was so strong that, in action, more Jews were shot in the back than the front. I am sure that this was not true, but I am equally sure that many Jews got a hard time from some other servicemen.

Whilst my father was fighting for democracy in the Palais de Dance in Cleethorpes, back in war-torn, dangerous London my mother and I lived between the shop in East Ham and the central London home of my maternal grandparents Peter and Annie Levenberg. My grandparents lived in a large flat in Bedford Square in the now trendy area of Bloomsbury. One of my earliest memories is clinging to my mother in a taxi as we drove there from East Ham through the blazing London docks during the Blitz. Grandpa Peter was a master tailor in the Mile End Road. I used to love going to his workshop where he and my uncle David would sit cross-legged on a counter, making bespoke suits built to outlast the Taj Mahal. There were huge heated pressing irons hissing on a gas range, the workshop smelled of tailor's soap, and I was allowed to sit cross-legged with my grandpa, pulling out basting stitches with an ivory pick.

When I was aged six or seven, my mother would often put me alone on the 106 bus at East Ham for my grandmother to meet me an hour later at the Tottenham Court Road stop, where the conductor to whom I had been entrusted would help me off. No thought of danger from strangers … different days.

Tottenham Court Road tube station was the nearest designated bomb shelter to Bedford Square. The trains stopped running, the electric rails were switched off and we slept on the station floor for many a night during air raids. I still have to resist getting undressed on platform three when I go down there to catch a tube train home from Soho.

I have a vivid memory of VE Day when the war was finally over. I was nine and my cousin Alan – who was five years older than me and was my boyhood hero – took me to join the celebrations on the streets of the West End. There was much spontaneous singing and dancing and I particularly remember a sailor. I assume he was a sailor because he was completely naked other than wearing a sailor's hat, his modesty barely covered by a skimpy Union Jack flag, as he pulled us into a circle of revellers for a knees-up.

Once the war ended, my grandparents' flat in Bedford Square was very much the focus of family life. We were a close-knit bunch. Grandpa Peter's brother Nussan had married my grandma Annie's sister Brandel. In the next generation, my father's brother Hymie had married my mother's sister Betty. Don't spend too much time trying to work that out, just be assured that there was no incest involved down the line. I was very close to my cousins Alan and Marlene Myers on my mother's side and Roy and Patsy Bloom on my father's side and we were socially pretty much self-contained. I had other cousins who were born after the war but we never had the opportunity to be that close. I was never that involved with my grandparents on my father's side, maybe because my father was not close to them himself.

On Thursday evenings my parents and my aunts and uncles, together with their children, all met at the Levenbergs' flat at Bedford Court Mansions. I have wonderful memories of the warmth and closeness of those family gatherings. Parents, uncles, aunts and cousins, eating, laughing, shouting and more eating. Grandma was a great cook.

When my cousin Alan was sixteen, his best pal was Marty Feldman, who used to come to my grandparents' flat and practise his clarinet – my first introduction to show business. Alan also introduced me to jazz and American big band music at a very young age, for which I thank his memory.

My father had worked as a hairdresser before the war and when he was discharged from the army in 1945, he got a job at a Mayfair salon. He was, by his own admission, a lousy hairdresser and claimed that his inept use of scissors inadvertently produced asymmetrical haircuts long before they became fashionable in the swinging sixties.

In spite of – or maybe as a result of – my patchwork education, aged eleven I passed my scholarship exams and spent a term at East Ham grammar school, before the family moved to Finsbury Park, where I attended Holloway County grammar school.

2. THE FIFTIES – THE FINSBURY PARK YEARS

My mother had been in a terrible traffic accident during the war and it was painful for her to stand, so being a hairdresser was not a great idea. My father was still a hopeless hairdresser and it was decided they should both change careers. In 1947, when we moved to Finsbury Park, my father bought a small tobacconist and confectionery shop.

Dad had an envious eye on his brother-in-law Len, who had three confectionery and tobacconist shops in north London. A multi-retailer! My parents had no capital and Len altruistically financed my father's acquisition of the Astoria Candy Stores, a small outlet opposite the Astoria cinema on Seven Sisters Road.

The Astoria was a showpiece cinema built in the thirties and was decorated spectacularly in the style of an Andalusian palace. There were silhouettes of Andalusian architecture around the auditorium and a large mosaic fountain in the foyer. When the house lights went down, the roof was a beautiful dark sky twinkling with stars. It was truly magnificent. I had a free pass to

The Astoria – if you kicked the third emergency exit door on the Seven Sisters Road side in the right place, it would open and allow you to pass freely into the splendid auditorium. In later years The Astoria would become The Rainbow rock venue and I would promote shows there. The first thing I did when I took over was to secure the third exit door on the Seven Sisters Road side. It is now a church and you can get in for free. Where's the fun in that?

Finsbury Park now has the wonderful Park Theatre, opened in 2013, a two-minute walk from where I once lived. Many years later I produced plays there. You can take a boy out of Finsbury Park, but you can't take Finsbury Park out of a boy.

My dad had a board outside our sweet shop that advertised the current weekly variety bill at the nearby Finsbury Park Empire. For this we were given two tickets for each of their weekly shows and I saw most of the acts that played there. There was always a mixed bill of supporting 'specialty acts', known in the trade as 'spesh acts': jugglers, acrobats, magicians, cycling acts, dog acts, knife throwers ... Variety in the true sense of the word. Table tennis was very popular at the time and Viktor Barna, the Hungarian world champion, used to tour the halls giving exhibition matches. Artists such as the Beverley Sisters were advertised as 'Decca Recording Stars' in recognition of having received the great accolade of a record deal, and comedians famous through radio often topped the bill.

The site of the Finsbury Park Empire is now a mosque where Abu Hamza, the infamous cleric with the hook for a hand, once preached his particular brand of brotherly love. On the spot where the cleric more recently spewed venom, Arthur

Askey, Jimmy James, Jimmy Wheeler, Max Wall and a host of other legendary comedians spewed jokes. These artistes toured the UK and usually played any particular theatre once a year so never had to change their act, and we would have hated it if they did. The comedians' routines, polished and refined by years of practice, were eagerly anticipated and if one was missed we fretted. Their acts were so good that over sixty years later I can still recite chunks out of most of them, and to my wife's dismay I frequently do. Their example taught me to insist that the acts that I managed always featured their hits in live performance, no matter how bored they were with performing them. 'Give your audience what they want.'

My favourite singer was Josef Locke: a large, usually drunk, Irish tenor with the voice of an angel. His big song was 'The Soldier's Dream'. There was a line in the song where he put his hand to his ear and shouted: 'Hear the guns' and we, the cognoscenti in the audience, shouted it out with him. I have tortured my children and, indeed, selected friends to this day by insisting on playing the song from my iTunes collection and expecting them to holler 'Hear the guns' at the appropriate moment.

Josef Locke did not believe in paying tax. In order to keep ahead of the Inland Revenue he would perform his sell-out concerts billed as Mr X. In 1991, Ned Beatty played him in a film called *Hear My Song*. Any of my kids who didn't go to see that film would have been cut out of my will. If you don't buy the DVD, you'll be cut out as well.

Comedian Max Wall was a particular favourite. He announced himself with: 'The name's Wall, Max Wall, my uncle was the Great Wall of China.' He used to come on stage clown-like as Professor

Wallofski, sporting a long and wild wig, wearing black tights and slap shoes. His absolute showstopper was the Max Wall walk. It is impossible to describe his act and I urge you to look him up on YouTube. His career was ruined in 1955 when, as a married man, he was caught in bed with Miss Great Britain, twenty-six years his junior – something that today would guarantee him a book deal, a spread in *Hello!* and a spot in *Celebrity Something-or-Other*.

In 1974 when he was quite old, I filmed his classic Professor Wallofski act at the Richmond Theatre before an invited audience, which included Richard Attenborough and many other celebrities, all devoted fans of Max. Max was a bankrupt and I paid him in cash, which he said 'saved his life'. He was also working by that time as a serious actor. I went to see him in John Osborne's *The Entertainer*. He was magnificent and a reviewer said, 'Max Wall makes Olivier look like an amateur.' Max died in 1990, but there is still a Max Wall Society and I have given them permission to distribute *Max Wall Funny Man*, the film I lovingly made, to its members.

From the age of eleven I received a steady education at Holloway grammar school, a ten-minute bus ride from home. My popularity there, I'm sure, had little to do with my parents owning a sweet shop and sweets being rationed until 1953!

After an undistinguished school career, I left at sixteen with a modest six O-levels. I had no idea what I wanted to do, other than becoming a Latin American percussionist. My preferred dream would have been to be a drummer but I could only afford to buy a set of bongos, hence the Latin American bias. Telling my mother that I wanted to be a drummer of any sort would have been an intriguing way to commit suicide, so I did not even suggest it. I had to choose from the post-war Jewish Mother's List: doctor, lawyer, architect, dentist, accountant. This was very brave on my parents' part as none of these professions provided a living prior to qualification and it was going to be a struggle for them to support me. I went down the list, rejecting the suggested professions for no sensible reasons. My mother threatened me with a career in hairdressing if I did not say yes to something, so I agreed to accountancy.

I became an articled clerk to a small firm of chartered accountants in Holborn. The firm consisted of two brothers, and I was their first and only employee. They did not even have a secretary and did all of their own typing. They were very nice men, but the practice was tiny and I received no real training. At a time when a sixteen-year-old school leaver was earning about five pounds a week, my pay was a Dickensian fifteen shillings, seventy-five pence in today's currency. Hard to believe now, this covered my daily fares of one shilling (five pence), and lunch money of two shillings (ten pence). It *was* a long time ago.

I earned the occasional few shillings as a newspaper reporter. Well, more of a tiny cub reporter. The *Daily Express* used to pay for contributions and if I saw a road accident I would call them from the nearest phone box, exaggerate the severity of the incident and get sent a five-shilling postal order. I used to walk about hoping to see a car crash, preferably fatal. Well, I was young and very broke.

As my parents could not afford to subsidise me, I earned my spending money working on Sundays in the street market on Club Row Waste, an extension of the famous Petticoat Lane market in London's East End. Sunday was a big, busy day in the Astoria Candy Stores so after the market I helped out in the

shop. I was no martyr, my parents worked hard and so did I. In
the market I rented a stall from which I sold mainly old confectionery provided by my father's connections. This was before the
concept of sell-by dates, which is just as well, because most of
my stock would have had Roman numerals. True to the Finsbury Park ethos of dealing in hooky gear, a man only known
to me as Cecil delivered my more current stock to our shop in
the middle of the night. I never questioned the source of the
remarkably cheap and invoice-free goods.

In the summer I sold cold drinks from a large, galvanised tin
bath on which I balanced a huge block of ice. The ice, which was
extremely heavy, was schlepped by my only employee, Reg, aka
Chicken. It was a ten-minute walk with the ice water melting
on his back, from an ice factory in not so nearby Wentworth
Street. Chicken was an illiterate meat-market porter, who could
be the subject of his own book as well as many a police charge
sheet. I went to his wedding to a hooker who was pregnant
with twins. Chicken proudly claimed that 'one's mine an' one's
me mate's.'

Market grafting is only romantic to those who have never
done it out of necessity. For me it involved borrowing a vehicle
that may or may not start; loading up at six o'clock on Sunday
morning come rain, shine or flu; and struggling to make about five
pounds, and there's not much romance in that. It was, however,
a most valuable part of my education, and the fiver a week that
I earned kept me in spending money. I could also afford my
first set of wheels, but only two of them, on a Lambretta motor
scooter. It cost about eighty pounds; more money than I had
ever possessed, so I bought it on hire purchase.

After a couple of years I became a multiple retailer, having rented a second stall on Club Row, an adjacent market, the stall manned for me by my pal Colin Levine. The doubling of my business outlet enabled me to double my wheels from two to four and I bought an Italian-made Isetta bubble car. Messerschmitt also made a bubble car but in those days Jewish people did not buy German cars or any cars that were green. The German antipathy was because of the recent war and green was considered to be unlucky.

Market grafters are a fascinating bunch of characters. Some, anecdotally, did so well that when they drove home to their mansions in the country, they swapped their beat-up old vans for their Rolls-Royces. On one occasion, the rarely seen but legendary Red-Faced Sam came to the market to work the 'run-out', a fraudulent auction resulting in some poor punter going home with a box full of swag (worthless junk) for which they had handed over their Christmas Club savings. I saw him avoid repaying a very large and very angry husband of a woman he had conned, who caught him as he was packing up. Sam explained, as well as he could with a docker's hand around his windpipe, that he would love to give a refund but he had 'closed the books for the purchase tax' and would get into trouble with the authorities if he gave the money back today. The docker, suckered by Sam's patter, and clearly ready to join up against the authorities, apologised profusely and agreed to return next week for the promised 'no-questions-asked full refund'. Needless to say, Sam had no plan to return to the market for some years.

Most market grafters had a philosophy that was 'As long as they don't cut my tongue out, I'll earn a living selling *some-*

thing.' I had a huge, warm duffel coat, which I wore for the cold winter mornings. It was really scruffy but even after I was married I kept it in my cupboard for some years until I felt confident that I could earn a living as an accountant. Some market grafters went to jail, some prospered, and one became Alan Sugar.

In 1948, when I was twelve, my brother Roger was born. At that time it was not unusual to have a large gap between children. The threat of war delayed families having children, and they were inclined to wait a few years after the war before starting again. Roger was a gorgeous baby and I loved him to bits. I still do. We were obliged to share a bedroom until I was about eighteen, but I never for one moment resented him. When I was sixteen I ventured up west to the Queensway ice skating rink, sometimes taking the cute four-year-old Roger with me as a pulling prop. It worked, and there I met fourteen-year-old Marsha Bloom, who would be my intermittent girlfriend for some ten years and, ultimately, my wife.

Marsha lived just off the Edgware Road. I called it Paddington but she called it Marylebone. The argument persists to this day but it was undeniably classier than Finsbury Park, and her family was so posh they had fruit on the table when nobody was ill. We were married in 1962 and – more than half a century later – she is still the love of my life.

My father's shop did well with the sweets and cigarettes because of the queue that formed outside of the cinema opposite. In the fifties there was no competition from television and everybody went to the cinema at least once a week. The Astoria was full every evening no matter what was showing, and the lines would form early. Sweets were on ration and had to be weighed up for sale out of seven-pound jars. Rationing required cutting out coupons for each sale, and from the age of eleven I had to work in the shop every evening to deal with the cinema pre-opening rush. I'm sure that I can still pick out a handful of sweets to weigh a quarter of a pound with great accuracy.

On the actual day that sweet rationing ended in 1953, we sold every single sweet in the shop. The shelves were absolutely bare and for some weeks to follow we opened for just an hour a day to sell the little stock my father had managed to find. Unlike now, where concessions are the major money-earner for cinemas, the venue itself did not need the revenue from selling any drinks or snacks. With rationing ended and TV inexorably taking cinema audiences, so the owners looking for more income introduced kiosks selling packaged sweets.

The disappearance of the cinema audience market caused the inevitable demise of the Astoria Candy Stores and in 1954 my father was about to go broke. It was not only our business that was threatened; it was also our home as we lived above the shop. My father was incapable of dealing with this, so aged eighteen, I had to. I went to Uncle Len, my father's brother-in-law, and begged him to help out financially, which he generously did. I went to see the bank manager and persuaded him not to fore-close. This episode took away what little confidence my father had and, at eighteen, I effectively became head of the family. We put a little hairdressing salon on the ground floor behind the shop and, enduring the physical pain from her bad leg, my mother went back to work as a hairdresser. For a while, my father still ran the sweet shop at the front. To accommodate the salon, we lost our bathroom and our only bath was moved to the middle of the kitchen. They say that you should never be ashamed of your own home, but I was acutely embarrassed at the thought of my friends seeing this.

After a couple of years we sold the shop, and my parents opened a proper salon in a parade of shops in nearby Manor House, where we rented a flat in the block above. Still living above the shop, but least I now had my own bedroom, and the bath was in the bathroom. My father – who had been such a lousy hairdresser before the war – now worked alongside my mother and eventually got back a little of his confidence and self-respect.

3. MANNERS MAKETH A MAN BUT A DARK SUIT DOES NOT MAKETH AN ACCOUNTANT

I am still entitled to use the initials FCA – Fellow of the Institute of Chartered Accountants – after my name, although I cannot remember the last time I did so. Each year when it is time to pay the annual subscription, I wonder why I am spending the few hundred pounds that it costs to continue membership. Then I think about how hard it was for me to get the qualification, and pay up.

I found studying for my exams really hard. We were prepared for exams by correspondence courses, which required great self-discipline, which I had heard about but did not have. I was supposed to study for an average of three hours an evening. I would tell my parents that I was going to the public library to study but then spend the time at friends' houses, listening to music or going to a film. At weekends, when not helping in the shop, I spent my evenings at clubs like The Poubelle, Cy Laurie's, the El Toro, the Whisky A Go-Go and the Cage D'or, perfecting my jive and bongo playing. Few of these clubs had licences to sell alcohol, it cost little to get in, and they were mostly rather grotty but I went to them because I loved to dance.

There is an unfair generalisation that accountants are boring. People can be boring no matter what their job is. I have known some famous actors who are really boring off-stage. However, I found that there was no quicker way of stopping the irritatingly chatty person sitting next to me on a plane than answering the inevitable 'and what is it that you do?' with: 'I'm an accountant.' If this did not work, I used to add, 'with the Inland Revenue' ... at which point they would move seats.

My lack of fascination with the structure of consolidated balance sheets meant that I struggled with my accountancy exams. There were intermediate and final exams that had to be passed, with six papers in each of the different subjects. If you failed in one, you had to take all six again. I twice failed one paper in each of the exams, resulting in my taking two years longer than necessary to qualify. For me, the problem of those years was that my life was on hold until I qualified, and there was no certainty that I would do so. I eventually earned my qualification at the end of 1960, and the day that my results came through was the most emotional day of my life. I started my proper grown-up life by becoming engaged to Marsha Bloom, the gorgeous girl that I had first met at the ice rink some ten years before.

4. THE EARLY SIXTIES – QUALIFIED, BUT FOR WHAT?

Whilst I was engaged to Marsha, Cyril Myers, a distant cousin, approached me with an opportunity to operate bingo one evening a week at the Rio cinema on Canvey Island. Showbiz called!

Cyril was an extremely nice guy about the same age as me. With a loan of four hundred pounds from Marsha's stepfather, the lovely Billy Levene, we ventured east to Canvey Island. It's a small mass in the Thames Estuary joined, I do not recall how, to the mainland. Canvey Island in the winter was decidedly lacking in sun-seekers and indeed sun. In the sixties, it was a drab wilderness of caravan parks and miserable stony beaches. The Rio cinema, a local fleapit, was generally patronised by holidaymakers and did not operate in the winter. Bingo was just becoming a big business, so where could we go wrong? Read on and find out.

We had an ambitious marketing campaign consisting of a couple of tiny ads in the local paper and a hand-made sign outside of the cinema. On our first night Cyril and I waited for the rush. Twenty-seven people – mostly Essex ladies with a definite resemblance to Les Dawson in drag – rushed to join the club and we were in business … sort of. I was the bingo caller, an experience which soon eradicated the tiny voice inside me that thought I could entertain in public. I had learned the bingo lingo: 'two fat ladies, eighty-eight', etc, and also decided that the way to build the audience was to tell a few jokes. I can tell you now that Jewish humour does not travel to Canvey Island. Our highest crowd was about sixty and we never made enough to pay the rent.

The law at the time was that you had to be a member of a club for twenty-four hours before you could actually play. This was to avoid the ladies going wild and squandering their sixpences without time to reflect on their folly. We were so short on punters that I let a middle-aged lady in without her having waited the statutory twenty-four hours. She was strangely pedantic. 'So, you are letting me in without my having to wait for the statutory twenty-four hours?' This should have rung a warning bell, but we were so short of members, I just patted her bum in a 'cheeky-chappy' way and waved her through.

The Essex constabulary force had a female sergeant of middle-age who looks like Dot from *EastEnders*. I was charged with offences against the Gaming Act and I had visions of headlines in the popular press along the lines of 'Chartered accountant in bingo scandal' ruining my future chances of a knighthood. In the event, my cousin Cyril, being a gentleman, took the main rap and I was fined five pounds for contravening the Gaming Act. Cyril was fined fifty pounds and that was the end of our bingo empire. Had I not been busted, I am convinced that we could have doubled our miserable attendance to about a miserable hundred and I could today still be calling, 'Number one, Kelly's eye,' to an adoring crowd of elderly ladies in Canvey.

5. HOW GOODMAN MET MYERS AND GOODMAN MYERS & CO., CHARTERED ACCOUNTANTS, WAS BORN

Having had a very poor training at the firm to which I was articled, coupled with my great disinterest in accountancy, I was untrained and fearful of holding down a job. I decided that the best option was to be my own boss so that only me could fire me.

In 1962, Alan Carter, a long-time friend from the ice rink days, had also recently qualified as an accountant, and he introduced me to fellow graduate Ellis Goodman. Ellis had been to public school and wore dark suits, which in my book meant he was a proper accountant. The idea was that the three of us would start up a new accountancy firm. In the event, Alan dropped out and Ellis and I decided to go into business together. Goodman Myers and Co., Chartered Accountants, was thus born.

In April 1962 Marsha and I were married. Marsha's father, Jack Bloom, had divorced her mother many years earlier. He was a very successful antique-silver dealer and made our wedding party a modest bash for three hundred guests at The Dorchester hotel in Park Lane. Most of our friends at the wedding we have kept to this day, and at our thirtieth anniversary I counted eighty people who had been at our big day three decades earlier. We are soon to celebrate our fifty-seventh wedding anniversary and inevitably there will be fewer of the original guests there. Jack and Marsha's other family helped us to buy our first home, a tiny house in Abercorn Place, St John's Wood. Jack was a wonderful and generous man and his support had a very positive effect on my life. He encouraged me to dare and, most importantly, he was someone I felt provided me with a safety net should I ever falter.

Goodman Myers & Co. initially consisted of Ellis, a secretary and myself. Ellis's father – a delightful man called Manny Goodman – was coming to the end of his career as a provider of posters for the film business and we based ourselves at his tiny office in Blenheim Street, just off Bond Street. The offices were on the third floor, and to get to it you had to walk up rickety stairs past a tailor's workshop and Bev's Blenheim Club, a tiny drinking establishment on the second floor. As well as buying a dark suit, I invested in a bowler hat and umbrella in the hope that I would pass as a city gentleman. We had very few clients but Ellis had managed to find some sub-contracting work from a large accountancy firm that he knew. Ellis's clients included Petula Clark, which – with my latent show-business aspirations – made me most jealous.

Soon we developed some clients of our own and were able to take on our first employee, a delightfully eccentric young Indian clerk called Mitra. Mitra came from quite a wealthy family in Delhi and was to go back and face an arranged marriage as soon as he qualified as an accountant. He therefore took a delight in failing his exams, thus ensuring an income from India and a continued pursuit of cricket and English girls. I once found him in the office, eyes closed, doing up and undoing a bra on a modelling bust that he had brought to the office. An explanation? 'Tonight, Mr Myers, I am taking a girl to the cinema and am therefore practising the removal of her brassiere in the dark.'

Mitra had a vivid imagination. He was always late and always had improbable excuses. His best, in his delightful Indian accent, being: 'I was thinking that I had the diabetes. The doctor told me to provide him with a urine sample, which I expressed into the small bottle that he provided. I left this in the toilet of the house I am sharing with some English girls. Later on, unbeknown to me, one of the girls had left her own urine sample in a bottle in the same lavatory and by some mistake I was taking her bottle instead of mine to the doctor. This morning the doctor asked me to urgently attend his premises where he told me, "Mitra, you do not have the diabetes but you are pregnant." That is why I am late.'

On another occasion I was sitting with one of our few clients, reviewing some accounts that Mitra had prepared. Having a small query, I called for Mitra to come into my office. This he did, immediately dropping to his knees, hands held protectively over his head, imploring, 'Please don't beat me, Mr Myers. Please don't beat me.' I have many Mitra stories but they really don't work without his fabulous accent. He eventually left us, before I did him actual bodily harm, and I often wonder if he ever returned to India to face his arranged bride.

Ellis ran the practice. There was no fight over this as he was much better at running a business than me, and I knew it.

In later years, had he run all of my businesses, he would have prevented me making many of the big mistakes that I made left to my own devices. Ellis went on to be an extremely successful businessman. He now lives in the USA, but we are still close friends and Marsha and I have enormous affection for him and for Gillian, his wife.

6. MICKIE MOST – MY PARACHUTE INTO THE HEART OF THE LONDON MUSIC SCENE

I t was my relationship with legendary record producer Mickie Most that got me into the music business. In 1964 my accountancy partner, Ellis Goodman, had a chance meeting on an airplane with a man who wanted to back Mickie Most in opening a record company to be called Warrior Records. The man was looking for an accountant to represent the company and Goodman Myers & Co. was duly appointed.

We were by no means a successful firm yet and we welcomed a new client. Aware of my personal passion for music – I had actually bought 'The House of the Rising Sun', the hit that Mickie produced for The Animals – Ellis agreed that I should take over the account.

As they say, the devil is in the details, and the Warrior Records deal was far from done. It quickly became apparent that Mickie and the potential investor had different views on how the venture should be run and Mickie decided not to go ahead

with the deal. A court case ensued, and the investor understandably thought that we would support him, but I really thought
that Mickie – who had no business experience at that time –
had been badly misled by his would-be investor, and Ellis and
I decided to support him. It would be hard to resist accusations
that ethically we had done the wrong thing. It is said that there
are three phases in a businessman's life. 'Dishons' is the time
when you do things that you would rather not, in order to get
on; 'Hons' is when you want to be regarded as an honourable,
'his word is his bond' type; and 'Honours' is when you want to
be recognised with some glory – be it a knighthood or being
enrolled in the Rock'n'Roll Hall of Fame. Backing Mickie Most
against the man who brought him to us was definitely in the first
category, but without Mickie I would not have had the entrée to
the music business that has given me a career.

Born Michael Peter Hayes to a military family in Aldershot,
Mickie Most had left school at fifteen. As a wannabe pop star,
he worked as a singing waiter at the influential 2i's coffee bar
in London's Soho, where, incidentally, Peter Grant – the future
Led Zeppelin manager – was working as a bouncer. Mickie, with
Alex Murray as his partner, had an undistinguished career as a
part of the pop duo The Most Brothers. In 1959 he followed his
wife Christina back to her native South Africa and had some
local success as Mickie Most and the Playboys. He came back
to London in 1962, where he briefly tried his luck again as a
singer, before deciding that there was a better future for him as
a record producer.

The producer's function was to choose a song, outline the
arrangement of the music, and then supervise all aspects of the

recording in the studio. A great producer is like a master chef. He just knows how to mix the ingredients, and what needs adding to season the dish. Most importantly he knows when to stop adding more. In 1964 the producer was, in most cases, pivotal to the making of a hit record. With the right song, a skilled producer in a well-equipped studio could make a great record out of the most limited of singing talents. Tamla Motown famously made great tracks of great songs and then decided which artist got to sing on the track. Phil Spector with his wall of sound – arguably the most influential record producer of his era – could have had his hits with almost any artist he chose to work with. Of course, there were exceptions to this very general rule. The Beatles had unlimited talent but even so, it was George Martin, their producer, who fashioned them into a hit factory.

Mickie's first successes as a producer came in 1964, with The Animals. 'Baby Let Me Take You Home' was released in April, followed by 'The House of the Rising Sun' in October. It was just after this release that Mickie came into my life.

It was a great time to be involved in the music business, which was going through a worldwide revolution starting out in England, and I was lucky enough to be involved at the heart of it. Popular music had changed in the fifties. And not just the music, but also the way the public heard it and bought it. The forties were the golden age of radio and being a radio star was an accolade second only to being a film star. The public bought records that caught the magic of an artist who had established themselves via film, radio or personal appearances. Frank Sinatra's bobbysoxers, the first of the hysterical girl fans, were created by his personal appearances and radio shows with the Tommy

Dorsey Band. Teenagers did not exist as a defined cultural group until the mid-fifties, when both in America and in the UK a very few radio programmes started catering to the younger audience. This was no doubt due to the fact that sponsors were recognising that teenagers had spending power and spots on their faces that needed clearing up. When teen-oriented programmes were on air, kids would be glued to the radio. Suddenly a recording by a relatively unknown artist could be a hit. Records by Frankie Laine, Johnny Ray, Eddie Fisher, Al Martino and their contemporaries were instant hits with kids, mainly young girls. The first chart published in the UK was in 1952 and the first No. 1 was Al Martino's 'Here In My Heart', a big romantic ballad.

Young boys were to find their own idols when rock'n'roll came in a few years later, pioneered by Bill Haley's 'Rock Around The Clock' in 1954 and exploded when Elvis released 'Heartbreak Hotel' in 1956. The British soon created idols of their own with Cliff Richard, Marty Wilde, Billy Fury and many others, nearly all pale imitations of the American pioneers. Radio exposure now made the record king. A star could be created by radio play alone, without the artist needing to rely on personal appearances or film.

A record producer was to a record what a director was to a film. In the world of early sixties' pop music, the independent producer picked the song, usually written by someone other than the artist, supervised the musical arrangements and the sound created in the studio. A good producer listened to a song that would be presented to him with just a piano or guitar accompaniment and had a vision of what it would sound like with a change of tempo or a specific arrangement. Most importantly the producer crafted a record that *the teen public would want.*

Previously, the best recording studios were owned by major record companies. The growth of the independent producer encouraged a proliferation of independent studios. The creative power of the major companies was being eroded, although they still controlled manufacturing and distribution as well as the all-important financial power to pay for recordings and marketing. Staff A&R men – their initials showing they were responsible for Artists & Repertoire – were employed full time by the major record companies. They were usually under-salaried and undervalued.

I knew Norrie Paramor, who was a staff producer at EMI records. He produced, amongst many other artists, Cliff Richard, Frank Ifield, Helen Shapiro and Ruby Murray; all top stars of their time. He had produced more No. 1 singers than any other producer of the day working in England. He once told me that, having heard that American producers got a royalty on sales, he approached Joseph Lockwood – the feared and respected head of EMI Records – and timidly suggested that, like his American counterparts, maybe he himself could get some small royalty on sales of the records that he had produced. He had heard that the going rate for top US producers was 2 per cent of the retail-selling price of a record so, not wishing to push it, he suggested getting a half per cent. Lockwood said that he would consider it. Norrie was later summoned back to the great man's office.

According to Norrie, Lockwood said, 'Paramor, we have run the figures. Do you realise how much money we would have paid you at a royalty of half a per cent?'

'No,' replied the frightened Norrie.

'Well,' thundered Joseph, 'it comes to over two hundred thousand pounds!'

Norrie told me that he was so appalled at the thought that he, a mere employee, could earn that sort of money, he had apologised profusely for his temerity and settled for a raise of a thousand pounds a year and a new Ford Cortina. Even George Martin is on record saying that he was on a salary of two thousand pounds a year from EMI when he started producing The Beatles – making millions for the company.

I could see that all of this was going to change and I was determined to be one of the people who helped make it happen.

Mickie was also producing Herman's Hermits, who were signed to EMI, and The Nashville Teens, who were with Decca. Although he had had some success, his deals were poor and he was not in a position to pay us any fees for the work we would have to do as his accountants. I was reluctant to let him go as a client, as I really believed in his talent, and I had a passion for the music that he was making. I suggested that instead of fees, we would take a 10 per cent stake in all of the companies, and Mickie happily agreed. We set up three companies: Rak Records, Rak Music Publishing and Rak Management. Peter Grant, his old friend from the 2i's, had worked for a variety of people as a road manager and tour manger, but he was currently unemployed and Mickie asked him to head-up Rak Management. Peter was a huge figure of a man who, long before he became the legendary manager of Led Zeppelin, tried his hand as a film extra and professional wrestler.

Mickie's younger brother Dave would take care of the publishing interest, having had no previous experience – but there was no school for music-business executives and the independent side of the business was so new that anybody could get a shot at getting involved. Mike Jeffery, who managed The Animals and later on Jimi Hendrix, was running a coffee bar and some music venues when he signed The Animals for management. The only company that had activity from day one was Rak Records, because Mickie was already recording artists. I was now unquestionably involved in the music business and was really enjoying my life.

State-of-the-art recording studios of today can record voices and instruments on a virtually unlimited number of different tracks and have the ability to infinitely vary the sound on each of those tracks in hundreds of ways and even auto-correct a singer's out-of-tune note. This technology was not available to Mickie, who used to record at the Kingsway Recording Studios in Holborn. Kingsway had a very basic four-track desk and this meant that there were only four separate mics available during recordings. In simple terms, he only had the ability to add a little echo and reverb. Sessions were booked in three-hour blocks and Mickie could make a hit single *and* a B-side in this limited time. 'The House of the Rising Sun', which sold millions, probably cost under two thousand pounds to record and mix. Today, many artists spend hundreds of hours and hundreds of thousands of pounds to make a record. Eventually Mickie opened his own recording studio in St John's Wood, and it is still run by his widow Chris today.

Mickie and Chris became close friends with me and my wife Marsha. We went on holiday together and frequented the trendy restaurants of the day. The most 'hip' was the trattoria Terrazza, where it was essential to be seated in the back room along with the likes of Michael and Shakira Caine, Roger and Luisa Moore and many stars of stage, screen and rehab clinics. The funny thing is that the back room was a late addition to the already fashionable restaurant, and Mario, the owner, once confided in me that he thought that nobody would want to sit in the space that was windowless and nothing particularly special. Alvaro, the manager, who later went on to open his own eponymous restaurant, worked the magic to make it desirable. Whenever anyone phoned for a reservation, he would say, 'Of course, but I regret I do not have a table in the back room.' In no time at all, being seen in the front room was unthinkable. This was a reminder of how easily we the public can be manipulated to be 'where it's at'.

Our most frequented clubs were Tramps, which is still going, and the Ad Lib, and it was a great thrill to hear the DJ play a record that Mickie had produced. There were lots of clubs where musicians hung out, like the Bag O' Nails and The Cromwellian, where you would often see a Beatle drinking with a Rolling Stone.

The legendary Marquee Club in Oxford Street, which moved to Wardour Street in 1964, was the venue to see great bands. the Stones, The Yardbirds, Jimi Hendrix, The Who, Led Zeppelin and other big bands of the sixties and seventies all played there and it was a hangout for A&R men who were looking for new talent.

One of my earliest memories of being with Mickie was on a flight to New York with Andrew Oldham. Mickie and Andrew commandeered a spare wheelchair and blanket before boarding the flight. Andrew sat on the chair, tucked his knees under his legs and covered them with the blanket. In those days, airplanes were always boarded by a flight of stairs and Andrew allowed himself to be carried up the stairs by two struggling stewards. Once on the plane, he jumped up, thanked the stewards for their help and walked jauntily down the aisle towards our seats. I was convinced that we would be thrown off the plane. We were not, but for me, it got worse. We were sitting in first class, and in those days you could smoke at the front of each cabin. Andrew produced a joint which he lit and shared with Mickie. There were not many passengers in our cabin and most had chosen to sit at the rear. I looked nervously towards to the passengers at the back, hoping that the plane's air-conditioning did not allow the smoke to drift backwards. There was only one other passenger in our row: an attractive young woman of about twenty. Mickie offered her a toke which she declined with a smile. I declined too – not out of morality, but out of fear. Before they finished the joint, he once again offered it to the young lady, who said 'I'd better not, my father's the chief pilot.' Uncharacteristically, I took advantage of the free bar to recover my nerves.

Early in 1965, Mickie, Chris, Marsha and I went to a party at composer Lionel Bart's house in Seymour Walk, off the Fulham Road. The house was wonderfully over the top, as you would expect from the outrageously profligate Lionel. There were bowls of joints everywhere and the finest of wines were served in abundance. We once met Lionel in Positano, where he had taken a suite and several rooms at The Splendido for the entire summer. The hotel was, and still is, one of the most expensive hotels in Italy, but Lionel had reserved one room for himself, one for his boyfriend and the other rooms for friends passing through.

Lionel was delightfully crazy. On one of the several occasions that his mate Liza Minnelli got married, he hired a private jet and took his entire crowd to the wedding in New York. UK taxation was high in the sixties and none of Lionel's wild extravagancies were tax-deductible. Even for the man who had written many hit songs including 'Living Doll' for Cliff Richard and *Oliver!* – the greatest ever British musical – he was spending way too much money.

Lionel was a lovely man and in the early seventies I would try to extract him from his self-created financial quagmire. He had already sold all of his future royalties, including his interest in *Oliver!* and he was being pursued by the tax man and many creditors. American Express ('Membership is a privilege') were particularly intransigent and, after exploring all other possibilities, I told him that he had no choice other than to declare himself bankrupt. Apart from the financial implications, this was a terrible blow to his ego and it was one of the most difficult conversations I've ever had.

Years later he came to our home for dinner so drunk and/or stoned that he bent his fork leaning on it as he fell asleep at the table. When he left he said that he wanted to go to a club to 'find some pretty company' and asked me if I would kindly arrange a car to take him. Of course, I said yes and, concerned that Lionel would not find his way home, told the driver to 'keep the car at Mr Bart's disposal for as long as he needs and charge the cost to my account.' Lionel kept the car throughout the night, the following day and the following night. It was impossible to be angry with Lionel. Marsha and I were both really fond of him and we were delighted when Cameron Mackintosh – a mensch if ever there were one – as a condition of producing a highly successful revival of *Oliver!* at The London Palladium, negotiated that, during his lifetime, Lionel would have his income back from the production.

We were at the first-night party and Lionel came over to me and said that he couldn't remember if he should love or hate me. They say if you can remember the sixties you weren't there. I assured him that he had no reason to hate me. Even though *Oliver!* was once again hailed as a huge hit for Lionel, he was not working productively and once again I tried to help him. Every composer wanted to collaborate with him, but he did not want to actually work. Don Black, the Tony and Olivier award-winning lyricist, told me that whenever they met for a work session Lionel suggested that they first had a cup of tea. He would then reminisce about the old days until the planned time was up. Don reckons that Lionel was afraid that his talent had deserted him and was frightened to put his head back above the parapet.

7. DON ARDEN

My first major music-business meeting involving Mickie Most was in 1964, with the legendary Don Arden, father of the now famous Sharon Osbourne. Don, who in his early days had been a singer/impersonator working the variety circuit, was by then a very successful promoter. He brought over Chuck Berry, Gene Vincent and other big US acts to the UK, and had recently promoted a UK tour by The Animals. Some months later, he had still not paid them the six thousand pounds that they had earned. The Animals' manager, Mike Jeffery, was in America at the time and asked Mickie if he could persuade Arden to pay up.

I wanted to show Mickie the great value of my accountancy acumen and suggested a meeting with Arden. Mickie explained to me that in the course of a dispute with the Bee Gees' manager Robert Stigwood, Don had dangled Mr Stigwood out of a window by his ankles. In Mickie's opinion the only thing that Don understood was violence, and this was something never covered in the exams to be a chartered accountant. Mickie had a plan B. He asked the mountainous Peter Grant, who had worked for Don as a tour manager, to come to the meeting. Being very confident the law was on our side in this issue, I was against bringing along a 'heavy', but as it was very early days in my relationship with Mickie, I went along with it.

I put my accountant's dark suit on for the meeting. Don had a posh office in Mayfair and as we waited, I heard Don screaming down the phone in his American gangster accent, threatening to have someone's legs broken. I thought that the accent was rather poor but smiled weakly as we were shown into his office. Don knew why we were there and without the usual formalities a screaming match kicked off between Don on one side and Mickie and Peter on the other. Even in my dark suit I was totally ignored but eventually plucked up the courage to nervously intervene. After all these years, the details of the meeting have stayed in my mind.

Me: 'Excuse me, Mr Arden.'

Don: 'Who are you?'

Me: 'I am Laurence Myers and I formally represent The Animals in this matter.' (Thus far, I was quite impressed with myself.)

Don: 'Oh, yeah?'

Me: 'Would you like to see my authority?'

Don: (To Mickie) 'Who is this schmuck?'

Mickie: 'He's their accountant.'

Don: (Looked at me as if I were an accountant.) 'So, Accountant, what do you want?'

Me: 'You owe my clients money arising from their last tour.'

Don: 'Do I now?'

Me: (Smugly I gave Don a pristine copy of the accounting I had prepared.) 'Yes, you do, Mr Arden. Six thousand three hundred and seventy pounds.'

Don: 'So?'

Me: 'So you have to pay them.' (I looked at Mickie, sure that he
was impressed.)

Don: (Without a glance, he tossed my beautifully presented
accounts into his bin. There was a pause.) 'Fuck off.'

This was not in my script. Pulling myself up in my chair and
pausing for dramatic effect, I said, 'Mr Arden, if you do not pay,
I … [another pause for dramatic effect] am going to issue a writ
on behalf of my clients.' I gave a self-satisfied 'get out of that'
nod and sat back in my chair.

Don replied, raising his eyebrows, 'Are you now?' He picked
up his bin, walked over to a window – no doubt the same one
as Mr Stigwood had been dangled from – and threw out the
basket. 'Listen, you little pisher,' Don growled. 'Get out of my
fucking office or you're next out of that window.'

I paused, before offering a weak, 'You'll be hearing from
our solicitors' and hurried out of the office. Mickie followed
me, laughing. Peter Grant stayed behind to execute plan B –
smashing up the office – but, to my knowledge, Don never paid
The Animals.

Later on, Don and I became friendly to the point that one
day he felt impelled to call me to warn that he was very sorry, he
liked me very much but he was going to have to give my brother-in-law Larry Levene 'a good smacking'. Larry had financed
the making of a record by an artist who had been through Don's
hands. The disgruntled artist had called the B-side 'Take the
Money and Run', and had credited the writer as being D. Arden.
Don, who was surprisingly sensitive for a man who hung rivals

out of windows, perceived this as a slight, hence his wish to reward Larry with a smacking. Larry had the good sense to call Don and resolve the issue without being smacked.

8. MIDEM – THE MUSIC INDUSTRY ANNUAL GET-TOGETHER

Midem, standing for *Marché International du Disques et de l'Edition Musicale*, is a music business market/trade show that takes place in Cannes, France. It has been going for fifty years and I went to the very first one and didn't miss a year until the eighties. We had a home in Cannes and by the seventies the Midem party that Marsha and I hosted was a very much sought-after invitation.

Before the demise of the independent music publisher, owners of music copyrights met at Midem to buy and sell territorial rights. There are two copyrights in a record. One is in the written words and music of the song and is owned by the music publisher, and a separate copyright is in the recording, owned by whoever paid for the session. If you own the music copyright in the song of, say, 'White Christmas' (you should be so lucky) you'd never have to work again. Every time the song was used on a record, or played in public by anybody, you would be paid a royalty. If you owned the Bing Crosby recording of 'White

Christmas', you would earn only from the sales of that record, from the public performance or use of that particular record, maybe in a film or in a commercial.

Midem used to be full of people who had owned a record master or a publishing copyright, licensing their product on a territory-by-territory basis. Now Midem is attended by tens of thousands of people and takes over the whole of Cannes. The focus is the Palais des Festivals where participants take small booths as offices. The first Midem in 1967 was attended by about five hundred people. The English representatives were Mitch Murray and Peter Callander, very successful songwriters in their own right. They had invited Mickie Most – being an important producer and user of songs – as an honoured guest. Marsha and I together with Chris Most went along for the ride. The rooms at the Martinez hotel had been turned into offices and small independent music publishers from all over the world scurried from room to room, buying and selling copyrights. This was before the Common Market and it was possible to own the rights to a song in any European country. Now it is mainly populated by the large companies who use the date to arrange their own international conferences, and there are more lawyers than what we used to call 'record men'.

The gathering was closed by a gala concert featuring Nina Simone, Sonny and Cher and a young singer called Oliver, one of the early one-hit wonders. Oliver's hit was 'Good Morning Starshine' from the musical *Hair*. The record was produced by the proudly gay Bob Crewe. Oliver had a wonderful voice but was not very charismatic. He was, however, very pretty. I'm just saying …

Miss Simone took the opportunity to rant to her audience about how the industry, i.e. most of the people in the room that night, had cheated artists in general, black artists in particular, and very specifically, herself. She was not entirely wrong in her assertions and it must have been an irresistible opportunity for her to vent her spleen, but it sort of killed her performance.

After the concert there was a big party and everybody including Sonny and Cher were on the dance floor. As was the style at the time, everybody danced with everybody else and I had my few minutes of bliss dancing with Cher. I think it is what inspired her to write 'Little Man'.

In 1973 Stig Anderson, a Swedish publisher, was working Midem, trying to place his recording of the Swedish entrant to the upcoming Eurovision Song Contest. It was a time when Scandinavian countries usually scored '*nil points*' in the contest and he only managed to get deals in a few territories because some small record companies were prepared to take on this certain loser as a favour to Stig, who was a well-liked and much respected individual. Also 'Waterloo' sounded like a terrible title for a pop song. Cut to 1976, three years later, and all of the territorial deals for Abba were up. I was chatting with Bob Summer – the worldwide head of RCA Records – when he excused himself: 'Sorry, Laurence, I have to run over to the Carlton hotel. It's nearly three o'clock. Stig now wants to make a worldwide deal and has told the head of every major record company that he will be available at three. I have to go and line up with the others outside his suite.' I guess that Bob was not early enough in the queue because Stig signed Abba to Polydor.

At one Midem, Marsha and I found ourselves playing late-night poker with a bunch of guys including Mike Stoller who – with lyricist partner Jerry Leiber – were arguably the most successful writers of the era. They wrote many of Elvis's early rock'n'roll hits including 'Jailhouse Rock', 'Hound Dog' and 'King Creole' as well as brilliant songs like 'Is that All There Is' for Peggy Lee. They also co-wrote 'Pearl's A Singer', one of my favourite songs of all time, for Elkie Brooks.

Mike and I became business friends and I often met with him and Jerry when I was in LA. We usually met at Nate'n Al's, a very famous deli in Beverley Hills. There, nobody had a prestigious table and the waiters were famously indifferent to celebrities who ate there. Mike always teased Jerry for parking in the public car park thus saving a few dollars, but they were as close as brothers, and for a songwriter groupie like me spending time with them was a joy. At one point, Mike's wife Corky, herself an accomplished musician, wanted to write a musical about lyricist Al Dubin. He and his composing partner Harry Warren wrote many of the songs for the hit musicals of the forties, including the outstanding *42nd Street*. Al Dubin was an alcoholic and he died, unrecognised, in a gutter when he was fifty-four, broke and forgotten. I thought that it was a brilliant project and offered to get involved but, for a number of reasons, it never made it to the stage.

For me the most amazing thing about our friendship was going to Mike's home where he and Jerry would pitch their latest compositions to see if they would be of interest to any of the artists that I was involved with in the UK. *Jerry Leiber* with *Mike Stoller* at the piano, singing and playing their songs, hoping they would please *me*. It was like me auditioning Shakespeare for a new play.

9. ALLEN KLEIN – THE MAN WHO CHANGED THE BUSINESS OF THE BUSINESS

Allen Klein, who was to be a huge influence in my business life, also first became involved in the music business as an accountant. He was studying for his qualification while working for Fenton & Co., a New York firm that specialised in the entertainment business. He was not a disciplined employee and was soon fired for always being late. He did not bother to qualify but started his own small accountancy firm with a friend who had the necessary licence for the firm to able to practise.

Allen earned a meagre living from accountancy for clients recommended by Don Kirshner, a close friend who was working for a small publishing firm in the Brill Building. This was the fabulous art deco office block on the corner of Broadway and 49th Street in Manhattan. The Brill Building was crammed full of music publishers and songwriters in small offices and studios; a one-stop-shop for anyone looking for a hit song. Don became one of the most successful music publishers of his era. He discovered and nurtured Gerry Goffin and Carole King, Barry Mann and Cynthia Weil, Neil Sedaka, Neil Diamond and Phil Spector. In the sixties, he was given the task of finding songs for *The Monkees* and called upon his old Brill Building writers to provide some hits. He was in no small way responsible for the incredible success of that show. Later on he did the same thing for *The Archies*, an animated TV series. It was for good reason that Don was known as the 'the man with the golden ear'. Don features heavily in *Beautiful*, the wonderful musical about Carole King. I enjoyed it hugely, although it was strange seeing somebody I knew being portrayed on stage. I remember being halfway through a New York call from him when he said, 'Hang on, Laurence,' the line going dead for a minute, 'I'm going through a tunnel.' This was 1964 and he was calling me *from his car*, a truly astonishing thing more than fifty years ago.

Both Allen and I used similar methods to audit record companies on behalf of our clients. I would start with the vinyl pressing orders. Having verified the number of records actually manufactured, I then established the difference between that number and the number on which they had actually paid royalties to the client, which was always considerably less. The record company would ascribe the difference to promotional copies, reserves for returns, discounts to retailers and other semi-fictional explanations, but in truth some of the major record companies institutionally cheated.

Allen also invariably found unpaid monies for his artists. His pitch to attract prospective clients never changed (except for the figures). He would say, 'I can get you a hundred thousand dollars.' Even if he didn't get that amount he always got them something substantial for which they were quite rightly grateful. Later, he refined this approach and the promised amount became considerably bigger.

This is how Allen got to Mickie and came into my life. Sam Cooke – whom Allen would later manage – was signed to RCA records. When The Beatles were at their most successful, Allen asked Joe D'Imperio, his contact at RCA, what he would pay The Beatles if they switched to his label from EMI. 'A million dollars advance and a royalty of 10 per cent' was the answer. Allen then contrived a meeting with Brian Epstein, The Beatles' long-time manager, and said: 'I can get you two million dollars' (he thought it was more impressive and figured that RCA would go for it if pressed) 'and a royalty of 10 per cent'. Brian had signed The Beatles and all of his other acts to EMI and, thanking Allen for the offer, said that he would stay loyal to EMI. They were paying The Beatles one old penny per single sold – about one-sixth of the payment Allen was offering, but Brian was not interested.

Allen's thinking was simple, but genius. If you asked a record company what they would pay an artist who was now successful on a rival company's label, the answer would of course be a huge amount. It was like betting on a horse when the race was finished. If you asked them what they paid their own newly signed and unproven artist, the answer would be very different.

I did not know Brian Epstein well but at a meeting we had some years later when I was trying to get his artists to record my writer's songs, he confided in me that Allen was not someone that he would want to do business with. Brian was the most charming man but did not pursue my offer to provide him with songs from my songwriters, so maybe he didn't want to do business with me either.

In September 1964, Mike Jeffery, the manager of The Animals, was in New York meeting with top agent Jerry Brandt about possible work for the group. Jerry was a business friend of Allen, and introduced him to Mike. Through Mike, Allen learned that Mickie Most produced The Animals and that Mickie was a hot producer. The Dave Clark Five were going to appear in *Get Yourself a Girl* with Nancy Sinatra. Featuring in a Hollywood movie was something that no other contemporary British act had ever achieved, and this impressed Mike no end. Allen – with no basis of truth whatsoever – told Mike that he could get The Animals into an MGM movie and that they would be paid ten thousand dollars for the day's work. Mike was definitely impressed and in return agreed to introduce Allen to Mickie.

Allen Klein arrived in London and asked Mickie and me to meet him at the Grosvenor House, a swanky hotel on Park Lane. His reason for asking us to go to where he was staying was that he had sent his clothes to the laundry. It sounded a bit strange, but so what. At the appointed time, the door to Allen's impressive suite was opened by his wife Betty: a petite, pretty brunette. She ushered us into the suite's parlour, where Allen sat wearing a bathrobe and holding a pipe. Allen was in his early thirties, and even with the pipe looked younger than I had expected for a guy who was powerful enough to get pop artists into movies. The pipe was not alight, and when we became closer he confessed that it was just a prop. Allen thought it made him look wise and he could suck on it if he needed a moment to think before answering.

He did not get up but said, 'Hi. Would you like some tea?'

We said, 'Yes, please', and exchanged pleasantries until room service delivered the refreshments. Allen gave the waiter a stack of silver coins from a row of such stacks that he had lined up on a table beside his chair. It was an obviously over-generous tip and I think that we were supposed to be impressed, but we were not. Betty left the room after serving the tea and Allen said, 'Mickie, I can get you a million dollars.' Now we were impressed.

What followed was, for me, a master class in the intricacies of the record industry. Allen knew the cost of every aspect of the manufacture and distribution of records. In 1964 the retail price of a single was six shillings and four pence, about thirty pence in today's money. The cost of manufacture was maybe five old pennies. Even taking into account the retailer's margin, royalties for music copyright and the cost of physical distribution, the record company's profit margin was about fifteen old pennies; they could easily afford to pay artists *and* producers much more than the few pennies they did. As mentioned above, *The Beatles* were being paid *one* old penny per record, and even this was subject to arcane deductions. Allen made us realise what huge potential power a successful artist had.

Mickie's deals for The Animals and Herman's Hermits were with EMI. Allen offered to renegotiate the deals so that Mickie would be guaranteed that million dollars for future productions. During the conversation it became clear that Allen had decided that I was the key to Mickie agreeing to take him on and he gradually switched his sales pitch from Mickie to me. We said little as he talked in thousands and millions and I told him that we would think about his million-dollar proposition. We thanked him for the tea and left.

Once outside the door, we practically fell about laughing at the thought of Mickie getting a million dollars, a sum equal to approximately ten million dollars today. Mickie was doing well, with an income measured in the tens of thousands, not millions. He lived in a small suburban house in Wembley, probably worth about four thousand pounds. I was drawing twenty-five pounds a week from my practice and gave Marsha eight pounds a week for housekeeping. The average wage was less than one thousand pounds a year and you could buy a nice family house in Chelsea or Hampstead for less than fifteen thousand pounds, so a million pounds was a *lot* of money to both of us.

In the 1960s, while getting a record deal was big, getting a deal with EMI – the leading record company in the UK – was huge. They had artists like Gerry and The Pacemakers, Helen Shapiro, Billy J Cramer, the Dave Clark Five and, of course, The Beatles. In those days, EMI presented artists with a standard contract that was *printed*, thus discouraging thoughts of changing it. To many, EMI was regarded as a major institution. Nobody tried to change their printed insurance policy with Prudential or the printed conditions of a Barclays Bank overdraft. Naive artists and equally naive advisors just checked the blank spaces in EMI's printed contracts, where the basic royalty rate was inserted, and artists eagerly signed the forms.

Not only were the basic royalty rates very low, but the small print in the contracts reduced them even further. Royalties were paid on 90 per cent of sales, because historically records had once been made from very breakable shellac, and there was an allowance made for broken records. The contracts were not changed when records began to be manufactured with more durable vinyl. Also, royalties in overseas sales were halved – an echo of music-publishing practice. No royalties were paid on stocks of records sold after they were deleted from the current catalogue … and so it went on. All recording costs were deducted out of the pitiful royalties that were paid, even if the record companies used their in-house studios. An artist had to sell an awful lot of records to get a meaningful cheque. Later on I realised that the value of a hit artist had an ever-greater benefit to a record company than the immediate profit. In the sixties, a large proportion of sales were through independent record shops. Record companies had sales reps who called on the shops on a regular basis and if the salesman had a hit record, it was easier to persuade the owner to take other records that were not such certain sellers. The shop owners had to settle their accounts if they wanted new releases, so a hit artist got the record company's bills paid *and* attracted other artists to the label.

Mickie believed that Allen was a bit of a joke, making ridiculous promises that he could not fulfil, but I had been impressed by his knowledge and his lack of fear in taking on 'the big boys'. I returned to Grosvenor House to meet Allen again. This time he was dressed and had dropped the pipe prop. He explained more about the power of artists. At that time EMI did not have their own company in the USA. They licensed their product to MGM Records, a subsidiary of MGM Films. 'The Animals and Herman's Hermits are the only two artists MGM have that sell any records. You're keeping MGM Records alive.' It sounded ludicrous. MGM! MGM who made all of those musicals that

I used to go to watch at the Astoria cinema opposite my dad's sweetshop. It was unbelievable.

By now I could see that confronting EMI with the knowledge of their chicanery would certainly get their attention. However, as I reminded Allen, Mickie had entered into binding agreements with EMI, which they had no legal obligation to change. This did not seem to be of any concern to Allen at all. He offered to take nothing from any deal made for Mickie if he did not get him the million dollars, and a 20 per cent commission if he did. I told him that I would not permit Mickie to enter into any written agreement at this stage, and that I would have to attend all meetings.

I told Mickie that Allen had agreed to a no-win-no-fee deal, and that I would be at all the relevant meetings. Mickie agreed that Allen should go ahead.

I wanted to know Allen better. He was a fascinating man, clearly extremely bright, and his analysis of the music business made absolute sense to me. I invited him and his wife Betty to dinner at our home. Marsha cooked a great meal and the four of us got on extremely well. We laughed a lot and Allen and I found some common ground in our upbringing. We were both from very modest Jewish family backgrounds and had found our way into the music business via accountancy, but our childhoods were very different. My brother Roger and I were brought up by loving parents, and our financial circumstances were no different from our friends' and did not seem to us to be a hardship. Allen was one of four children. His mother had died when he was nine months old, his father could not cope with a baby and Allen, aged barely a year, was sent to live with his grandparents. When

he was four he and his sister Naomi went to Newark's Hebrew
Orphanage and Sheltering Home for five years, until their father
remarried and was able to take them back. Understandably, this
experience would have a lasting effect on Allen and I believe it
was the breeding ground for his exceptional drive and ambition.

We definitely struck a bond and the next day Allen called
to thank us for dinner and said that the four of us should go
to dinner. 'Your town, you choose a restaurant.' Marsha's father,
Jack Bloom, used to take us to Les Ambassadeurs, a very expensive members' dining club off Park Lane, where they had dinner
dancing (it *was* fifty years ago). The club was housed in what
used to be the home of a Rothschild and it reeked of elegance.
If I wanted to impress Allen, and I did, this would do it. I asked
Jack to arrange a booking at Les A. Always keen to advance my
business career, he promised a great table and generously offered
to charge the bill to his account. I declined, explaining that the
Kleins were reciprocating our invitation to dinner at our home
and therefore would pay for the evening.

On the way to the restaurant, Marsha made me promise
not to pick up the bill. 'He's the rich guy with his suite at the
Grosvenor House and it was his idea that we go to dinner. We
have entertained him at our home and obviously it's his place to
pay for us. Don't you be a big shot, we can't afford it.' I promised
not to pay.

Meanwhile, Betty was having a similar conversation with
Allen. She had made enquiries about Les A and had been told
it was the most expensive restaurant in London. She was not
sure that Allen had enough money to pay for their suite at the
Grosvenor House and they certainly couldn't afford dinner for

four at Les A. 'The Myers wouldn't be so bad-mannered as to choose the most expensive restaurant in town and expect us to pay. Don't be a big shot, we can't afford it.' Allen promised not to pay.

As arranged by Jack, we were ushered into the restaurant by William, Les A's famous maître d' who, no doubt on Jack's instructions, fussed over us and seated us at the number one table by the dance floor. Once again we had a fun time together, and when the meal was finished and it was time to call for the bill Marsha was furiously kicking me under the table to make sure that I did not call for the bill. On the other side of the table Betty was similarly abusing Allen's knee. There was an embarrassing few moments while I carefully avoided the waiter's eye.

Suddenly Betty said, 'Allen, let's dance.' Allen hated dancing but before he could protest, she dragged him away. Not sure what to do, I looked at Marsha.

'Don't you dare call for the bill,' she said with wifely authority.

'Right,' said I. 'I'm going for a pee.'

Thinking how clever I was to have outwitted Allen, I delayed my return until I could hear the song finish, waited for a few minutes to give Allen a chance to return to the table and call for the bill, then sauntered back to our table. But no. The band had started a new song and Allen and Betty were *still* dancing. The waiter rushed over to pull out my chair and I had no alternative other than to ask for the bill. Betty told me that she looked over Allen's shoulder, saw me pay, and gave Allen permission to stop dancing. On the way home Marsha asked me why the hell I paid, to which I replied. 'Allen could dance all night, how long could I pee for?'

This was a story that we all told time and time again whenever we were asked about how we first became friends. It was
also the story I told when I spoke at Allen's funeral in July 2009.
We had been friends for forty-five years and I owed him much.
Allen's last few years were cursed with Alzheimer's and it was
heartbreaking for me to see this giant of a personality mentally
waste away.

In 1964 I was excited at the thought of going with Allen to EMI
to see if he could get Mickie his million-dollar deal. Mickie was
still dubious and nervous that Allen would spoil his relationship
with EMI, but having spent time with Allen I was confident
that he would pull it off. Ron Tudor, EMI's managing director,
and Clive Kelly, the company's in-house head of legal affairs,
greeted us politely.

'Would you like some tea?' asked Clive.

'No,' snapped Allen, 'We don't want tea.'

I was shocked by his rudeness; it was a bit like refusing to
shake Clive's hand. I was expecting a little warm-up before the
main event but Allen went straight for the jugular.

'Mickie's not going to make any more records for you.'

'I beg your pardon?' said Ron.

Allen repeated it again more slowly. 'Mickie is not going
to make any more records for you.' Then he added, 'No more
records from The Animals or Herman's Hermits.' The two executives could not have been more shocked if Allen had stood up
and peed on the carpet.

'But we have a contract with Mickie,' said Clive, definitely a
little red-faced.

'You may or may not have a contract, that is for a court to decide, but you're not getting any more records.' He paused. 'Now we'll have a cup of tea.'

This was the essence of Allen's standard negotiations. Even with a binding contract a record company could not enforce personal services. They could stop an artist recording for any other company, but they could not make the artist record for them. Even if they could, they would have no control over the quality of product they had forced the artist to record. It was a huge bluff, but it made no sense for a record company to call it. If they wanted to keep the artist, they simply had to pay more, which they could easily afford to do.

I subsequently used the formula with great success many times myself when renegotiating clients' contracts or doing a deal for my own company Gem. I was a little less brash, substituting 'My client is not happy' for the blunt 'You're not going to get any more records'. But the effect was usually the same. After a while I became a gunslinger whose reputation was so fearful he never had to take his gun out. As I walked into some negotiations with major record companies, they would produce a Laurence Myers draft contract that I had negotiated for a previous artist. It contained all the revisions that I required and all we had to talk about was the basic royalty rate and the advance. I learned a lot from Allen, but I worked out for myself what was probably the most important aspect of dealing with major record companies.

We all know that politicians' decisions are for the most part based on what they need to get themselves re-elected rather than what is good for the long-term future of the country. Well, the same premise applies to most of the heads of record companies. They put their personal need to hit their annual targets above the long-term interest of the companies. I was invariably able to negotiate the return of ownership of the copyright in the recordings five years after the contract ended, because the person that I was negotiating with believed that they would be long gone from the company by then. This is something that my grandchildren should really be happy about. The income from the catalogue that I retained has diminished over the years, due in no small part to streaming, but after I go to the Great Recording Studio/Theatre/Film Set in the Sky, they will still have something to thank Papa for, when the royalty statements come in.

Allen indeed renegotiated a deal for Mickie that came to a million dollars, albeit advanced over years and dependent on Mickie delivering artists in addition to The Animals and Herman's Hermits. He tossed aside the EMI printed contracts and agreed a new one line by line. Gone were the spurious deductions from royalties, and the rate payable to Mickie was increased considerably. Mickie had the rights to The Animals' and Herman's Hermits' recordings under contracts made with those artists before I became involved with him. He was in no hurry to pass on to those artists more favourable terms. That could be done when *their* representative told us that 'the artists were unhappy'.

Allen's plan was to be an owner of some of the masters that were the subject of his renegotiations. His greatest ally in achieving this was HM the Queen, or more specifically, Her Majesty's collectors of taxes. In 1964 the highest rate of tax was 83 per cent and in some cases 98 per cent. People who could flee, like Michael Caine and Sean Connery, fled to America, but most people had to make such arrangements as they could to legally minimise their tax liability.

Allen proposed that the rights to artists' recordings would be split between the USA and the rest of the world. He would be the owner of the rights in America. The Animals and Herman's Hermits were re-licensed to MGM on much improved terms and future artists that Mickie would produce were licensed for America to CBS Records. Allen's company would retain 20 per cent of advances and pay the balance to Mickie over a period of years. The rest of the world income was also spread over a number of years, but Mickie retained the ultimate rights through the ownership of the company that we set up to deal with them. It was legally tax-effective and I advised Mickie to do it.

After the deal was struck, Allen's family and mine carried on our transatlantic friendship. On 20 July 1966, Peter – our second son – was born. This was shortly after Betty Klein gave birth to their daughter Beth. We had sent Betty a small but tasteful bunch of congratulatory flowers. Allen, as ever over the top, sent six-dozen red roses to Marsha in her room at the London Clinic. The nursing staff thought that she was a major film star.

More kindness followed. In 1967, my nineteen-year-old brother Roger was working with me at Goodman Myers and was very involved with a girlfriend. She was nice enough, but he realised that he was too young to get seriously involved. I called Allen who, without hesitation, gave Roger a job in the New York office of his firm ABKCO (Allen And Betty Klein COmpany) for a couple of months, which gave him a reason to break up with his girlfriend. He loved living in New York, and it was a great experience for him. A few years later, he met Lee Spencer Morris, an attractive young lady who was working for a UK country music promoter. I knew that this was real love because Lee was going to work at Midem and Roger asked me to look after her, which I did. Roger and Lee married in 1974.

Allen continued to be a good friend to me until he died. He has been much maligned over the years for his perceived unethical dealings with the Stones and The Beatles. The day before I spoke at his funeral there were adverse comments in lots of the press and a particularly vicious and damning obituary from Ray Connolly in the *Daily Mail*. In my eulogy, I recited my dishons, hons and honours theory and how it very much applied to Allen. Allen had certainly gone through all three of those stages and his honour came when he was inducted into the Rock'n'Roll Hall of Fame. I also told the story of Allen sticking me with the bill at Les A., which got a laugh. The service was attended by hundreds of mourners, including the great, the good and a few of the not-so-good in the music industry. At the end of the service both Yoko Ono, John Lennon's wife, and former Stones manager Andrew Oldham came up to me and thanked me for my comments, saying that I had summed up Allen's character completely.

I know that I have already told you how much of my business success I owe to Allen, but I am saying it again, so there, and it all began with the EMI deal he secured for Mickie.

Now that Mickie was fully financed by EMI, the Rak Records group really started to motor. In addition to continuing with The Animals and Herman's Hermits, Mickie produced records with

Lulu, Jeff Beck, and Donovan. Most of the songwriters already had a publishing deal, but the hope was that Rak Publishing, headed by Mickie's brother Dave, would pick up the rights on some of Mickie's records. Mickie was very smart and he never let the publishing rights influence his choice of songs.

In June 1966, I was asked to conduct an audit of Pye Records, on behalf of The Kinks. The Kinks were currently hot with 'Sunny Afternoon' and 'Dedicated Follower of Fashion', written by Ray Davies. They were, I thought, original songs and Ray sang them in his natural London accent, which I found a delight at a time when guys who spoke broad Geordie sang like they were born in Mississippi. As a fan, I was eager to meet Ray. They say never meet your heroes and avoid disappointment, which isn't always true, but in Mr Davies' case it was. Considering that he had written 'Sunny Afternoon', Ray turned out to be less than sunny. This is something that others have remarked upon. Years later I met with Ray again to discuss the possibility of him writing a stage musical and charming he was not. Some would call him taciturn; I would call him a miserable bastard but not – of course – to his face.

The Pye audit was most revealing. Amongst other more minor discrepancies, the good old 'payment on 90 per cent of sales' came up. This anachronism of royalty reduction for break-ages in transit, when records were no longer inclined to break, was standard in contracts of the time. What I discovered was that the Pye accounting system took 10 per cent off *all* sales before the income was reported in an artist's account. They then took *another* 10 per cent off royalties payable to each artist. As I mentioned earlier, it was institutional cheating. Most of the record companies were established icons, and the thought that they would be in any way dishonest was outrageous. In more recent years the same could be said about high-street banks.

10. THE GREEK TYCOON

Although this story is more to do with my life in film, Allen Klein was integral to getting *The Greek Tycoon* made as a Hollywood movie made so I will tell it now. In 1976 I was really in the movie business. My record companies were doing well and I had started GTO Films in 1974. It was a major player in the UK film scene and we always had a big presence at the Cannes Film Festival. Allen had dabbled in the movie business – mainly spaghetti westerns – but we had never tried to do any films together.

Some few months earlier, Nico Mastorakis had been in my office trying to sell me some low-budget, soft-porn films that he had made in Greece. I declined his offer as we did not deal in pornography – obviously a huge mistake. Nico, a small-time writer/producer had had a career as a TV personality in Greece, but I later found out that it was during the time that his country was governed by the right-wing military junta so he was not particularly popular in Greece by the time he came to see me. He asked what sort of thing I was interested in. I said broad-appeal commercial movies. Nico rummaged around in his bag like a travelling salesman and after examining a few scripts produced a film treatment entitled *Onassis*. 'What about this?'

He wanted to write and produce a film of the life of shipping magnate Aristotle Onassis and needed seed money to get
the project under way. He had, he said, a commitment from
Anthony Quinn to play Onassis. My disbelief was obvious so
Nico asked me if I would like to speak to Quinn directly, right
now, and get his confirmation. Of course I would! Right there
and then, Nico made a call to Rome. In no time I was talking to
Anthony Quinn who – having convinced me that he was indeed
that Anthony Quinn – confirmed that, subject to script, director
etc, he was eager to make this movie.

I had not so long before this read Willi Frischauer's
wonderful and fascinating biography of Onassis. Onassis – a
charismatic figure who had been the richest man in the world
– had died in March 1975, so he was still very much of interest to the general public. I looked at Nico's treatment, which
was obviously stolen from the Frischauer book. Nico insisted
that the information was the same because Ari, as we were
both now calling him, had told them both his life story. Nico
explained that when he was a journalist he had 'interviewed
Onassis extensively'. As I recall, Nico confessed that the
interview was him with a group of other scrambling photographers snatching a paparazzi-type photo of the great man
and being removed by bodyguards before he could get a question in. Internet research reveals that Nico smuggled himself
onto Onassis' yacht as a musician and hid a camera behind his
guitar strings while Onassis was entertaining Teddy Kennedy.
He was discovered and thrown off the boat. Nevertheless, I
was interested. I just knew that we mere mortals are fascinated
with the lifestyles of the rich and famous, and Onassis was as

rich and famous as they came. I doubted that Nico could write the script, but thought that finding someone who could would not be a problem.

The idea was that we would take Quinn to the upcoming Cannes Film Festival and – with the help of Bobby Meyers, a well-respected film salesman – we would create enough pre-sales of the movie to get it financed. The budget for promoting the film at Cannes was not big. Nico had already met with important sponsors in Greece: the Epirotiki cruise line, the Metaxa liquor company and the Greek tourist office who, between them, would provide at no cost to us 'the most spectacular party ever thrown' at Cannes. All I needed to finance was travel and the publicity campaign. Believing this would not cost more than ten thousand pounds, I went to Athens with Nico to obtain confirmation from responsible authorities that what he had told me was true. And it was. It was all very plausible.

Epirotiki had Cannes as a stopover on their scheduled route. Their five hundred passengers would disembark for an evening ashore and we would promptly board the passenger-free vessel for our party. As the ship provided catering three times a day already, our party guests would not be a problem. The tourist office loved the idea of a film showing the glamour of Greece. They promised to give us goody bags for our guests with ouzo, brochures, food samples and worry beads. They could not do enough. We met with Mr Mataxa of Mataxa spirits fame, who promised to provide enough ouzo for us to fill the swimming pool. I could see the headlines, as film starlets cavorted in my ouzo-filled pool. It was all just wonderful and did not impact at all on my ten-thousand-pound budget.

Back in London, I spoke to Quinn's agent and said that I
wanted to contract Quinn before I went to Cannes. No problem,
they said, but I would have to pay 10 per cent of Quinn's fee up
front. This was thirty thousand pounds. I was now completely
carried away. In for ten grand – in for forty. I sent the cheque.
I then found out that Quinn's agent also represented Jacqueline Bisset. Jacqui loved the idea of playing Jacqueline Kennedy
and – subject to script and director – she would also commit to
the movie. Yes, she would go to Cannes with us to promote the
movie. As with Quinn, I would have to put up 10 per cent of
her fee. So that was another fifteen thousand pounds from my
already-busted coffers.

Nico was in Athens where he arranged for well-known Greek
actress Irene Papas to commit to play Maria Callas. There would
be no upfront fee for Irene but we would have to pay for her
first-class travel and accommodation for the film festival. Nico
also arranged for a bouzouki band to come to Nice from Athens,
courtesy of Olympic Airlines. We would only have to pay for the
overnight stay of eight musicians. 'Why not?' I said.

By the time we set off for the festival I was in for around
sixty thousand pounds, which is probably half a million pounds
in today's money. I had to mortgage my house to cover it. This
was one of the few secrets that I ever had from my wife. The
festival had to be a financial success or I would have to sell my
family's home.

Thankfully, once we arrived at Cannes, our project was a
talking point for those in the trade and the party on the boat
was the hottest ticket in town. Invitations were delivered by
foot soldiers to hotels. They would ask (bribe) the concierges

but – huge mistake – we did not put the names on the actual invitation cards, only on the envelopes. The concierges sold the invitations (why didn't I think of that?) and I was obliged to send out a further few hundred invitations properly addressed. There were now some eight hundred invitations in circulation.

Allen Klein was in Cannes for his own business and inevitably I received a call from my friend and mentor. He asked me if he could get involved in the film but I said no. Allen would not be capable of being a partner, he would have to run the whole deal, and I was determined not to abdicate control of this golden opportunity to break into big-time movies. I was honest with Allen about my thoughts on this and he was fine about it. He asked if he could read the script anyway and was surprised to learn that I had not got around to having one written.

There is a golden rule in filmmaking that the three essentials are: the script, the script, and the script. I was aware of this but before getting around to it I had lined up the stars, the stars, and the stars. I was the shmuck, the shmuck, and the shmuck who – like Sinatra – would do it My Way. In my defence, I would say that I had been spoiled by my reputation in the music business. If I had gone to a record company with, say, Tom Jones, they would have given me the deal knowing that I would find the right material and producer. But this was the film business and very few producers could get the finance for a film without a good script, director and cast attached and I was fairly unknown to Hollywood studios.

As if there was not enough going on for me in Cannes that year, I had to deal with Angie Bowie, who called me from London to ask if I could put her up for one night. She was David Bowie's wife so I could hardly refuse. My head of distribution Bill Gavin was staying in a suite at The Majestic hotel and agreed to share with her. Angie arrived with eleven suitcases and ran up a phone bill the size of the national debt. She asked me if I could arrange for her to be the date of someone famous for a red-carpet film screening, which I could not.

Anthony Quinn arrived the day before the party. His Italian lawyer and one of his many agents were in town and Anthony suggested that Nico and I had dinner with them. He suggested the Moulin de Mougins – one of the finest and most expensive restaurants in the whole of France – and asked if my office could make the reservation. I said that it was impossible to get a reservation at the Moulin de Mougins during the festival as people booked from year to year but he said that he was a friend of the owner. Sure enough his name got us the reservation.

It was a fun evening. The restaurant was packed with people I knew and I rather enjoyed the kudos of sitting with one of the biggest stars in the world. Anthony was a great raconteur and regaled us with wonderful stories of the golden age of Hollywood. He carried on with his stories after we had finished dinner and – as entertaining as this was – it was getting late. With the big day ahead, I wished that he would call for the bill so that I could go home. The head waiter came to the table and informed Mr Quinn that his car was here. Mr Quinn stood up, thanked me for dinner and swept off with his guests leaving me with a bill which I remember could have paid for the dining room suite in my unfinished and now heavily mortgaged home in London. I subsequently also got the bill for his car.

I had sent Bill Gavin's wife Jane to travel with the cruise ship from Naples to supervise the onboard arrangements en route. On the morning of the party, a distressed Jane called me from Naples with news from the captain. Firstly, the guests on the boat would have to stay onboard unless I paid twenty dollars a head shore supplement. If they remained, the maximum number of guests allowed to attend my party would be two hundred and fifty. I had sent out eight hundred invitations! I had written confirmation from the owners of the boat that I could invite five hundred people and told Jane to inform the captain of this and that I refused to pay any shore allowance.

We had planned that the ship's tenders – smaller boats used to transfer goods and people to and from shore – would collect my guests from the jetty of the Carlton hotel. This was printed on my eight hundred invitations. But the captain said now that the tenders could not be used at all. Only tenders licensed by the Cannes municipality would be allowed. I was given the name of the man I should contact in Cannes to discuss this, a Monsieur Davide, from Havas Travel. I had written confirmation from Epirotiki, the boat's owners, for using the boat's own tenders and told Jane to inform the captain that I would ensure that the bill from Havas was sent to them.

Pretty sure that Havas would not send the bill to anyone other than me I rehearsed what I was going to say to Monsieur Davide. '*Bonjour, Monsieur Davide, je m'appelle Laurence Myers et peut-être que je ferai une grande soirée ce soir,*' etc.

I telephoned Monsieur Davide on the dot of nine that morning. '*Bonjour, Monsieur Davide, je m'appelle Laurence Myers et peut-être ...*' He interrupted me immediately and in perfect

English said, 'Ah. Mr Myers, I was expecting your call. You are the gentleman who is obliged to hire our tenders this evening. Time is short, I suggest you come and see me immediately.'

I jumped on my little Honda motorbike and drove like a TT rider to see the man. A thanksgiving turkey riding his motorbike to the butcher. On the way, I tried to estimate what this was going to cost me. This was the Cannes Film Festival, where a Coca-Cola cost a week's wages and the local sport was ripping off festival attendees. By the time I hurtled in to see Monsieur Davide, I was near hysterical. Trying not to sob at his feet I maintained a calm exterior. Monsieur Davide had already worked on the '*petit problème*' and gave me the '*grande image*'. The cost of the tenders was six thousand pounds for taking two hundred and fifty people to the boat from the Gare Maritime (not the Carlton's jetty), and he had strict instructions to take no more. Then there were the buses that I would need to take the people who would be following their invitations' instructions to gather at the Carlton jetty to the Gare Maritime, a mile or so away. That was another thousand pounds. So a total of seven thousand pounds needed to be transferred from my bank account before a single tender pulled away from the shore. Wishing to be helpful, Monsieur Davide would accept a telexed confirmation from my London bank that the transfer had been made.

Back at my apartment, I called my bank in London and persuaded them to send the money from my already overdrawn account. I then summoned a council of war, attended by my partner Nico Mastorakis, Bill Gavin, and Dennis Davidson our PR. It was impossible to change our arrangements at such short notice and anyway Nico had telexes confirming the boarding arrangements that had been agreed with the ship's owners. The telexes were in Greek – obviously Greek to me – so Nico telephoned Athens and tried to resolve the issue. Nobody at the shipping line would take his call. The rest of the day was spent sending costly foot soldiers around all of the hotels with costly (everything at the Cannes Film Festival is costly) flyers informing guests that the departure venue had changed.

I had lunch with Anthony Quinn and Jacqueline Bisset who – having no knowledge of the '*l'heure des crises*' that I was dealing with – chatted happily about the project as I sat with a fixed and foolish grin on my face, counting in my head the cost to date of the 'free party'.

In the afternoon the bouzouki band called from Rome. The free tickets provided by Olympic Airlines were only valid for the Athens–Rome leg of the trip and I would have to pay for the Rome-Nice leg. By now I was simply nodding at any requests for money, provided they could be met by my credit cards.

At eight o'clock in the evening, my stars were in the bar of the Majestic hotel, drinking the finest champagne my money could buy. Eight hundred people were lining up at the entrance to the Gare Maritime singing, 'Why are we waiting?' in an assortment of languages. The invited TV cameras and paparazzi were waiting on the dockside and patrolling the waters in hired boats ready to board the ship pirate-style. Bill Gavin was at the Gare Maritime, offering the captains of the tenders obscene bribes to take all of the guests out to the ship. Monsieur Davide was grabbing the money from their hands and giving it back to Bill, who gave it back to the tender captains as soon as his back was turned. Allen Klein was asking if he could bring a couple of extra guests to the party. Of course he could!

Originally, the cruise ship was due to arrive in Cannes at five in the afternoon. We then received a message saying that it would not arrive until 7 p.m. It did not. At 7 p.m. I was standing at the edge of the quay, scouring the empty horizon. I might have thrown myself into the sea had I not been wearing my new white film producer's suit. At 7.15 p.m. the ship arrived. Too big to dock in the port, she moored close by.

I hurried the advance party onto the first tender out. This was Quinn, Bisset, Papas, the bouzouki band and me. Everybody wants to be a star in their own country and Nico was heavily engaged with the Greek press. We arrived alongside the ship where there was a proper boarding platform manned by smart sailors. I felt a little better. I was first up the ladder. My first sight was the deck beautifully decorated with fairy lights and a vast spread of party food. I felt a lot better. My guests would party 'till dawn' as stated on the invitations.

My second sight made me feel worse. A prominent notice at the top of the boarding ladder stated 'ALL SHORE VISITORS MUST BE OFF THE BOAT BY 10.30 P.M.' There was a man with lots of gold on his uniform nearby, repeating the message, over and over again. 'What does this mean?' I asked. He read the notice out slowly as if I was a child.

'Oh no,' said I. 'I have a contract. My guests will be dancing 'till dawn.'

'Fine,' said he, 'but they'll be dancing in our next stop, Marseille.'

Jane, my representative, came to greet me. I am not a great drinker but, on this occasion, I was in desperate need. I asked her for a drink. She did not look happy. 'Laurence, there is no drink.'

'Of course there is,' I snapped. 'You told me you saw it loaded on.' She explained that our ouzo, wine and brandy was indeed on board but held in a bonded hold. Because the ship had arrived so late, French customs had closed and it could not be released from the bonded hold without them.

Eventually the ship's purser appeared and told me that the ship's bar could be opened at discount prices and charged to me but – huge but – he could not keep out the passengers, all of whom were eager to join my stars. I would be buying drinks for five hundred holidaymakers and as many of my guests who could fight their way onto the ship.

As I was desperately trying to deal with the escalating disasters, the bouzouki bandleader had been following me around, trying to get my attention. He informed me that there was no power on the bandstand and as they needed amplification nobody would hear them. Nico was still busy giving interviews to the Greek press, so could not help me. The bandleader said that he was an artist and refused to play. Remembering Peter Grant's great line to Led Zeppelin's drummer, I asked if he could play in a wheelchair, and he huffed off.

So this was the situation thirty minutes after the party started. The guests who had managed to get to the ship were fighting to get up the narrow ladder, just as the guests who were on the ship, fearful of ending up in Marseille, fought to get down. I was having to pay a bar bill for several hundred cruise guests. The only press that had made it onboard were Greek and a local TV crew. The band were playing silent bouzouki music. The PR man for the cruise line was trying to make Quinn wear a branded T-shirt (which was one part of the contract that they had remembered!) and in the process ripped Quinn's shirt. Quinn then – not unreasonably – refused to do any interviews. Jacqui Bisset and Irene Papas sensibly hid themselves away and I realised that Allen Klein was one of the hundreds of guests who had been stuck at the Gare Maritime, unable to join the party.

PR man Dennis Davidson, who was more used to Cannes Festival party debacles than I was, actually got together *the* photo opportunity. QUINN THE GREEK (actually born Mexican of course) WAS GOING TO DANCE AGAIN. We were about to invoke that iconic dance scene in *Zorba The Greek*. The TV and photo press stood by and the unamplified bouzouki band strummed with their bloody, torn fingers as loudly as they could.

Quinn was in fact a terrible dancer with little sense of rhythm but he was a pro and knew that this was the shot everybody wanted. He stood up and – looking around – said that he could not dance alone. He looked at me and said, 'Hey, kid, come and dance with me.' I grabbed Jacqui Bisset and we joined the man. Nico, who had been nowhere to be seen during the earlier dramas, suddenly appeared. Just then, the whole thing seemed worthwhile. Here was I, the boy from Finsbury Park, about to be beamed around the world in my white producer's suit dancing with Anthony Quinn and Jacqui Bisset. The dance began, everybody started clapping, and I was smiling like the cat that got the cream. Then somebody shouted 'Whoopa!' in true Greek style. Then everyone shouted 'Whoopa!' and a glass of red wine came hurtling through the air, all over my white producer's suit. I have the photo. It was an appropriate end to the party. I wanted my mummy.

Notwithstanding the fact that the party was later described in one of the trade papers as the Greatest Disaster in the History of the Cannes Film Festival, we had created a great interest in the project. The next day, Allen Klein once again asked if I needed any help. Once again, I declined. I had a hot property and was determined to run with it myself.

A month or so later, me and my newly cleaned white suit went to Los Angeles where we were installed in an expensive bungalow at the Beverley Hills Hotel. Not any old expensive bungalow at the Beverley Hills Hotel, but the super-expensive Bungalow 5: the one with a dining room and two or three bedrooms. Such was the interest in *The Greek Tycoon*, I actually had appointments with the heads of most of the major Hollywood studios. The meetings were cordial, but brief. They all said the same thing. Nice cast – come back when you have a script and a director. I was shattered. I, of course, knew that these elements were absolutely vital to the making of a good film but I had naively believed that the cast was so strong, the studios would trust me to get them right. Dispirited, I tried some of the smaller studios and distributors but with no success. Everybody wanted to see the script and be sure of the director. By now I was desperate. There was a young Englishman working in LA called David Blake who worked for Cinema Shares, a two-desks-and-an-empty-filing-cabinet type of operation based in New York. I asked him if there was any point in meeting with his boss in New York, but he was quite certain that this would be a waste of time, so I had no idea what my next step should be.

I really was in serious financial trouble. I had literally bet my house on this project and the options on Quinn and Bisset would soon evaporate, making my investment worthless. I decided to go home via New York for no good reason other than I did not want to immediately face the problems that were waiting for me in London. I checked out of the Beverley Hills Hotel. As I closed the door of Bungalow 5 behind me, I heard the telephone ring. Thinking that it could save me tipping the bell captain, I went back to answer it. It was Allen Klein asking how I was doing. The last thing I wanted was an 'I told you so' from my mentor so I told the first lie that came into my head: 'Great, I'm flying to New York to make a deal with Cinema Shares.'

'Never heard of them,' said Allen. 'If you don't go with a major, I'd like you to go with me. Whatever Cinema Shares are giving you, I'll give you a dollar more.' Not wishing to give me a chance to refuse him, as if I would under the circumstances, he rang off and I nearly fainted with relief. I was close to Allen until he died some forty years later, but I never told him of my deception.

Allen was nervous that I would meet with Cinema Shares and he had his driver meet me at the airport in New York and whisk me straight to his office, where he immediately asked me what my proposed deal was with his 'rival'.

'First,' I said, 'I get my investment of seventy-five thousand pounds back.'

'Of course,' said Allen. 'What else?'

'I get it back very soon,' I said.

'Yes, yes, what else? What is your deal with Cinema Shares?'

'Well, first I get my money back.'

'And then?' said Allen

I, of course, had never even spoken to Cinema Shares and had given no thought to anything beyond getting back my money. 'I can't deal with you as I would with them,' I said, 'What do you think is fair?'

Allen laid out a proposal but – such was my relief – that I did not even absorb it. I just nodded a lot as the blood returned to my veins. In the event, his offer was fair. He gave me my seventy-five thousand pounds back and the film got made, scripted by Mort Fine and directed by J. Lee Thompson.

As expected, Allen took over the running of the project but – as he personally financed the production and the golden rule was He Who Provides The Gold Makes The Rule – this was his entitlement. Universal Studios had expressed a serious interest in the film and I begged Allen to do a deal once shooting started but he figured we would do better when the picture was finished. By that time Allen was in for eleven million dollars, which I knew he could not afford to lose. I persuaded him not to wait until the film was fully edited as he would have to stand by the film he had made. He took my advice and we showed Universal a rough cut – an assembly of the scenes without the final music, sound effects, etc. Universal went for it. We shook hands with the studio before Allen and I celebrated by going to Nathan's on Broadway and each eating two of their famous hot dogs.

It was not a great film. We claimed that the film was not about the Onassis family but a Greek ship owner called Tomassis who married the widow of a fictional American president. The film anyway had the usual disclaimer that 'All the characters are fictitious', but we were chary about upsetting the Kennedy and Onassis families, so we made a bland film where all of the characters were nice, which, of course, they were not. The film was released in 1978 but did no real business. Years later, *Dallas* and *Dynasty* proved my theory of the commercial value of stories about the rich and nasty.

I never received a penny profit from the film but I still have the poster with my name on it, and I still have my house.

The other benefit of the whole debacle was that when I was in LA Jacqui invited me to lunch with her and her then boyfriend Victor Drai at her home in Beverley Hills. She was a most charming and unassuming host and after lunch we all swam in her beautiful pool. The next film that Jacqui was going to appear in was *The Deep* – remembered by many because she spent a lot of the film in a wet T-shirt. Jacqui was finding it hard to swim underwater, a requirement for her part in the film. She asked me to help her practise by putting my arms around her and holding her underwater, which I did. I don't remember what we had for lunch.

11. PIRATE RADIO AND THE STAR-CLUB

In the 1960s, pirate radio was booming in the UK. Operated from ships outside of territorial waters and so beyond regulatory control, they filled the gap left by the BBC, which had a limited output of pop music. Radio Caroline had made a fortune and Mickie Most and I were convinced that we could do the same in Germany. The idea was brought to Mickie by Henry Henroid – a wonderful cockney character who had spent years working as a road manager for Don Arden without being hung out of a window or smacked.

Henry's job was to look after American acts that Don brought over to Europe and he had wonderful stories about his tours with Gene Vincent. Vincent was a notorious hellraiser, despite having a steel sheath around one leg following a near-fatal motorcycle accident. 'Now 'e was a bleedin' lunatic. You should 'ave 'eard 'im when there was a full moon. I had to smuggle the bastard out of the 'otel in a laundry basket and his bleedin' leg wouldn't fold in.' Henry also toured with Little Richard: 'I was wiv 'im on the plane when he saw the bleedin' light and got religion. He got down on 'is knees in the middle of the bleedin' aisle, 'allelujahrin' to God, and renounced his material possessions. I copped 'is gold watch in all 'is tomfoolery. Lovely man.'

Henry had looked after many of the acts that Don had booked into the Star-Club in Hamburg, the place where The Beatles famously honed their craft. Henry got to know Manfred Weissleder, the owner of the club, well. The Star-Club was in the red-light district of Hamburg and Manfred, who – according to Henry – was involved in soft pornography and all manner of shady deals, was open to any kind of business. Either Henry or Manfred – both claimed the honour – had come up with the idea of starting a pirate radio station under the Star-Club banner, broadcasting from a ship to be anchored outside German territorial waters off of the coast of Hamburg. Henry told Manfred that he could 'raise the readies no prob' and came to see Mickie and me.

Henry and Manfred had already done some spadework. There was a German rum importer who was keen to come in on the deal. He owned a ship moored in Flensburg, a fishing town in the north of Germany, which was being used as a dormitory for imported Turkish labour. Telefunken, the enormous German electronics company, were, it seemed, keen to do a deal for the necessary broadcasting equipment.

I did some preliminary research and it seemed that there was no German law that would inhibit the venture so Henry and I flew to Hamburg. We stayed in a hotel that Henry knew near to The Reeperbahn, where the Star-Club was situated. The Reeperbahn, the centre of Hamburg's red-light district, is a walled-off street near the docks. It is lined with bars, dance clubs and brothels, and the Star-Club was one of the most successful operations. Manfred, eager to attract the custom of the young merchant seamen who frequented the area, had started booking English rock groups. Much has been written about The Beatles who, fuelled by amphetamines and God knows what else, played their fourteen-hour shifts alternating with one or two other bands doing the same. When I was there the policy had not changed, although the now-famous Beatles had not played for about three years. I saw lots of bands, the most memorable of whom were Freddie & The Midnighters. I had a drink with Freddie between sets and he was like the ball in a pinball machine, pinging from flipper to flipper and lighting up whatever he touched. I thought that he was on some sort of speed but later this zaniness found him fame back in England as the comedian Freddie Starr. All the bands played similar sets of American rock'n'roll standards and it seemed as though finishing with 'Walkin' The Dog' was obligatory.

Henry introduced us to Manfred in his best cockney German: '*Das ist Herr* Myers, *dein Geschäftsführer von dein Animals und das 'Ermans 'Ermits.*' I was not the manager of The Animals or Herman's Hermits, just a business advisor, but it seemed to impress Manfred, who had his thriving porn-film business and no doubt many other enterprises which in the UK would not have gained him a knighthood. He was in fact your basic dodgy geezer. He was, however, a shrewd dodgy geezer and recognised the financial potential of a pirate radio station.

We drove to Flensburg, where the rum importer's ship was moored. For six months I'd owned a half-share in a rarely functioning twelve-foot speedboat so I was, of course, the expert in all matters maritime. We climbed onboard and it seemed to me to be big enough compared to the photos I had seen of Radio Caroline's vessel. Being the maritime maven, I demanded to see the engine (this from a man who cannot change a lightbulb or a car tyre). I was invited downstairs – they call it 'below' – where the smell from the dormitories was, as Henry put it, 'absofuckinglutely reels' (reels of cotton: rotten).

Back on deck, I dug my heels into the planking a couple of times and pronounced that the ship had passed my preliminary survey. We returned to Hamburg for a meeting with executives of Telefunken. As Henry had indicated, they were prepared to barter the supply and fitting of all of the required equipment in return for favoured advertising.

The next day Manfred went on national television in Germany where, by use of graphics showing sweet little white-dot radio waves beaming from the radio mast of a ship, he demonstrated the proposed reach of the station. By the time we got back to his office his phone was ringing off the hook from people interested in taking advertising. We went back to London in a happy frame of mind. In just three days we had lined up a ship, the equipment and a line of probable advertisers.

My interest in Mickie's music companies was 10 per cent but in recognition of my efforts in this venture, Mickie offered me 25 per cent. Henry Henroid would also have 25 per cent ('Tasty, tasty,' said Henry) and Mickie, who would be overseeing the programming, would have 50 per cent. We would follow Radio Luxembourg's example of taking song-publishing rights in return for special promotions. We were going to be very rich. Then it occurred to me that we should get a proper survey of the boat, find out the specifications of all required equipment and obtain advice on the legalities of the operation. The cost of this preparatory work was considerable, so clearly we were going to become very much poorer before we became very much richer. Fortunately, before we actually spent any money, I received a call from Manfred saying that he had been informed that the German government would vigorously oppose our scheme. I explained that – subject to verification and further research – the law was on our side. He explained that Telefunken and the Rum Man were not prepared to take on the government. Also because of his own 'rather specialised business interest' he was reluctant to do so himself. Bearing in mind that the FBI got Capone on tax evasion, and presuming that the German taxman had seen one of the relevant movies, I could see he was right.

I thought about taking the project forward on my own. I imagined myself standing proudly on the bridge of my own pirate radio ship, an Englishman once more defiant against German aggression. I then imagined a periscope cutting towards me through the waves and forgot the whole thing.

There is no doubt that my involvement with Mickie was the key to my later success in the music business. I was Mickie's consigliere at a time when there were no other accountancy firms specialising in the world of popular music, a relatively new industry. Many of the artists in Mickie's musical circle became clients of Goodman Myers. The most important to me personally was Mike Leander, a young writer-producer who, in 1970, would have an absolutely life-changing effect on my career.

Mickie was sixty-four when, tragically, he died in 2003 from a form of cancer relating to asbestos, which had been liberally used in the walls of recording studios. We had drifted apart over the years, but for some time he had been very much part of my life. I was very moved when I learned of his death.

12. TETRAGRAMMATON RECORDS AND TINY TIM

I had first met Greg Smith when he was an office boy for some theatrical agents who took temporary office space at Goodman Myers' Albermarle Street premises. In 1968 he became the London representative for Tetragrammaton Records, a new-ish record company in Los Angeles. Tetragrammaton was planning to open London offices and Greg kindly recommended that I should represent them.

They flew me out to Los Angeles first-class to meet up – always a good start. Then they put me up in a very nice room at the Beverley Hilton and even provided a hire car for my use. Tetragrammaton was a strange name for a record company. It is the Hebrew theonym (name for God), a translation of which is used by observant Jews who do not wish to say 'God' aloud. Now you know too.

The driving force behind the company was Roy Silver who, with his partners Bruce Post Campbell and Marvin Deane, ran a very successful management company in LA. They managed Bob Dylan, Joan Rivers, Richard Pryor and other stars. Bill Cosby was Roy Silver's personal client and I suspected that Mr Cosby was the major financer of the Tetragrammaton record company.

The offices on Canon Drive in Beverly Hills were astounding, a low-built block nesting amongst lush trees, surrounded by a parking lot that looked like a sales agency for Mercedes. My meeting was with Roy Silver himself, a charismatic man with an extraordinary personality. I thanked him for the extremely generous travel and hotel arrangements but he brushed my words away, indicating that he had merely asked his secretary to make the necessary bookings. There was clearly no ethos of budgetary control in the company coming from the boss.

The label had two successful artists. Deep Purple were doing well with their debut album *Shades of Deep Purple*, the single 'Hush' from the album having made the Top 10 on the American charts. The only other successful act they had was Tiny Tim, whose novelty recording of 'Tiptoe Through the Tulips' – sung in a high falsetto – had made the Top 20.

Commenting on the number of staff, and noting the number of Mercedes in the parking lot, I asked Roy how the company could afford such a large overhead out of its relatively modest success. Roy said his LA accountants were dealing with that and he only wanted to talk to me about the cost of setting up in the UK. I went through some figures but he was obviously not focusing on what I was saying. I had the distinct feeling that he had given no thought as to why I should be brought over at great expense. On the way out he introduced me to Tiny Tim, a very strange-looking young man. His American mother was the daughter of a rabbi and his Lebanese father was the son of a Maronite Christian priest. Mr Tim had managed to parlay his falsetto one-hit into something of a career. Other than the dubious honour of meeting Tiny Tim, the trip was a waste of my time and Bill Cosby's money. Tetragrammaton never opened a London office, and predictably went bankrupt in 1971.

Roy Silver was, however, a naturally talented chef of Chinese cooking. Later on, in 1976, when his showbiz career was somewhat in tatters, he opened an eponymous restaurant, which quickly became a very popular hangout for the LA glitterati. The Chinese food was excellent – he only used kosher chickens – but the real draw was that if you were a friend – and he had no enemies – he dragged you into the cloakroom and encouraged you to help yourself to cocaine from an extremely large jar that he kept behind the coats. Predictably, his restaurant followed his record company into bankruptcy in 1982. Not the last restaurant to disappear up the owner's nose in a cloud of white powder.

As with most LA restaurants, where you sat at Roy's was an important statement of status. I was once there as a guest of an important film agent who, of course, had been allocated an appropriate 'I am an important film agent' table. During the course of our meal Tony Curtis came into the restaurant. Mr Curtis must have been well into his fifties at the time and arguably well past his box-office prime, but I was excited beyond belief to see him in the flesh. When I was a teenager I wanted to look like Tony Curtis, as did any boy my age that did not want to look like Elvis or Marlon Brando. Apart from the fact that as Jewish boys we were both circumcised, Mr Curtis and I had very little in common. Tony Curtis was slim, handsome and looked fantastic on screen. Laurence Myers was overweight and did not even look good in his wedding photos. Anyway, Curtis was now sitting a few tables away from me in the company of a very attractive blonde lady and I could not take my eyes off him. My host was sitting with his back to the focus of my attention and he asked me what I was looking at. In reverential tones I told him that I was looking at Tony Curtis. He did not even look round. 'Tony Curtis? Can't get arrested.'

I was shocked at his callous attitude. 'But it's Tony Curtis, the one from *Some Like it Hot* and ...'

My host turned around, looked at him, turned back to me and said, 'Look where he's sitting. I told you, he can't get arrested.'

I love LA but I regret to say that the incident was, and no doubt still is, typical of the town. When you're hot you're hot and when you're not you're relegated to a 'not hot' table. Many years ago there was a wonderful sketch on *Saturday Night Live* which, for me, sums up the LA view of showbiz status. It went something like:

Chevy Chase, playing a snotty maître d' is standing at his greeter's desk. John Belushi, playing an actor, asks if he could have a table for two. Chevy Chase, without looking up says, 'No. Go away.'

'I'm an actor,' says Belushi.

Chevy Case points to a long line of people standing patiently against a wall. 'Go to the back of that line.'

Belushi meekly does as told. After a while Chevy Chase goes over to him. 'You working?' asks Chevy Chase.

'Yes.' He gets moved up a couple of places.

'Speaking part?'

'Yes,' says Belushi.'

He gets moved up a bit more.

'How many lines?'

'Four lines,' says Belushi.

He gets moved down the line.

And so it goes on, with Chase moving Belushi up and down the line until the famous producer Aaron Spelling, playing himself, comes in and gives Belushi a big 'Hello', at which point the Chevy Chase character physically removes a couple of diners by the scruff of their necks and ushers Belushi to a good table. It is one of the funniest sketches I have ever seen and I urge you to try to find it on YouTube.

Saturday Night Live was, and remarkably still is, a huge and important TV show and in 1978 I was privileged to go and see the live taping, which was a great experience. I had gone to New York with John Goldstone, the producer of the Pythons' *Life of Brian*, Eric Idle and Terry Gilliam to try to help them to find the money to finance the film after EMI Films suddenly pulled out. Allen Klein had put up the money for my film *The Greek Tycoon* and he was my best shot. He read the script, but did not think it was funny. I admired Allen for many things, but not his sense of humour. Eric Idle is a really nice guy and even though I didn't get the film financed, hanging with some Pythons was a great few days in New York. John and Eric took me along to the after-show party that *Saturday Night Live* always held after the broadcast, at No. 1 Fifth Avenue. I got to rub shoulders with the cast, and actually chatted a little with John Belushi. I think of that privilege whenever I watch *The Blues Brothers* on TV.

In 1979 George Harrison put the money up to make *Life of Brian*. By then I owned GTO Films, a film-distribution company, and John Goldstone really wanted me to distribute the film and offered very favourable terms. Unfortunately, Bill Dunn, the American schmuck who was then running GTO

Films for me, did not like the film and did not feel he was the right person to do it. He was an idiot for turning it down and I was a bigger idiot for not replacing him with someone with a sense of humour.

13. THE LATER SIXTIES – SHOWBIZ, HERE I AM!

Another client I got through my growing reputation as accountant/nanny/psychiatrist to the songwriters was Geoff Stephens, born in north London but then living in Southend. He was trying to earn a living as a songwriter and comedy writer and had some of his sketches accepted by the BBC.

In 1964 he discovered Donovan, later to become a huge international star. Geoff told me he was walking along the front in Southend with Peter Eden – a pal who was also trying to get involved in the music business – when they saw a young man in blue denim and a cap, carrying a guitar. They stopped to chat to him and he played them a couple of songs. His music was very folky, and he was clearly a huge Bob Dylan fan, but he had a certain quality that encouraged Geoff and Peter to sign him for management. In 1965 they produced two albums, *What's Bin Did and What's Bin Hid* and *Fairytale*, for Pye Records. Both albums were folk-influenced. The first album included Donovan's original recording of 'Catch The Wind,' which was released as a single and made No. 4 in the UK charts. The Pye albums were not particularly successful, probably because Pye was a crap record company. Geoff and Peter decided that they were not natural record producers and they brought Donovan to meet Mickie Most, which was when I met Geoff. The first album that Mickie produced with Donovan was *Sunshine Superman*, a change of direction away from folk and a huge hit.

Inevitably, Donovan sought new management and Geoff concentrated on his songwriting. His first big success was writing 'The Crying Game', a big hit for Dave Berry. It was a very classy song and in 1992 inspired director Neil Jordan to make a film of the same name. Geoff wrote that one by himself, but then concentrated on lyrics, and collaborated with a variety of composers, writing great songs like 'There's a Kind of Hush' for Herman's Hermits, 'Semi-Detached Suburban Mr James' for Manfred Mann and 'I'll Put You Together Again' for Hot Chocolate.

In 1966, Geoff came into my Regent Street office and played me a record called 'Winchester Cathedral'. He said the record came about because he was tinkling on his piano with a half-developed song. It was going to be about a guy being despondent about a girl. He got the second half of the first line, '… You're bringing me down', but couldn't come up with who was bringing his protagonist down. There was a picture of Winchester Cathedral on his wall and, as many composers do, rather than get stuck on a line he carried on writing the song with the dummy lyric, 'Winchester Cathedral, you're bringing me down.' A bottle of vodka later he had finished the song in the style of Rudy Vallee, a twenties' megaphone crooner. He went into the studio with John Carter, a multi-talented singer and composer who replicated the twenties' vocal sound. The record cost Geoff three hundred and eighty pounds. In sober mode he was not at all confident that he could get a novelty record released and asked me if I wanted to put up half of the money and own half of the record.

As fond as I was of Geoff, I had no wish to piss away a hundred and ninety pounds on a piece of nonsense. As Geoff often reminded me after the event, I didn't even decline grace-fully. I just laughed.

There was no group so Geoff made up the name The New Vaudeville Band. The record went to No. 4 in the English charts, was No. 1 in the US charts for four weeks and sold over three million copies. Geoff made so much money from the record that, on my advice, he became a non-resident and went to live in Switzerland. I try to never think about 'if onlys' but that one was quite hard to put aside.

The New Vaudeville Band was soon a household name, but there was no band to cash in on the success. Peter Grant was still the head of Rak Management without much to do. Manager and producer Simon Napier-Bell had asked Peter to take over the management of The Yardbirds, who were struggling finan-cially in spite of their undoubted talent, but that hadn't worked out. The Yardbirds split up and Peter needed to find an act to manage. I asked him if he wanted to put a band together, manage them and exploit the success of 'Winchester Cathedral'. Peter did not pretend that he liked the record, but he pulled it off brilliantly until the public tired of the novelty. As a 10 per cent owner of Rak Management, I earned a little from The New Vaudeville Band, but nothing compared to 'if only'.

Probably as a consolation, Geoff allowed me to write the lyrics of a New Vaudeville Band B-side. My song was called

'Uncle Gabriel' and I wrote it under the name of Peter James –
the names of the two children Marsha and I had had by then.
The A-side was 'The Bonnie and Clyde'. The record sold very
few copies, probably just two, to Peter and James. It is so rare
that even I don't have a copy.

Peter Grant then put together Led Zeppelin based around
ex-Yardbird Jimmy Page and John Paul Jones, a first-choice
session musician who had played on Yardbirds recordings. John
Bonham joined as drummer and Robert Plant was the charismatic lead singer. You may recall from my Don Arden story
that Peter was not averse to using the threat of physical violence
and his management style reflected this. There are many stories
about Peter's use of intimidation, some apocryphal, but I was in
the room when he resolved a dispute with John Bonham, the
Led Zeppelin drummer, by threatening in a voice to be believed:
'Listen you c**t, can you play drums from a wheelchair?'

As a shareholder in Rak Management, I enjoyed a small
financial interest in Zep's early career. Once, when I was in
New York, Peter asked me to bring back a very large amount
of cash. I was staying at The Americana hotel and I carefully
placed the money in one of the safety-deposit boxes that were
situated in the wall behind the reception desk. I was leaving the
next day so that only gave me about eighteen hours in which
to lose the key. Eighteen hours was enough, and when I went
to check out the next day they had to call the safe company to
break open the lock. The considerable cost of this was of course
charged to me but was a small price to pay for not having to
face Peter Grant and tell him that I had left his cash in a wall-
safe in New York.

Whilst still in practice I took over the management of The Tremeloes. They had started off as the backing band for Brian Poole, but had since gone out on their own. It was well after 'Silence is Golden' and they were no longer making hit records, but they had done very well and their financial affairs needed sorting out. They were also the publishers of 'Yellow River,' a song that they were going to record themselves but gave to a band called Christie, who had an enormous hit with it. I licensed it to Yellow Pages for an advertising campaign for six thousand pounds. It was probably far too little, but it was hard to get a guide. I liked the boys immensely, especially Alan Howard and Chip Hawkes, and I was sorry that I could not revive their recording career, but they were very sensible in accepting that they were a pop band and their time was over. They were very bright and carried on in the music business, writing, producing and managing other bands.

Most pop artists had a three-year career. Typically, a band would put out four singles a year and then a best-of album. Containing all twelve tracks. The reason for this was that pop artists appealed to early teens and pre-teens. As the kids grew into their later teens, their musical tastes changed. This is, of course, a generalisation and I could do an analysis of the charts to prove my point but, to be honest, it would be a lot of work that I do not want to undertake, so just take my word for it.

14. THE SOCIETY OF DISTINGUISHED SONGWRITERS – THE SODS

As you may have gathered, I had a passionate admiration for songwriters. In the early sixties few artists wrote their own material. Top artists of the day like Tom Jones, Shirley Bassey, The Hollies, Cliff Richard, Adam Faith, Dusty Springfield and even Elvis Presley depended on songwriters for their ongoing success. The Beatles were the real start of the singer/songwriters movement and now of course it is rare to find a successful artist who does not write their own material.

America had Goffin and King, Leiber and Stoller, Barry Mann and Cynthia Weil, Neil Sedaka and others, most of whom were Jewish – as were Irving Berlin, the Gershwins, Jerome Kern, Oscar Hammerstein, Sammy Cahn and most of the other writers of the great American songbook. There must have been something in New York bagels.

In the UK there was a coterie of successful songwriters, many of whom wrote with each other, swapping writing partners as might be expected in London's swinging sixties. I thought that

the artists whose careers they had started with a great song did
not always appreciate how much they owed to that writer. I knew
many UK songwriters well and I devised a scheme whereby,
as a condition of a new artist being given a song that became
a big hit, the songwriter would have some sort of interest in
the artist's subsequent career. More importantly, as part of my
scheme, leading songwriters would pool a part of their income
in a company owned by them – and me, of course – thus sharing
in each other's success. The high-earning managing partner of
the company would also, of course, be me.

Just before I left my accountancy practice in 1971, I invited
some of the hottest songwriters in London to a dinner: Tony
Macaulay, Mike Leander, Geoff Stephens, Don Black, Bill
Martin, Barry Mason, Les Reed, Mitch Murray and Peter
Callander. If I listed the songs that they had written between
them it would take up the rest of this book. Don Black concentrated on films and theatre, working with Andrew Lloyd
Webber, John Barry and many other of the best composers
around, collecting Oscars, Tony Awards and an OBE on the
way. I find it annoying that the contribution of lyricists is often
forgotten when songs are credited. *Sunset Boulevard* is known
as an 'Andrew Lloyd Webber Musical' but it would not have
worked so well without the lyrics and book of Don Black and
Christopher Hampton. Bert Bacharach's 'songs' may never have
come to light without the genius of Hal David's lyrics. Similarly,
Elton John and lyricist Bernie Taupin.

At great, unaffordable expense, I booked the private room
at the fashionable trattoria Terrazza in Soho. Every one of the
invitees turned up and found my carefully prepared document,

explaining my brilliant scheme, on the table in front of them. They all looked through it, some of them more carefully than others, and all promised to take it home to study. I quickly realised that my scheme was a non-starter. These were all ambitious young guys with great faith in their own abilities and they were not ready to be unionised. My scheme was quickly forgotten and they got down to eating and drinking ... and drinking ... and drinking some more. I did not try to keep up with them. I kept myself unamused, totting up the cost as my guests ploughed through the restaurant's expensive wine list.

After the meal someone suggested that we should go somewhere and play poker. I had drunk enough to think that it was a splendid idea. In 1967, we had moved to a flat in St John's Wood and I invited them all back there, where they added to the expense of the evening by cleaning me out at poker. Some of the writers had never met before and socially it was a great evening. Mitch Murray had such a good time he thought that they should all meet on a regular basis. He came up with the idea of forming The Society of Distinguished Songwriters (The SODS) and all of those who were at my dinner joined. There would be a King Sod and other offices. The membership of SODS has since expanded rapidly. Lionel Bart, Andrew Lloyd Webber and Tim Rice, Abba's Bjorn and Benny, Queen's Brian May and many other leading songwriters were later inducted into the society. They would meet on a monthly basis and, once a year, have a SODS' night bash at a grand hotel when the members invited family and friends. I went along to the first of these, where Mitch Murray was the first King Sod. Marsha and I were invited to many SODS' nights thereafter and they were great fun. The SODS themselves performed a cabaret that was always entertaining and the food and wine were of the highest order. The society is still going and quite rightly now dominated by a new generation of songwriters, but I have not been to a SODS night for many years.

15. TONY MACAULAY

Unquestionably my greatest contribution to the song-writers' cause was my orchestration of Tony Macaulay's case against his wicked publisher Schroeder Music.

When Tony first came to me for management he was contracted exclusively to Pye Records for his services as a producer. Using the technique I had acquired from Mr Klein, I told Louis Benjamin, the head of Pye Records, that Tony would no longer be making records for them. Louis did not put up much of a fight, and in return for a very reasonable ten thousand pounds, Tony was free.

For his songwriting, Tony had signed for an advance of fifty pounds exclusively to Schroeder Music Publishing. It was a small firm owned by the American husband-and-wife team of Aaron and Abby Schroeder. The contract was patently unfair. Tony could not place a song with any other music publisher, the Schroeders had no obligation to pay Tony any sort of retainer and they had no obligation to actually do anything with the songs that Tony was obliged to give them. He had made them a great deal of money with songs that he had written with John Macleod including 'Baby, Now That I've Found You', and other hits which he produced for The Foundations.

The traditional split between a songwriter and the publisher was 50/50. This harked back to the days before songs were recorded and publishers had to promote the sales of printed sheet music. They would try to get the songs sung by popular artists, in the hope that the public would want to buy a copy. The publisher would also employ people to sing the songs at a piano inside shops selling sheet music. A publisher's hard work justified his 50 per cent. Almost every home had a piano, and a popular song could sell thousands of copies and make a decent sum to be divided between publisher and writer. In order to get a song exploited in a foreign territory, the UK publisher would license the song to a local publisher in the foreign territory. The local publisher was obliged to work as hard as the original publisher to get the song known in their own country, sending the other 50 per cent of their income back to the original publisher, who would then divide the 50 per cent between himself and the writer. This was all perfectly fair until songs could be exploited on gramophone records and radio, at which point sheet-music sales became just a tiny part of income derived from hit songs.

In the sixties, unscrupulous publishers still applied the 50/50 formula even if they had their own company in the foreign territory. The Schroeders licensed Tony's copyrights back and forth between their own companies to contrive that Tony and John shared 12.5 per cent of the income on foreign sales, as opposed to 50 per cent. The Schroeders also held on to royalties in each country so that the writers might have to wait for years for foreign income to filter through. Other publishers, including some of the majors, also indulged in this practice.

Aaron Schroeder was himself a songwriter who in the past had written songs recorded by Frank Sinatra and Elvis Presley. Abby was the businesswoman who ran the company and she was not at all interested in my threat that Tony would not write any more songs for them. Under the then UK law, the contract was binding and she was both unpleasant and immovable. I discussed the problem with my American lawyer Normand Kurtz. Normand was a passionate man who railed against injustice. Such a contract would not be upheld in the USA and he urged me to take the Schroeders to court in the UK. Nick Kanaar was our UK lawyer and he recommended that I go to see Robert McCrindle, a barrister who was England's leading expert on contract law. Mr McCrindle told me that Tony's contract was indeed unfair *but* binding as English law now stood. If we wanted to get Tony out, we would have to change the law. He really fancied our chances of doing this and would have been delighted to take the case, but he was about to retire and, as the case would take months if not years to run its course, he advised me to find another barrister.

I recommended to Tony that he should sue the Schroeders. John Macleod was on the same unfair contract but he was too meek take them on and Tony decided that he would bear what might be the considerable cost of such an action himself.

The music business is replete with contract disputes and I had become somewhat of an expert in the field. One of the most important things that I had learned was that often it is the best prepared, not the virtuous, who win the day in court. I went to QC Morris Finer. He was under fifty, a young man by legal standards. I made it a condition that I could call him directly, unheard of when protocol demanded that a barrister could only be seen in the presence of the instructing lawyer. I even had his home telephone number. I drove everybody mad with detail and when the case started I sat behind Mr Finer in court, frequently handing him notes on points of the proceedings. I called councils of war with Morris and Nick on a regular basis to discuss strategy.

The Schroeders' lawyer was the notoriously outspoken Oscar Beuselinck. He admitted to me that he had told his clients that they would lose but they ignored his advice. He was right.

We won the case with Macaulay's costs awarded against the Schroeders. Our jubilation was short-lived because they appealed. We won the appeal and once again our costs were awarded against the Schroeders. They appealed yet again, this time to the House of Lords, then the highest court in the land in the days before the Supreme Court. There they lost yet again, with costs awarded against them once more. Not only did they lose the future copyrights of a great writer, their intransigence cost them several hundred thousand pounds in legal fees.

The House of Lords ruling is rather wordy but just in case any of you are interested I am setting out a summary below. It is easy to skip if you are satisfied to know that, as a result of this case, music publishers were obliged to be more transparent and fairer in their dealings with writers.

In 1974 five of England's most senior law lords held that the Schroeders' standard form agreement could not be justified as moulded under the pressures of negotiation, competition and public opinion. Macaulay had no bargaining power. The defendants purported to be able to arbitrarily decline to exploit the plaintiff's work in which event the plaintiff's remuneration under the agreement would be limited to a £50 advance payable hereunder during the five-year period. The defendants' power to assign precluded the argument that the restrictions would not be enforced oppressively. The defendants had failed to justify restrictions which appeared unnecessary and capable of oppressive enforcement.

Morris Finer, our QC, came to the celebration party at our offices and let his wig down a little. He later told me that he had allowed my unconventional approach of dealing with him directly because he admired my enthusiasm and passion for the case. In the seventies Morris successfully represented The Beatles against Allen Klein. He went on to be Sir Morris Finer, a senior judge.

Tony was free from the Schroeders but unfortunately was not returned his copyrights. To do this, the Schroeders would have to have been guilty of fraud as opposed to being dishonest exploiters of young talent. Macaulay v Schroeder became the test case that enabled many writers to escape from unfair contracts, including Elton John.

Nowadays, established singer/songwriters can get as much as 90 per cent of the income, and the copyright in the songs reverts to them after relatively few years. This is because – other than executing the paperwork necessary to register the copyright with the various collection bodies – there is little for the publishers to do. Led Zeppelin's Peter Grant made deals with publishers where the writers got 100 per cent of the money and the companies paid huge advances for the privilege of being the band's publisher and the right to hold on to the money that they collected for a few months until they accounted to the writers. Eventually music publishers just became bankers for writers.

In the 1980s, George Michael's UK publisher Dick Leahy, my ex-partner in GTO Records, asked me to assist him in the negotiating of a new deal for George's non-UK songwriting services. His contract with Warner Music was about to expire and just about every international publisher wanted to sign him. The competition to sign him drove the price so high that I could not see how the publisher could ever earn its money back before the copyrights reverted to George. Eventually Warner Music paid the price to retain him.

Tony Macaulay was one of the best UK writer-producers of his era. He co-wrote and produced a string of hits, including 'Build Me Up Buttercup' with Mike d'Abo; 'Let The Heartaches Begin' with John Macleod for Long John Baldry and 'You Won't Find Another Fool Like Me' with Geoff Stephens for The New Seekers. He is a very intelligent man, very driven and wanted to be involved in every aspect of his records. He used to help plug his own records in answer to his complaint that one wasn't selling, I told him that I couldn't get a machine gun and make people go into a shop to buy his records, to which he replied: 'Why not?' He was a complex man but had a great sense of humour as he demonstrated when the guitarist on one of his records was unhappy with his solo. The record had gone to be pressed and Tony, with his tongue firmly in his cheek, told him that the only way the guitar break could be changed was if the guitarist plugged his guitar into the pressing plant and replayed his bit as each record was pressed. According to Tony, the guitar-ist offered to do it!

Tony desperately wanted to be a star artist himself but was smart enough to realise that he was a lousy singer. He was very demanding of my time and attention and when I started GTO Records in 1974 I diplomatically asked him to find another manager. His attitude changed and he became cold. But I will always be grateful to Tony because he co-wrote and produced 'Love Grows (Where My Rosemary Goes)', Gem Produc-tion's first release in February 1970, very soon after I started the company. A huge hit, it was like going to the casino for the first time and having a big win. This of course can be dangerous but I managed to continue on a winning roll for some time. Anyway, it was 'Love Grows (Where My Rosemary Goes)' that set Gem on the path to success, so thank you, Tony.

16. MUSIC PUBLISHERS, FREDDY BIENSTOCK AND ELVIS

For those of you who are interested, this is how a song actually earns income for the publisher and songwriter. For those of you who are not interested, skip the next couple of pages.

Still with me? Good. There are three sources of revenue from copyrighted music.

Mechanicals. This is pretty straightforward. Any company that wishes to manufacture a record is legally obliged to get permission from the copyright owner to use the song. There is a statutory rate, which is the royalty that legally has to be paid by the manufacturer. The current UK rate is 8.5 per cent of the price charged to a record dealer. More songs are downloaded than physically bought and the online site is obliged to pay the copyright holder a royalty on every download. In the USA the mechanical rate is paid per track – so the more tracks on an album, the greater the cost. British albums were usually twelve tracks and, until UK artists were powerful enough to insist that their albums were released as recorded, the US record companies used to drop two tracks to save money. The current rate is 9.1 cents per track, so by cutting out two tracks the record company saves 18.2 cents on each album sold. The Beatles sold about one hundred and eighty million albums. You do the maths.

Performance royalties. This is a little more complicated. The songwriter assigns the right to collect income from public performances to the Performing Rights Society. The board of PRS is mainly made up of songwriters. Television and radio companies pay PRS a substantial fee for the right to broadcast music. Live music venues have to pay a fee. Even a shop that plays music that its customers can hear is obliged to pay the PRS a fee for doing so. Fees vary depending on the size of the potential audience. Over many years, the PRS have developed an algorithm by which they distribute the considerable amount of money they have collected between the songwriters.

'Points' are awarded for chart positions and plays on radio and TV. For example, a Saturday-night, prime-time TV show will accrue more points than an afternoon chat show. A big hit song can earn its writer several hundred thousand pounds over a number of years. In 2017, PRS announced record figures including payouts of £527.6 million to its members. It was the first time it surpassed half a billion pounds. To put it in context, Noddy Holder and the bass guitarist from Slade earn around a million pounds a year from 'Merry Christmas Everybody'. Writing a perennial Christmas song is the holy grail for song-writers. Irving Berlin was the first to do so with 'I'm Dreaming of a White Christmas', a song which he anecdotally wrote in ten minutes.

In the days before the public bought records, a publisher would distribute sheet music to bandleaders and end-of-the-pier concert parties, to encourage them to use the song. A bandleader was obliged to file a report listing all the songs that they had played. Many put down songs that they had written themselves, even if they had not played them.

Similar societies to the PRS all over the world collect performance income in their own territories and, after deducting a fee, pass it over to the PRS. Obviously, the allocation of PRS income is somewhat arbitrary but over the years it has been refined to the satisfaction of the songwriters.

Synchronisation fees. This is now a huge revenue earner. If a film or TV commercial uses a song, the producers negotiate a fee with the publisher for the copyright-holders, who can take home a seven-figure sum. I recently saw a TV documentary that purported to list the top ten earning songs. 'Happy Birthday' predictably is the highest at thirty million pounds and 'White Christmas' is next. In terms of pop music 'You've Lost that Loving Feeling' is the highest at No. 3 and 'Yesterday' is next. Obviously the longer a copyright is around the more it can earn and some more recent hits may well be up there in the fullness of time.

At a time when very few so-called publishers actually understood the intricacies of the business Freddy Bienstock was a proper exception. Most importantly he knew how to maximise income from the less obvious revenue streams. Freddy spent twenty years learning about his trade. He ensured that those who were supposed to pay did so. In the sixties and seventies, the publisher also took responsibility to 'plug' a song on radio and TV. Unlike some of his contemporaries, my friend Freddy was an expert in copyright law, to the point that he spotted a rather obscure court ruling which enabled a writer's estate to claim back a copyright years before its natural expiration. Freddy's companies own the copyright of important songs from the biggest hits of rock'n'roll to standards from the great American songbook. Freddie died in 2009, leaving his family a company that I am sure is worth many hundreds of millions of dollars.

In the same way as a lot of amateurs jumped on the property development bandwagon of the sixties and seventies, almost everybody in the music business – including me – started a publishing company. There was no real skill required. The key was to persuade writers to sign a copyright over to your company and then sit back and watch the money come in. The records went out and the publisher collected the income generated. The way publishing developed, copyright owners could contract with major publishing houses to administer and collect on their behalf at a small cost. All you needed was a bank account.

Had I been the publisher of the artists I managed, I could now have a single filing cabinet holding copyrights that, without my lifting a finger, would have generated enough income to keep me and my descendants in a luxury lifestyle until the copyrights expired. But most of the writers I knew had existing contracts with publishers, and in any event, I had decided that I could not be all things to all people and had elected to concentrate on management and records. I did have a 50/50 publishing company with Freddy, mainly B-sides or album tracks that we had picked up via our recording activities. There was one decent copyright, for 'The Pushbike Song', acquired for the company by my partner David Joseph, of whom more later.

As a general rule, copyrights become PD (in the public domain) seventy years after the death of the last living writer of a song. This may vary from country to country. If someone makes an arrangement of a PD song, the copyright in their version belongs to the arranger. 'The House of the Rising Sun' was a traditional American folk song, but Alan Price was credited as the arranger on The Animals, recording and he therefore earned the royalties.

Freddy Bienstock was the last of the old-school independent publishers. Born in Switzerland in 1923, his family lived in Vienna before moving to New York just before the outbreak of the war. Freddy started work in the stock room of Chappell Music in the Brill Building. He worked his way up to being a song-plugger before going to work for publishers Hill & Range, where one of his jobs was to find songs for Elvis Presley to record. In 1966, Freddy bought their UK subsidiary and changed the name to Carlin Music. He was also partner in Elvis's music publishing company. Although Elvis was not a songwriter, his manager Colonel Parker made it a rule to get the company the publishing of every new song that Elvis recorded. Freddy ran the company, and Elvis had such respect for him he would ask his opinion on almost everything that he recorded.

After 'Hello,' the next thing that Freddy said to a talented songwriter was 'I can get you an Elvis cover.' In fact sometimes this even preceded 'Hello.' I used to tease him incessantly about this. If we were in a restaurant I would nod to the waiter and say: 'He can get you an Elvis cover.' Most of us hang our gold discs on a wall. Freddy would have needed the Great Wall of China to hang his and he only had one gold disc on his office wall. It was a gold disc I had specially made for him with 'I can get you an Elvis cover' on the plaque.

Geoff Morrow, a good friend of mine who I managed as part of the writing team Arnold, Martin and Morrow, had several songs recorded by Elvis thanks to Freddy. One of them, 'Let's Be Friends', was the title song of an Elvis album. The team also wrote 'Can't Smile Without You' for Barry Manilow, a huge hit which is still the high point of Barry's act. Our business paths crossed again when Geoff started writing for theatre. Geoff is now an extremely successful businessman.

I went with Freddy on three occasions to see Elvis's opening night in Vegas. Elvis was inclined to coast a little on his Vegas dates, but not on the opening night, which was always an occasion with a celebrity-packed audience. On one trip, Marsha came with us. She was not an Elvis fan so I should never have married her, but when he took his bows after what was an unforgettable performance, she was on her feet screaming his name with the rest of us.

Freddy had a very clever way of dealing with the dissolution of publishing partnerships. He asked the partner he was splitting from to divide the copyrights into two lists, and Freddy decided which of the lists he wanted to retain. It is a brilliantly fair way of dividing assets, which I have since used myself. The other effective way is for Partner A to name a price and Partner B to decide whether he wants to buy or sell at that price. When I decided that we should administer our own copyrights, it was necessary to 'divorce' from Freddy's Carlin Music. At the time,

Keith Potger, one of the original Seekers – a hugely successful group from Australia – was running our publishing company. Keith made up the two lists and Freddie chose the one that included 'The Pushbike Song', the only song that was of any real value. Some people are gifted with musical talent; some people are gifted with brains. Keith could play the guitar and sing. I should never have put him in the ring with Freddie. It was like putting Julian Clary in the ring to fight Mike Tyson.

17. THE ROLLING STONES

I am not trying to compete with the many excellent books written about the Rolling Stones, some of which I have researched (if a writer gets facts from one book it's called 'plagiarism'; if he gets facts from lots of books, it's called 'research'). I will restrict my history of the Stones to stories in which I was personally involved.

In my brief career as a partner in a firm of chartered accountants, nothing was more exciting than Goodman Myers being appointed as accountants to the Rolling Stones. My only previous encounter with the Stones was when they and The Animals were both appearing on a TV show called *Ready Steady Go!* The show was shot in a TV studio in London, and I was in with The Animals, who were sharing a dressing room with the Stones. Eric Burdon grabbed Bill Wyman's camera while the Stones were performing, dropped his trousers and had Chas Chandler take a photograph of his own not inconsiderable appendage. Eric then put the camera back exactly where he had found it. In those days one sent one's films off to be developed, and God knows what problems Eric's prank caused Bill Wyman.

Needless to say, I didn't mention the subject of Eric Burdon's cock when, in 1971, Bill came to see me about an album he had produced with The Walker Brothers' John Walker (whose real last name was Maus). John, Scott (Engel) and Gary (Leeds) split in 1968 – although they would reunite in 1974, when the brilliant talent-spotter Dick Leahy signed them to GTO Records, the record company that we owned together. We had a huge hit with the single 'No Regrets' and the album of the same name. More about GTO Records later. Scott was the real singing talent of the Brothers and after their break-up nobody wanted to release a solo album by John. When Bill came to see me it was to ask if I could place the record for him in Japan where The Walker Brothers had huge success. He hoped I could get him an advance of ten thousand pounds.

The Japanese generally never attended the Midem music festival, but I agreed to take the album to see what I could do. There were rumours of a Japanese guy being seen in Cannes and I eventually tracked him down. He was leaving early the next morning but when I mentioned John of The Walker Brothers he agreed to meet with me at 7 a.m. Now, you should know that a lot of Midem business is conducted in the late-night bars and that night I was at The Martinez hotel bar until the early hours of the morning. I dragged myself out of bed and met my Japanese contact for breakfast at the five-star Carlton hotel, a place he had suggested. There was a lot of exchanging business cards and bowing which went on too long because I did not know the etiquette of who should bow last. Eventually we sat down.

'Are you staying here?' I asked.

'No.' He mentioned a hotel on the outskirts of Cannes that I had never heard of. This should have been a clue. He ordered a huge breakfast. 'I will not eat on the plane.'

I ordered a large breakfast too. I was very bleary-eyed, but as the discussions progressed I perked up considerably. The guy said yes to everything.

'The royalty will have to be 16 per cent.'

'Yes.'

'You will pay an advance of twenty thousand dollars.'

'Yes.'

'In addition to the royalty you will pay me a commission of 2 per cent.'

'Yes.'

This was too easy for words. Bill was going to be delighted with me. I had got him double his hoped-for advance and even got the Japanese to pay my commission. I stood up and leaned forward to shake hands.

'So we have a deal?'

'No. I must report back to my superior in Tokyo.'

I sat down again and he left, leaving me to pay the outrageous price of breakfast for two at one of the most expensive hotels in Cannes.

Needless to say, I never heard a word from the gentleman again. I later learned that in Japanese culture 'Yes' means 'I understand' not 'I agree'. Make a note of this if you ever meet a Japanese person for an early-morning breakfast meeting.

Andrew Loog Oldham left school at sixteen for a menial job with Mary Quant (who almost single-handedly invented the fashion of London's swinging sixties). He then got a job in a PR company, a world that he loved. In 1961 he became a freelance PR, at one point doing PR for the fast-emerging Beatles. He and Tony Calder, another freelance PR guy, started Image, a PR company specialising in pop music.

Andrew often visited The Crawdaddy Club, a popular venue where the Rolling Stones often played. The audience reception was extremely enthusiastic, almost at Beatle level, and Andrew was impressed. Image PR was not making him any money and he decided that he wanted to manage the Stones. Concerned that his lack of knowledge might put them off signing with him, he did not approach them that evening. He went to see Eric Easton, a well-respected theatrical agent, and persuaded him to come and see the band perform. Easton was also impressed. Together they approached Brian Jones, the founder and leader of the Stones, who agreed that that Easton and Oldham would manage the Stones. They charged 25 per cent of the band's earnings. Mick and Keith were underage so Brian signed on behalf of the band. It was 1963 and Andrew was barely *twenty years old*.

Andrew and Eric made the Stones huge in the UK. They had half a dozen hit singles, a number-one album and their tours sold out but they were nowhere near as successful in America, where The Beatles were a phenomenon and The Dave Clark Five, Herman's Hermits and Freddie and The Dreamers were all huge. the Stones' comparative lack of success was a problem and Andrew struggled to find an answer. In the spring of 1965, he was in New York on Stones' business. He had fallen out with Eric Easton and, in partnership with his old PR partner Tony Calder, was planning to start Immediate Records in the UK, a venture that he found more exciting than his management endeavours. He was due to have a breakfast meeting with J. W. Alexander, a partner in Kags Music, Sam Cooke's music publishing business.

He was hoping to get a rebate for the Stones on the royalties paid to Kags for the use of 'It's All Over Now', which was Kags' copyright. There was no reason why Mr Alexander should agree to this after the event, but Andrew thought that he would try.

Sam Cooke's manager, Allen Klein, was also sitting next to J.W. and Allen later told me that he had had his eye on the Stones for some time and was shocked at how young their manager was. Andrew's request for a rebate on 'It's All Over Now' was dismissed out of hand, but they carried on chatting and Andrew told him of his plans to start Immediate Records. He also intimated that he was not getting on with Eric Easton. Allen's main objective was to get to the Rolling Stones, but smart man that he was, he never brought them into the conversation. He offered to help Andrew get distribution deals for Immediate Records. His parting shot to Andrew was, of course, 'I can get you a million dollars.'

Allen called me to ask me if I knew Eric Easton, which I did not. He told me what had happened with Andrew, and his belief that he would soon be managing the Stones with him. I knew that Mickie Most knew Andrew, but Allen did not want to ask him to help snare Andrew. It was important to Allen that Mickie believed that he was getting most of his attention. I understood this, as I was in a similar position myself. Allen asked me to 'be aware' and keep him advised of any information that came my way that would be helpful to his cause. I was a little amused at Allen's Machiavellian style of operating and admiring of his dedication to getting what he wanted. Inevitably, Allen usurped Easton as Andrew's partner. Easton sued Allen and got a court order freezing the band's back-royalties.

After long litigation, Allen paid him off with two hundred thousand pounds in September 1971.

At the time that the Rolling Stones business took up residence in my office, Brian Jones had still been the leader of the band, but in title only – it was clear to everyone, including Brian, that this was changing and that Mick was now The Man. Andrew arranged for Allen to meet with Mick and he did his thing, successfully gaining the singer's confidence. Allen then met with all of the Rolling Stones at the Hilton hotel on Park Lane and they enthusiastically agreed that he should become co-manager of the band with Andrew.

the Stones' business had been run out of Easton's offices, and as this was clearly no longer viable, in January 1967 we gave them some space in Goodman Myers & Co.'s offices in Regent Street. Stephanie Bluestone, the Stones' general assistant, moved in with us to run their office. We hosted them for a few months until they set up their own office in Maddox Street, but those few months were an exciting time in the history of the Stones, and I was privileged to be at the heart of it: this was the period in which Allen renegotiated their Decca deal, Mick and Keith famously got arrested for drugs, and the band firmly established themselves as the 'bad boys' of rock. Brian Jones was confirmed to no longer be the band's leader and some months later died in the swimming pool of Cotchford Farm, his house in Essex. The inquest recorded death by misadventure, arising from Brian's abuse of drugs and alcohol, but there are many other theories still around which dispute this, including murder. If this is of interest to you, the internet is full of conflicting 'maybes'.

The Stones were signed to Decca Records, via Impact Sound, a company owned by Andrew Oldham and Eric Easton. Decca paid Impact a royalty of 8 per cent and Impact paid the Stones 6 per cent. Andrew and Easton also took 25 per cent of the Stones' 6 per cent in their capacity as managers, leaving the band with 4.5 per cent. Clearly the Stones did not have a great deal and the whole mess had to be sorted out.

A meeting was arranged with Sir Edward Lewis, owner of Decca Records. The main Klein party consisted of Allen and myself with Andrew Oldham and all five Rolling Stones. We went to the meeting at Decca House in two Rolls-Royces that Allen had hired for the occasion. He believed in arriving in style.

Sir Edward, Bill Townsley (Decca's MD) and people from his legal affairs department greeted us. Allen, Andrew Oldham and I (the good guys) sat at the boardroom table and the Stones stood around behind us, looking sullen and angry, as had been rehearsed. Without preamble, Allen turned to each of the Stones and asked if he was authorised to speak on their behalf. As rehearsed, each said 'Yes,' and then, as also rehearsed, they trouped out. Sir Edward was clearly dismayed by the pantomime he had just witnessed. His previous negotiations had been with Eric Easton, a businesslike gentleman. He looked at Andrew.

'Is Eric not coming?' Andrew, who had also been rehearsed, did not speak. But Allen did.

'Eric doesn't play in the band. You can speak to me.'

Allen was purposefully aggressive. He wanted Sir Edward to know that he was difficult to deal with and had no wish to be liked. I could see Sir Edward struggling to maintain his composure. 'Very well, what is it that you want, Mr. Klein?'

Allen demanded copies of all of the Stones' royalty statements and contracts, including the draft contract that Eric Easton had negotiated for future renewal. Sir Edward went red enough to double as a traffic light. I do not know what he said because I do not speak splutter but I suspect that he did not wish us a 'good day'.

I later reviewed Decca's proposed contract, negotiated by Easton and it was clear that it contained all of the unnecessary royalty deductions that were standard record-company practice, and committed the Stones to Decca for up to five years. The contract provided that the Stones would get an advance of the equivalent of $300,000 recoupable against all royalties including pipeline royalties. These are royalties on past recordings recently sold around the world, but not yet included in quarterly account-ings. I could see that Decca were offering to pay the Stones an advance out of their own money.

Allen negotiated a new deal for Impact Sounds with Decca that guaranteed the Stones $1.25 million for a one-year contract, with more advances for any extensions. $600,000 was to be paid on signing. Andrew agreed that the Stones' royalty from Impact Sounds was increased to 7 per cent and they would pay no management commission on record royalties. Allen's cut came out of what would have been Eric Easton's share and, as he said to Mick, 'I have made you rich and it hasn't cost you a cent.'

As mentioned before, UK tax was at a punitive level and, as with the Mickie Most/EMI deal, it made sense for the Stones to get their money paid over a number of years. Allen, somewhat craftily, structured the spread in such a way that he ended up being the owner of the Stones' recordings for the US and Canada, paying them 80 per cent of the royalty income arising. He also made a deal to be the publisher of Jagger and Richard's songs, giving them 70 per cent of earnings as opposed to the standard 50 per cent. He gave them a writer's advance of a million dollars, an astonishingly large amount even if it was payable over twenty years, to shelter the advances from UK taxes. With success, the spreadable advances went up to three million dollars. Any sums they earned above the advances were to be paid at the end of the twenty-year period.

The net result of these two deals was that Allen had legal control of the vast monies that were generated by the Stones' record sales in America, subject to paying them the contractual advances. In later years – after he had ceased to manage the Stones – they launched several legal attacks on Allen and his company ABKCO, trying to wrest ownership of the master recordings and music copyrights away from him. All the attempts failed and ABKCO still owns the American rights to all of the Stones' hits recorded in the sixties and the copyright in the songs.

Allen was even smarter. Record contracts traditionally provided that the company would own recordings made by the artist 'manufactured out of vinyl' – the current practice – 'or by any means now invented or to be invented in the future'. Allen pointed out that as nobody knew what the economics of unknown future production would be, Decca could only have the rights for vinyl, which was the existing medium. Decca, too weary to fight for a future contingency that might never happen, agreed. This meant that when cassettes and later CDs replaced vinyl, the record company had no rights to the product and his company ABKCO, as the owner, was free to control manufacturing and distribution of the recordings. He arranged for the Stones' records to be distributed in the US by Decca subsidiary London Records, but ABKCO Records became the Stones' de facto American record company.

The relationship between Andrew Oldham and the Stones had been deteriorating for years. There was no question that his faith and flair had launched them but his perceived desire to be famous in his own right had caused the Stones to believe that he was more interested in his own celebrity than theirs. In 1968, he sold his interest in the Rolling Stones to Allen for $750,000. Now there was not even the pretence that Andrew was involved with the career of the band that he had made famous, and Allen had total control of the second-biggest band in the world. The biggest band was, of course, The Beatles and it was still Allen's firm ambition to manage them.

One of my first jobs as the Stones' accountant was to prepare the figures for their past tours for submission to the UK Inland Revenue. These were not the hundred-million-dollar world tours that they undertook in later years. In early January and March of 1964, they did two tours of one-nighters that I had to report on. The January tour was fourteen dates in twenty days and the March tour was thirty dates in thirty days. The accounts I prepared showed that the Stones made very little money from the tour. Brian claimed expenses for the use of his own car and the rest of the boys travelled in a beat-up old van, squeezing between Charlie Watts' drum kit and the instruments. They were one of eight acts that each did about twenty minutes. They played two shows a night and a comedian told a few jokes as the acts changed over. For one 1965 tour, the comedian was Ray Cameron, father of Michael McIntyre, now one of the most popular comedians in the UK. Ray went on to write for *The Kenny Everett Video Show* and in the seventies I produced *Bloodbath at the House of Death*, a spoof horror film starring Kenny that Ray directed.

Mickie Most had toured with the Stones as a performer on a 1963 tour when the crowd-pullers were American acts The Everly Brothers, Bo Diddley and Little Richard. Like most UK pop stars, Mickie's act was a pale imitation of American rock acts in general, and the Stones used to play Bo Diddly songs at their gigs. Mickie and the Stones were both low down in the pecking order. The second tour was largely with UK acts: Marty Wilde, Dave Berry, and The Swinging Blue Jeans. the Stones were not popular enough to close the show.

I had to go through the accounts with each of the Stones to clarify certain expenditure. Mick, Charlie and Brian were very vague but Bill Wyman had kept meticulous records, down to how much of the room service charges were for him in the room he shared with Brian. Bill was always the keeper of records and he never threw anything away. His book *Stone Alone* is full of minutiae of his life with the Stones, and is well worth reading.

There was no tax liability but the man from the revenue demanded a meeting, which was quite unusual for such a small turnover. I duly attended the tax office in Soho Square on crutches, having damaged my ankle on a trampoline in the garden of Mickie's new house in Totteridge. I overplayed my limp, hoping that sympathy for my plight would help me in the meeting. The man from the revenue showed no concern what-

soever about my condition but expressed great interest about an
item of cash disbursement described as 'sundries'. It was a very
small amount and it became clear I was only there because the
young man from Her Majesty's inspector of taxes was clearly
a Stones fan. I told him that the cash was used by the band to
buy tickets to their own performances – to give to girl fans who
would scream. I had made this up, but I swore the guy to secrecy
and he passed the accounts, no doubt happily believing that he
was in on a Rolling Stones secret.

The bank account for the tour had all of the Stones as signa-
tories. In those days, banks returned cheques that had been
issued on the account. Once I completed the audit there was no
need to keep them so, in accordance with standard practice, I
threw them out. Can you imagine what a cheque signed by all of
the Rolling Stones would fetch at a memorabilia auction today?
Who knew?

During the time that the Stones were run out of the Goodman
Myers offices, Allen Klein seldom visited England. He spent
his time and energy berating London Records for not doing
a better job, and berating concert promoters for not treating
the Stones as superstars. It was working. Les Perrin, an established UK PR person, dealt with the considerable media issues.
The Beatles were perceived as the 'good boys' and the Stones
were cast as the 'bad boys' and Les, following a pattern set by
Andrew Oldham, did a brilliant job maintaining the Stones'
image as being rebellious and anarchic on both sides of the
Atlantic and beyond. Parents disapproved, so of course the kids
loved them.

The Stones were technically rich but Allen was holding their money. When he received the big advance from Decca, he opened American bank accounts in the boys' names, depositing fifty thousand dollars for each them. There were tax implications if they brought the money into the UK and exchange control regulations, which made it illegal to have bank accounts abroad. Easton had sued the Stones and Allen, tying up pipeline royalties from Decca, so one way or another the Stones had yet to directly benefit from their impressive new deals.

I would talk to Allen often, and warned him that his lack of attention to the financial needs of the London office was causing great resentment. His response was always words to the effect of 'I'm busy making the Rolling Stones bigger than The Beatles. I'll deal with these little problems later.' the Stones' financial needs were real. Assured by Allen that they were now rich, the boys started to spend money but, as they could not bring any funds back to the UK that Allen had deposited for them in their American bank accounts, they were as good as broke. The UK exchange control regulators attacked the Stones for holding money abroad, and I had to get them out of trouble by explaining that the accounts were opened in their names but the signatory was Allen Klein. As a consequence, they were then obliged to bring the money over to the UK.

In the meantime, Allen had given vague assurances that if they needed money he would get it to them. the Stones office had to deal with calls for money from the boys as well as from general creditors. The fastest form of international communication was the telex machine. You could dial up any telex number and anything typed your end would instantly appear on the machine at the other end of the line. With a secretary manning each machine it was possible to have 'conversations'. Goodman Myers had such a device and Stan Blackburn, the Stones' long-time bookkeeper, was constantly sending telex messages to Allen's office in New York, asking for money. Allen foolishly did not even acknowledge the requests. Eventually I sent a telex to Allen saying, 'Does my telex have bad breath?' which prompted him to call me. I explained the situation, and he started to take the requests more seriously.

When Allen did concentrate on keeping the Stones happy, he did so with style. I was in New York in August 1965 when The Beatles played Shea stadium, a legendary concert. Allen decided that we should take the Stones to see the show and spent hours trying to get permission for our party to arrive by helicopters and have seats in the dugout. This could not happen so we did not go at all.

Determined to take some public attention away from The Beatles – a lost cause if ever there was one – he rented a huge boat and took the Stones on a cruise down the Hudson River and I was lucky enough to still be in town so I joined them. Whenever we passed another boat Andrew Oldham stood at the prow, his long hair streaming in the wind, preaching to anyone that could hear him that he was Jesus and that this was how He had decided to make His second coming. My great memory was the Stones' non-stop playing and replaying of Wilson Picket's recent release, 'In The Midnight Hour'. They just loved that record, as did I.

After the Stones set up their own offices in Maddox Street I frequently went there to discuss their affairs. Mick had set up a small teepee tent in the middle of the office, which he used when he needed to be shut out from the general hubbub. Jo Bergman, a powerhouse of a lady who was by now running the Stones' office, told me that he spent hours in there talking to a young American guy who had walked from Heathrow airport into London to see him. The young man, who clearly had mental issues, believed that Mick was some sort of messiah. Mick showed extraordinary patience and compassion in dealing with such people. He was also patient with intrusive fans. I once had to have a meeting with him while he was waiting for a plane at what is now Kennedy airport. I was not travelling, so we could not go to a private lounge. We found a quiet table in the public area and settled down to discuss some important matters. A drunk American redneck came over to us and rudely interrupted us.

'Hey, Mick, my girlfriend wants your autograph.'

Mick was in mid-sentence and politely held up his hand in a 'give me just a moment' gesture. The guy wasn't having that. 'I don't even know why she likes your shitty music. You too big for your fans?'

Mick did not say a word. He signed the piece of paper that this rude pig had stuck under his nose. The rude pig walked away without a thank-you, and Mick carried on with his conversation. When I expressed my surprise, he shrugged and said, 'It happens all the time. If I react, there could be a fight and it won't be that arsehole's name that makes the headlines.'

One of the things on the agenda was a pension plan. Mick had considered going into the insurance business when he left the London School of Economics. Ellis, my partner, had a good connection with a blue-blood firm of insurance brokers and Mick actually asked Ellis if he could effect an introduction 'just in case'. Ellis would of course have been delighted to do so, but Mick soon created his own insurance policy via his talent, and the introduction never took place. Mick is a very smart man, which is why he is still singing rock'n'roll in his seventies.

In February 1967, following an anonymous tip-off, the police – armed with a search warrant – raided Keith Richards' home Redlands in West Sussex. Mick and Marianne Faithfull and some other friends were Keith's houseguests. George Harrison and his then-girlfriend Pattie Boyd had popped in but left before the police arrived. It was a major raid with carloads of coppers. Mick and Keith were very polite and cooperative. Marianne, who was upstairs at the time of the raid, appeared at the top of the stairs covered in a rug, which she dropped revealing her naked body shouting, 'Search me!'

The police found four amphetamine tablets – which actually belonged to Marianne – and some hash in the possession of a friend known as Acid King David. Mick, ever the gentleman, claimed that the tablets were his to protect Marianne. In March, Mick and Keith were informed that they would be charged with offences against the Dangerous Drugs Act. I went with Allen and a small army of lawyers to the Chichester court, where the charges were put to them. They were released on bail pending trial and I have a photograph on my wall of a very young-looking me, peering over the shoulders of Mick and Keith, laughing on the steps of the court.

The offences were not serious but Allen and I did not take the charges lightly. If the boys were found guilty of drug charges it could affect their entry into the United States. It was clear that the Stones were going to be constant targets for the police,

and indeed Brian Jones' flat was raided on the evening of the day
they were charged. Jagger and Richards seemed to think that it
was all a hoot, but they followed Allen's advice and went abroad
to avoid being hounded by the press until they were obliged to
appear before a Chichester judge.

On the 27 June Mick was found guilty of possession of four
amphetamine tablets and a day later Keith was found guilty of
allowing cannabis to be smoked on his property. They were both
sent in handcuffs to Lewes jail to each serve a month's sentence.
Released on bail the next day, they appealed and Keith's sentence
of one year in jail was overturned. Mick's sentence of three months
was also reduced to a conditional discharge. There was a public
outcry of support for Mick and Keith. Even *The Times* weighed in,
with illustrious editor William Rees-Mogg writing an eloquent
leader column in their defence, headed 'Who breaks a butterfly on
a wheel?' Brian was also sentenced to jail but on appeal was fined a
thousand pounds and ordered to seek professional help.

The Stones were now trophy targets for police forces all over
the world. Keith's excellent autobiography *Life* is, amongst other
things, a fascinating record of the ingenious ways he managed to
get his heroin as he toured the USA, in spite of the district attorney of each state being determined to be the hero who caught him.
He makes the interesting observation that he survived the drug
itself because he was rich enough to buy only the purest-quality
heroin and cocaine. In spite of, or maybe because of, my proximity
to serious drug-takers I have never been tempted to try it and I
have no idea if there is any truth in his claim.

Because I was a sympathetic ear, Brian Jones would sometimes
come in to see me. He was now very aware that he was no longer

the leader of the Rolling Stones, nor was it musically the band that he had started. Brian was a true blues fan and wanted to play the music of his heroes. His relationship with the rest of the band was not helped when it was discovered that he had made a secret deal with Easton/Oldham to get five pounds a week more than the other band members when they had first signed with them for management. Brian had started a blues band with the still semi-pro Mick and Keith and, from his point of view, the deal he had signed with Oldham and Eastman led to their ultimate success. Without him there would never have been the Rolling Stones, but he was never invited to write a song for the band and now he was not even wanted at recording sessions.

Brian spoke very quietly and would ramble on, often incoherently, about what he perceived was the injustice heaped on him by the world in general and by Mick and Keith in particular. Keith had stolen Anita Pallenberg, his girlfriend. (Keith famously commented, 'Shit happens in the back of a limousine.') I am not sure why Brian confided his woes in me but I suspect that he did so with anyone who was prepared to listen. Even though his woeful condition was self-induced, I felt very sorry for him.

The housekeeper at Brian's home at Crotchford Farm had my home number as one of the people to call in the case of an emergency. On 3 July 1969 I got an early-morning call from her to tell me that Brian had drowned in his swimming pool. It was the middle of the night in New York, but I called Allen to tell him the news and he was extremely distressed. I was personally very saddened by Brian's death. He was only twenty-seven years old and it seemed to me that there had been little joy in his life, other than his music, and even that had been tainted when the purist blues band that he started was taken in a more commercial direction by Mick and Keith. There was no indication if Brian's death was an accident or suicide, and much has been written since. I personally believe that his death – like that of so many of his contemporaries – was due to the mind-altering drugs that were too fashionable and too freely available to those who could afford them in the sixties.

Apart from my professional relationship with the Rolling Stones, I am to this day a fan. They are, in my view, the greatest rock'n'roll band ever. Mick is astonishingly fit and contrary to that discussion that we had some fifty years ago, he *is* still singing rock'n'roll. Many of their current following were not even born when the Stones had the big hits that the fans demand to hear today.

18. RUPERT LOEWENSTEIN COMES ON THE SCENE AND THE STONES BREAK WITH KLEIN

O n the day that Brian Jones died in July 1969, Mick went to a white ball at the Holland Park home of Prince Rupert Loewenstein. Antique dealer Chris Gibbs had introduced them in 1968. Chris thought that Rupert might be of use to sort out Mick's money affairs and Rupert then met with Mick a few times to generally discuss this possibility.

As can be deduced from his full title, Rupert Louis Ferdinand Frederick Constantine Lofredo Leopold Herbert Maximilian Hubert John Henry zu Löwenstein-Wertheim-Freudenberg, Count of Loewenstein-Scharffeneck, was an aristocrat, from minor Bavarian royalty. He was educated in England and was a partner in Leopold Joseph & Sons, a prestigious boutique merchant bank.

Mick had become disenchanted with Allen's obsession with The Beatles and his apparent neglect of Stones' business, and appointed Rupert as advisor to himself and the band. Rupert and his wife Josephine were fixtures in the upper echelons of society and introduced Mick and Marianne to their world, which

Mick rather enjoyed. Mick now became familiar with Antibes, Mustique, St Barths and other watering holes that were once the exclusive haunts of the beau monde. Now these places are frequented by tattooed footballers, girls called Tracy and Cheryl, and even people like me.

Rupert kicked out the UK and American lawyers that had been put in place by Allen and brought in a new team of his own, choosing those who would help him analyse and review the band's legal affairs. I escaped the cull and worked closely with Mrs Stacey, Theodore Goddard's highly regarded tax lawyer, helping her restructure the Stones' tax affairs. The rate for high earners was still about 90 per cent and Mrs. Stacey advised the Stones that they should become non-resident, which they achieved by moving residencies to the south of France.

I got on well with Prince Rupert. The only Prince I had known before was Prince Monolulu, a black racing tipster who used to go to race meetings dressed in exotic Zulu chief garb shouting, 'I got an 'orse.' On Sundays he used to try to sell his tips at the Petticoat Lane market where I had my market stall and he occasionally bought sweets from me. Keeping a straight face, I once asked Rupert if he knew Prince Monolulu. He searched his memory for African aristocracy that he had known and said he did not. Before he became involved with Mick Jagger, Rupert was only interested in classical music but he very quickly became enamoured with rock and pop. He sent me demo tapes of a band called Gypsy and I promised to go to their next gig. Some days later my secretary handed me a priceless message that said, 'Gypsy are playing for the Prince tonight.' It was like something out of a Franz Lehár operetta: I did not go to the gig, but I kept the piece of paper for years.

I warned Allen that Rupert was amassing forces against him, but he did not seem to be unduly perturbed. The way Allen had structured his deals with the Stones' recordings meant that he did not need the goodwill of Mick Jagger or any of the Stones for ABKCO to continue to benefit from their recordings. the Stones' share of income had not changed, but by buying out Oldham and Easton, ABKCO effectively received 50 per cent of the income on every record sold. The three-year deals that Allen negotiated with Decca were about to run out and I told Allen that Prince Rupert's influence was becoming stronger and the Stones might look to him to negotiate a new deal. Allen's ego was his downfall. He was sure that all he needed to do was spend time with Mick to reclaim his loyalty. He tried, but it was too late. the Stones appointed Rupert as their new manager. Allen went into in denial, but as much as he tried to convince himself to the contrary, he was out.

Rupert and Allen both reached for their legal guns. They ultimately came to a preliminary settlement but there was an orgy of lawsuits between Allen and the Stones. As they say in the biz, 'Where there's a hit, there's a writ,' and here there were lots of hits, so the litigation went on for twenty years.

Allen's reign was the golden years for Stones music, producing classic hits like 'The Last Time', 'Paint It Black', 'Ruby Tuesday' and 'Satisfaction'. Stones fans still demand to hear these old hits and none of the records that Jagger made as a solo artist have had any real success. Allen's son Jody now presides over ABKCO on behalf of the Klein family and the money still rolls in.

Prince Rupert negotiated the new deal with Decca, which – with Allen out of the way – gave the Stones all of the royalties. In

America he negotiated a profitable new deal for future recordings with Ahmet Ertegun, the charismatic head of Atlantic Records. I have written earlier about my close relationship with American publisher Freddy Bienstock. Freddy's wife Miriam, a formidable woman who became a good friend of my own wife, started Atlantic Records with Ahmet. She had introduced me to him some years earlier and I got to know him and his brother Nesuhi quite well. Rupert had asked me to advise him in his negotiations with Ahmet, but I felt that helping move them to another record company was disloyal to Allen who was still a close friend, so I diplomatically declined his request.

Allen broke the Stones in America and his deals made them financially secure. Rupert made them personally very rich. He successfully guided all aspects of the Stones' careers until 2007, since which time Mick has effectively managed the band. the Stones' live performances became huge money-makers, and even at an age when they are all entitled to a bus pass, their world tours gross about half a billion dollars. It's a long way from the few thousand pounds from their UK tours in the early sixties, and a long time since that meeting at Kennedy airport when Mick said to me 'After all, Laurence, I'm not going to be singing rock'n'roll when I'm sixty.'

In the same way that I had gained knowledge about the music business, Ellis Goodman, through his clients, had gained knowledge and expertise in the whisky business. We both quit our practice in 1971, but, for years after, we kept a 50/50 interest in each other's work. In all of the years that we were together, we never had a written contract, never exchanged a cross word and we are still close friends.

It's hard to be good at something you don't like and I hated being a chartered accountant. The statute of limitations is six years for a simple contract, so I can now confess that my advice to clients was not always sound. I used to come home to my wife and say, 'Thank God I'm not a doctor, I might kill people.' Aware of my shortcomings, I relied a lot on the knowledgeable people around me, but it is not easy to keep on saying, 'Just got to pop to the loo,' to a client so I could nip next door to a colleague and ask their advice. I remember on one occasion when I was obliged to advise 'Yes' or 'No' to a client there was nobody around to ask, so I gazed out of my office window looking profound and thinking that if a bus goes by before a taxi I'll say 'Yes'. There was a 50/50 chance of being right, and I've acted on worse odds for myself. Another problem for me was that professional etiquette at the time prevented me from going after other accountants' clients. You had to wait until the client approached you, and it was difficult for me to meet people in the music business that I believed needed my help and not be able to say words to the effect, 'I can get you a million dollars.'

Roger, my brother, at the age of twenty-three replaced me as a partner in Goodman Myers & Co. and he continued to look after the Rolling Stones. Roger left the practice in 1974 to go into business with Tony Visconti, producer of Marc Bolan and David Bowie. They started a company called Good Earth. Tony was married to Mary Hopkin, the sweet-voiced girl who had a surprise hit in 1968 with 'Those Were The Days', produced by Paul McCartney. This came about because Paul's friend Twiggy had seen Mary sing on *Opportunity Knocks*, a UK talent show, and brought Mary to Paul's attention. Paul had the song 'Those

Were The Days' in his head for years. He had heard it sung by Gene and Francesca Raskin, an obscure American cabaret duo who worked at the Blue Angel, a small club in Mayfair that Marsha and I occasionally frequented. He instantly fell in love with the song and thought that he might record it himself. Well, the Blue Angel did serve alcohol.

Paul spotted that Mary's voice was perfect for 'Those Were The Days' and he signed her to Apple Records to record it. The result was a No. 1 record in the UK, sales of 1.5 million copies in the US and only 'Hey Jude' kept it off the No. 1 spot in the American charts. It was the magic combination of that voice and that song that had interested McCartney. They subsequently made a few records together, which did not work, and he called in Mickie Most, (small world), who produced a couple of records including 'Knock, Knock, Who's There?' for Great Britain's entry in the 1970 Eurovision Song Contest. Mickie told me he couldn't stand being in the studio with Mary, and Apple brought in Visconti, who made an album that was closer to her folk roots. The album got no support at all from the now disarrayed Apple Records, and she left the label.

The Raskins cabaret duo never wrote another successful song, but financially they did not need to and they retired, very rich, to Pollença – a small village in Majorca. Mike and Penny Leander had a house in Pollença and they and the Raskins were part of small circle of expats. Marsha and I often stayed at the Leanders' house in Majorca, and one year Penny Leander, who loves to cause mischievous fun, told the Raskins that their friend Laurence 'the important record company man' was their houseguest. As a result, wherever we went to dinner, the Raskins would unexpectedly appear to play and sing their current summer song 'When Manolo Played Guitar (In the Café by the Sea)'. There was usually a crowd of us at the table and we all had to stop eating to listen to what was a terrible song. For all the wrong reasons, I had 'When Manolo Played Guitar' in my head for years,

Roger and Visconti's Good Earth made records with Mary and Judie Tzuke. They managed Argent and were agents for The Average White Band. Then Roger started a promotions division, bringing James Brown, Jerry Lee Lewis and Chuck Berry to Europe. Roger never mastered promoter Don Arden's trick of hanging difficult artists from windows and he shortly moved on to what would be a spectacularly successful career in the restaurant and hotel business. In 1978, with his friend Alan Lubin, he opened Peppermint Park in London's Covent Garden. It was an American-style diner/soda fountain, revolutionary at the time, and it really took off. It became even more famous after a party that I gave there for *The Buddy Holly Story*, a film that I distributed through GTO Films. Guests included wild-man Keith Moon, The Who's drummer, who died at his home the next day, and the press was full of photos of Keith and Paul McCartney at the party with their wives.

Roger later started the Café Rouge restaurant group, building it to a chain of 130 restaurants before selling it to the Whitbread pub group. He then, with some partners, started the Punch Tavern group, one of the largest pub owners in the UK. Punch went public in 2002 and Roger cashed in and moved to St Lucia, where he and his wife Lee own The Sugar Beach, one of the best hotels in the Caribbean.

The three generations of our families are all very close, which is one of the great joys of my life.

19. THE JEFF BECK BAND AND ROD STEWART

In 1967 Mickie produced 'Hi Ho Silver Lining' for Jeff Beck. It was a great song written by Scott English and Larry Weiss, two highly successful Americans. Larry Weiss wrote 'Rhinestone Cowboy' and in the seventies I did a deal with him to develop the song into a film. At the same time I also did a deal to make Elton John and Bernie Taupin's 'Bennie and The Jets' into a movie. I got close, but neither of them got made into films.

One of the many curses of being a film producer is that you often *nearly* get films made and it keeps you in the game. There are lots of other curses, too many to mention here, but if you get the chance, have a look at the 2002 documentary *Lost in La Mancha*, the story of Terry Gilliam's doomed attempt to get a film based on *Don Quixote* off the ground. At the time of writing, he had finally completed it as *The Man who Killed Don Quixote* and it was awaiting distribution.

Singer/songwriter Scott English (along with Richard Kerr) wrote 'Mandy' for Barry Manilow. Scott actually recorded it himself in under the title of 'Brandy', and had a modest hit with it. Arista Records owned the rights to Scott's recording for America and when Clive Davis, the legendary boss of Arista heard it, he changed the name to 'Mandy' and gave it to Barry Manilow to record. Scott told me that he was initially pissed off that his own version was not put out, but when he received his writer's share of the multi-million-selling Manilow version, he felt better.

Scott came to live in London and we became quite friendly. He was a very funny guy who said that he wanted to write a song called 'Don't Fuck Around with Love', which appealed to my sense of humour. In November 2018 I had dinner with Scott after not seeing each other for some forty-five years and it was great to catch up. He told me that he had sent an unfinished version of 'Hi Ho Silver Lining' to Mickie Most and Mickie had asked him to finish it. He told Mickie that he thought that the song was crap and he did not want to finish it. Mickie, who knew a hit song when he heard one, summoned Scott to the office, called in his secretary and made Scott dictate some lyrics there and then. Scott assured me that this was the reason that the song had lines like 'Flies are in your pea soup baby, they're waving at me.'

I was in the studio when Mickie was mixing 'Hi Ho Silver Lining' and he asked me what I thought of it. I told him that I loved it but thought he should drop the guitar solo in the middle. This is why I am not a record producer.

Jeff Beck went on the road as The Jeff Beck Group with Ronnie Wood on rhythm guitar and Rod Stewart as his singer. I was the accountant. The band members were Jeff's employees and, like any other PAYE employee, a payroll tax had to be deducted from their wages. They were paid on a performance basis and, as there was not a gig every night, the band's wages varied from week to week. The plan was that each Monday Jeff would give us money to place in our clients' account, to cover the band's previous week's wages. We would then calculate the statutory deductions for tax and provide cheques for the band members.

Rod wanted his cheque on a Friday and he would come to Goodman Myers's office to collect it. The problem was that Jeff's Monday payment into the Goodman Myers client account drifted later and later into the week, to the point where I would be phoning Jeff on a Friday to tell him that Rod Stewart was in reception waiting to be paid. I explained to Rod that we could not be expected to pay him if we had not received the money and maybe he would like to come back on Monday. Rod assured me that he would not like to come back on Monday; he would like to wait at our offices until he had been paid. Jeff, being a musician, was not an early riser and Rod would hang around our reception, chatting up our pretty receptionist whilst waiting to be paid. Eventually a roadie would turn up with the amount due to each of the band members, and we would quickly calculate Rod's wages after tax and give him a cheque.

One Friday, my partner Ellis had a prospective client, an important city type, coming to see him. Every time Ellis passed through reception he saw this tall, lanky lad in tight tartan trousers, sprawled out in reception with his feet on our reception coffee table, disturbing the nice piles of business magazines that Ellis had set out to impress the prospective client. He asked Rod what he was doing. Rod explained that he came in to see me on Fridays to collect his wage cheque. Ellis, fearful that his prospective client would be deterred by such an untidy and unwholesome sight, popped his head around my office door to ask me to have this person removed. I was not in my office so Ellis went back to reception and politely asked Rod if he would kindly remove his feet from our coffee table, go away and only come back when he had a proper appointment. Rod, who is actually quite a gentleman, apologised and left. Throwing Rod Stewart out of your office was not a smart move. Who knew?

20. THE BEATLES AND APPLE CORP

When Brian Epstein died in 1967, Allen Klein was so convinced that he would become the manager of The Beatles, he even put a date on it: the end of 1968. To many this seemed like wishful thinking and Chris Most bet him a thousand pounds that it wouldn't happen.

Fast-forward to January 1969, and Allen Klein had his first meeting with John Lennon, who asked him to look after his business affairs. The following evening he met with all of The Beatles, when Ringo and George asked him to look after their affairs as well. Paul vociferously declined. Allen was now effectively managing three-quarters of The Beatles. It was a month later than the date of his bet with Chris Most, but she wouldn't let him off. I suggested that she should only claim a quarter of the bet, but she insisted on full payment, which I thought was rather mean of her.

At the time, Paul was engaged to be married to Linda Eastman, the daughter of a prominent New York lawyer who had extensive interests in both art and the music business. Linda's brother John was a partner in the firm. The Eastmans loathed Allen, no doubt because when Brian Epstein died they fancied taking control of The Beatles affairs themselves. The Eastmans were from a very uptown background and they made no attempt to hide the fact that they looked down on Allen, regarding him as a Jew with no class. This made Lennon, who was very conscious and proud of his own working-class background, an even stronger supporter of Allen. There were vicious confrontations between Allen and the Eastmans and eventually it was agreed that Allen would look after The Beatles' business affairs and the Eastmans would become their American attorneys.

Brian Epstein had run the management of The Beatles and his other artists through a company called NEMS. He had named the company after North End Music Store, which had been opened as part of the family's thriving furniture store in Liverpool, where Brian had his office. There was often a crowd of excited teenagers waiting to get into the Cavern Club, a short walk away from Brian's office. Intrigued, he went down into the small basement space to see what all the fuss was about, and the rest, as they say, is history.

His elder brother Clive had taken over the running of NEMS after Brian's death. Clive was thrown in at the deep end to a world which he had no knowledge of and in which he had no real interest in, and The Beatles were left without anyone to give them direction and guidance. It was no secret that the Apple finances were totally out of control. The news of the profligacy had reached New York and that was when Allen got on a plane to London.

No doubt flushed with their new 'freedom', the four lads from Liverpool had decided to start their own company, which they called Apple Corp. Allen asked me to go to their offices to prepare a report on the company's current financial position and make recommendations for its future running. The Beatles' wanted Apple to be a company that any creative people could come to – not just musicians – to get financial support. Lennon described it as, 'Artistic freedom within a business structure'. You are already wincing, and you are right.

They had taken over a beautiful period building at 3 Savile Row. It was on its roof that they famously gave their last performance in 1969, filmed by Michael Lindsay-Hogg. Although totally unannounced, the word quickly spread and the surrounding rooftops soon filled with lunchtime office staff who could not believe their luck. The streets became blocked with traffic as passers-by stopped to look up to see where the music was coming from. The Savile Row police station was a couple of hundred yards away and the police reluctantly asked The Beatles to stop so that order could be restored to the West End streets. Unfortunately, I was installed in the Savile Row offices too late to witness this historic event.

I started my investigation and what I learned was astonishing. Under the Apple brand, the boys started a record company, a film company and a music publishing company, all to be run by them out of the Savile Row offices. In the basement was the workshop of Alex Mardas, who at The Beatles' expense was developing amazing inventions that could never work. He installed a 'state of the art' recording studio, which also never worked. They opened a fashion boutique in Baker Street, which I had often passed on my way to work. The building was painted with psychedelic designs and looked amazing and the shop was stocked with the tie-dye and Indian-influenced fashions of the day. Clothes flew out of the store, most of it stolen by staff and customers. There was no control whatsoever and the shop was closed after six months, with The Beatles instructing that any stock left should be given away. An experienced American music executive called Ron Kass had been hired to run Apple Records but he had not managed to exercise much control and one of the first things that Allen did was fire him.

The Beatles themselves seldom turned up at the offices, other than George Harrison, who was sequencing his new album. It was a time when unreleased records were sampled on individually recorded acetates which could not be played too often without loss of quality and George sat alone in a room for days surrounded by piles of acetates of each song, trying to decide the running order. The acetates would have cost a fortune but George only played each one once, selecting a fresh one for each play. John once came into the office where I was working. He had no idea what I was doing there, and I explained that I was trying to find out what had happened to The Beatles' money. Anxious to find a reason to spend time with him, I started talking to him about my preliminary findings, but he did not seem to be interested, surprised or concerned. He just said, 'Really?' and wandered out again.

I did get to spend time with Lennon when Marsha and I had dinner with Allen and Betty and John and Yoko at the very plush Le Gavroche restaurant in Mayfair, Allen's favourite haunt. Yoko, who had yet to become the self-confident lady of later years, mostly clung monkey-like to John's arm and communicated with us by whispering in John's ear. John was very relaxed and chatted away about his early life when he, Paul McCartney and George Harrison played skiffle music in a group called The Quarrymen.

I told him that when I was about sixteen I had played in a skiffle group myself. I had to admit that sadly I wasn't on guitar (which would have required me to buy a guitar, which I could not afford, and learn three chords) but rather the lowly washboard. Skiffle as a musical force never took off in America, and John and I had to explain to Allen that it was a usually played by a few guys who knew three chords on a guitar, accompanied by a tea-chest bass player and someone creating a beat with thimbles on a washboard. Skiffle repertoire was mainly Lonnie Donegan songs or folk songs borrowed from American heroes Pete Seeger or The Weavers. The skiffle craze only lasted about three years in the mid-fifties and Allen was surprised to hear how many other early English pop groups had been inspired, including the Stones and the UK's first young pop idol, Tommy Steele.

Lonnie Donegan outgrew skiffle and became a wide-appeal entertainer. Coincidentally, when I wrote this in March 2018, I had been on the set of *Judy*, the film I am producing about Judy Garland, starring Renée Zellweger in the title role. In the scene I was watching, Lonnie Donegan was standing by to go on stage instead of Judy Garland at The Talk of The Town, a popular London cabaret club in the sixties. Miss Garland was going through a terrible period of addiction to drink and prescription drugs and was incapable of reliably turning up. Lonnie was a big enough star to appease the audience in her absence. Sadly, Judy Garland died of a drug overdose a few months later.

At the dinner, John discussed the problems that he was having renovating Tittenhurst Park, an early Georgian mansion near

Ascot that he had recently bought as a home for himself and Yoko. The house was Grade II-listed, and he could not get the permissions that he needed to make sweeping changes, including removing most of the walls. In that wonderful Liverpool accent, he told us, 'I can't see the point of having separate rooms to sleep in, eat in, fuck in and piss in.' Considering his predilection for 'bed-ins', it was maybe more than an idle thought. In the meantime, he and Yoko were living in a caravan parked in the seventy-two acres of ground that came with the house. He ultimately had to compromise but he did put a lake in the grounds without bothering to get planning permission and an unauthorised recording studio where he recorded some important albums for The Plastic Ono Band. When he moved permanently to America in 1971, he sold the house to Ringo, who had more traditional taste. I once went to see him there, and it was indeed beautiful.

John's most memorable remark of that unforgettable evening at Le Gavroche was about the time he was leaving school and his headmaster advised, 'Stop spending so much time playing the guitar, Lennon, you'll never make a living with that.'

The cost of running Apple's Savile Row operation was ridiculous. Many of the mainly overpaid staff made free use of Apple Corp's account with a minicab company to take them to and from work. The company had an account with a wine merchant, which was also cheerfully abused by staff. There was no semblance of discipline and staff came and went at their own convenience. The Beatles were paying for the good time that was being had by all. My report showed how and where substantial savings could be made and, armed with the specifics, Allen waded in and sorted out the mess.

I ran into Ron Kass again – the guy Allen had fired – in the mid-seventies. He was by now husband No. 3 for Joan Collins, who I met socially from time to time. One evening, we bumped into each other at the Tramp nightclub and I mentioned to Joan that we were planning to rent a home in Los Angeles for a month in the summer. She suggested that I rented hers. I had been to her London home, close to where we lived in Highgate, to pick up our son who had been to her own son's birthday party, and it was not a modest place. I had never been to her home in LA but I remembered that Sue St John, a mutual friend who was close to Joan, telling me it was spectacular. It was certainly big enough to take my family and I would be sleeping in Joan Collins' bed, so it sounded a great idea. Joan asked me to 'be a darling and talk to Ron about the business side'.

Joan was pretty broke – this was before she made *The Bitch* and *The Stud*, and a long time before *Dynasty* – and Ron asked for four thousand pounds, a very reasonable sum, *in cash*. As further enticement, Ron offered to throw in the two cars that they kept in LA. Then, in what he clearly thought was a clincher, dropping his voice to a conspirator's whisper, he promised to speak to Walter – the all-powerful maître d' of the Polo Lounge at the Beverley Hills hotel – to make sure that I had Joan's booth whenever I went there. You may recall that one's positioning in a fashionable LA watering hole was vital to one's prestige in town. The red leather booths at the Polo Lounge were up there with the window tables at Spago, and Ron assured me that Joan was always afforded the *No. 1 booth*. This was an offer I clearly could not refuse. And I didn't.

I went to the house a couple of days before my family arrived to make sure that all would be in order for their arrival. Ron's sister was staying and she showed me around. The house was in Bel Air, a very exclusive gated community. It was close to the house that was used in the filming of *The Beverly Hillbillies*, a popular comedy TV show about a country man who strikes oil on his land and moves his family to Beverly Hills. Most of the people who live in Bel Air have struck oil in some form or other and there is no social housing on the estate.

Ron's sister left and I turned on the TV. There was a remote, something that we were yet to get in England, and I clicked the button and sank into a couch the size of a small ocean liner to watch TV. The TV did not go on but the doorbell rang. Fighting my way from under the cushions I went and opened the door. A mountainous security guard in uniform, a huge gun at his hip, blocked the ever-present Californian sunshine out. He asked if the owners were at home and I said no, I was alone. He asked me for the security code, which I did not have. He asked me some other security questions, none of which I could answer, but I did offer to give him Joan's telephone number in London. He got on to his walkie-talkie and I thought he was going to call for back-up. I had visions of being read my rights, cuffed, and placed in the back of a 'black-and-white' by Starsky and Hutch. Disappointedly after listening to his walkie-talkie, he told me to 'have a nice day' and drove off.

I went back to my couch and tried again to turn on the TV with the remote. The doorbell rang, it was the BFG again. My TV remote was not remotely connected to the TV. It was a panic alarm connected to the Beverly Hills security patrol. Who knew?

The house was indeed spectacular, if suited to a particular taste. Huge, its roof-height living area dotted with silver lamé faux-palm trees, the place had more glitz than Ziggy Stardust's make-up box. There were photos of Joan everywhere and for Marsha's arrival I had carefully arranged a large photo of Joan by my side of the bed, with a single red rose next to it. She was so amused I discovered another spare bedroom.

We had a great time there. We had a big party for Marsha's fortieth birthday, which was a huge success. I told all my LA friends that we could 'do lunch' at my reserved booth at the Polo Lounge. They were very impressed.

21. MIKE LEANDER – THE MAN WHO ENCOURAGED ME TO CHANGE MY BUSINESS LIFE

I think that Mike Leander really understood my frustration at being an accountant, in a career I did not really enjoy. He had started his own working life in a solicitor's office but his first love was music, so he gave up law after a year and got a job as an office junior for a small music publisher. He had a natural gift for orchestration, which he studied in his spare time at Trinity College London. He tried his hand at songwriting and production, without much success. When he was twenty, Dick Rowe of Decca Records gave him a three-year deal as a musical director. Dick famously turned down The Beatles, a fact that has become synonymous with his name. His home electricity bill was probably addressed to Mr Dick Rowe-Turneddownthebeatles Esq.

Dick Rowe was by no means the only one who passed on talent. About twenty years ago, Jocelyn, a close friend of ours, had a holiday home in a small village in Tuscany where her Italian neighbour had a son who was a singer. Jocelyn told the neighbour about her friend Laurence, the *grande uomo nel mondo della*

With Marsha at our engagement party, 1960.

Left: Marsha and me on holiday in Acapulco, 1974. *Right:* With Marsha at our son James's wedding, 2018.

With Allen Klein, my music business mentor in the 70s.

Marsha and me with Mike Leander, the man who persuaded me to go into the music business full time.

Mike Leander and Marianne Faithfull at Decca, 1964 (photo: Gered Mankowitz).

Left: Wearing my trademark cowboy hat in the mid-60s. *Right:* A young me looking over the shoulders of Mick and Keith at Chichester Crown Court after their drugs bust. (Photograph copyright Alamy images)

Tony Defries and Tony Macaulay on either side of me at a Gem celebration, 1970.

Tony Burrows, lead singer of Edison Lighthouse, receiving a Gold Disc for 'Love Grows (Where My Rosemary Goes)' from songwriter Tony Macaulay (*left*) with co-writer Barry Mason (*right*).

With Larry and Michael Levene and The New Seekers at an Arcade Records presentation.

With Nicky Chinn, the man who brought me The Sweet.

Top row: D.J. Ed 'Stewpot' Stewart, Andy Scott of The Sweet, Gary Glitter.
Bottom row: Three members of Springfield Revival and Brian Connolly of The Sweet.

Left: David Essex and me in the late 1970s. *Right:* With Tony Macaulay, Geoff Stephens, Johnny Johnson and Anya Wilson, a record plugger.

Above: With Alan Price. *Below:* Top row: Me, Glenn Wheatley, Senior V.P. GTO Inc., and my partner David Joseph. Bottom row: Three GTO Inc. artists and Eileen Bradley, V.P. GTO Inc.

With Dick Leahy on my boat 'Ziggy Stardust' making the GTO deal.

Left: With Phil Daniels, who starred with Ray Winstone in the GTO film *Scum*.
Right: With Hazel O'Connor, who starred in the GTO film *Breaking Glass*.

With D.J. Alan 'Fluff' Freeman.

Left: Signing the Gem Records deal in 1978, with RCA's Bob Summer. *Right:* Dancing with Anthony Quinn at *The Greek Tycoon* film launch party on a boat in Cannes.

musica'. Suitably impressed, the neighbour asked me if I wanted to manage her son Andrea, who was struggling to earn a living as a cabaret singer in Tuscan holiday resorts. I responded '*Grazie* but no *grazie*,' because, as I said to my wife, 'what am I supposed to do with a blind Italian opera singer?'

It gets worse. In the 1970s, Norman Sheffield and his brother had a management company within his Trident Studios group of companies. Norman asked me if I wanted to buy the management company, whose main asset was its contract with a band called Queen. Norman claimed that he wanted to concentrate on the studio, which was his core business. I had heard rumours that the band were unhappy with the Sheffields and if they had come to me of their own accord I would, of course, have been interested. But I was sure that the band would not want to be 'sold on' as part of a company, I was up to my ears with my existing successful artists, and I did not think that it was worth pursuing. My only regret is that, had I pulled it off, I would have featured in the huge hit film *Bohemian Rhapsody*. I would fancy George Clooney to have played me, but I fear that they would more likely have cast Danny DeVito.

In 1988 I got to know Brian May a little. He was a regular after-show visitor to the delightful-in-every-way Anita Dobson who, at the time, was starring opposite Adam Faith in *Budgie*, the first musical that I ever produced. Brian was about to get divorced from his first wife and Anita did not feel secure about her future relationship with him. This is when I learned that the duties of the producer of a musical extended to reassuring your lead actress that she would marry the man she loved, so please stop crying. There was a lovely Don Black/Mort Shuman ballad in the show called 'In One of My Weaker Moments', which Anita told me she sometimes struggled to perform because of her romance with Brian. I would sometimes chat with Brian as he waited for Anita after the show. It was all a bit teenagery, as Anita would later ask me 'Did he say anything?' Brian and Anita made their own record of 'In One of My Weaker Moments' in 1989, which made me very happy. Indeed, they did marry and are still together, the marriage having run a lot longer than the show did. *Budgie The Musical* closed in three months, losing all of the investors' money.

The extraordinarily talented Brian May was a lovely gentle man, unlike Adam Faith who, whilst mildly talented, was a nightmare in so many ways that I could write a book entirely about him. Maybe I will. All right, one story now. He was impossible about publicity. His test was 'Would Marlon Brando do it?' To which my answer should have been, 'Of course not, you schmuck, but you're not Marlon Brando.' Instead I felt obliged to cajole and beg him to promote *Budgie*. We were offered *Russell Harty*, then the top TV plug programme. The show's format was to feature three guests, but Adam would only do it if he had the show to himself. I pointed out that the line-up for the previous week had been Dustin Hoffman, Sting and Dave Allen, to which he replied 'Well they're c***s.' This was just one example of his delusional sense of importance, and even though he was the star of the show, I should have fired him before we opened. It was my first production. A later, more experienced version of me would have done so.

In 1981 Brian Brolly, who was then managing Andrew Lloyd Webber, asked me if I wanted to invest £130,000 in *Cats*. He was quite desperate and offered me the record rights and an interest in all future productions. Comfortable in the thought that nobody would be interested in a musical using the poetry of T. S. Eliot, I said, 'No'. To add to my foolishness, when I went to the opening night I was convinced that I had made the right decision. The show of course has played for years in every major country in the world and those bloody cats' eyes advertising the show follow me round at every airport. *Please* don't tell anyone about this.

Back to Mike Leander. Whilst he was with Decca, Mike Leander worked with the Rolling Stones, Billy Fury, Marc Bolan, Shirley Bassey and many other stars of the day. He released two albums under the Mike Leander Orchestra banner without great success, but to enormous critical acclaim. Jerry Wexler, the revered head of A&R at Atlantic Records, flew Mike over to New York to work with Ben E. King, The Drifters and other artists on the Atlantic label.

At the time I first met Mike, he was working with MCA Records as an in-house producer. He had already written 'Lady Godiva' for Peter and Gordon (with Charlie and Gordon Mills), 'Early in the Morning,' a big hit for Vanity Fare written with Eddie Seago, and a couple of hits for Paul Jones. He had done the fabulous string arrangement for The Beatles' 'She's Leaving Home' for the *Sgt. Pepper* album, the creative work that he was most proud of until the day he died. Mike was executive producer of *Jesus Christ Superstar*, one of the first concept albums and the vehicle that set Andrew Lloyd Webber and Tim Rice on the road to success.

I have a theory about why the *Jesus Christ Superstar* album was so successful. At the time of its release, there was a strong movement amongst young Christians in America known then as 'Jesus freaks', maybe born out of the general hippy philosophy of peace and love. The telling of the story of Christ in such a modern manner had enormous appeal to them and they made the album a huge hit, leading to a Broadway production in 1971. This is not to take away from Andrew and Tim being in tune with the times or the commercial bravery of Brian Brolly, the head of MCA in the UK, in financing the recording.

Apart from this, not a lot was happening for Mike but Dick Leahy, the UK head of Bell Records – a recently formed subsidiary of Bell Records in the USA – was well aware of Mike's talent. Dick, unquestionably one of the best 'record men' of his era, had just had a successful spell as A&R manager of Philips Records and was keen to sign UK artists, including Tony Macaulay. I was by now establishing myself in my career as a manager and both Tony and Mike were clients of mine. There was a deal to be done.

Dick was obliged to go to his New York-based boss Larry Uttal, who had started the company, to do any significant deal. By now, 'significant deal' was my middle name. I negotiated a terrific three-year deal to finance recordings produced by Mike and Tony. Dick Leahy at Bell UK, later my partner in GTO Records, would be our point of contact. Mike had committed his exclusive services to me via Gem and he urged me to quit accountancy and devote my time to the company. Altruistically, he knew that I was unhappy with the accountancy side of my work and that I wanted to leave Goodman Myers. Selfishly, he wanted me to have more time to devote to him. Either way it was a meeting that I had with him towards the end of 1969 that made me decide to make the move. He sat in my office, lecturing me to 'get out from behind that boring desk' and go and compete with the 'old farts' who then dominated the business side of the UK music industry (it was amazing how quickly the years flew and I became an 'old fart' myself).

I went home and told Marsha that because of the deal I had made with Bell Records, I had a unique chance to go full-time into the business. Beth, our daughter, had been born in 1968 and we now had three young children but I recklessly wanted to give up a financially secure future for a leap into the unknown. Marsha, of course, knew how much I wanted to do this, and she encouraged me to grab the chance. I would never have made that leap without her blessing and encouragement. It was only the first of many occasions in more than fifty years of marriage that Marsha supported me taking business risks. My wife really did help me succeed. She smiled at gigs that she hated and graciously entertained people that she did not necessarily like. When I wanted to monopolise the attention of one or two people at a business dinner, I would identify the possible diversions and ask her to 'take them out', which she did without them even being aware of it. Smart and funny, she is an amazing woman, and I am lucky to have found her.

Ellis had given up trying to make me even look like an accountant – I had taken to wearing cowboy hats and boots at the office – and he also supported the idea of me devoting my time to the music business. Happily, for me, and maybe more so for my clients, I quit being an accountant in practice in 1970.

Bearing in mind what Allen Klein had taught me about giving the artist 80 per cent of yours rather than taking 20 per cent of theirs, under the deal that I made with Mike and Tony, Gem Record Productions Ltd would own the records that they produced. They would receive 80 per cent of Gem's revenue from records that they recorded after deducting payments to the artists.

Gem's first release was by Edison Lighthouse in January 1970. It was 'Love Grows (Where My Rosemary Goes)', written and produced by Tony Macaulay with co-writer Barry Mason. Barry's then girlfriend Sylvan Whittingham was credited as co-writer, which later became a general issue as to whether helpful comments by a writer's girlfriend during the writer's creative process entitled her to be a credited collaborator.

Macaulay's brilliant production used Tony Burrows as lead voice to make what was a perfect pop record. Burrows was a talented and versatile singer who could sight-read music and he was much in demand as a session singer. The other musicians on the recording were all seasoned session artists. I later managed Tony as a solo artist, but never got him the success his talent deserved. (I met with him in the course of writing this book and he referred to me as his 'damager'. It was with affection – I hope.)

At that time Tony Macaulay's girlfriend was Anya Wilson, who was working as an independent record plugger. Tony promised her that if she worked on the record and it became a hit, he would recommend that I took her on as a full-time in-house plugger. With the help of Anya, the record got immediate airplay and shot into the charts at No. 12 for the weekend of 24 January 1970. Anya met with Mel Cornish, the producer of *Top Of The Pops*, whose weekly average audience of fifteen million could almost guarantee to make a record a hit. She hoped to persuade Mel to use the record for a routine with Pan's People, a group of sexy and talented dancers who had a regular spot on the show. To her surprise Mel loved the record and did better, offering to put the band itself on the next *TOTP* going out in a few days' time.

This would have been great news had Edison Lighthouse actually existed, but of course Anya could not admit this slight hiccup to Mel. Fortuitously, she bumped into an agent who represented a little-known band called Greenfield Hammer, who immediately agreed to morph into Edison Lighthouse. Macaulay rehearsed them solidly for a day and on 29 January 1970, with Tony Burrows singing lead, they appeared on the show miming to the original track. On that same show Tony also appeared as featured singer with White Plains and Brotherhood of Man. Appearing on the same *TOTP* in three different bands was a feat achieved by no singer before or since. In the chart for the week following the show, 'Love Grows' shot to No. 1. It was the fastest-ever climber to the top spot. It stayed there for five weeks and continued to sell, becoming the 'summer hit' for the year.

Gem's second hit, also produced by Macaulay, was 'Blame It on the Pony Express', a song that that he wrote with Roger Greenaway and Roger Cook for Johnny Johnson and His Bandwagon. It got to No. 2 in the charts in January 1970 and established Gem as a serious player in the world of independent production companies.

I was busy with the hits that Tony Macaulay was producing, working with Mike Leander on his projects, whilst still being involved with Mickie Most's Rak Records, as well as looking after the affairs of my other accountancy clients including the Rolling Stones. My time was clearly stretched. Mickie Most was unhappy that I had left my practice to set up my own production company and he thought that I should give him back the shares that I owned in the Rak group of companies – I had 10 per cent of all his companies in lieu of fees. I hated having to account for the time that I spent on each client's affairs and this meant I didn't have to bill him in the same way. I offered to sell Mickie the shares for the recorded time that I had accumulated over the years. It was about five thousand pounds, a small fraction of what the shares were actually worth. He refused to do this for a long time until reorganising his own affairs forced him to do so.

I had no obligation to stick to my original offer but I did. There was a saying amongst the literati of market grafters: 'If they're gonna hate you anyway, fuck 'em.' The advice was right. Mickie would have disliked me no more had I held out for the six-figure sum that the shares were actually worth, but I have never regretted my decision. I had earned the true value of my shares, but Mickie was my entrée into the music business, and in any event, it was my choice to leave him.

I had been in practice for five years without getting found out. I was known and respected in the music business and I had enormous faith in the talent of Mike Leander and Tony Macaulay. I was thirty-five years old, I had a great family and I felt wonderful.

22. GEM PRODUCTIONS – MIKE LEANDER, TONY MACAULAY

I said earlier that the sixties were a great time to go into the music business. It was, in fact, a great time to go into *any* business.

Post-war, the fifties were austere and grim but the sixties were booming and colourful. Anybody who wanted to work could get a job and if you worked hard you prospered. Most of my friends were lower-middle-class, as was I. We were all state-educated, none of us went to university and, with almost no exceptions, all of us did OK. As a matter of interest, most of us stayed married too. Maybe the two are linked?

As the business grew, I concentrated on music and Ellis continued to build up his contacts and expertise in the wine and spirits business. He had already formed ADP Ltd to take care of our interest in that industry, and he was about to take that company public. Ellis had a 50 per cent interest in Gem and I had 50 per cent of the shares in ADP. He was also ready to fly the Goodman Myers' nest and set up a new office in Sackville Street. In January 1970, I walked about two hundred yards out of my office at 273–287 Regent Street, across Oxford Circus, to the space I had taken for Gem at 252–260 Regent Street.

Nineteen-seventy proved to be a truly amazing year in my career. People spend their whole lives in the music business without being attached to major success. By the end of my first year, I'd had a No. 1 record with Edison Lighthouse, two Top 10 hits with Johnny Johnson and His Bandwagon and had signed David Bowie. A single could sell 300,000-400,000 copies and Gem's end might come to well over ten thousand pounds (about £100,000 in today's money). By contrast, today sales of singles are so low that, even with downloads, nobody makes much money and they are largely seen as promotion for the album.

My offices were about three thousand square feet on the top floor above Dr Scholl's footwear store, about a hundred yards from Oxford Circus. Formally the London headquarters of Warner Brothers' Corset Company, you walked into a space with a large reception and a showroom on the left. I took that as my own office/meeting room, and to the right there was a corridor with four small offices on either side. The initial occupants were Mike Leander, Tony Macaulay and Tony's secretary – a very posh gel called Jane Hickey who went to Fortnum & Mason to buy the office tea supplies. The space was much too big for my immediate needs but ... I had a dream.

I have already mentioned the famous Brill Building in New York, where there were eleven floors crammed full of publishers, writers, song-pluggers and executives who were the heart of the New York music industry. Hits poured out through the windows onto Broadway. I was going to have my own little Brill Building-ette where I would give space to creative people who, in my plan, would create hits that would pour out through the windows onto Regent Street.

23. DAVID BOWIE

I had my new office and the most significant hits that drifted out of my Regent Street windows were created by David Jones, aka David Bowie.

As with the Stones, I have no wish to write a version of David Bowie's life story, only that part of it that relates to my personal involvement. There are dozens of books written about David but I particularly recommend *Alias David Bowie*, by Peter and Leni Gillman, who interviewed me extensively in 1986. Also read *Stardust: The David Bowie Story* by Henry Edwards and Tony Zanetta and *Any Day Now* by Kevin Cann. This last book contains some very specific accounting information that I do not have and the author told me that he had got it from the Gillmans. They told me that they had been given copies of the accounting by the widow of Peter Gerber, who was my in-house accountant until he was seduced away by Tony Defries. In a way I was getting information back that had originally belonged to me. It was very bizarre.

As we all know, success has many fathers but failure is an orphan. David's talent may well have brought him success, but the road to stardom is littered with the bodies of talented people who were never afforded the break they deserved. The financial risk that I took on when David was by no means a star, entitles me to proudly claim to be one of the fathers of his success.

The first manager to be meaningfully involved in David's career was Les Conn, at a time when David Bowie was still David Jones of Davie Jones and the King Bees. I first met Les in 1965 when, as a sometime artists' manager and wannabe songwriter, he was a peripheral figure in Mickie Most's circle of business friends. Les came from Stamford Hill, a Jewish area in north London close to Finsbury Park, where I had been brought up. There were not many north London Jewish boys in the music business, so there was something of a bond between us and, although I was a little younger, I became something of a confidant. Les had not managed to achieve any real success for the King Bees and they had recently amicably parted company.

I later met with Les Conn after the struggling David Jones had become the superstar David Bowie and he never showed the slightest bitterness about what might have been. In fact, he laughed when he told me that David and another young hopeful, Mark Feld (aka Marc Bolan), had painted his kitchen. Les was fond of introducing himself as 'Conn's the name and con's the game' – referring to hype rather than financial misdeeds – and Bowie (who had worked briefly in the advertising industry) was not hype-adverse when it came to advancing his own career. He actually used the name The Hype for a short-lived band that he formed with Tony Visconti and Mick Ronson. He also learned the value of branding, which no doubt influenced his successful self-reinvention during the course of his career.

Les was an extremely easy-going and affable guy, which could be why he never really achieved his potential in the music business. When Les died in 2008 David wrote a very warm obituary acknowledging the important part that Les had played in his early career.

I first met David Bowie, briefly, at the Ivor Novello Awards in The Talk of the Town in May 1970. Tony Macaulay was receiving an award as the British songwriter of the year. Peter Sarstetd won best song with 'Where Do You Go To (My Lovely)?'. Peter would be a GTO Los Angeles-managed artist in later years as one of the Sarstedt Brothers, along with siblings Robin Sarstedt and Eden Kane, the stage name of another brother. David's 'Space Oddity' won the special award for originality and without doubt it was the talking point of the evening. I went over to David and congratulated him on writing not a love song, but a great theatrical song with a story. I also mentioned the fact that he did not sing with an American accent, which I greatly applauded. Actually, he sang very much like Anthony Newley, an entertainer I admired immensely. David freely confessed that he was a huge Newley fan, and I recall that in an *NME* interview in the early seventies, he said 'I was Anthony Newley for a year.' It was not only Newley's voice that David admired. Newley was an actor who could sing and had used mime to great effect in the avant-garde musical *Stop The World – I Want to Get Off*, written with Leslie Bricusse, a show that I went to see three times. I think that I got brownie points from David because of our shared Newley fandom.

Newley was the artist I would most like to have managed simply because I was a huge fan of his talent. He was a great actor, songwriter and a great performer. I was in contact with him in the early nineties about a musical project with Don Black. He once left a message on my home answerphone which started:

'Anthony Newley here, I was very big in the sixties.' Such was my fandom, I kept that cassette for years. He was a great talent and a lovely man. Newley was by then working in UK cabaret venues that, sadly, were a far cry from his days topping the bill at Las Vegas. Joan Collins, who was married to Newley for eight years, once told me that he was the love of her life, but she could not take his philandering. Tony died in 1999, aged 67. It was a great loss to the world of entertainment.

When I met fellow Newley fan David Bowie at the Novello awards, I had no idea that the wheels were already in motion that would eventually lead him to my office. It was Tony Defries who brought Bowie to see me. I will call Defries by his surname in this book, not to be derogatory but because there are far too many Tonys involved in Bowie's story and it will get confusing.

I met Defries when he worked for Martin Boston and Co., a law firm that I had recommended to Mickie Most in his fight with Warrior Records. Defries definitely made an impression on people. He always wore a strange type of frock coat, slightly Dickensian in style. He smoked big cigars, but certainly not the Havanas that he could later afford. He had a huge Afro hairstyle and a slow, rolling gait. He moved slowly, but he thought quickly. Although he was not a qualified lawyer, I thought he was very bright. Soon after I moved into my Gem offices in Regent Street, Defries came to see me. He had left Martin Boston and moved to Godfrey Davis and Batt, a respected firm of lawyers who had engaged him to represent the Association of Fashion Advertising Photographers (AFAP) who were seeking to retain the copyright in the photographs that were commissioned by advertising agencies. He switched sides and decided that models should have a share of the copyright in their photographs. Also, it seemed that the top models were often kept waiting to be paid by their agent and were treated badly in other ways. Defries was aware of the manner in which I had improved the lot of music artists and thought that I might be interested in doing the same for these girls. Why would I not want to meet with some of London's top models? I was soon hosting a dinner at La Trattoria Terrazza surrounded by about ten of the best-looking girls in London.

In essence these girls were all unhappy and desperately wanted to improve their financial relationship with their agents. I explained how I improved the lot of recording artists by threatening to withdraw artists' services and offered to meet with the agents in question and tell them that these girls were not going to work for them any more. I stressed that they would have to back me up by refusing further work until the agencies met what we thought were reasonable demands. We would form an Association of Fashion Models, which of course I would manage. The last time I had hosted a business dinner at the Trattoria was to propose a similar arrangement for songwriters and it had occurred to me that that had not worked out particularly well, but these were beautiful models so, of course ... well, of course.

In spite of the mistreatment, it seemed that all the girls loved their agents. One of the girls said that if they did not work her agency might go broke, to which I replied, 'So be it.' One said that they thought it was a horrible thing to do to the agent; another started crying at the thought of my nastiness and that was pretty much the end of my managing models. Whoever said men were from Venus and women from Mars must have, at some point, tried to help models.

After the models fiasco I did not see Defries again until April 1970 when he came to see me about David Bowie. After leaving Leslie Conn in 1965, the singer was managed by Ralph Horton, a young guy from Birmingham. Horton did not have the money or resources to effectively manage a band and approached Ken Pitt, an established agent, who had brought Manfred Mann his first success. Horton wanted Ken to put some money into promoting David, who was by now performing as Davy Jones and the Lower Third. Ken initially said no, but advised David to change his name to the more distinctive David Bowie. Ken did help Horton with money and advice and gradually became a bigger influence on David himself. In February of 1967, David split with Horton and Ken Pitt became his manager. Ken, in my opinion, did a lot of good advancing David's career. Most of all he was a fan and you cannot successfully manage an artist if you do not admire his or her work. But by 1970 David had decided that it was time for a change of management and I can imagine how Ken must have felt. He had risked money, shown faith and given good guidance.

Artists often leave a manager who has done a good job for them. The reasons are sometimes valid but as often as not it is because someone has whispered in the artist's ear that they are not as rich as they should be or are being taken for granted, neither of which might be the case. There are very few managers, including myself, who do not bear some scars as the result of disloyalty. Mickey Duff, in his day a leading manager of boxers, once advised me, 'If you want loyalty, buy a dog.'

Ken's problem was that David had come under the influence of Angie, the powerful American lady he had married in March of that year. They met at The Speakeasy Club, a music-business hangout, about a year earlier. She was with Lou Reizner, an American record producer and Calvin Mark Lee, a Chinese-American friend of Lou's – one or both of whom she was romantically involved with. I am confining my recollections to matters which concern my relationship with Bowie, but for those of you who are interested in the fascinatingly liberal sexual machinations between these characters and many other people in David's life, I would refer you to *Alias David Bowie* which deals in some detail with the web of David and Angie's sexual preferences and relationships.

The introduction of a new wife/girlfriend in a pop star's life is not always positive. Some ladies think that they can do a better job of management than the manager. On the few occasions I was faced with this problem, I encouraged the lady concerned to test her talent by going out and finding someone to manage. This issue is best illustrated in *Spinal Tap*, Rob Reiner's satirical but definitive film on the subject of rock bands. If you are considering managing an artist I urge you to watch it every night. In the years after I gave up management I was occasionally tempted to go back by an artist who I believed had talent that I could nurture. I would watch my copy of *Spinal Tap*, take a cold shower and go to sleep – undisturbed by any 3 a.m. phone calls about the artist's van broken down outside Sheffield (as if there was anything that I could do about it) or the drummer being arrested for assault, which was the *good* news because the police had not yet found the drugs taped to the inside of his bass drum.

Angie, who was very bright, unquestionably had a positive influence on David's public persona, providing a level of energy and urgency that he lacked. It was she who encouraged him to do something about leaving a manager he was not happy with. They discussed his dilemma with Olav Wyper, the marketing manager of Philips Records, which released 'Space Oddity', and he recommended his own lawyer. Enter Defries, who drafted a letter to Ken from David, informing him that he was terminating their business relationship on the basis that Ken had not fulfilled his management obligation to further David's career.

Gem had got off to a flying start and the UK music industry was certainly aware of my presence when Defries came to explain that David was free, and that he would like to stop being a lawyer and get involved with managing the star himself. As he had had no music-business experience he did not think that David would go for it, but he had enthused about me and Gem, my hot new management/record production company. Defries offered to bring David up to meet me, on the understanding that he could come and join the company if David signed with us. My experience as an accountant in the music business had taught me that where there's a hit there's a writ and, irrespective of getting involved with David Bowie, I quite liked the thought of having Tony Defries as an in-house business affairs person.

We agreed that Defries would work for me for a salary of thirty pounds a week. I would sign David to Gem and – if everything worked out – I would give Defries 20 per cent of the company and make him a director. It was difficult to define what 'worked out' meant but Defries said that he was happy to trust me to 'do the right thing' and there was no paperwork between us. It is worth noting that I would never have signed David Bowie had Defries not brought him to me, and equally it is my belief that David would never have signed with Defries in a management capacity, had he not been working with me.

Before I committed to sign David I, of course, wanted to get to know him a little and we met a few times to discuss his relationship with Ken Pitt and what his hopes were for the future. My first impression of David was that he was quietly spoken, very gentlemanly and very polite. He was, however, very firm in his ideas about how he wanted to present himself to the public.

Most artists, encouraged by their management, base themselves on precedents. In the fifties, stars like Johnnie Ray, Frankie Laine, Eddie Fisher and their contemporaries dressed like cabaret singers in glitzy tuxedos with lots of white teeth. Elvis set the mould for undulating hips in tight trousers and English pop stars like Billy Fury, Cliff Richard and Marty Wilde happily followed The King. Brian Epstein put The Beatles into cute uniforms. the Rolling Stones were the scruffy rebels – although Jagger was very choosy about his stage gear. By and large, the management's hope was that the artist looked 'sexy' to the teenage girls who were a large share of the record-buying market. Part of that sex appeal meant you shouldn't seem to be gay. Many Hollywood stars disguised their homosexuality or bisexuality, including male pin-ups Marlon Brando, Montgomery Clift and Rock Hudson.

I touched on this issue lightly but David just laughed and told me not to worry about it. He obviously thought that I was too conventional in my thinking, and he was probably right. It was obvious to me that David was very bright, had a clear vision of his stage persona, and he was not looking to be moulded into any of the perceived 'looks' of his predecessors. In fact, he was clearly not looking to be moulded in any way at all. I had to

decide if I wanted to sign this self-determined artist who was
going to be very different from the norm and was going to
stretch my limited resources.

Please understand, this was not Laurence being a shrewd
businessman looking to make an adequate return on investment.
This was Laurence worrying how he would pay his mortgage
and feed his family if he lost too much money supporting
Bowie. I liked his songs and admired his being his own man, a
pioneer and all that. The problem was that pioneers tend to get
arrows up their arses, and financially it was my arse that was the
potential target.

I was somewhat encouraged by David's reaction to a sign I
had on my desk, which read: 'Art for art's sake – money for fuck's
sake'. He picked it up and looked at it and I thought that he
would disapprove, but he laughed and said, 'I like that, I'll bear
it in mind.'

David only owed one more album to Philips records and his
songwriting contract with Essex Music had expired in June of
the previous year. Whilst he was signed to Essex Music, Geoff
Heath – who ran the company for owner David Platz – brought
David a song he had heard at Midem called *Comme d'habitude*.
The song had been written and recorded by Claude François, a
successful French pop star, who was tragically electrocuted at the
age of thirty-nine when an electric heater fell into his bath. Bowie
wrote new lyrics and called it 'Even a Fool Learns to Love.' It
did not really work and eventually Paul Anka wrote new lyrics
to the song, now called 'My Way', for Frank Sinatra. The song
fitted his persona like a glove, but I personally think that whilst
the sentiment is wonderful, the actual lyrics are embarrassingly

contrived and I find listening to it quite painful. I don't think my view would bother Mr Anka or indeed the late Mr Sinatra. Incidentally, I feel much the same about 'Strangers In The Night', which to me sounds like a pastiche crooner's song written for a B-movie. Who doobee doobee knew? Certainly not me.

Now to the exciting bit … The end of David's publishing deal with Essex was a perfect time for a new manager to take over. David was by no means a star at this point in time but there was a slight buzz about him in the industry. I was a big fan of 'Space Oddity' and had heard 'The Man who Sold the World', another great song that was not about love.

Defries moved into my new offices at Regent Arcade House and on 1 August 1970 David signed a six-year recording agreement with Gem Productions. He also signed a management agreement under which Gem would take 20 per cent of his earnings. A very standard deal. Defries insisted that there was a key-man clause in the management agreement allowing Bowie to walk away if Defries were to leave Gem. I considered this to be perfectly reasonable, as it was Defries who had brought David in and Defries had no contract with Gem to give him security. However, no record company would accept a key-man clause for a recording agreement, so Gem signed David with no protection for Defries if his star ever walked away from me.

Gem also signed Dana Gillespie, a singer who was an ex-flame of Bowie and now a close friend of his and of Angie. Dana had starred in *Jesus Christ Superstar* and was, I thought, a very talented artist. She was at the heart of the Bowie crowd during the time that I was involved, and has been kind enough to recently meet with me and fill in some background information.

24. THE PLAN TO LAUNCH BOWIE

In 1970 the cornerstone of an artist's career was a record deal. The major companies provided the money to make records, had marketing departments to exploit them and the ability to distribute the physical recordings to record shops. Remember record shops? They were where teenagers would meet on Saturday mornings, crowding into little sound booths to listen to records through headphones.

Music is still the centre of most teenagers' lives but of course owning a record is not, which I think is sad because in the olden days, having a record collection was a big deal. The first album I ever bought was in 1956 when I was twenty. It was Frank Sinatra's *Songs for Swingin' Lovers!* and the cost was more than my weekly salary of about one pound. I made a label with my name on, which I carefully stuck to the album sleeve so that when I took it to a friend's house it would not be confused with their copy. All of my friends had a copy or they would not have been my friend.

I created space in the shelf above my bed for my record collection and it filled *very* slowly – it fact it never really filled at all. When I got married and moved my 'collection' to my marital home it was not very heavy. In a way, it was one of the few downsides of being successful in the music business that I was gifted almost any record that I wanted by the record companies. I even persuaded some of them to put me on their reviewers' list, sending me a copy of every release. The result was I gradually ceased to value having an album/CD in my personal collection and didn't even hold on to them all. If I had kept them for my home I would have had to live in a warehouse.

David Bowie's own record deal was with Mercury Records and it had expired. There was general interest in him from other record companies, but they were not exactly knocking on my door. My initial interest in David was as a songwriter and I was keen to develop this side of his career. Gordon Mills, who managed Tom Jones, was always looking for songs for the Welshman to record and – with no imminent record deal in sight – I sent him demos of some of David's songs, but he did not like them. In the meantime, Tony Defries was busy planning gigs to showcase David to record companies and was also dealing with ex-manager Ken Pitt's claims that David had breached his contract.

The Man who Sold the World was released in the UK by Philips Records in April 1970 and flopped. If anything was to establish David's casual approach to androgyny it was that album cover, dominated by a large image of a blond-wigged David Bowie lolling on a chaise longue wearing a dress designed by Michael Fish, a fashionable designer of the day. David's look on the album was frequently referred to as pre-Raphaelite, but now I find it more pre-Grayson Perry. The album was produced by Tony Visconti who, for whatever reason, did not work with David again until Defries was moving out of the picture in 1974.

The album was free for publishing and was about to be delivered to Mercury Records. This, together with the prospect of a deal with a new record company, strengthened our hand with any potential music publisher. Chris Wright of the highly successful Chrysalis Group had just started a new publishing company. Neither Chris nor his partner Terry Ellis knew much about publishing, and they had appointed Bob Grace, a young man with a good background in publishing, to run it. I knew Chris and Terry well, admired them very much and was confident that Chrysalis Publishing would be an active publisher and not just a banker, as many of the larger publishing companies had become. I called Chris to alert him that David would soon be recording a new album and we would be looking for a publishing deal. It is to be remembered that David was by no means a hot artist at this time. Chris was not particularly excited, but I persuaded him to arrange for Bob Grace to meet with us.

Tony Defries went to see Bob Grace and played him 'The Man Who Sold the World' and some of the unrecorded songs that David had written. Bob Grace was very interested. Nick Blackburn, Chrysalis's money-man, called me to talk a deal. Defries and I decided that we wanted five thousand pounds, and Chris was very much against paying such a substantial advance. He had never imagined giving such a hefty amount to an unproven songwriter but he was swayed by Bob Grace's enthusiasm. Under the terms of the deal that Defries cleverly negotiated in October 1970, once Chrysalis recouped the five-thousand-pound advance, half of the copyright would be assigned to Titanic Music, owned by Bowie, increasing his share of the income from the then standard 50/50 to 75/25 in his favour.

Titanic would not be party to Chrysalis's existing obligations to sub-publish with publishers around the world, for which it would have received substantial advances. Bob Grace was concerned that this was a ploy by Defries to allow Titanic to negotiate separate advances, which if true, was a move that he reluctantly agreed to even though he thought it was immoral. He later said that he was green and allowed Defries to push him into the agreement. Defies always maintained that the purpose of setting up Titanic was primarily to gain David an increased share of his copyright income, not to circumvent Chrysalis's existing contractual arrangements.

David could have been signed to Chrysalis Records then, but according to Chris's excellent autobiography, Terry Ellis did not like the material that David had written for *Hunky Dory*, and Kenny Bell, who ran the record company, thought that David would never make it as a live act. Nick Blackburn is now in the theatre business and I bump into him from time to time. He never fails to rib me about selling Bowie's publishing for a mere five thousand pounds. It is important to realise that in today's money that is about fifty thousand pounds, and Gem's 20 per cent commission at least made a small dent in the money I had laid out on Bowie. David now had four thousand pounds – about forty thousand pounds today – so was now less financially dependent on Gem, and there was now a company other than mine who could give support if needed. David's obligation to Chrysalis was to write a minimum of one hundred songs of which seventy must be commercially recorded.

Bob Grace, a good music man, worked closely with David and the singer had more faith in Bob's creative opinion than he did in that of Tony Defries or me. Bob sent David's song 'Oh! You Pretty Things' to Mickie Most, who recorded it with Peter Noone as his first solo record after parting with the Hermits. I kept well in the background for this, knowing that Mickie would not favour a song submitted to him that had my thumb-print anywhere near it. I subsequently learned that Bob tried to convince David that Defries and I were unproven managers and that David would be better off being managed by him. Fortu-nately, at that time, David had absolute faith in Tony Defries' guidance and resisted Bob's advances. I had sent David to Chrys-alis and it was wrong of Bob to do this, but having been guilty of similar actions myself it would be hypocritical of me to have held this against Bob. There's no business like show business.

Anya Wilson was now employed by me full-time as a record plugger, and she worked on the singles from the album released in the UK, but 'Memory of a Free Festival,' with Marc Bolan playing piano, and 'Holy Holy' weren't successful. 'Memory of a Free Festival' was seven minutes long, making it difficult to get airplay. Radio liked a three-minute single and we later always told stations, if asked, that the length of every song we submit-ted was always three minutes and twenty seconds – whatever the actual length. I even had 3'20" written on the sleeve of the acetate. I will tell you another little secret: A&R men at record compa-nies often felt they needed to contribute artistically and when presented with a record would often say things like, 'The bass needs remixing.' We always agreed with them and would then re-submit exactly the same version in a sleeve labelled 'remix', thanking the A&R guy for his input. It was important to make the record company feel some ownership of the creative process.

About this time, Anya brought a man called Jon Brewer in to see me. He and his partner Robert Patterson were managing a band called Czar whom I quite liked and I thought Jon, in particular, was bright and personable. They used to drive around in an old hearse that at some point was used by the Belgium royal family – presumably when one of the royals was past driving. They had had some experience of putting a band on the road, something that neither Defries nor I were familiar with. Jon's sister Liz, a socialite party planner/publicist, was a friend of Penny Leander, Mike's wife, so I knew that Jon was a 'real' person. As part of my 'Brill Building in London' ambition, I gave them an office on the understanding that they would offer me involvement in any acts that they signed and help out with Gem acts if needed.

I introduced Jon to Defries, and as I recall, he was indeed very helpful in this area. He booked some of David's early gigs and David enjoyed being driven around in the ornate hearse, and the two of them became quite close. Robert left the Brewer/Patterson partnership and Jon devoted a lot of time to helping Defries. He was never on the Gem payroll but has since told me that Defries had promised a financial interest in Bowie's gigs. Jon claims that he was never paid by Defries but he went on to manage Alvin Lee and Gerry Rafferty, so the Gem experience obviously helped him. He produced and published Rafferty's huge hit 'Baker Street', a smart move. Jon is now a maker of important documentaries on music legends, including B. B. King, Nat King Cole and Mick Ronson. Jon has been very helpful to me in filling in some details of his time working with David at Gem.

Mercury Records took David to America in February 1971 to promote *The Man who Sold the World* and it is my belief that, although it did not help record sales, it was an important episode in David's career. Starting in Washington, he toured major cities, frequently wearing one of his Mr Fish-designed dresses. The reactions of outrage from the more conservative press, DJs and public balanced the delight from the thinly scattered outré among them. David finished his tour in Los Angeles, an experience which I believe was pivotal to his career. He was hosted by Rodney Bingenheimer, who at the time was Mercury's main promoter in southern California. Rodney would become a great fan of David and helped promote his career when he later opened a trendy music venue on Sunset Strip in LA. Rodney borrowed a friend's Cadillac convertible and drove David on a tour of radio stations. To David's delight, he was refused entrance to an LA restaurant because he was wearing a dress. In 1973 Richard O'Brien's *The Rocky Horror Show*, about the sweet transvestite from Transylvania, was first staged and demonstrated yet again that the younger public was not disturbed by transgender entertainment. So much for my initial concern, when David first came to my office, that openly incorporating gay imagery could affect record sales.

In San Francisco he was asked to pick some songs to be played as a guest host on a local radio station. He was urged to pick a record by The Stooges, Iggy Pop's band. He had never heard of Iggy but learned that he was the idol of the 'in the know' music media for his outrageous behaviour as much as for his talent. This registered with David, himself no stranger to outrageous behaviour. David was then interviewed by *Rolling Stone*, the hugely influential music magazine. You will read later that it was this article that inspired a group of avant-garde American actors in a play about Andy Warhol to go to see the not-yet-famous David perform in London. They then introduced David to Andy Warhol in New York, resulting in David becoming a gay icon in the Big Apple, which was instrumental in his success.

As *The Man who Sold the World* did nothing in America, Mercury were clearly not passionate about having Bowie on their label and Defries brilliantly negotiated the transfer of the Mercury albums to Gem in return for repaying the cost. I took a deep breath, wrote a cheque for eighteen thousand dollars and the albums belonged to Gem. I subsequently recouped this when Gem licensed them to RCA as part of the deal for future Bowie product.

When he returned to London, David continued to write material for the album that would be *Hunky Dory*. The American trip definitely got his creative juices flowing and I thought that the material that he was writing for this album was just terrific. I particularly liked 'Changes', 'Life On Mars' and 'Kooks', the song he had written for his new baby son.

In June 1971, Defries and I agreed that we would make David's next record without record company finance. Obviously, this was a great risk for Gem, but this would enable us to make a beneficial new deal *if* the record was great when completed. David wanted Ken Scott, a well-respected recording engineer, to help him co-produce the album. I was a little nervous about this because, whilst Ken had engineered for The Beatles, Elton John and many others, he had not actually sat in the booth as a producer.

I will overcome my desire to bang on about Bowie not being an artist in demand at this time, but you must permit me to occasionally do so. The golden rule in business is 'he who provides the gold makes the rules.' Whilst I never berated Defries or David about my increasing financial exposure, they were very aware and appreciative of the artistic freedom that I allowed them. I had seen the magic that great producers like Mickie Most, Tony Macaulay and Mike Leander brought to a recording, but they were producing pop acts who did not write their own songs and were totally reliant on the taste of their producers to pick likely hits written by others. Bowie was an artist with a distinct view of how the songs that he wrote should be recorded. Tony Visconti would not return whilst Defries was around, so I agreed that Ken could co-produce with David. Ken has subsequently admitted that he was very nervous about stepping up from engineer to producer and that both he and David were both unsure that they could do the job, but the more they worked together, the more confident they became that they had done the right thing. They recorded at Trident Studios in Soho, the most in-demand studio in town because it was one of the few with an eight-track desk.

My relationship with David was very comfortable. We would chat about his business life, but I never attempted to socialise with him. I would not have felt at ease hanging out with the habitués of El Sombrero (a gay-friendly club called Yours Or Mine in Kensington High Street which had a sombrero above the door) or participating in the smorgasbord of drugs that were freely available. I did go to his flat in Bromley. He was very involved in the local arts scene and had starred in the Arts Lab at the nearby Beckenham Recreation Ground – a mini-Glastonbury of its time. Bowie's home reflected his interest in music and art. He and Angie had no money to spend on decor but it was furnished in a very quirky and eclectic style. They lived in the huge ground-floor flat of Haddon Hall, a large Victorian villa. Until their professional split, Tony Visconti and his girlfriend shared the flat with the Bowies. In later years, when Visconti was in partnership with my brother in Good Earth, he told Roger that both he and his girlfriend were terrified by the bewildering array of bedfellows that David and Angie invited to Haddon Hall. Gender seemed to have little to do with who did what to whom.

David and Angie once came to my flat in St John's Wood. Angie gave us a small, mirrored duck that was sort of fashionable at the time, which was very sweet of her. David politely expressed an interest how we had done out the place and I showed him around whilst Angie chatted with Marsha. We had only lived there for a few months and I was naturally proud of our new home. David did say all the right things but I could tell that had I rolled back his sleeve I would have heard the laughter. I did not take offence; he would never warm to the middle-class decor of our home, no matter how chic we thought it was.

David and Ken started recording at the beginning of July and were in and out of Trident until August. This was lengthy – I was used to producers like Mickie Most, who got a single and a B-side down in a three-hour session and usually only needed one more session to mix the tracks. But when I went to the studio I liked what I heard and I did not impose any budgetary restrictions.

David booked Rick Wakeman, the piano virtuoso, then a session musician who would go on to be part of mega-band Yes. Although Rick was a fabulous musician, David wanted Dudley Moore, the film star who could easily have had a career as a pianist, to play piano on 'Life On Mars'. This was a very commercial thought, but Dudley did not respond to Gem's letter of invitation so the very fine piano you hear on the final version is Rick's. Four of Dana Gillespie's songs were recorded for her own album and she also did a version of Bowie's 'Andy Warhol', but later told me she preferred lyrics with emotion and her recording didn't work. David's own take on it ended up on *Hunky Dory*. Dana didn't reach her potential at the time but later developed into a fine blues singer.

There was still little interest in David from record companies, although I was constantly in touch with the right people: no one was asking me about Bowie. His gigs were sparsely attended and I could tell from those I saw myself, in truth, that he was not particularly exciting. This is hard to believe considering the dynamism of his stage act in later times, but in June 1971, after David played the second ever Glastonbury Festival, he told his small audience, 'I don't do gigs any more because I got so pissed off with working and dying a death every time I worked.' His offstage, gentle manner did not really change when he performed. David really exploded when he could hide behind a character. Ziggy of course was the most dramatic and remains the most iconic to this day. I firmly believe that had David not been so brilliant at reinventing himself he would never have achieved the almost god-like level of success that he did.

David's study of mime with Lindsay Kemp had taught him how to put on a mime face and Angie was certainly a huge influence on David's look. It was, however, the brilliance of David to actually inhabit Ziggy and his later alter egos and deliver the quality of music that enabled him to make such an impact on the world. I also believe that David Jones, the boy from Becken-ham, invented a superstar identity called David Bowie who he could call on to be his face to the outside world.

In June, David and Mick Ronson played the first Glaston-bury Festival organised by Michael Eavis on the fields of his farm. It was then, by contrast with the world-beating extrava-ganza it has become, an unambitious event with one stage, but it was still quite important and I was eager to know how it went for my artist. I had to wait until David and Defries came into the office the following day to learn how they had got on.

The pair, along with Angie, Bob Grace and Dana, took the train to the nearest station to the site. They walked to the farm for miles along country lanes. David was due to go on at 7.30 p.m. but the organisation was lacking and he only took the stage at 5.30 a.m, by which time it had poured with rain, creating the unavoidable sea of mud for which the festival is still famous. Understandably there was a very small audience, most of whom were wet and cold – but David and Mick went down well. I think that one of the highlights was when Defries tripped and went sprawling in the mud, David and Bob Grace giggling together like naughty schoolboys. More seriously, Defries told me on his return that he was sure Bob was trying to steal David away from us, which I did not doubt. Bob had been very involved with David's creative path and I am sure that he continued to stress how much more of a 'music man' he was. Jon Brewer has since told me that Bob Grace made a point of telling David that we were pursuing Stevie Wonder and would lose interest in David.

Defries complained vociferously to Terry Ellis that Bob was trying to create a rift between David and us. Terry called to assure me that Bob was just doing his job as David's music publisher. I expressed my doubts and reminded Terry of the law relating to 'incitement to breach a valid contract'. Later, when Terry and I became good business friends, he admitted that my reminder was timely. Five years later, when David's songwriting contract with Chrysalis was up, he did not renew. Under the original deal, Chrysalis retained 25 per cent of the copyright of the songs that David had written during the contractual term, so Chrysalis continued to enjoy a great income stream with no responsibility whatsoever. They took the chance, so good for them.

Having signed a publishing deal that required David to secure commercial recordings, it was now even more important to make a record deal. We needed something to attract some interest from major record companies. The new material that David was writing was exciting and David and Ken mixed down tracks for a Gem promotional/sample album, seven songs performed by Bowie and five Bowie-produced tracks of Dana Gillespie. This was a very unusual step to take and, at considerable cost, we pressed five hundred copies that are known to collectors as *BOWPROMO*. The album was presented in a gatefold sleeve that had a pocket in which we put selected reviews and interviews.

(A word about *Hunky Dory* test pressings and acetates. Research shows that the various acetates that Gem produced at the time are sometimes offered on eBay and other auction sites, fetching astoundingly high prices. A *BOWPROMO* was reportedly sold for ten thousand dollars. I no doubt had copies of them all cluttering up my office, which I would have thrown away when having the occasional tidy-up. Who knew? To add insult to injury, my son James recently gifted me with a replica copy of *BOWPROMO* that was released to mark Record Store Day in April 2017. It was a limited edition of fifteen thousand copies and my son paid fifty pounds for it. I have no idea how the releasing company got the rights to do this. It certainly was not from me. I should probably pursue them but I do not have the energy to take on issues that are not important to me. (It is, by the way, surprising how quickly old age happens.)

We started to line up record companies by sending them the sampler acetates. There was definitely antipathy in the UK. Bowie had created a high expectation with 'Space Oddity' and the failure of *The Man who Sold the World* meant that most record companies in the UK wrote him off as a one-hit wonder. But 'Space Oddity' had done nothing in the USA and it was decided that we should look there for a company to sign David, where hopefully he would have no 'previous' and could be judged on his new material. My New York attorney, Normand Kurtz, arranged August meetings for Defries with RCA, CBS, United Artists and Columbia. I set up a meeting for him with Bell Records. Being pop-orientated, they were not really the right label for Bowie, but because of the already successful deal that I had with Bell for Macaulay and Leander productions, I felt Defries should at least speak to them. The quality of the tracks on the sampler, coupled with Defries's unwavering faith in Bowie, attracted positive interest from everyone.

A few people recommended RCA. They had bought Elvis in 1955 from Sam Phillips, who had first signed him to his Sun Records, a tiny label in Memphis. Elvis had stayed with RCA and Defries was particularly impressed by the staying power because he admired the way Colonel Parker managed Elvis. David felt the same because even though Elvis was now recording some really crap songs amongst his classics, he was in the DNA of every UK artist who ever picked up a rock'n'roll guitar.

Dennis Katz was head of A&R at RCA and saw David Bowie as that weird transvestite guy who made 'Space Oddity', a record that had done well in the UK. He was a good A&R man and listened to the Gem sampler with care and without prejudice. Dennis enthused to Rocco Laginestra, head of RCA, who was not that taken with the material but supported Dennis. He had recently taken him on to find some interesting acts, and Bowie was nothing if not interesting. Rocco was aware that there was no desperation on the part of any other companies to sign David, and Mel Ilberman, his head of business affairs, was told to make a tough deal. He offered Gem $37,500 as an advance for each album and a royalty of 11 per cent of the retail price, excluding any taxes. Eight per cent would go to David, from which we would not deduct management commission, 1 per cent to producer Ken Scott and 2 per cent would be retained by Gem.

When the Rolling Stones signed to Andrew Oldham's company they were paid 6 per cent. Andrew Oldham used to deduct his management commission of 20 per cent, leaving the band about 5 per cent, which was shared between them. Reputedly, when The Beatles had signed to EMI a few years earlier, they were paid one old penny per single, also shared between them. Under my deal with David, he was paid about four pence per single. By any standards, David had a fair deal from Gem. No royalties were to be paid until RCA recouped its advances, which was a standard provision in all record deals.. It was a two-year deal for three albums, with options for RCA to extend with increased advances of $56,250 per album. David had committed to Gem for six years so I would be able to renegotiate with RCA after their term ended or negotiate a new deal with a different company. Clever me!

The advances were not high by RCA's usual standards, who were known to pay advances of a hundred thousand to two hundred thousand dollars for some American artists, but the royalty rates and lack of spurious deductions was fine, and David was keen to be with them. RCA also agreed to pay twenty thousand dollars for the Mercury albums that Gem now owned, approximately the amount Gem had paid for them. There was also an advance of $18,750, 50 per cent of the amount due on delivery of the next album (what would be *Ziggy Stardust*).

All in all, Gem would receive a cheque for around seventy-five thousand dollars from RCA. Aside from the advance on the next album, the money would go towards recouping my initial outlay on Bowie. True to my credo, the albums were to revert back to Gem five years after the deal ended.

About the time that *Hunky Dory* was finished, a play called *Pork* came from New York to London. It was based on conversations recorded by Andy Warhol in his New York studio, The Factory. The play was outrageous, and controversially pornographic. Andy Warhol was played by an actor called Tony Zanetta and the rest of the cast played other characters from Andy Warhol's Factory cabal. *Pork* played at The Roundhouse, a cool venue in funky Chalk Farm, north London, down from Haverstock Hill and The Country Club, where David was performing with Dana Gillespie.

One of the *Pork* company members had read the article in *Rolling Stone* magazine referring to David wearing a dress, so of course the entire company went to see him perform. It was love at first sight. David was invited to go to see *Pork* and a bond was established between all concerned. David and Angie went to see the play nearly every night but, despite the opportunity to see simulated masturbation on stage, I declined his offer to join them. David was hanging out with the *Pork* cast at El Sombrero most nights and he invited them to make themselves at home at my office in the day. Like-minded characters from the dark side or the enlightened side – depending on your point of view – seemed to be drawn to my offices, a corner of which became a mini-outpost of Andy Warhol's Factory.

25. STEVIE WONDER – AN INTERLUDE IN THE BOWIE STORY

One of the people who frequently appeared at the Gem offices in early 1971 was Don Hunter. I cannot remember how he came to us but he was there a lot. He produced a band called Milkwood that we had signed to Gem for management. Maybe he brought Milkwood to us, I don't remember. They did not have any great success, which is probably why I don't remember.

Don was an educated, rich, young white man from Minneapolis who had worked extensively in the studio with Stevie Wonder, co-writing and producing. I think that he was also employed by Berry Gordy, the head of Motown, to look after Stevie on the road in the UK. Don told us that, other than Diana Ross – who was Berry Gordy's great love – Motown treated their artists really badly. Don was very close to Stevie, who, according to him, was deeply unhappy and was thinking about leaving Motown and moving to England.

Stevie was part of a Motown revue that was touring the UK and was hankering after a state-of-the-art Sony music player, which unbelievably he could not afford to buy for himself. Don suggested that we buy it for him and he would bring him in to meet us and say thank you. In Don's opinion we could then start to woo Stevie for management. I thought that this was highly unlikely, but Defries had spent time with Don and assured me that they were really close.

We bought the gift and – to my great surprise – Don brought Stevie up to the office. Defries and I declared ourselves to be fans, which was not difficult because who wasn't? That first meeting was particularly memorable because Stevie felt our faces. He loved Defries's afro hair and we chatted about what we were doing. The fact that I had been involved with the Rolling Stones seemed to impress him and he left saying he would come and meet with us again. Don had obviously been selling us hard because Stevie did return. He told us he had made 'Fingertips', his first hit for Motown, in 1963, when he was about eight years old. Since then his hits included 'Uptight (Everything's Alright)', 'For Once in my Life' and 'My Cherie Amour'. He had done many tours but astonishingly he had no money, was living in a very modest house in Detroit and had no idea how much, if anything, he had coming to him in the future from the trust that Motown told him had been set up for him. He was twenty years old.

Stevie said that he wanted to get away from Motown and Berry Gordy and he felt that the only way he could do this was to move away from the USA. Don had told him that if he signed with us Don would move to London to look after him, and Stevie agreed. As much as I understood the logic behind Stevie's motives, I still did not believe that it would actually happen. I told him that I wanted him to call Berry Gordy there and then and tell him of his intentions. He made the call in private while

Defries, Don and I waited nervously. He came out of the room in tears. He told us that Berry had told him that he was like a son to him and he would never stand in his way, whatever he wanted to do.

I was still unsure and got *Music Week,* the bible of the UK music business, to run an article saying that Stevie Wonder was coming to live in London and was signing to Gem for management. I sat back waiting for a call from Motown's lawyers or a visit from two large gentlemen carrying baseball bats but there was no reaction whatsoever. There was no question, legally, that Stevie was free to leave Motown. He had been signed when he was blind and underage. He was going to be twenty-one in May and could disavow his Motown contracts with absolute certainty. First he would be touring the US and we made plans to take over his management on the day of his birthday. Defries sent Motown the appropriate paperwork, advising them of our plans and yet again there was no response. By the time it had gone out Stevie was in the middle of his tour and there were practical issues to deal with. We wanted to ensure continuity and put money into an American bank account so that there would be no problems when we took over.

Don recommended a Minneapolis-based lawyer to advise Stevie on the new contract, away from the gossip of New York or Los Angeles. The details were finalised and the contract had to be signed. Stevie told us that on his actual birthday he had been given a day off from the tour and was going home to Detroit for a big party organised by Syreeta, his wife. Lots of his friends from Motown would be there and he would feel uncomfortable if we were there too. We, of course, understood and flew to

Minneapolis on the day after his birthday to sign our copy of the contract. The lawyer was then going to meet with Stevie and get his thumbprint of approval.

Stevie, who had enjoyed his generous one-day-off, was back in New York, staying with his crew at The Hilton. We called the hotel and asked to be put through to the room in the assumed name under which he was registered. A voice, not Stevie's, answered abruptly. Stevie was not there. The phone was put down. Don had the room numbers of various crew who were staying at the hotel. He called them one by one and each put the phone down on him. We called Syreeta who said, 'I can't talk about it,' and she too put the phone down. It was obvious to me that Stevie had been 'got to' by Motown at his party the night before and Gem were no longer going to be managing Stevie Wonder. Defries and Don wanted to fly to New York but I was not going to incur any more expense in chasing what I knew was a lost cause. Sure enough, a few weeks later there was a full-page ad in *Billboard* magazine in Stevie Wonder's name stating, 'Motown is the place for me.'

Stevie had gone to Joe Vigoda, a legendary American music-business lawyer who was one of the great characters of his era. He looked like he was dressed by a charity shop and carried his office around in a beat-up old rucksack. He once gave me all of his contact phone numbers; homes and offices in Los Angeles, New York, and other places of interest around America. He took a full page of my Filofax (remember them?). I have no doubt Joe negotiated a fair deal for Stevie to stay with Motown, part of it being a reputed thirteen-million-dollar advance on signing. I'm sure that Joe also secured a bigger financial interest in Stevie's past success and a degree of ownership, which of course we could never do if we had taken him to Gem, a different company. I never really blamed Stevie for what he did, although because of him I missed seeing Arsenal winning the double, a very rare feat in football, and there was a very brief moment when I wished he'd go temporarily deaf, just in one ear.

Some months later, Normand Kurtz bumped into Joe Vigoda and complained to him how badly Stevie had behaved in his dealings with me. Joe said nothing, but a few days later he sent Normand a ten-thousand-dollar cheque for me, together with a brief message of apology on behalf of Stevie Wonder. Normand told Joe that I had spent a lot more than that in the pursuit of Mr Wonder, which was true, but Joe advised us to take the money and run, which I did.

Now that Stevie Wonder was no longer a diversion, all the focus was back on David Bowie. Before Gem was paid its seventy-five thousand dollars under the agreement with RCA, the masters of *Hunky Dory* had to be delivered to the record company and David had to sign an 'inducement letter' to RCA, confirming his formal agreement to his personal obligations under the Gem agreement. In September 1971 David and Angie, together with Mick Ronson, went to New York with Defries. We sent them all over first-class, something none of them had experienced, and on arrival RCA arranged for them to see Elvis Presley perform at Madison Square Garden. David was now beginning to feel like a star.

On 9 September in the RCA boardroom, the *Hunky Dory* master was formally delivered to Rocco Laginestra, the head of RCA. As was their style, David and Angie were both dressed similarly. Both had identical red hairstyles and there was a slight hitch when the RCA head of publicity thought that Angie was in fact David. That resolved, David signed his inducement letter and RCA handed Defries the cheque for seventy-five thousand dollars, made out to Gem. It was quite a moment in my business life and I rather wished that I could have been there myself. Defries called me as soon as he was out of Rocco's office to tell me that he had the cheque. It was obviously a great relief to me personally – in addition to covering recording costs, Gem paid David, Mick Ronson and the rest of the band weekly wages. Not only that, but so far not one of David's recordings had ever recouped its cost, and he was earning a pittance from personal appearances.

Tony Zanetta or 'Zee' as he was generally known, enthusiastically welcomed David and his party to New York. Zee took them to The Factory and introduced them all to Andy Warhol and Paul Morrissey, the film-maker who was closely associated with the artist. After the meeting, Defries called me to say that he thought we could get involved with the distribution of Warhol's films. In Defries's view, Warhol was not exploiting his commerciality and he was certain that he could help. In Zee's recollection of the meeting, Warhol gave Defries no reason to think that he was interested in any assistance.

After a dinner where David and Defries met Lou Reed, the crew went to Max's Kansas City, a New York club where they were introduced to Iggy Pop. The next morning Iggy was invited to breakfast with Defries and David, resulting in Defries soon signing Iggy, a proud heroin addict and general wild-man, as a Gem artist. The Warhol/Reed/Iggy/Bowie relationship was a forge that made David a major talking point within the

New York gay community, who were a very influential force in Manhattan's movers and groovers. It did him no harm at all in advancing his career.

Defries returned to London full of his fantastic trip to New York. He was convinced that we could manage Warhol and Lou Reed as well as Iggy. He brushed aside my concerns that we were taking on more than we could chew. He also became somewhat dismissive of other Gem artists. I became concerned about Defries' enormous belief in his ability to achieve world domination of the 'alternative' music business and began to think that I might not want to bring Defries into my company as a partner. When he first came to see me, I believed that he was hoping to attach himself to my rising star. Now just over a year later, he clearly thought that his personal comet had eclipsed me. We still had a warm relationship but I was wary of the change.

In November we all went to The Rainbow theatre to see Alice Cooper – maybe the first successful rock'n'roll artist to wear character make-up. The Rainbow was previously The Astoria cinema, just across the road from the Astoria Candy Stores – my parents' business, my home from the age of twelve to eighteen and now a very tacky dress shop. I explained to David that I used to live above it and I think he was surprised by my humble origins.

The Alice Cooper show was groundbreakingly great and spectacularly theatrical, but David promised that he could do better. He was already in the studios, recording tracks for the album to follow *Hunky Dory* and there was no doubt that he was influenced by his contact with Iggy, Lou Reed and the Warhol cabal.

Hunky Dory was released in the UK in December 1971. It had a Gem Productions logo on the back, which was dropped without my permission in later pressings and on the CD. I could have taken legal proceedings but it did not seem important to me at the time. My kids, now grown up, have copies of the original, which is enough for me. I have the gold disc that was presented for sales of a hundred thousand copies. I also have a gold disc for the *The Rise and Fall of Ziggy Stardust and the Spiders from Mars*, which was also a Gem production. I have three children and, unfortunately, only two Bowie discs to leave them, so to be fair I will have to work out how many New Seekers, Donna Summer and Heatwave gold discs equal one Bowie. I also have Gary Glitter gold discs, but suspect these would probably be a minus in the equation.

Hunky Dory did not do well on its initial release, selling barely two thousand copies in the first month. RCA London boss Ken Glancy was very concerned at the amount of money being spent on the promotion of the album at the insistence of Defries. To everybody's relief, it had a surge in sales after the release of *Ziggy Stardust*, accumulating sales of three hundred thousand. *Hunky Dory* did get great reviews in the music press and was widely acclaimed by the industry.

Choosing the first single off the album was important and – in a rare nod towards my success at having selected hit singles for other artists in the past – I was asked to choose a track. 'Life On Mars' was clearly a masterpiece but I was concerned it did not have the instant appeal to producers of radio, especially BBC Radio 1, the station that was then vital for exposure to the pop-buying public. I settled on 'Changes', which I thought better fitted the radio-play requirements, and 'Life On Mars' would be the second single. 'Changes' did not make the Top 40 … so much for my reputation as a pop picker.

The album definitely created a Bowie buzz, and the material that David was writing for *Ziggy* excited us all. The relative failure of *Hunky Dory* was a disappointment against that but was not a major setback for me personally. Tony Macaulay was producing hits for Johnny Johnson and Mike Leander was in the studio producing albums for David Essex and Marianne Faithfull, so I was fully occupied on positive projects.

In January 1972, Michael Watts – an important music journalist – came to Gem to interview David for the *Melody Maker*. This was quite a serious weekly paper and I remember standing in the Gem reception afterwards with David, who told me that he had just come out to the writer. He reminded me about my initial concern that being openly gay could affect his popularity with female fans, laughed and said, 'Laurence – we're about to find out.' David's announcement was no great shock, bearing in mind his penchant for wearing dresses and his general lifestyle, but it was hailed as a statement of pride by the gay community and many gay men who were not particularly aware of his music became instant fans. In some quarters, his coming out was seen as a publicity stunt. David had a big UK tour coming up and there is no doubt that the article was a huge help.

Shortly after the article appeared, a letter came to the office. It was in a brown envelope marked On Her Majesty's Service (OHMS), presumably from the taxman, so it came to my desk. It was in fact from a gay man who described in great detail what he would like to do to David and what he would like David to do to him. I still blush at the thought of it. The remarkable thing is that the sender continued sending letters in similar OHMS-marked envelopes almost every day for some months, presumably all written in working hours ... and we wonder why the UK has a trade deficit.

I took Marsha to see David playing in Aylesbury that same month. He still showed no confidence on stage and was frankly disappointing. I remember saying he needed someone to help him create a stage act. A couple of weeks later he played the Imperial College in London. The gigs were chalk-and-cheese – he had now really got into his Ziggy character. He was in front of a small, studenty crowd but I remember 'Suffragette City' bringing them to their feet. I had taken the whole office along to support David. Paul Gadd – soon to be Gary Glitter – came with Mike Leander. After the show we all offered David our congratulations. David was patronising to Paul, which upset me a little at the time.

By now Defries' spending – of Gem's money – was getting totally out of hand. He always insisted on having a large amount of cash on his person so that he could be magnanimous to David and other artists (albeit with my money). At Gem's expense, people were flying back and forth across the Atlantic, studios were being hired and musicians employed. Gem was like an avant-garde musicians' benefits office and, having investigated the profligacy of The Beatles' Apple Corp in my previous life, I clearly had to get my own house in order. Any concerns that I expressed to Defries were met with a shrug and, 'I'm building us the biggest artist roster in the world, Laurence.' My problem was finding the time to properly address this issue. Apart from working with Leander and Macaulay, I was starting to put together

Arcade Records, the compilation company that would become the most profitable business venture I ever undertook.

One of the most important and interesting of Defries' signings was Iggy Pop. David was keen to work with Iggy, who arrived in London in February to collaborate on David's new album. We initially put him up at The Royal Garden hotel in Kensington. Iggy did not like the poshness and I was not mad about the cost. My tiny house in St John's Wood was currently unoccupied as we had recently moved. I foolishly agreed that Iggy and his guitarist James Williamson could move into the house for the rest of their stay. 'What a stupid thing to do,' I hear you say, and you are right, but it seemed like a good idea at the time. Iggy was very charming when I took him to the house – no sign of the wild-man of rock who appeared on stage – and he thanked me most politely for allowing him to stay in my house. He repaid me by leaving burn marks on our carpet where he had made little fires, no doubt to warm spoons for eating soup.

The Rise and Fall of Ziggy Stardust and the Spiders from Mars, to give it its proper title, was produced by David and Ken Scott, and was released in the UK in June of 1972. The album artwork featuring David, dressed in a stunning jumpsuit, was brilliantly photographed by Brian Ward on a rainy night in Heddon Street, a cul-de-sac off Regent Street. It's now full of trendy restaurants, but in 1972 it was something of a seedy backwater where Brian could work undisturbed. Such is the importance of the album, there is now a plaque on the wall where the photograph was taken.

The album was immediately a success in the UK, selling eight thousand copies in the first week and peaking at UK No. 5. The music press had enormous goodwill towards David. They wanted him to produce a great album and *Ziggy Stardust* did the job. The alien had landed and had conquered the world.

It is important to acknowledge the contribution that Mick Ronson made to Bowie's music, not just as one of the Spiders from Mars, but as a general contributor. He was not only a great guitarist who gave Bowie's recordings a distinct sound, he was a brilliant arranger and producer who should have received much more formal credit for his work. Mick was quite an enigma. Very much a salt-of-the-earth northern lad, he was inclined to stand up when I – the guv'nor – entered the room. Classically trained from childhood to play piano and violin, he wanted to be a cellist until, influenced by the distinctive sound of guitar virtuoso Duane Eddy, he switched to guitar. From 1963 he played with a variety of bands in the Hull area, while working as a gardener for the Hull City parks department between gigs. He did a lot of session work and toured briefly with Van Morrison, Bob Dylan and others. In 1970, he joined David as a member of his backing band, The Hype, and was a huge influence on David's music until he left him in 1973 to pursue a solo career.

Mick's arrangements included the lovely string arrangement on 'Life On Mars'. He was also, of course, part of the controversy when David famously simulated fellatio on his guitar on the tour to promote the *Ziggy* album – something that Mick was not happy about. But he was unquestionably one of the great guitarists of his era. He was a thoroughly nice bloke and I was deeply moved when I heard of his death from cancer, aged forty-six, in 1993. Mick was something of an unsung hero and I was happy to contribute to *Beside Bowie: The Mick Ronson Story*, Jon Brewer's excellent film.

Based on the success of the album I had bought a twenty-two-foot motorboat, which I named *Ziggy Stardust*. I thanked David for his 'gift' and he urged me to commission a paint job by George Underwood, a childhood friend and one-time fellow band member. It was hardly a practical idea, and the boat would never have lasted until now, but I sometimes wonder what a boat painted by George – now a successful artist – would be worth these days.

Success was a double-edged sword. On one hand I was delighted that the expectation and hype that had surrounded David had at last come to fruition and that I no longer needed to be concerned about my financial exposure. The downside was that Defries, vindicated in his belief of Bowie's stardom, was paying less and less attention to my advice to concentrate on our other artists. He was now trying to get more deeply involved with Iggy, Mott the Hoople, Lou Reed and various other artists within that circle. David sat on my office floor playing 'All The Young Dudes' for Ian Hunter, the lead singer of Mott. Ian loved it and David produced the single and the following album. With my approval, Tony Defries signed Mott the Hoople to Gem.

My offices were now a home from home for a motley collection of musicians – now including Mott the Hoople – outré hangers-on and arguably weirdos, who sucked up so much of the oxygen of Gem that the other occupants – including me – were made to feel like background characters. I had no wish to fall out with Defries, but clearly I had to make some changes. I had promised him 20 per cent of the company 'if things worked out well' and at some level things had worked out very well indeed, but it was clear that if I did not change my relationship things could work out very badly.

There was no question that if David was to be a worldwide star he had to conquer America. America had by far the biggest market for music. As a generalisation, a US hit sold more than five times as much as a UK hit, and a successful US tour could make ten times as much as a UK tour. Through his marriage to Angie, a US citizen, David was allowed to work in America and it made sense for him to physically establish a base there. Defries was completely in love with the New York scene and had been nagging me to open a Gem office in New York, which he would run. I was unable to contain his extravagance when he was in an office five yards from where I sat, so clearly my chances would not improve if he were three thousand miles away. I was also very much aware that once he was that far away – human nature being what it is – at some point Defries would start to resent being a 'junior partner' and things could well become nasty. I had been increasingly convinced that I could not live with Tony Defries as a partner in my company and the timing of his wish to move to New York suited me very well.

The Defries coterie of artists was still in deficit to Gem. Pay attention to this next bit because it introduces irony into my story. I did not keep copies of my old Gem accountings – who knew? – but Kevin Cann's book *Any Day Now* sets out some very specific balances of Defries-signed artists from around 1972:

Bowie's deficit: £29,062.

Mott the Hoople's surplus: £2,603

Iggy Pop's deficit: £5,767

Dana Gillespie's deficit: about £2,000

I called Kevin Cann and asked him how on earth he had come by this information. He told me that he had been given copies of accountings by Peter Gillman, who with his wife wrote *Alias David Bowie* in 1986. I called Peter who told me that he had been given some files by the widow of Peter Gerber, who was my internal accountant until he was seduced away by Defries. So essentially, the information that I have set out above was generated in the seventies by a member of my staff, passed on to Peter Gillman for the book he published in 1986, and passed on to Kevin Cann for the book he wrote in 2010. I was upset at the time that Defries had approached Peter to work for him without asking me if I minded, but on the other hand – and there is often another hand – I thought that Peter would protect my future interest, so I did not make an issue of Tony's poor behaviour.

Having decided to change my arrangement with Defries, we had to agree a 'divorce' deal. If it came to a fight, in the left-hand corner was David Bowie's contract with Gem, which provided that if Defries left Gem, David could walk away. But – big *but* – in the right-hand corner we had David's obligation to RCA, which was through the recording contract that he had signed with Gem. Even if Gem lost David for management, it would still own his recording services and most importantly, the Gem/RCA contract provided that outright ownership of the albums reverted to Gem five years after the contract ended. Gem would win. Happily, Defries acknowledged my contribution to his position at that time and there was no fight.

Defries had decided to go it alone under the name Main-Man. There was to be a MainMan London and MainMan New York. He had no money so I loaned him forty thousand dollars to finance his New York operation. Gem assigned to MainMan all the rights and benefits that it owned in David and the other artists brought in by Defries. Gem would receive all outstanding amounts due plus 20 per cent of the gross income from all of David's earnings for five years. After the deal was agreed, Defries asked if there was a point at which I would be satisfied to give up my financial interest in David's gross income. Without giving it too much thought I said that if he repaid the loan and paid the deficits on the assigned artists account, plus – a big *plus* – five hundred thousand pounds within eighteen months, I would then give up any future interest. Before you conclude that I was a schmuck to make this deal, a few points in mitigation:

1. Five hundred thousand pounds was an enormous sum of money then and approximately five million pounds in today's terms.

2. David would have to generate two-and-a-half million pounds in eighteen months for me to get five hundred thousand at my rate of 20 per cent, which at the time seemed very unlikely.

3. With the benefit of hindsight, I should have insisted on keeping a 5 or 10 per cent interest in David's future, which I am sure would not have affected the amount I was to get under the deal that I had agreed. It would probably have earned me another five million over the years. Who knew?

4. Read on and I will tell you how I pissed away most of the five hundred thousand pounds opening and running an office in Los Angeles.

Defries now had to make his own deal with David. He had often expressed his admiration for the Colonel Parker/Presley concept of a 50/50 partnership between manager and artist and he told me that this is how he intended to operate with David. The Colonel only had Presley, so I could see how this might work but I questioned how it could work when you had an office looking after multiple clients. This was answered with a typical Defries don't-you-worry shrug. It was no longer going to be my any of my business, so I did not worry. We will get to the actual deal that David might have signed with MainMan in Tony Zanetta's recollection of the crisis meeting that he had with David in 1974, a full account of which is set out a little later in this book.

David, who of course desperately wanted a career move to America, was delighted that I was facilitating Defries' opening of a New York office. He and Angie came to express their appreciation of all that I had done to help them in the past and what I was now doing to help David's future.

In August 1972, Defries moved from Gem to a home/office in Gunter Grove – between Fulham and Chelsea and an almost fashionable part of London – to plan the American venture. I felt good about the departure of the Bowie circus. Everybody in my office clearly felt that I now had more time to spend with them and the general atmosphere was more 'one family'.

MainMan's New York offices opened on East 58th Street, with Tony Zanetta, the actor Defries had first met the year before in *Pork* at the Roundhouse, running the company. Dana Gillespie also went to New York with Bowie and both she and Zanetta tell how Defries hit the ground running. He now had what he wanted – a stable of talented artists who had complete faith in his apparent Svengali-like ability to progress their careers. He no longer had an obligation to answer to me and his business ethos

of 'live like a star to be a star' flourished unchecked. This philosophy was not confined to MainMan's artists. Defries obviously
believed in leading by example, with cigars flown in from Cuba
and general profligacy. His twenty-six employees were allowed to
charge any expense they chose to the company account, including – I've been told – cosmetic dental work and plastic surgery.
According to Zanetta all, even maids and chauffeurs, had the
use of a fourteen-room suite of offices in uptown Manhattan,
an Upper East Side penthouse, a duplex on East 58th Street, an
apartment at The Sherry-Netherland hotel and a loft on Lower
West Side (now part of the trendy Tribeca area). There were also
four apartments for the use of clients. Defries lived in a twenty-
six-room estate in Connecticut where his customised Cadillac
limousine was available to him twenty-four hours a day.

Tony Zanetta told me that David was surprised by the
extravagance of the MainMan offices when he arrived in early
1974, but he had complete confidence in Defries' judgement and
went along with the set-up. Tony ensconced David in a suite at
the very chic and very expensive Sherry-Netherland, which is
as nice a place as any to go along with anything. When David
toured America, Defries made sure he enjoyed a similar level
of high-profile luxury. For instance, most bands when in Los
Angeles stayed at The Sunset Marquee, a reasonably priced
rock'n'roll hotel, but David and his entourage stayed at the five-
star Beverly Hills hotel, very much the haunt of A-list movie
stars. I must confess that in later years I often stayed there myself.
There is something about breakfasting with Paul Newman and
Dean Martin at nearby tables to add a frisson to one's morning
– but I was paying the bill with my own money.

Within months the Defries/Bowie honeymoon was over. The catalyst was the Diamond Dogs Tour. Defries authorised a highly-paid West End/Broadway design team to create an amazing set without budgetary restrictions. This of course is like setting kids free in a candy store. The design team created a set that cost four hundred thousand dollars and took thirty men a full day to erect. Madness for a touring set. The rehearsal was a shambles and the tour was a nightmare for the crew. During a break, David would go off to record *Young Americans* with soul and R&B musicians, where he was to catch a bit of roots soul, and decide that he should present himself in a back-to-basics way. He would then dump the set without reference to Defries.

MainMan had debts piling up. Defries lost three hundred thousand dollars producing *Fame*, a play about Marilyn Monroe, which came off after one night on Broadway. The UK bank account was overdrawn and debts were piling up on both sides of the Atlantic. Peter Gerber resigned from MainMan, unable to cope with Defries' cavalier attitude to pressing creditors. Peter died suddenly a few years later from a heart attack. He was in his thirties. At his wife's request, I spoke at his funeral, which Defries did not attend.

Back at the beginning of the Diamond Dogs Tour, Angie had flown to New York, and was summoned by Defries to his penthouse to explain how she had spent a hundred thousand dollars in a year on travel, limos and hotels. He told her to stop and that she must no longer meddle in business affairs. David then summoned Tony Zanetta to his suite at The Sherry-Netherland hotel, furious with Defries for his treatment of Angie.

Henry Edwards related Tony Zanetta's recollection of the meeting in their book *Stardust – The David Bowie Story*. It is quite a long extract, but it is a major event in David Bowie's career. I was not there, but Tony Zanetta was. It happened to him, and I think that his recounting brings it to life. I am most grateful to have received Tony's permission to use it.

David finally came into the living room, dressed in a kimono. Angie snuggled up next to him on the couch. She looked adoringly at him and stroked his hand. The roles they had elected to play with each other that evening were man of the house and loving wife.

David emptied a vial of cocaine onto a mirror and chopped it into lines. Using a hundred-dollar bill, he snorted a line or two. He enjoyed the drug-taking ritual, chopping the cocaine and deciding how big each line should be. He especially liked the fact that he controlled the stash and could decide if and when to offer Zanetta a line. Angela neither took drugs not drank. The cocaine binge between David and Zanetta would last fifteen hours.

Even when he was relaxing, David had an agenda; there was always a scenario, a script to act out, with David triumphant at the third-act curtain. Looking back at that meeting, Zanetta realises that Bowie had several intentions. He wanted firsthand confirmation from an eyewitness of what he had been told was going on in the MainMan offices. He was also engaged in a subtle but deadly war with Defries. Now David wanted to win Defries's right-hand man over to his side; he wanted Zanetta to work for him and not Defries.

'Every day I wake up to face a nightmare,' David began, 'a nightmare I don't understand. I once had a dream, and Tony had that dream. It's a dream we shared.'

He looked knowingly at Zanetta. His dream automatically was everyone's dream, his quest a mission shared by all who knew and loved him.

'But I had to do my part,' he continued. 'I had to create; I had to do my work. I've done my part, haven't I? I've upheld my end of the bargain. I don't understand why he has done this.'

Overcome with confusion, he paused. 'Is this the time to abandon me?' he finally asked. 'Is this the time to abandon the dream? This is the moment that is supposed to be triumphant.' It was impossible not to believe along with him that he was a victim of a colossal betrayal.

'Z, I don't have a dollar in my pocket,' he said incredulously. 'It's ridiculous, laughable, a bloody nightmare. When Tony spoke to Angie like that he was meddling in my personal life,' David declared. 'I don't advise him on the subject of Melanie's [Defries' wife] spending. Where does he come off telling Angie how to spend her money? He's crossed his boundaries with that one. He's in charge of my business, not my personal life or my work. All I know is I don't have the money to give Angie to spend while he has all the money in the world to give to Melanie.'

Angela looked lovingly at her champion. 'I was never so insulted in all my life,' she said sadly. 'He really hurt me.' They cuddled up to each other. They looked so childlike and wounded they could have been posing for an orphanage poster.

Although they slept in separate bedrooms Angela and David had enormous loyalty, neither tolerating criticism of the other.

In the proper mood they could give stunning performances of husband and wife. They acted the roles so well they convinced not only everyone around them but also themselves that they were deeply in love.

'I can't get through to Tony on the phone. I can't see him. He doesn't have time for me or my career. He's too busy getting the price of gold, too busy worrying about how many nights I'm going to play and counting heads. Everything, everything, has a dollar sign on it. It's diabolical!'

There was a pause. He stared at Zanetta. 'Z, I feel very alone. I feel totally defenceless.'

Zanetta was touched by David's surprising display of emotion. He replied, 'I'm willing to do anything I can to help. I can talk to Tony for you.'

'You're the only one I can rely on. You're the only one in that office I can trust, whom I can expect to give me answers about what's going on. I'm financially dependent on Tony. I have no idea what I've got, I don't know what I'm worth. I don't know who's paying for everything. Where's the money coming from for all the projects? Who's paying for the Wayne County film? Who's paying for the Broadway production of Fame? Who's paying for Mick Ronson's campaign? Who's paying for Dana's campaign? Who's paying for the billboards? Half of this company is mine, but I have no say in anything. I don't know what's going out, I don't know what's coming in.'

'David,' Zanetta said, 'your deal is no secret. You are to receive 50 per cent of the profits – after your expenses are deducted – of the monies generated by you and you alone. You own no portion of MainMan. MainMan belongs exclusively to Tony.'

It was as if David had erected a soundproof booth around himself. His look grew determined, and he jutted out his jaw. 'I don't understand,' he said. 'Tony and I are partners, our agreement has always been 50/50.'

'You own 50 per cent of your income after all expenses are deducted. Tony is under no obligation to pay you anything other than your salary and to support you, your family, and your staff. The money you generate is MainMan income, not Bowie income. It remains MainMan income until Tony decides to distribute it. You have given him permission to use this money to develop other acts and to build MainMan. All your money goes to him, and he has total control over it. You have never had any control over your money.'

'I own 50 per cent of MainMan.'

'That's not your agreement. You own no portion of MainMan.'

'I know I own 50 per cent of the company.' Nothing could make him change his mind.

'Surely you always knew what your deal with Tony was?' said Zanetta.

David looked confused. To admit that he had not known the truth was to admit that he had behaved irresponsibly, to admit that he was less than perfect. 'I never understood it,' he said stubbornly. 'I know I own 50 per cent of MainMan.'

Once again Zanetta told him the exact terms of his deal. 'David, it's the deal you made. You could always have renegotiated it; you can still renegotiate it.'

'I own 50 per cent of MainMan, I know I do.'

'If you think Tony's cheating you, hire an accountant and audit his books. See where the money is going. Decide which expenses you think are legitimate.' Zanetta was talking to a wall. David stared silently into space. 'If you have suspicions about anything, hire a lawyer and conduct a full investigation,' urged Zanetta.

Bowie didn't want lawyers and accountants. He wanted to maintain his fantasy that Tony had become involved with him out of love and a belief in his talent, not as part of his empire-building.

It was almost dawn but the cocaine had filled David with speedy energy.

Angela curled up on David's lap and fell asleep.

Later, while Angela dozed, the two men watched the sun rise over Manhattan. Everything seemed peaceful and happy for a few moments. Then David again became crestfallen. 'How did it come to this?' he asked quietly. 'Why did it come to this? It shouldn't have. You know it shouldn't have. I don't understand any of it.'

I met with Angie in May 2017 whilst doing research for this book. She had been invited to London by the filmmaker Jon Brewer to help promote *Beside Bowie*, his film about Mick Ronson. Our meeting was interesting. She is no less of a force of nature than she was when I first met her almost fifty years ago. Angie was born in Cyprus to American parents. She was well educated in Cyprus, Switzerland and England and then went to Connecticut college where she was expelled for having an affair with someone of her own sex. She was, by her own admission, brash and opinionated. She now lives in Atlanta with a long-term partner – male! In some quarters she has been exclusively cast as a bad influence in David's life, which I think is unfair. I have no view of who was 'the bad guy' in their personal relationship, and by conventional standards I think Freud might have given up psychiatry had he taken the case. But I firmly believe that she was extremely important in prompting David to make the initial breakthrough from talented musical artist to chameleon-like, world-famous icon. He was a low-energy individual and she provided high energy for them both.

I first asked Angie why it took so long for David to actually take any action against Defries. The relevant meeting with Tony Zanetta was in the summer of 1974 and it took six months before David instructed his attorney Michael Lippman to start any proceedings. She told me that David was on tour, doing a lot of cocaine and it was a big decision, requiring careful thought. Apparently, John Lennon and Mick Jagger had both advised him that no managers were to be trusted.

Angie told me that Defries was determined to get rid of her as soon as he felt he had a hold on David. Corinne Schwab – Coco – a MainMan employee who had become David's assistant, was also a great influence and was also determined that Angie should go. Coco became David's fiercely loyal gatekeeper for many years. Angie physically split from David around 1977, although they were not divorced until February 1980. By then she was in Switzerland and Angie told me that she was not given enough to live on and was deprived of any relationship with her son Zowie (now Duncan Jones). I asked her if she was proud of his success as a film director. 'Good for him,' she said, 'but David poisoned him against me, and I have not seen him for forty years. I don't know him so it gives me no thrill.' Tony

Zanetta later told me that Duncan, who had been sent by David to be educated in Switzerland, used to visit Angie in school holidays until he was about thirteen. Angie was still very much living a rock'n'roll lifestyle and, in Tony's view, Duncan was not comfortable staying with her. David sent him to be educated at Gordonstoun, the Scottish school attended by the Duke of Edinburgh and Prince Charles, from which time Angie and her son were totally estranged.

Angie told me of the sexual merry-go-round of her circle in the early seventies. David was certainly a busy boy. He had 'fucked countless women, and there were also many men,' said Angie. David had 'fucked Corinne once, to make her feel good'. She said that Defries and Dana Gillespie were also, at some point having sex. Defries had married Melanie, who had met him via Rodney Bingenheimer. Angie said of Defries and Melanie, 'I fucked them both. Well ... not fucked, but ... you know?' In truth I did not know, but nodded, not wishing her to think that I was naive – which in this area I was and am. A middle-class background and the leftover sixties' hippy trippy/free love/do-your-own-thing/ let-it-all-hang-out lifestyle had passed me by. She actually said that she had always admired me for being 'the most honest man she had ever known in the music business, with a wife and family that gave stability'. She also said that when the MainMan carnival moved to America she missed my steadying influence, and told David so. She may have just been telling me what I would like to hear, but I liked to hear it, so that's OK.

I did not meet David again until 1975. I had received a call from Mel Ilberman of RCA Records, whom I liked very much.

'Where there's a hit, there's a writ' was manifesting itself in a tsunami of litigation. In addition to the bitter fight between David and Defries, Defries and RCA were also actively engaged in litigation. Following the fallout with Defries, David was trying to get RCA to deal with him directly. Record companies invariably support artists who are in a fight with their manager as, invariably, managers can't sing. In this case, Mel would have been delighted to bypass Defries, but the manager had a powerful legal position which complicated the situation. There seemed to be no hope of David releasing a new album until the legal issues were resolved, a stalemate which could have gone on for years.

This would have been a problem. No matter how big the artist, if the fans' interest is not maintained with a new album there is a danger that they can eventually be forgotten. It genuinely concerned me that David's career would be harmed if this logjam was not resolved. I no longer had any financial interest in David, having happily banked my half-a-million-pound pay-off at the end of 1974, but I had started my relationship with David in 1970 because I was a fan, and I still was.

Even though there were things about Tony Defries' conduct that had upset me, I had maintained a cordial relationship. I knew Michael Lippman, David's new attorney/manager, so I was in a unique position to calm things down. I told Mel that if RCA would host a 'peace conference', I would do my best to get the warring parties together. Negotiations followed that made organising a Middle East summit look like a doddle, but eventually RCA took a huge suite at The Century Plaza hotel in Los Angeles. The Defries camp had a room, the David camp had a room, and RCA and I had a room, the neutral ground, where we met. It had a living area that looked like a forerunner of an IKEA show-room. The two warring parties sat on sofas at either end of the room, which could easily have accommodated five-a-side football. If I'd have had a whistle I would have blown it to start the game.

The essence of my referee's instructions was something like this: 'If you carry on fighting you are going to make some lawyers a lot richer and yourselves a lot poorer. You two have made me a lot of money and it concerns me that you are both wasting time, money and energy fucking up David's career. I have no financial interest in the outcome of this meeting. Both of you have to be prepared to give a little and both of you have to want to resolve the issues. I do not wish to act as any sort of mediator and will not be present during your discussions.'

They agreed to talk and I went and hid in the RCA room with Mel Ilberman. After a long time Michael Lippman came in to see me, looking a little shamefaced. 'I am very embarrassed but David insists that I ask you to sign a piece of paper confirming that you have no financial interest in Defries' affairs any more.'

I was furious, and replied, 'Tell David to go fuck himself.'

I am pretty sure that Michael did not pass on my specific choice of language, as on the few occasions I subsequently ran into David he was his usual polite self. But as Oscar Wilde once famously said, 'No good deed goes unpunished' and in later years when I wanted to get David involved in some theatre projects, my approaches were ignored. Maybe he *was* told of my sugges-tion to 'go fuck himself' and was returning the compliment.

As I recall, the peace and reconciliation meeting came to a premature end when Mel Ilberman received a call to say that Defries' lawyers had just served another formal notice on RCA, pursuant to his general campaign, that they were not to deal with David's recordings other than through MainMan. But dialogue had, however, begun between David, via Lippman, and Defries, and eventually a very long and detailed settlement agreement was signed giving MainMan a substantial interest in Bowie's future earnings and granting them joint ownership of his album masters (full details of the agreement are set out in the Gillmans' *Alias David Bowie*). The agreement was far-reaching and in 1997 – more than twenty years after their split – Defries was still profiting hugely from David's work.

It was also in 1997 that the star raised fifty-five million dollars – not a misprint; fifty-five million dollars – by issuing 'Bowie bonds'. Put simply, these were loan notes paying 7.9 per cent interest, maturing after fifteen years, secured on his future earnings from his albums. As Defries was half-owner of the masters, David would have needed his cooperation and he presumably received half of the full amount raised, to buy out his interest. Under my Gem deal with RCA, the masters were to revert to my company and that benefit I passed on to MainMan for a lousy half a million pounds. Who knew?

Tony Zanetta told me that the MainMan offices were closed in 1975 and he and many others felt cast adrift. It seemed that he had never had a proper salary working for Tony. He had his rent and credit card paid by Mainman, and was given a few dollars walking-around money. The same had applied to the Spiders' Mick Ronson, bass guitarist Trevor Bolder and drummer Woody Woodmansey.

After a hugely successful tour playing sixty-one venues in seven weeks, the final date was at London's Hammersmith

Odeon in July 1973. Just before they finished with 'Rock'n'Roll Suicide' in front of a star-studded audience, including Mick and Bianca Jagger, Paul and Linda McCartney, Lou Reed, Keith Moon, Barbra Streisand and me, David made an announcement that shocked the audience. 'Not only is this the last show of the tour, it is the last show we will ever do.' The band was over. Woody and Trevor had no idea that they were now out of work. Even Mick Ronson was only told earlier in the day. Like Tony Zanetta in New York, the three Spiders From Mars had never been paid a proper salary. Their expenses were covered generously: Mick was given fifty pounds a week and Trevor and Woody were each given thirty pounds a week. Mike Garson, the American jazz pianist who had been brought in for the tour was paid eight hundred dollars a week, more than the rest of the band put together. After the tour David was taking time off from recording so Mick was also going to be out of work. Defries took Ronson on as a solo artist, but according to Suzanne, Mick's then wife, they didn't have any money until Mick produced the *Your Arsenal* album for Morrissey.

After the Century Plaza un-peace talks, I next met David at the Cannes Film Festival in 1978. David Hemmings was there with David, promoting *Just A Gigolo*. Marsha and I had met David and Prue Hemmings in the summer of 1977, through Mike and Penny Leander. This was when we had been due to go and stay with the Leanders in La Barracca, their villa in Majorca. On arrival, they told us that their house was not completed and we were to stay with David and Prue, who had rented a large house not far away. We had met the Hemmings socially a few times, but were hardly proper friends. The Leanders had not told us of this switch in accommodation until we arrived, because obviously we would not have wished to impose ourselves on people that we hardly knew.

David Hemmings came to prominence as an actor in Antonioni's *Blow-Up*, one of the seminal films of the sixties. He went on to make dozens of films before turning to directing. In addition to being a superb actor, he had a great voice and had started his career as a boy soprano working with Benjamin Britten. He starred in Andrew Lloyd Webber's musical *Jeeves*. He was also a gifted artist and a superb raconteur. Most of all he had a huge sense of fun, as indeed did Mike Leander. They were both inclined to drink *a lot*, which often fuelled their naughtiness. Hemmings, offered a drink, would say, 'Well, it is a warm day.'

The Hemmings made us extremely welcome and we had a great time. David played all day but had enough energy to work late into the night. Though around forty and past the youthful beauty of *Blow-Up*, he was still an extremely handsome and attractive man. I noted that if Marsha needed to get up in the night to go to the lavatory she spent some time fixing her hair and make-up before she ventured out of our room. There must have been something in the Majorcan water because she never got up in the night to pee when we were at home.

David and I did become friends and we also worked together. In 1981 he directed *The Survivor*, a film that I had developed based on a book by James Herbert. Hemmings changed the story so much that James Herbert, quite rightly, never forgave me.

Hemmings and Mike Leander were like brothers. They even looked alike. One evening at Tramp, when Mike was being treated for the cancer that would eventually kill him at the too-young age of fifty-five, he complained that the chemo had made him bald. Hemmings roared with laughter, 'Your hair will grow back, but these won't,' as he took out his false teeth and slapped them on the table. This in a crowded Tramp club was a true measure of friendship. Hemmings also died young, at the age of sixty-two. They had both smoked, drunk and enjoyed life to excess. Personally, I do not believe in heaven or hell but would like to think that Leander and Hemmings are together somewhere, along with Peter O'Toole, Oliver Reed, Richard Harris, Richard Burton and others of that ilk whose way of life we mere mortals condemned but wished we had tasted.

Just A Gigolo starred Kim Novak and Marlene Dietrich as well as David Bowie. It was made in Berlin and Hemmings invited me to come and see him on set. It was 1978, the Berlin Wall was still up and I jumped at the chance of having a glimpse of life in the besieged Berlin. I flew into Tempelhof airport feeling very 'spy who came in from the cold' and went straight to the studio. I had not seen David Bowie for some years and I was intrigued to see how he reacted to me. I was particularly excited at the thought of meeting Marlene Dietrich and Kim Novak, the other stars of the film. I was very disappointed – David was not on set. Marlene Dietrich had never been on set. All her action had been shot in Paris and cut in to her scenes with David.

David would probably not have taken a part in the film had he not been living in Berlin. He had recorded *Heroes* there, produced by Tony Visconti, in a studio about five hundred yards from the Berlin Wall. Hemmings confided in me that other than his 'close relationship' with Miss Novak, things were not going well. He was over-budget, he was unhappy with the script – there had been four different screenwriters – and it was not a happy set. Bowie was understandably pissed off because one of the main reasons he had said yes to the film was to work with the legendary Dietrich, whom he never even got to meet.

Anyway, Hemmings took the film to Cannes in 1978 and David was there to promote it. By then I was a regular participant in the festival. Mike and Penny Leander were also there and we all saw a lot of each other. *Just a Gigolo* was a poor film but Hemming's optimism was infectious and we all celebrated its upcoming release as if it had Oscar potential.

There was one memorable night when I took David Bowie and the Leanders to the Whisky À Gogo, Cannes, hip disco. David did not raise his differences with Defries and actually thanked me for his 'great times' at Gem. David seemed quite philosophical when I explained that I could not accommodate his request to get 'my artist' some cocaine. The Whisky was full of music-business people, and I must confess to enjoying the looks of jealousy/admiration as I sat chatting to one of the great glam-rock pioneers I had helped to fame. David took Penny on the floor for a slow dance, and she was not best pleased that Mike did not appear to be the least bit upset. Hemmings was supposed to join us but had been obliged to spend the evening with potential buyers of his film.

Just A Gigolo was released to such universally terrible reviews that it was withdrawn from circulation, causing Bowie to later quip: 'It was my 32 Elvis Presley movies rolled into one.'

That evening at the Whisky was the last time I spent time with David and I am glad that it is such a pleasant memory.

26. POSTCRIPT ON DAVID BOWIE AND TONY DEFRIES

Since I began writing this book, David Bowie has died. I had not seen him for forty years, and it would be hypocritical to say that I was devastated by the news in a personal way, but David had been a big adventure in my business life and I was certainly saddened and shocked by his unexpected death.

What shocked me even more was the effect that David's death had on people around the world. The outpouring of grief was extraordinary, and the worldwide media coverage was equal to that following John Lennon's murder.

I think that it was not David's musical ability, special though it was, that had such a profound effect on his fans and followers. In the sixties, The Beatles and the Rolling Stones had caught the wave of youth revolution and became the symbols of change from the older generations. David had not caught a wave, he had created one. Through his music, performance and lifestyle, he articulated that people should be what they wanted to be, and that conventions were made to be broken. Though forever a chameleon, he was always quintessentially English and when we were together in private, he never appeared to take himself too seriously. He also wrote songs that were not love songs.

I have not seen Tony Defries for some thirty-odd years. He is, I believe, a highly intelligent man. In the 1970s, he predicted that every home in the developed world would have a personal computer for general family use, an outrageous idea at the time. Sadly, after I helped him set up MainMan, I only ever heard from him when he needed my help. Around 1978 he called me to ask if I could assist him in getting a record deal for John Mellencamp, an artist whose name, against his wishes, Defries had changed to Johnny Cougar. I was unhappy with the offhand way that he had dealt with me once he had fled the Gem nest, and I did not feel that this was something that I wanted to do. Mr Cougar had little success under Defries' guidance but subsequently became an important artist when he left Defries and changed his name back to Mellencamp.

About eight years ago, Defries called me again, out of the blue. He told me that he had become a self-taught scientist and had developed a technique that would revolutionise solar-panel heating. He was urgently looking for substantial monies to develop the project and asked me if I could help him find an investor. Still a respecter of Defries' intellect, I did not doubt his ability to come up with something brilliant but had no inclination to be involved with him in business again.

Since the demise of MainMan, as far as I am aware he did not manage any other well-known artists other than those he met during the time he worked with me at Gem and John Cougar Mellencamp,. Maybe he chose not to. According to Wikipedia, Tony Defries lost twenty-two million dollars in an offshore tax-evasion scheme. He was also sued by Capitol Records for copyright infringement – a case that he lost, costing him nine million dollars in damages and costs.

I do not think that Defries behaved particularly well with me but I do not rejoice in any woes that may have befallen him. He brought David Bowie into my business life and, in the early days, before he began to believe his own publicity, he was fun to work with.

27. GTO INCLUDING DAVID JOSEPH AND THE NEW SEEKERS

So, how did I manage to go through the five hundred thousand pounds that I received from the Bowie deal? It is a cautionary tale.

One of the reasons that I was not unhappy that Defries and his entourage were moving out in the summer of 1972 was that I was actively considering a merger with the Toby Organisation. It was a company started by a young man named David Joseph, who had brilliantly taken three boys and two girls, named them The New Seekers and guided them to major success with 'I'd Like to Teach the World to Sing'. This had become a worldwide hit thanks to a Coca-Cola commercial.

David was the opposite of Defries. He was conventional, serious, obviously reliable and a proven success as a manager. I was still aware of my own lack of experience of managing a group on the road, getting the right gigs, arranging tours etc, and I was interested in working with him. He, on the other hand, had negotiated a poor record deal with Polydor Records for The New Seekers and I could see that we complemented each other. At the time he was based in St James Street, London, sharing offices with Slim Miller Entertainments, a successful agency who booked the group's live performances in the UK. David had an interest in Slim's company but his ambition was not to help grow a company involved in cabaret acts. He wanted to be a player on the international pop music stage.

David was born in England but his parents soon moved to Australia. He worked in radio and then became a successful TV producer, marrying Robin, an accomplished and well-known Australian jazz singer who then raised their family. They moved to the UK in 1970 and when we met, he and Robin had three daughters and a dog called Toby – hence the name of his company. One of the reasons I had been outside the Bowie/ Defries circle was that I was married with children and in the evenings I wanted to have time to devote to my family while they were happy to spend their leisure time at the somewhat louche Sombrero club. Like myself, David Joseph was a family man. We were not close friends, but we had a lifestyle in common.

The New Seekers were a five-piece harmony group born out of The Seekers, a hugely successful sixties Australian, folk-influenced act led by the amazing voice of Judith Durham. They had a string of hits including 'The Carnival is Over', 'I'll Never Find Another You', and 'Georgy Girl'. Judith left in 1968 and the group broke up. David had the idea of forming The New Seekers and organised Keith Potger – one of the original Seekers – to front the group and to 'resign' once The New Seekers were established. Keith retained a financial interest in David's business.

I suggested that David and I merge our two companies on a 50/50 basis. Even though the skills that David brought to the merger were important, the 50/50 agreement now may seem a

poor deal on my part, bearing in mind the subsequent success of
Bowie, Gary Glitter, GTO Records and others. *HOWEVER* –
purposely in *bold* capitals – in July 1972 when I made the deal,
David's New Seekers were a star act who had broken through big
time, were touring for good money and generating substantial
income. They were bigger stars than David Bowie. They were the
UK entry to the European Song Contest (a very big deal at that
time). My existing artists – Bowie included – had great potential
but were an overall drain on my limited resources. *Ziggy* had just
been released, and whilst we all thought it was rather special,
nobody could anticipate the way it would set his career alight. I
felt comfortable working with David and felt that acquiring the
Toby Organisation was a safety net for GTO.

The joint company was called Gem Toby Organisation Ltd,
which soon became GTO. Keith Potger had a minority share-
holding in Toby and was therefore a minority shareholder in the
new joint company but, in practice, I was the dominant partner.

Following the success of The New Seekers, David tried the
same formula with The Springfield Revival. The original Spring-
fields, featuring Dusty Springfield and her brother Tom, had
been a big success in the early sixties. Mike Hurst – one of the
original group – fronted the new band to get it going. Dusty of
course had gone on to have a brilliant solo career, but The Springfield Revival was not a success, and we lost all of our investment.
I did get to keep one of the guitars that we had bought for them,
which I call my 'fifty-thousand-pound guitar'. In the same vein,
I still have some very costly mementos bearing the name of my
various artists and films that failed at spectacular cost. I have a
very expensive paperweight from my Broadway production of

End of the Rainbow. It was a play about Judy Garland, which I have since had made into a film starring Renée Zellweger called *Judy*, so maybe I will get some of the play losses back after all. It is no bad thing to keep reminders of one's failures, along with the trophies of one's successes – pride of place in the former category definitely goes to my four-hundred-thousand-pound *Breaking Glass* T-shirt, from the film starring Hazel O'Connor that sent my film company broke.

Hazel wrote and performed the songs in the film. The soundtrack album went to UK No. 5 and two or three of the singles from the album also charted. It was a good film and I organised a double royal charity premiere on two screens at the Odeon Shaftesbury Avenue. Prince Charles attended one screening and Princess Anne the other. Hazel arrived in a military tank – of course! It was the highest promotional budget I had ever committed to a film, but we promoted its punk aspect and the film failed to attract a wide audience.

When she came to the film, Hazel was under contract to a small record company called Albion Records. They had one release with her, which did nothing, and she was working as the company's receptionist to earn some money. Somebody brought her to the attention of film director Brian Gibson when he was about to start on *Breaking Glass*, financed by Dodi Fayed and produced by Davina Belling and Clive Parsons. The pair had produced *Scum*, which had been a hit for GTO Films some three years earlier and gave Ray Winstone his big break. Hazel auditioned for Brian, but it was some time before she heard from the producers that she had the part. John Finch was *Breaking Glass*'s male lead and Jonathan Pryce had a smallish part, as a saxophone player. After the film Hazel would have a long personal relationship with John Finch.

After her audition, Hazel signed an agreement with Albion as a recording artist and songwriter, for which she was paid forty pounds a week. Albion licensed her services to A&M Records – the successful US company – to make and release the film's soundtrack, which was produced by Tony Visconti. Although Hazel maintains that she never received any money from Albion for her work on the soundtrack, the film and the successful soundtrack gave her great exposure and she was poised to have a very good career. Hazel was convinced that small-thinking Albion Records were incapable of helping her find her potential. Tony Visconti presumably agreed with her view because he declined to produce her on the Albion label and Albion refused to let her go.

Eventually, Hazel came to me for help. I met with Albion heads Dai Davies and Derek Savage and tried hard to negotiate a deal under which Albion would have had a significant financial interest in any record deal that I made for Hazel with A&M, who were desperate to sign her. Cutting off their corporate noses to spite their corporate faces, they flatly refused to let her go. I had also introduced her to my old GTO Records partner Dick Leahy, who now had a very successful publishing company in partnership with Bryan Morrison, who published Pink Floyd and other important acts. Morrison Leahy Music would go on to be George Michaels' publisher and, in 1990, Bryan would become my producing partner in my stage musical *Matador*. Morrison Leahy offered a very generous deal to buy Hazel's publishing from Albion, but they too were met with a flat refusal. Eventually Hazel's contract came to an end, with Albion having earned very little from hanging on to an artist who, with some reason, did not want to be with them.

Hazel remains a uniquely talented writer/performer. She still has a career, with a devoted fan base called Hazelnuts but, in my opinion, she never fulfilled her potential because of Albion's intransigence.

The one good thing that happened with The Springfield Revival was that in 1973 they appeared at the Academy Awards ceremony, having been asked to sing a song that was nominated for an Oscar. We all went along and it was a fabulous night. The song, 'Come Follow, Follow Me', was very forgettable as was *The Little Ark* – the film it came from – but the evening was not forgettable at all and I have a photo of Raquel Welch and me up on my wall to remind me. Impressed? Don't be. Bob Levinson, our LA publicist, had offered to introduce me to singer Glen Campbell that night and I facetiously said that I would rather meet Raquel Welch. Later in the evening, Bob came and got me from the really unimportant people annex where we were all sat and – with photographer in tow – marched me through to the main room where Raquel Welch was sitting at a table with other luminaries. He shoved me in against the unsuspecting Ms Welch, clicked his fingers for the photographer to take the picture, said, 'Thank you, Raquel,' and schlepped me away. The whole thing must have taken less than thirty seconds. Without question, the most embarrassing thirty seconds of my life.

David closed his St James office and, together with his wife and three children, moved to a very nice home in Beverly Hills that was bought for them by the company. There was a deal to be done with an American record company for the American rights, but this would in no way meet the expenses of a GTO Inc. office in Los Angeles – as part of my renegotiation with Polydor, I had freed The New Seekers' recording rights for the USA. I suggested that David initially ran our business from his home, but David insisted that we 'do it right' and demonstrate to the industry that we were 'serious players'. He took a suite of prestigious offices in Century Plaza in the heart of Beverly Hills and staffed up, ready to deal with the yet-to-be-discovered stars of tomorrow which he hoped to sign. The company also bought him a Lincoln Continental, which David assured me was the car that 'serious players' drove. In fairness to David, whatever my private reservations were, I did not object to him setting up our LA operation as if it were already a huge success. He thought that if you wanted to be a success in LA you had to present yourself as if you already were. Defries thought that if Bowie was to be a star he should live like one. Same principle.

David was right. I love LA but it is a shallow town where people can, and do, rent a Rolls-Royce for an afternoon so they can arrive at a business meeting in style. Before I bought my own little house in LA I stayed at a bungalow at The Beverly Hills Hotel or the Chateau Marmont and shamelessly rented a Cadillac Eldorado or the like for myself. I kidded myself that I too was obliged to keep up the façade of success, but the real truth was that I just loved briefly living a lifestyle that I could only have dreamed about in my Finsbury Park youth. When I was later in the film business, I sometimes had meetings at the big film studios. I cannot fully explain to you the thrill I

got turning up at the Paramount or MGM studios to have the
gateman say, 'Welcome, Mr Myers, you are expected,' and being
directed to park on the lot.

David moved The New Seekers and The Springfield Revival
to LA and provided them with nice living accommodation
and weekly living allowances. He staffed up the office, taking
Glenn Wheatley, an old Australian associate he had brought to
London, over as vice-president. (I have to say that in corporate
America, every employee seems to be a vice-president. If a VP is
meeting with you, you are supposed to feel that you are important. You soon learn that the VP in charge of internal/external
transit is what we would call a doorman. GTO Inc. had a staff of
four, two of whom were VPs.)

Glenn was twenty-three and in Australia he had been a
member of a very successful band called The Masters Appren-
tices and, as is the way with pop stars, he was married to a
successful model. Glenn was ambitious and eager to learn
and I liked him immensely. He did not get on with David,
whom he claimed was unreasonably abusive and aggressive. If
so, I certainly never saw this side. At the end of 1974, Glenn
went back to Australia. He soon became hugely successful
there, managing some of the country's biggest music stars and
owning a major radio station. By 1987, he was included in
the Top 200 rich list in Australia's *Business Review Weekly*. In
1999, he published his autobiography that was almost embarrassingly fulsome in his praise for me as his guide and mentor.
He inscribed the book to me: 'Without you this would never
have happened'. In 2000 I received a call from *This Is Your Life*
in Australia. Glenn was to be the subject, and they wanted to

fly me over as the 'surprise guest'. Unfortunately, I was in the middle of my production of *The Seven Year Itch*, starring Daryl Hannah, and could not get away.

In the 2000s Glenn got into trouble with the Australian tax authorities for putting his money in a tax scheme on bad advice. He called me from time to time and I gave him what little advice I could. Unfortunately, as he was a public figure, the Australian revenue decided to make an example of him. He was given a jail sentence and went bankrupt. After he was released from jail he struggled to get back on his feet. He came to London and I loaned him ten thousand pounds, no paperwork, no payback date, no interest, which he said 'saved his life'. According to social media Glenn is now extremely successful again, but in spite of my several requests to do so, he has not seen fit to repay the loan. Disappointing.

Back to LA, where The New Seekers were signed to MGM Records, which was headed up by twenty-seven-year-old Mike Curb – a very right-wing Republican who was active in politics and would later become lieutenant governor of California. He was sometimes known as Mr Clean for his vehement anti-drug stance. Richard Nixon gave Mike Curb the job of coordinating the entertainment for the inauguration of his second term as president in 1973. Glenn was given the job of getting the talent to Washington. Glenn and The New Seekers flew in a jumbo jet of celebrities and retainers including Sammy Davis Jr and Pat Boone. Glenn made sure that everything went to plan on the night. The Nixon administration were famous for their appreciation of services rendered and Spiro Agnew, the vice-president, thanked Glenn and asked if there was anything he might be able to do as a thank-you. Glenn mentioned that he had been trying unsuccessfully for a year to get green cards – American work permits – for himself and his wife. Two weeks later, the cards arrived.

The other vice-president of GTO Inc. was Eileen Bradley, who had previously worked as a magazine journalist and had a good feel for the teenage market. Many years later I saw Eileen again when she was working as a well-connected agent for magic acts. I had an idea to make a musical based on the life of the famous escapologist Houdini. Magic was all the rage in Las Vegas entertainment and, ever the opportunist, I asked Eileen to fix me up with a meeting with the management of a large hotel and casino to see if they would put it on. The man I saw thought it was a great idea. He asked me what the running time would be and how much the show would cost to mount. As the show had not been written, I did the honest theatre producer thing and made up my answers. An average stage musical lasts around two and a quarter hours and, wishing to sound real, I said 'Two hours twenty.'

'No good,' he said. 'No show in our casino can last more than an hour, it keeps people away from the tables.'

'We can have a one-hour version,' I hastily replied.

'How much would it cost to put on?'

In those days, you would aim to budget a West End musical at no more than four million pounds, but knowing that Las Vegas loved things lavish, and not wanting to sound cheap, I said. 'Ten million dollars.'

He shook his head. 'You have to spend at least forty million dollars on a Vegas show,' and that was the end of that conversation.

Another ex-GTO Inc employee I met in later life was Billy Sammeth, a very talented man whom David had hired. Bill would later go on to manage Cher and Joan Rivers. Some time in the eighties, I popped in to see Billy at his office when he was managing Cher. He was sitting with his head in his hands. Cher was due to open that night in Vegas – a very big deal – but was two pounds over her desired weight and refusing to go on. Eventually she relented, but Billy probably lost more than two pounds in weight from aggravation. Billy ended up having lawsuits with both Ms Cher and Ms Rivers. The joys of management.

David and his team worked hard on improving the awareness of The New Seekers in America. They arranged tours including supporting Liza Minnelli in 1973. They appeared on the Johnny Carson show and also did a three-week stint in Las Vegas, but these activities contributed little to the coffers of GTO Inc. David signed some local acts including Angel, a handsome-looking rock band cast as the goody-goody antithesis of Kiss, just as The Beatles were perceived in relation to the Rolling Stones. They were signed to Mike Curb at MGM, who was keen on having wholesome artists on his label. He had signed The Osmonds to cash in on the success of The Jackson 5 and was generally into what you might call white-bread acts.

I introduced David to Alan Price, the brilliant keyboard player who was having a good career as a solo artist. I had been an admirer of Alan's talent from his days with The Animals. In fact, he totally changed my opinion on the musical ability he had, as well as that of many of his contemporaries, when I watched him playing around on the piano between recording at a Mickie Most session. Growing up, I had been a great jazz fan. My idols were musicians like Oscar Peterson and Errol Garner. I really liked the pop records that I heard in the sixties, but I was somewhat patronising about the musicians behind the voices. I always assumed that the players were experienced studio professionals, which, of course, they often were. Alan, who was truly a gifted musician, made me much more respectful of the music-makers of his generation. Because these guys often only needed three or four chords, it did not mean that they were not masters of many more. My humble apologies to all concerned for my unspoken thoughts at the time. When Alan asked me to manage him in 1973 I jumped at the chance. He wanted to break America and I booked him on a short promotional tour. Alan was petrified of flying and he took a strong cocktail of whisky and Valium to get himself on the plane from the UK. The tour ended up at The Troubadour, LA's most famous small venue. The tour was too short to have any real impact on the American market and, sadly, Alan did not like David's management style and asked me to release him from his contract, which of course I did.

David also put together The Sarstedt Brothers. Peter Sarstedt had had huge success in 1968 with 'Where Do You Go To (My Lovely)?' It reached UK No. 1 and fourteen other countries, but he had had little success since then. His elder brother Rick also topped the UK singles chart under the name of Eden Kane, with 'Well I Ask You'. The youngest brother, Clive, had made records under the name of Robin Sarstedt but by 1972 none of the siblings had much of a career. Their sister Lorraine worked as David's personal assistant. David put them in an LA studio and they made *Worlds Apart Together*. They toured a little in the

UK but the album was not a success, and they eventually went their separate business ways.

Rick (Eden Kane) had married Charlene Groman, a nice Jewish girl from LA. (In certain circles – my mother – the phrase 'Jewish girls' is *always* proceeded by 'nice'.) After GTO Inc. closed down I kept in touch with Rick and Charlene and in an oblique way Rick was a catalyst that helped me persuade Dick Leahy to sell GTO Records to CBS in 1978. It is quite a nice story, which I will relate when I get on to writing about GTO Records. In researching this book, I discovered that Charlene was a half-sister to the actress Stefanie Powers of *Hart To Hart* TV fame – also a nice Jewish girl: who knew? Stefanie Powers starred in my West End stage production of the musical *Matador* in 1991 and I had no idea of the connection.

In May 1974, The New Seekers no longer wanted to teach the world to sing in perfect harmony, and disharmoniously broke up. It was front-page news in the UK, and a great disappointment to their thousands of fans around the world. The most probable reason was that, after years of success, they had no money. The group formally declared that they no longer considered GTO to be their managers. They were signed to us individually and we sued them for breach of contract. Where there's a hit there's a writ, and the writs were soon flying back and forth like kids fighting with paper airplanes. They sued us for under-accounting. They employed a top firm of accountants to audit our books, but nothing untoward was found. One of them told me that he thought that I was just smarter than his accountants. A backhanded compliment if ever there was one. The audit did show that, strictly in accordance with the provisions of the management contract, the group's earnings had been eaten up by their regular cash advances and expenses.

As a standard management agreement of the time, we took 20 per cent of the gross income, and all of the expenses incurred on their behalf were deducted from the balance. Please note that our own expenses of running our offices substantially reduced our commission. The New Seekers were on wages from the day that David put them together. Unlike so many of their contemporaries, they never had to starve before they had success.

When a band starts on the road, they are usually happy to travel economy, share rooms and generally live a modest lifestyle. As they become more successful, understandably, they want to travel in more comfortable style. Now here is the thing. Every manager of a reasonably successful band has the same problem. Having risked a great deal of money in the band's development, you sometimes get lucky, they have some success and you start to recoup. The band become stars and want to live like stars. If the manager is responsible, he warns them gently, and then not so gently, that they should be aware of their financial position. *But*, people – some sincere, some hangers-on – surround the bands and sow the seeds of discontent. Why, they ask, does the artist not have big cars/houses/drug supplies, whatever? Often a wannabe manager adds fuel to the flames.

I present you with the manager's classic dilemma. If you responsibly restrict your artists' spending, eventually they feel aggrieved and want to leave you. If you let them spend recklessly, they will end up broke. You may recall that Bowie fell out with Tony Defries because he had no idea that he alone was paying for the lifestyle that Tony encouraged him to adopt. Elton John eventually had a falling-out with his long-term manager, John Reid, as did Bob Dylan with Albert Grossman. It is easier to make a list of the artist/manager relationships that did not end in financial acrimony. Peter Grant and Led Zeppelin, Jim Beach and Queen, and Bill Curbishley and The Who quickly come to mind. The Beatles were loyal to Brian Epstein until the day he died, even though he had made terrible deals for them.

So, faced with the dilemma, what would you do? Would you do the 'right thing': protect the artist from himself and take the chance that he would leave you? I don't think so. Like me and most other managers I knew, after your due warnings had been ignored, you would pragmatically keep your artists happy and your own family secure, by letting the artists indulge in the lifestyle they wanted. Of course, if the artist is hugely successful for years they get rich in spite of themselves or their cynical management. Elton John is richer than his ex-manager. He's quite probably richer than you and he is certainly richer than me.

With The New Seekers there was another possible reason for their break-up. After five years together they had had enough of each other. In my own view, any discord was not helped by the fact that although Eve Graham had been the lead voice on every previous hit, Lyn Paul took the role on 'Beg Steal or Borrow', the Eurovision Song Contest entry, and 'You Won't Find Another Fool Like Me,' a No. 1 hit in 1973 written by Geoff Stephens and producer Tony Macaulay.

As a Christmas present to me, the girls in my office went into the studio with the track and recorded 'You Won't Find Another Boss Like Laurence'. The line 'Those Cuban heels for high-pow-

ered deals' sticks in my mind. I plead guilty to the Cuban heels
... well, it was the seventies.

The break-up became extremely acrimonious between the
group members themselves. Peter Doyle, one of the original
members, who sadly died young of throat cancer in 2001, had left
the group in 1973. Marty Kristian and Paul Layton bought the
rights to the name from Eve Graham and Lyn Paul. In subsequent
years, they reformed the group in various incarnations, including
some ex-members of The Springfield Revival. Eve Graham briefly
rejoined The New Seekers in 1976, in a line-up which included
musician Kevin Finn. Eve subsequently married Kevin and they
had a happy marriage until Kevin died in 2016. Lyn Paul went
on to have a career on stage, starring in *Blood Brothers*. Marty
and Paul took advantage of owning The New Seekers' name by
making soundalike re-recordings of all of The New Seekers' hits,
without using Eve or Lyn and licensing the recordings to Polydor,
who had the original recordings. This seriously devalued the original recordings that I owned, but it was a smart move and I do not
blame the boys for doing so. The dispute spluttered on for years
until Marty and I eventually ruined the day of several West End
lawyers by coming to an amicable settlement.

The London office had been financially supporting GTO
Inc. since the day it started and David had not managed to sign
anyone to contribute at all significantly to the running of the
LA operation. I had no animosity towards David, but after the
breakup of The New Seekers, I decided that it made no business
sense to carry on draining our resources indefinitely. I put it to
David that if GTO Inc. were not self-supporting by 31 December 1974 we should close the office down, even if there were a

promise to sign The Beatles on the next day. David was not happy. I bought Keith Potger's minority holding in the controlling company of the group so that I had a majority vote. I was never obliged to legally use my controlling vote to ride roughshod over David but – as with all divorces – it was a little messy. David did manage to walk away with the house in Beverly Hills and a nice sum of money and I kept the company. We were both a little unhappy with the deal that we made, which is always a good sign of fairness. Most importantly, we remained friends.

David decided to get back into radio and moved Robin and his four children to Hawaii. That did not work out as planned and he moved his family back to LA. He got involved in film production and in 1982 made *The Pirate Movie* based on Gilbert and Sullivan's *Pirates of Penzance* in Australia, and was co-producer of *Flight of the Navigator* for Disney. Neither of the films were box-office successes and he did not manage to get another film made. He went back to Australia and went into the restaurant business.

I had stayed in touch with David after GTO Inc. closed and tried to be helpful where possible. In 1993, whilst in LA, I met up with him again. He had moved back without his family, which did not surprise me as I figured that Robin had had enough of packing up the kids on yet another major move. I met with him for lunch at a restaurant in Beverly Hills, expecting him to tell me that he and Robin had split up. He said that he had something to tell me which he found difficult and I, rather smugly, said that I thought that I had worked out why he had moved to LA alone.

'Well,' he said, 'I have always been gay.' I was so shocked that my pasta went all over the restaurant's mirrored walls.

David's story was not unusual, but it was nonetheless heart-breaking. He had felt that he was gay since he was a teenager but thought that it would 'go away' when he married and had a family. It did not, and having had the painful life of keeping his secret for twenty years of marriage, circumstances in Australia obliged him to come out to his wife, kids and mother. I was extremely fond of David and Robin and felt great compassion for all of the family. To make matters worse, David soon found out that he was living with AIDS. This was in the nineties, when the illness was more debilitating and more life-threatening than medicine has made it today. David was unable to work but still endeavoured to support his family, all of whom stayed close to him. I helped him out as much as I could. At one point he planned to move to Spain with his boyfriend, a Mexican, and I offered our house in Majorca for him to live in as a first step but he didn't make the move. Eventually I became weary of supporting his schemes, all of which revolved around the gay community and in my view were highly unlikely to succeed. Unkindly, I just stopped calling him.

In 2011, I got a call from Marty Kristian. He and David had made up after some thirty-odd years, David was coming to London, and they were having a New Seekers reunion. Marty wanted me to appear as a surprise guest, which he thought would be 'the icing on the cake' for all concerned. I was not proud of the way I had treated David in the later years and would love to have gone along to try and make amends. Unfortunately, it was impossible for me to get there, but I asked Marty to give David my number so that we could arrange to meet. I got a very cold call from David saying that he was not keen to meet with me because

I had failed to keep in touch with him for the last few years. I did point out that phone calls work two ways, and that maybe it would be nice to meet up. I then received an email from David saying that he had no wish to meet with me. I had told a mutual friend in Australia that I had stopped calling David because I was fed up with his mainly gay-based business ideas. The friend, who was obviously not a good friend to David, had felt impelled to tell him so. I would have liked to have had a chance to explain to David that I had no homophobic prejudices; I just did not believe that his ideas were commercially viable.

If David had a business fault it was a blinkered persistence, which could sometimes work against him. He would go on and on browbeating Mr A to agree to something that Mr A really did not want to do. He would then do the same thing with Mr B and Mr C, until they also reluctantly agree to be part of the deal. Inevitably one of them would have second thoughts and pull out and the deal would collapse like a pack of cards.

David died in 2012 following a hip operation. He was surrounded by his still-loving family – none of whom, I am sure, will think kindly of me, which is a shame because, probably unknown to them, I did help David out financially quite a lot in the years following his illness.

I led into the GTO Inc. story by saying that it had eaten up the five hundred thousand pounds that I had received from the Bowie deal with Defries. In truth, I do not recall what the losses of GTO Inc. actually were but it was not, as they say, chopped liver. Looking back, I do not regret the cost to me of having supported an LA office that failed. Gertrude Stein once famously said of LA, 'I went there, and there was no there, there.' This was not true if you were involved in the entertainment business in the pre-Silicon Valley seventies and eighties. GTO Inc. was struggling but my other business ventures made me a perceived success, something vital to make it with the LA in-crowd.

I guess I have enough shallowness within me to have thoroughly embraced the bullshit of LA. For me it was exciting and vibrant. I had lots of friends there, many of them UK expats and we did not take ourselves or each other too seriously. The Chateau Marmont, now a five-star hotel, but then delightfully seedy, was the hangout for visiting Brits. Peter Brown, the ex-Apple publicist, an extremely urbane English gentleman, used to arrange a monthly dinner for the expat community at The Dome restaurant on Sunset Boulevard. One such occasion was to celebrate the Queen Mother's birthday. My 'date' for the evening was Hermione Gingold, a once extremely famous English actress who starred in *Gigi*, *The Music Man* and many other major films. Now in her eighties and living in LA, in her youth Hermione was a friend of the Queen Mother who, before she became Queen of England, was the Charleston-loving Betty Bowes-Lyons.

Hermione, in spite of her age, was as bright and feisty as a teenager. She clearly shared her old friend's alleged love of a gin and tonic, and during the dinner she regaled us with wonderful stories of the twenties when she and Betty were leading lights in young British society. Of course, the names she scurrilously bandied around were meaningless to us, but she several times confided in me in her cut-glass English accent, that 'Betty was a bit of a gel, dontcha know.' Just for the record, when I dropped Hermione home, I did not go in for a drink.

28. ARCADE RECORDS

For those of you who are too young to remember, there was a time when you could not buy compilations of various artists. In 1972, I was instrumental in the birth of the compilation business. In fact, I have been credited with actually creating it. A bold accolade that I would be foolish to deny.

There were a number of factors that serendipitously came together to cause me to get into the compilation business.

1. In 1972, I had reel-to-reel tapes in my offices that were capable of taking tracks that I chose from different vinyl recordings and putting them onto one cassette. More importantly, I had a kid in the office who knew how to do it. I used to make my own cassettes of music I liked by different artists and also made up compilations requested by friends.

2. The brothers-in-law. Every successful Jewish businessman has at least one brother-in-law. Sometimes one he has to support and sometimes one who contributes to his success. I got lucky with both of mine. Marsha had two half-brothers, Michael and Larry Levene. They had inherited their father William Levene's business, which supplied market grafters

with product lines to be sold via demonstrations. By 1972, they were in the business of selling TV-promoted kitchen gadgets and the like to the retail trade.

3. The Levene brothers' big competitor was a company called K-Tel, a Canadian company also owned by a family brought up in the market grafting business, selling similar products.

So how did it all come together? One day in early 1972 Michael Levene told me that one of his spies had reported to him that K-Tel had put out a TV-promoted record of polka music in the US that had sold phenomenally well. Could I come up with something similar in the UK for the Levenes? I explained that there was a huge descendant population of middle-European immigrants in America and the polka was the music of their heritage. The nearest thing to polka I could think of in the UK was clog-dancing, the knees-up, or Morris dancing, none of which was ever going to be a winner.

There was a company called Pickwick Records, which I had noted did very well making soundalike recordings of twelve recent chart hits and quickly getting them into Woolworths and other mass outlet stores. What if I could persuade record companies to license us the original hits that we could put on a single LP?

Michael was insistent that not only would the content have to be good, the record would have to be a genuine bargain. We came up with the idea of pricing the records at the same retail price as conventional albums, but putting twenty tracks onto one record rather than the usual twelve. Squeezing that many tracks onto a 12-inch vinyl album would slightly reduce the quality of the playback, but not, I thought, enough to spoil the listening of the average consumer. Anyway, the ethos of the TV marketing industry was 'It's for selling not for using.'

My first call was to EMI, the company with the biggest roster of artists at the time. I met with Ron Tudor, the MD, who was not enthusiastic but said that he would look into it. At our follow-up meeting, Ron told me that his legal affairs department had told him that there was no provision in their artists' contracts that allowed them to be put onto albums with other artists and there was a further doubt – twenty tracks on one LP, sold for the same price as a current album, would be a budget album and that meant a different royalty rate. Generally, EMI were living up to their reputation as being the Ministry of Pop, so I tried RCA – with a similar outcome.

All this took some time and I then got a panic call from Michael to say that his spy had told him that K-Tel's own spy had told the company's founder and boss, Ray Kives, that I was trying to put together a complication of hits, and they were now trying to do the same. The competition between K-Tel and the Levenes was intense and sometimes I got confused as to who was spying for whom.

I was close to John Fruin, the head of Polydor, who were The New Seekers' record company. He loved the idea, railroaded his legal department to make it happen, and it did. The Levenes were great believers in the approach now known as 'Does what it says on the tin' and we called the album *20 Fantastic Hits by the Original Artists* – to distinguish it from the Pickwick soundalike releases. I had three of my own recordings on the LP, The New Seekers' 'Beg, Steal or Borrow,' Johnny Johnson's 'Blame it on the

Pony Express,' and Edison Lighthouse's 'Love Grows …', and an interest in the publishing of two other tracks, so I was also earning as a supplier. Happy days! K-Tel's *20 Dynamic Hits* hit the market a week or so before us but – slight puff of the chest here – our content was much better than theirs and we easily outsold them.

The Levenes and I became partners in a company called Arcade Records, named after Arcade House, GTO's building. Our first release was announced to the trade in a front-page article in *Music Week* in July 1972. In the same edition, there was a report that Pickwick had obtained an injunction against a company called Multiple Sound, who were also releasing soundalikes, for using the name 'Pick Of The Pops'. Multiple Sound was owned by Ian Miles, who later started the record arm of Ronco – a company in competition with Arcade and K-Tel – but they had little success with their releases. They did, however, do well with TV merchandising of weird gadgets like a device that made your old wine bottles into vases.

The Levenes did all of the marketing and distribution for Arcade Records, and my office made the repertoire selections and negotiated with the record companies. The Levenes' marketing was quite brilliant. On the basis that our TV campaign was driving customers into the shops, he offered the retailer a smaller margin. In addition, unlike conventional record companies, they offered the retailer full sale-or-return privileges. The pitch was that the retailer had nothing to lose by stocking our records. This was true, although some chains were initially resistant to the smaller margin before eventually realising that they were losing out on sales. All retailers, even Woolworths, the biggest mover of records at that time, gave in and stocked Arcade Records.

In no time Arcade had fully staffed offices in Germany and Holland. Larry opened an office in Paris but was frustrated by being unable to buy cost-effective TV time and soon closed the operation. We also became partners in PPL in Germany, a company making TV commercials. PPL was based in an abandoned swimming pool in Munich. It was a very creative atmosphere and I loved to spend time there.

Germany was by far the biggest market. K-Tel continued to be strong rivals but we usually won when it came to fighting for the most current hits. I really understood the record industry and used this knowledge to great advantage. I knew that one of the more difficult financial problems for a major record company was managing their pressing plants. They were obliged to have the capacity to deal with the demand created by a hit, but often were not aware of the extent until a record was released. This meant that most majors had idle capacity that they were obliged to keep in case. I would offer the record companies the contract for pressing a particular Arcade release, which could utilise their spare capacity. If they had an artist whose advance was unrecouped, I would offer to get that artist onto one of our records to help with the recoupment. I also had existing relationships with many of the writers, producers and managers of artists we wanted. If the record company was reluctant to give us a particular track, I could call one of the people behind the record and tell them that they were missing out on income because their record company would not license it to Arcade. Wherever possible, I chose a track in which a business friend had an interest, and that generally helped me within the industry. I was still seen as a hot source of talent so the record companies preferred to keep me happy.

K-Tel knew that Arcade was a family business, but at the 1975 Midem, Ray Kives, one of the owners, frustrated with usually coming second in the race for product, asked me what I would want to defect to them, which of course I would not even consider.

I did not want the record companies who were licensing us their product to realise how successful we were. In the UK I had managed to keep Arcade releases out of the charts, but in Germany both Arcade and K-Tel records were listed and the trade magazines also published their market share. In one quarter, Arcade and K-Tel had almost 25 per cent of the German market between them. When we made compilations, the majors sort of understood that it would be difficult for them to compete as they would have to agree with their rivals how many tracks each would have, who would do the pressing, etc. But when we started to make best-ofs for single artists, the majors began to wonder why they could not do this themselves. Over the years I persuaded major record companies to license us Elvis, the Rolling Stones, The Beatles, The Kinks, Hot Chocolate, The Beach Boys, The Everly Brothers, Johnny Cash, Diana Ross and some big local artists. We convinced them that there was some mystique about our operation. They believed that we had a secretive market-research department helping us to choose the less obvious compilations. In fact, with my trusted and brilliant lieutenant Sylvia Curd, I simply used to browse the record departments of the major department stores, Kaufhof in Germany and Vroom & Dreesmann in Holland, to see what was selling well in the budget record department.

We learned that the Germans, for instance, liked trumpet and saxophone records. There was a little-known American saxophone player called Billy Vaughn. I put together an album of familiar old songs like 'Sail Along Silv'ry Moon', 'Lili Marleen' and 'La Paloma' and it sold around half a million copies. An album of Nini Rosso, a trumpet player, featured a similarly unfashionable repertoire and almost was as great a success. One of our biggest-selling artists was the dolorously voiced Jim Reeves, an album that I could never listen to past the first track without falling asleep.

What kept the majors from entering the TV-selling market for a long time was their need for a business plan, especially in Germany, before they risked investment. What they did not know was that K-Tel and Arcade never had a business plan. We both operated with the market grafter's mentality that we all grew up with. Those of you who read my early history may remember that I worked in the market for about five years while I was a poorly paid accountancy articled clerk.

When an album was launched, Arcade had to commit to buying TV time and also make sure that we had reserved pressing capacity to meet the hoped-for demand. We would put an album out and if it was not working, Michael Levene would cancel the TV time and the pressing orders and worry later about the flack that inevitably came his way. There was a lot of schmoozing and many generous Christmas presents. We were very much a seat-of-the-pants operation, and the majors could not operate that way.

The biggest seller we ever had in the UK was *Elvis – 40 Greatest Hits*. The tracks that I licensed from RCA were pretty much already available on Camden, their low-volume budget line. Once again my inside knowledge of the business was the key.

I knew that RCA had recently bought out all of Elvis's future royalties for a huge sum of money and I convinced them that this was a way of quickly getting some back. I agreed an advance of just sixty thousand pounds, but eventually the record was so successful, Arcade paid them several hundred thousand pounds. We sold over two million copies, and at that time it was one of the highest-ever selling albums in the UK. As was normal, we had a three-year deal with RCA to exploit the rights. Elvis died in August 1977, two weeks after our deal ended. Had we still had the rights, we could have sold another million. In 1978, RCA put out a pink vinyl version of the same compilation, with a different cover but the same name.

There is a kicker to the *Elvis – 40 Greatest Hits* story. I had become close to RCA executive Mel Ilberman, who was then Colonel Parker's contact man at the company. Arcade Records had a gold disc made for Elvis that I took to Mel in New York, in the hope that he would pass it on to The King. He had a better idea. 'I'm flying to LA tomorrow to make a courtesy call on the Colonel. Why don't you come with me? You'll be doing me a favour, I really have nothing to talk to him about.' An offer I could not refuse.

I called my friend Freddy Bienstock, a partner in Elvis's publishing company, who promised to ask the Colonel if there was a chance of presenting the disc to Elvis in person. That evening Freddy told me that the Colonel's office was on the MGM Studios lot and Elvis would be there for costume fittings for his next (awful) movie. The Colonel was going to ask him to stop by. I was more excited than a sophisticated music executive should be – meeting Elvis was something that was as close to meeting a deity as this agnostic Jew was ever going to get. But the Colonel the next day gave the devastating news that Elvis's costume-fitting had been cancelled so he wasn't coming in. I was obviously disappointed, and as I recall so was Mel. I was about to leave them to their business but Mel asked me to stay. He was right – they really had nothing to talk about. Mel went through the release schedule for the next album, the Colonel whinged about RCA's slow accounting and that was it. Mel, no doubt eager to get away, excused himself but suggested that I stay for a few minutes and chat to the Colonel about the success of the Arcade release.

I had earned a living working as a market grafter. Colonel had at some point pre-Elvis also worked as a market grafter at county fairs where punters paid to watch his 'dancing chickens'. The chickens were placed on a heated plate and danced, as one would. The Colonel saw the two of us as kindred spirits and I was with him for a fascinating two hours. He ran the merchandising wherever Elvis appeared, and always stayed by the sales booth taking the cash. One wonders if he accounted for this to Elvis as part of their 50/50 agreement. One suspects not. He kept a stock of all of the merchandise in his office and gave me a range of samples as a going-home present. The gifts would not have been of interest to my young kids, so rather than carry them home, I gave them to the maid at my hotel. Who knew? I do know that Elvis got the gold disc. Very recently a friend of mine visited Graceland and sent me a photo of the Arcade gold disc on a wall, with hundreds of others that had been presented to Elvis over the years.

In 1982, a fourteen-page supplement in *Billboard*, the most important international music trade magazine, celebrated ten years of Arcade success. They reported that Arcade's turnover in 1981 was fifty million dollars. I cannot remember if that was true or something I made up to impress the industry. Probably the latter.

The major record companies, helped by ex-Arcade employees, eventually realised that there was no real mystery to our operation, and that they were mad to supply Arcade or K-Tel with product. They gradually went into TV marketing their own catalogues. Arcade got the dregs and began to lose money on some of our releases. It was obvious that our days in the record business were numbered. In 1983, Richard Branson – a smart man if ever there was one – made a deal with EMI to start releasing compilation albums for UK majors. *Now That's What I Call Music!* is, at the time of writing, up to *Now!* No. 96. Arcade, wisely, had already given up the UK market, by the time *Now!* arrived, and the series rang the death knell for K-Tel and Ronco.

We initiated the *Billboard* magazine supplement partly to promote the fact that I had taken Arcade Germany into the video business. In 1980, home VCR was exploding, and shops were opening all over the country to meet the public's demand for films to be played at home. The problem was that the major film companies were not yet making their product available. They had not worked out if the market was to be in rental or sales, if their rights even provided for home use, what the division of income between the various stakeholders in a film in this new media would be, etc. I realised that the shops had to fill their shelves with films. By now I was in the film world and I was able to source titles not owned by the majors, which the shops grabbed even though the content was generally awful. Inevitably, as with the record business, the majors soon worked out their problems, made their films available to the video market and that was the end of Arcade Video.

Arcade itself folded in 1983 and Herman Heinsbroek, the bright man I had poached from CBS Holland to run our Dutch company, took over the valueless company and re-launched the brand into the mainstream music business with great success.

In 1991, Michael Levene and I had another shot at working on a record together. Larry Levene had gone into the property business and Michael had a successful online sales company called Best Direct. As the name implies, products were not available in stores and customers bought directly in response to clever TV commercials and infomercials. You will remember them well. In fact, as a genre, they are still going. These ads had a key moment, the CTA – Call To Action – triggering the punter, sorry, the customer to, 'Order now and be sent absolutely free a ... '

Michael was nostalgic for the happy days in the record business and both of us were nostalgic for the money that we earned from Arcade Records, so he asked me if I could think of a record package that he could sell. Not an easy task, as by then the majors had ceased to license any of their catalogues to outsiders. But the radio station Classic FM had started in 1992 and was proving a great success broadcasting best-known melodies from classical music. Clearly there was a market for popular classics, which we could combine with the public's desire for 'collectables'. I decided to put together a ten-CD set of the most well-known composers, knowing that there would be a wide choice of snatches of instantly recognisable melodies that could be used to make a great TV commercial. The package would have to be good value, which was not a problem. The actual cost of manufacturing each CD was less than fifty pence. The value to the consumer was what was on it, so the challenge was to pay as little as possible for the content.

Decca Records had by far the best roster of classical artists, but I realised that they would be expensive to deal with and, quite rightly, very fussy about the quality of the recordings. By now, I was completely indoctrinated by the Michael Levene mantra of 'They're for selling not for using', so I bought the content from Henry Hadaway, who owned a huge catalogue of schlock recordings by well-known names – or at least featuring artists whose names were to become well-known even if they weren't at the time of the recording. Henry's 'Frank Sinatra records' were by the Tommy Dorsey Orchestra in the forties when Sinatra was the unaccredited singer with the band. Their Beatles recordings were when they were the backing band for Tony Sheridan. If Henry could have found a recording where Chuck Berry had clapped along, it would have been sold as a Chuck Berry record. You get the picture. Most of his product was retailed through garage forecourts and other retailers who sold purely on price.

For very little money, I bought the best-known recordings of the ten most popular classical composers including Mozart, Beethoven, Chopin, etc. The recordings were by such 'quality' names as the Bratislava Radio Orchestra or the equivalent of the Huddersfield Philharmonic, if there had been one. They made up ten CDs which could be sold on TV for a very large margin of profit. I had to come up with the additional 'absolutely free', something as an incentive to order. *Now!*'s classical music had been given a boost when the legendary trio of Pavarotti, Carreras and Domingo appeared on worldwide television in a concert broadcast at the time of the 1990 World Cup. The Three Tenors' recording of the evening had sold in its millions. Obviously a CD of the three tenors would be an amazing incentive to 'Call and order NOW'. Back to Henry Hadaway.

Sure enough, Henry sourced recordings by each of the three famous tenors. They were not singing together as they did on the famous World Cup concert and the quality of the recordings was awful, but it was for selling, not for using. Some had been pirated from radio broadcasts, some recorded illegally from live concerts. You could actually hear an audience member coughing on one of the recordings. *But* I had a CD that could legally be called 'The Three Tenors'. Am I proud of creating this really inferior compilation? Absolutely *not*. But in 1992 my glory days in the music business were long behind me and my income from my old catalogue was diminishing. Luciano, Placido and Jose, or 'the boys', as I like to call them, saved my financial arse.

Michael made a great TV commercial, the collection was an enormous success and I did very well out of it indeed. There were very few complaints about the quality of the recordings. I believe that most consumers bought it with the coffee-table book mentality, that it was for displaying rather than for listening.

Michael Levene died in 2009 after a very long and debilitating illness. I had known him since he was ten years old and he was best man at my wedding to Marsha. He was not only my brother-in-law and a good business partner, he was also my friend and I still mourn his loss.

The power of TV is now even greater than it was during my days with Arcade. Radio play used to make instant record stars.

Now it is reality TV that spews out telegenic chart toppers. But the choreographed manipulation of audience reaction bothers me. Voting for the back-story as much as the talent. The boom-boom-boom-boom heartbeat before the tearful winner inevitably declares, 'It's like a dream come true,' and the losers glottal-stop, 'I'm guh-ed.' I have a horror that one day the election of a new Pope will not be announced by white smoke coming from the Sistine chapel. Instead the eligible cardinals will be lined up on that famous balcony overlooking St Peter's Square. There will be the boom-boom-boom-boom heartbeat before His Holiness, newly elected by viewers' telephone votes, is announced to the world by a deep, echoing voice from the sky.

Why am I so incensed by reality TV? To be honest, partly it is because starting a pop music talent show was an obvious opportunity, open for all. Like many of my contemporaries, I am consumed with envy/rage/bitterness that I did not think of doing it myself.

29. MIKE LEANDER –
ROCK AND ROLL PT. 2

Mike Leander's musical talent really bloomed in the sixties. He helped Keith Richards with the arrangement for the 1964 record of 'As Tears Go By', the song written for Marianne Faithfull by Keith and Mick Jagger. He also did the string arrangement for The Beatles' 'She's Leaving Home'.

Marianne made ten singles for Decca Records between 1964 and 1969. The producers included Andrew Loog Oldham, Tony Calder and Mike Leander. Mike worked on the tracks variously as studio engineer, arranger and orchestra director. Some records were released under the name Marianne Faithful with The Mike Leander Orchestra. RCA released 'Migration', a highly acclaimed orchestral record by The Mike Leander Orchestra. Decca released a single by The Mike Leander Orchestra of 'The Letter'/'Hey Jude', all now collectors' items. By the time Mike started working with me at Gem, Marianne was at the height of her dance with heroin. She was literally living on the streets, but Mike thought she might still have some of her early magic. He brought her to see me and I agreed to take her on as a Gem artist. She had no home, no possessions and no hope. We found her somewhere to live, paid the rent and gave her some money to buy food. From my point of view, this signing was as much an act of charity as a commercial decision.

Unsurprisingly, the Marianne Faithfull sessions did not work. Mike found it difficult to get a decent performance out of her. She often did not turn up to the studios, where we had expensive studio time, technicians and musicians booked and waiting. Mike brought her to see me in the office. Pasty-faced and sweating, she promised that, if I gave her another chance, she would turn up to the studio straight. She did not keep her promise and it was all very sad.

One night, Marsha and I were sitting at a table at Tramp, a fashionable disco of its time. Marianne made an entrance into the club, escorted by Richard Cole, Led Zeppelin manager Peter Grant's archetypal rock-soldier roadie. I knew him from my past involvement with Peter and the band. Marianne, who looked like an emaciated black-and-white sketch of herself, acknowledged me with a perfunctory nod and sat at a table across the room. A while later, Richard came over and requested that I send a bottle of champagne to 'my artist's table'. I knew that 'my artist' had a recording session scheduled with Mike the next day and I declined to buy the champagne. My counter-offer to arrange for a car to take Marianne home at a reasonable hour was rejected and, *quelle surprise*, she did not turn up at the studio the next day.

Drug addiction is of course a terrible disease, and I have real sympathy for those it afflicts, and even more sympathy for the family and friends who have to look on. But, on a business level, it is really difficult to deal with an addict whose behaviour wreaks havoc with other people's careers. Alcohol, of course, can be just as destructive. Mike did manage to finish an album with Marianne called *Masque*, but I did not think that it was good enough to deliver to Bell Records for release. Years later, I licensed the album to a budget label, who retitled it *Rich Kid Blues*. I will never recoup my costs, which does not concern me, but it would have been nice if my altruism had helped Marianne with her drug issues. Sadly, it did not. There was an attempted suicide in New York in the eighties, before Marianne got herself into rehab and bravely straightened herself out. Since then, to her great credit, she has managed to survive not only being Mick Jagger's ex, but also all the drugs and her scandals du jour in the sixties, including the alleged novel use of a Mars bar. In her teens, she was the pulchritudinous fantasy behind many a young man's locked bedroom door. If you want to know why, look up clips of *The Girl on a Motorcycle* on YouTube. Marianne is now taken seriously as a singer and has celebrated her fiftieth anniversary in showbiz with a world tour. According to an excellent BBC documentary about her, broadcast in February 2019, she is enjoying her current musical success and her family life with her son and grandchildren. Good for her. In the documentary she also acknowledged her debt to Mike Leander and Gem for getting her off the streets in 1970. So, I suppose, good for us.

At this time, Mike would book studio time to work with no particular purpose other than to experiment with sound, with the help of studio engineer John Hudson. It was to encourage creativity like this that I had started Gem/GTO. Very few record companies would allow their signings to just fool around in a studio without knowing why they wanted the time and without

budgetary restrictions. I was content that neither Mike nor Tony
Macaulay would waste my money to no purpose, and they were
never obliged to seek my 'permission' to book a studio.

Mike was a multi-instrumentalist who could play drums,
guitar, bass and piano. I once popped into Mayfair Sound where
Mike, alone in the studio, was recording and found that he had
placed wet towels on the drum skins in an attempt to get a
sound that was in his head but that he was struggling to repro-
duce in the studio. He had looped his drum sound time and
time again and he and John Hudson were experimenting with
moving the mic around and using the technical effects that the
studio's recording desk had to offer. Mike had also multi-tracked
some guitar riffs using a technique that I had seen him practising in his office. When alone, Mike – a brilliant musician who
was not a great guitarist – sat there for hours experimenting
with retuning a guitar to enable him to play chords by using
his cigarette lighter like a steel guitar slide. We had a running
joke of me popping my head round his door almost daily, saying,
'Anything that you want me to hear?' and Mike replying, 'Not
yet, old bean.' For that studio session, he had also had in musicians John Rossall and Harvey Ellison to lay the down the horn
sound. I was yet to hear the melody to go over it, but the drum
sound went through my body as if the bass drum were inside my
head. It was an unbelievably exciting track.

Around April 1972, Mike booked in at Mayfair Sound to
work with David Essex, who unavoidably cancelled at the last
moment. Rather than waste the studio time, Mike went to the
studio to continue to work on the track that he had been sweating over for the past few weeks. He took a singer called Paul

Raven that he occasionally used for demos to put a voice on the track. When he had completed his mix, Mike came into my office and said, '*Now* I have something that I want you to hear.' The track featured Paul's voice, which was not great, but the record was not about his voice. It was Mike mixing it onto the track that he had taken hours and hours to perfect.

Rather than waste time and money recording a B-side, Mike played me a remixed version of the same track with the drum sound brought up and instrumental apart from the chorus, bringing up the guitar for the basic melody. We decided that it would make an interesting – and cheap – B-side. Logically the A-side was called 'Rock And Roll Pt. 1', and the B-side was 'Rock And Roll Pt. 2'.

Singer Paul was not physically pop star material. He was nearly thirty, a little overweight and balding. We discussed the advisability of finding a younger singer with a more appealing natural look to re-voice the track for release. Mike told me that he would give Paul a writer's credit to soften the blow of not being on the released version. In the event, Mike – a kind man – decided that it would be too cruel to Paul to replace him. Paul had been working as a singer for fifteen years without success and it would have been a big blow. This is the story of the record that morphed Paul Raven – born Paul Gadd – into Gary Glitter.

Almost twenty years later, Glitter was charged with child pornography. He rightly became persona non grata to the rest of the world, as he is to me and this book. Glitter cruelly damaged the lives of his victims. He also damaged the financial position of many of his professional associates. With records produced by Mike, his backing musicians had carved out a good career of their own as The Glitter Band and that was halted overnight. Sadly, Mike Leander died in 1996 and Glitter's criminal conviction cut off the flow of royalties to the Leander estate.

The success of 'Rock And Roll Pt. 2' in America in a way lead to the creation of GTO Records. The record went to US No. 7 and Dick Leahy at Bell Records UK urged his boss Larry Uttal, head of the American Bell Records, to quickly take Gary over to the States to promote it. If he had done so, there was every chance that the record could have been an US No. 1 and paved the way for Glitter to have the string of hits there that he had in most other countries of the world. The problem was that Larry had sold Bell to Columbia Pictures three years earlier. He had taken Columbia shares for the sale and the quoted price of Columbia shares had now dropped by about 75 per cent. Larry had a three-year contract to run Bell and was insisting that Columbia made good his loss before signing a new contract. In the meantime, he was purposefully doing nothing to help the company

Larry Uttal was not a particularly likeable man and had overplayed his hand with his bosses. Instead of giving him the deal that he demanded, they let him go and appointed Clive Davis, one of the best men in the record business, to take over as the new head of Bell. Clive Davis had been the uber-successful head of CBS Records in New York, having signed a string of major artists to that company, including Bruce Springsteen, Simon & Garfunkel, Billy Joel, Chicago and Aerosmith. Clive had been fired by CBS in July 1973, ostensibly for charging the cost of his son's bar mitzvah to the company. This is a ridiculous offence, and something that Clive denies to this day. Even if it were true, Clive was making millions for the company, signing big-selling, prestige artists, and sacking him for charging fifteen thousand dollars of personal expenses made no business sense. To his immediate bosses, this would have been like you or I using the company phone for personal calls.

The truth was that CBS Records was owned by the company that owned CBS News, a station that was constantly critical of President Richard Nixon. Tricky Dicky, as he was rightly known, was determined to have CBS reigned in. He seized on the fact that CBS Records' black music arm might be using drugs as payola, something that was common to most record companies. The CBS corporate board – concerned that they might lose their broadcasting licence – did what they considered to be the right thing by immediately firing the head of their record company. Using the excuse of his financial malfeasance, Clive Davis was actually marched out of his office by security guards. The whole record industry was aware that his vilification was a farce, and he was soon appointed as a consultant to Columbia Pictures, a company that at that time was not associated with CBS. Clive was the hottest record executive in the world and it was quite likely that Columbia manipulated the situation to get Larry out and Clive in.

The changes at the top of Bell made Dick Leahy reconsider his own position and I seized the opportunity to offer him a 50 per cent partnership in the new GTO Records. I had been most impressed with him. Apart from the product I supplied, and Bell's US acts, he had signed a number of good UK-based artists, most notably the hugely successful Bay City Rollers. He was passionate about records, understood the business inside out, had 'great ears' – industry shorthand for an ability to pick hits – and most importantly he had great rapport with artists. I had been flirting with him for a while about him someday joining me in starting a GTO Records division.

I told Dick that I would make a deal with a major record label to finance the company but he would have complete autonomy in the choice of artists and running of the business. This had obvious appeal to Dick, but by the same token if he chose to leave Bell, he could have walked into almost any job in the UK record business. He was a cautious man and he wanted time to consider his options. Clive Davis had asked him to fly to New York to discuss his staying on with Bell, and I wanted to see Clive to discuss the missed opportunity of bringing Gary Glitter to America.

We flew over to New York together to meet with Clive. He is a remarkable man, a couple of years older than me, and even today when most of our contemporaries are long retired from the music business or in the Rock'n'Roll Hall of Fame in the sky, he is still an active force to be reckoned with. I understood Dick well enough to not bring up his joining me, leaving him deep in thought as to what his next career move should be. Privately, I thought that he would stay with Bell. Clive Davis was a music executive legend. He loved his artists, and fought for them, as did Dick. There was no question that as soon as Clive got behind the desk, the calibre of artists that Dick would be looking after in the UK would be among the highest in the world.

The meeting that we all had was one that I particularly remember. Backed up by Dick, I complained about the fact that Bell had blown Gary Glitter's chance of making an impact in America by refusing to bring him over. Clive had signed major international artists to CBS and he was totally disinterested in what he considered to be a one-hit disco dance record performed by a strange-looking man dressed in tinfoil and a dodgy wig. He was dismissive to the point of rudeness, as he focused his attention on trying to persuade Dick to stay. Clive's ego was apparent as he explained that he was changing the company's name to Arista and would have unlimited backing to sign any artist that he wanted. He saw Dick as being a vital part of his plans to make sure that his artists were properly looked after in the UK, as well as relying on Dick to raise the standard of artists that were signed in the UK office. I felt sure that Dick would say yes to what was obviously a great opportunity. I said nothing during Clive's proposition, which was just as well because he talked to Dick as if I were not there. I was not offended. Indeed, if anything, I admired Clive's line of seduction, clearly perfected by his pitch to artists, and I took mental notes. The meeting lasted a long time. I was convinced that Dick would stay with Clive and – thinking of the pastrami sandwich I could get at the Stage Deli across 6th Avenue – I was near to excusing myself.

Clive finally sat back, a smug look on his face, and asked Dick, 'So what do you think?'

To my amazement, Dick pointed his thumb in my direction and said, 'Thanks for the offer, but I think I'll start a record company with him.' The look on Clive Davis's face was priceless. I said a cheery goodbye to the dumbstruck Clive and we left.

Clive, however, managed to do quite well without Dick, signing Aretha Franklin, Whitney Houston, Hall & Oates, Barry Manilow and many other big stars to the Arista label. Later when I asked Dick why he had turned Clive down, he said, 'He was dismissive of our artist, he was rude to you, and he fancies himself a bit too much.' So GTO Records was born. Under Dick's guidance it would be an important player in the UK business, and it deserves, and will later get, a chapter on its own.

Some time in 1977 Nicky Chinn came to see me about managing The Sweet. Nicky wrote the band's hit songs with Mike Chapman. They were also managing the band but finding it difficult to do so, possibly because of lead singer Brian Connolly's severe drink problem. Nicky was an interesting man. He came from a family that was successful in business and I felt that he did not have the pride that he should have in his own achievements. Although his songs sold millions of copies, he seemed somewhat embarrassed by their bubblegum nature. I assured him that he should not have been as he was responsible for some of the greatest glam-rock hits of the era, like 'Blockbuster'.

The Sweet were a great example of how a record can be a huge hit with a song that does not stand up on its own. There are very few, if any, cover versions of The Sweet's 'Blockbuster', which was a huge No. 1 record when it was released in 1973. The same anomaly applies to voices. Nobody would deny the value of Jagger's voice to Stones records, but neither would you hear a good song and say, 'I'd like to hear Mick Jagger singing that.'

It was not difficult to put together an extensive tour for The Sweet. I took James, my then seven-year-old son, to see them and naturally went backstage to meet the band. As we went into the dressing room, there was such a groupie fest going on, I had to spin him round and take him out.

I was also asked by Maurice Oberstein head of CBS Records, to manage Sailor. The band had had a couple of hits with 'Girls, Girls, Girls' and 'A Glass of Champagne'. 'Girls …' was particularly successful, knocking 'Bohemian Rhapsody' from No. 1 in 1976. I had met the group's leader Georg Kajanus and guitarist Phil Pickett some years earlier when I had signed them to Gem as Kajanus Pickett without getting them any success. Georg was a difficult man. CBS had brought over ex-Beach Boy Bruce Johnston to produce a new album, and early on in the recording process Bruce told me that he was giving up as he was 'too old and too rich to put up with Georg's shit.' Phil Pickett went on to write and work with Boy George, co-writing 'Karma Chameleon', one of the best-selling singles of all time worldwide. I still see Phil from time to time. Nice man.

30. GTO RECORDS – DICK LEAHY, DONNA SUMMER, BILLY OCEAN, HEATWAVE

Dick Leahy was born a year after me and was raised in Dagenham, east London – very much the town of the Ford motor company. Most of his family worked for Ford and it was expected that Dick would do the same. However, he had no wish to follow the family path. Passionate about pop music, he got a job in the A&R department of Philips Records. Dick soon established himself as having 'ears'. He was poached by Larry Uttall, who was setting up a UK office for Bell, and part of Dick's job was to look after my Gem output.

Dick was good at his job and extremely well respected within the industry. I soon had it in the back of my mind that, should I ever want to start a record company, I would want Dick to head it up. I casually planted this idea in Dick's mind when it was obvious to me that Larry Uttal was having trouble with Columbia, his parent company in New York. Dick did not react to my suggestion. He was a very contained man other than when he was talking about music, and I was content to let the thought of running a GTO record company stay with him.

I have already told you how Dick spontaneously accepted my job offer during a meeting with Clive Davis, when he turned down a very attractive job. I was aware that once it was known that Dick was leaving Bell, he would have many offers to join other companies and I had to move quickly to get him to come and join me before he changed his mind. I offered him a 50/50 deal with the promise of great autonomy. For the first time in his business life he would, to all intents and purposes, be his own boss. Dick was very happy with this proposal, but I knew I had to get the deal signed before he was seduced away by offers from the major record companies.

I used my frequent practice for getting deals concluded: get the principal and their lawyers in a room together with a secretary and have no one leave the room until the deal was agreed and signed. In this case – to make the process more seductive – I took Dick, his lawyer Tony Russell, my lawyer Martin Walford and my secretary Pat Grace to the south of France. I kept a twenty-two-foot motorboat in Cannes called *Ziggy Stardust*, courtesy of Mr Bowie. I anchored *Ziggy* in a very pleasant bay, and the five of us plus Pat's typewriter sat on the boat, enjoying the Mediterranean sunshine and some nice white wine from a chiller bag until we agreed the partnership deal and signed off the contracts. It was a happy negotiation and would prove to be a happy deal.

There was no problem in finding a major record company to finance the operation. Dick was highly rated and I had established myself as someone to do business with because of my success with Bowie, Glitter, The New Seekers and the other hits that had emanated from Gem/GTO productions. Although we were yet to sign an artist, there was competition amongst the major record companies to secure our product. Eventually we settled on Polydor Records, who financed the company through advances against royalties that we would earn from future product. We gave Polydor the rights to distribute our product throughout the world, excluding America, where their operation was not particularly successful. We decided that instead we would licence our product on an artist-by-artist basis in the US.

Although Dick was happy to be in business with me, he was very keen not to be seen as an employee running my record label. With my support, he took offices in Mayfair and had a distinctive logo designed for GTO Records. He put together a great staff, many of whom went on to have brilliant careers in the music industry after GTO was sold to CBS Records: Di Graham, my ex-secretary, ran the international division. She went on to become a top executive at CBS in Paris and then head of BMG International and eventually head of Arista Records. Paul Kinder – who was my office boy – asked if he could also move over to work for Dick. I happily approved and Paul became head of A&R. He went on to have a successful career with Virgin Records. The head of regional promotion was Edward Christie, who had started working for me as a chauffeur, then moved on to my film division to be in charge of print movement. But music was Edward's first love and I persuaded Dick to take him on.

GTO Records were in business before the EU and it was not unusual to own rights only for the UK. We were offered distribution for many artists owned by American record companies, most notably Donna Summer, the most successful artist that we licensed. When 'Love To Love You Baby' was a hit, we bought Donna a mink coat as a thank-you gift. Donna's recordings were owned worldwide by Casablanca Records. Casablanca was owned by Neil Bogart and he and I got to know each other quite well. He once told me one of the great stories of the music business: when he started Casablanca, he had no success for a long time. He had put all of his money into the band Kiss and nobody was buying their first album. He was so low that he went to the beach and walked into the sea with stones in his pocket with the intention of ending his life. He told me that he stood in the sea for hours then said to himself 'Fuck it.' He went back to his office and rented a Rolls-Royce to cheer himself up. A few weeks later Kiss suddenly took off big time, and Neil was in business. Casablanca then went on to become one of the most successful disco record companies of the time, signing the Village People as well as Donna Summer.

I almost took Neil Bogart into the film business. I had acquired the rights to make Elton John and Bernie Taupins's 'Benny and The Jets' into a film and Neil was going to finance it. As with most film projects, it did not happen – but that didn't stop us having a great time talking about setting the story on LA's Venice Beach where roller disco was the craze of the month. I tried it myself but my portly five-feet seven-inches did not feel comfortable amongst the tall, slim, blonde Californians. Tragically Neil died of cancer at the age of thirty-nine and he was much mourned by all who had known him.

GTO's first hit in 1976 was 'Only You Can' by Fox. The band's lead vocalist – British-Australian Noosha Fox – went on to make a cameo appearance in *Side By Side*, a film I produced which was directed by Bruce Beresford. It was his first film outside of his native Australia. Bruce went on to be an A-list Hollywood film director and never mentions *Side By Side* in his credits. I can understand why … it was a rubbish film!

GTO Records' most successful homegrown artists were Billy Ocean and Heatwave, both major artists in the seventies. Billy Ocean, who is still going strong, was a great coup for the label. He is the biggest-selling UK black solo artist. A great singer, and a lovely man, Billy was managed by Laurie Jay. In the 1980s when I was not doing well, I almost went into the management business with Laurie. He had lost Billy as a client but he had a nose for talent and there were a couple of his acts that I thought showed great promise. Unfortunately, Laurie was far too cavalier in his business dealings, which is probably why Billy left him, and I did not pursue a relationship. Laurie died in 2017 and I have been told that in recent years when he was struggling financially, Billy helped him out.

Heatwave were an extremely important and influential band in the UK disco/funk scene. It was Paul Kinder who brought the band to GTO Records and they were a fantastic signing. Formed in Germany by ex-American serviceman Johnnie Wilder Jr, they moved to the UK where Johnnie teamed up with Cleethorpes-born Rod Temperton. Dick signed them in 1976 and put them into the studio to be produced by Barry Blue – real name Barry Green (not much of a change!). Barry had a hit as a singer in 1973 with 'Dancin' on a Saturday Night', but was more comfortable behind a sound desk than in a TV studio. Barry produced a string of hits for Heatwave but much of the band's success was due to Rod's writing and their dynamic stage act.

Johnnie Wilder was an incredible performer and always brought the audience to their dancing feet. His performance was almost acrobatic. His career took a different turn after a tragic car accident left him paralysed from the neck down. A true musician, although no longer a dancer, he carried on for many years and became a successful gospel artist. He died in his sleep in 2006.

The band had already suffered a dramatic loss when guitarist Jesse Whitten was killed in a stabbing incident in 1978 and the band's Swiss bass player Mario Mantese was also stabbed after a party at Elton John's house. He was left in a coma and became blind, paralysed and mute but miraculously recovered his health and has gone on to write about his near-death experiences. Even by the standards of rock'n'roll, Heatwave certainly had more than their fair share of tragedy, but they left a great legacy with their music. Rod Temperton, of course, went on to be a major songwriter – most famously writing 'Thriller' for Michael Jackson.

GTO Records had thirty-seven hit singles and fifteen hit albums in the four years before we sold the company to CBS (now Sony Records) in 1978. Dick Asher, the American head of CBS UK, had asked me a few times if GTO Records was for sale. Although we had an important roster of artists, Dick's main reason for wanting to buy GTO Records was a desire for Dick Leahy to run CBS in the UK. I really wanted to make the sale because in my opinion the price bandied around very much reflected the anticipation of Dick's services as head of CBS. For me it was an easy 'Yes' but as part of the deal Dick would be obliged to enter into a long-term service agreement to run GTO as part of the CBS group, in the hope that he would soon take over the running of CBS UK. Once again, I did not pressure

Dick into selling. He knew of CBS's interest and I just bided my time, whilst reminding Dick that a big cheque was only a phone call away.

One memorable day, when Dick and I were in LA, we were invited to a pool party at a large Norma Desmond-style mansion that was for sale on – where else? – Sunset Boulevard. I was shown around and it was really incredible. A hallway that looked as big as the Albert Hall, and countless rooms. The standout memory was the huge ballroom. At one end there was a wall, which at the touch of a secret switch opened to reveal a speak-easy-type room where, in the days of prohibition, there would have been a bar stocked with illicit booze. A door in this room opened to a blocked-off tunnel which led to the neighbouring estate. Apparently there was a network of these tunnels between all of the estates on Sunset which guests could use to escape from any police raid.

It was a typical LA party, scattered with tall, tanned California blonds both male and female. There was a bar next to the pool, dispensing chilled white wine and champagne. As we lounged – or frolicked may be a better word – in the pool, by anyone's standards, it was better than being in Dagenham, Dick's home town.

Dick, his face in the sun, said, 'I could get used to this, Laurence.'

'It's a phone call away,' I reminded him.

'Make the call.'

And so I did. A few weeks later, Dick, Tony Russell and I were ensconced in a large suite at a Park Lane hotel, along with Dick Asher, his business affairs team and a secretary. It was a

Laurence Myers-style meeting with everyone agreeing not to leave until the deal was done. Proceedings started at about 10 a.m. Negotiations went smoothly but by one o'clock there was still one huge sticking point, which was something to do with Heatwave. I cannot remember exactly what it was but Dick Asher said that it was a deal-breaker. Some two hours later, Dick Asher conceded and the deal was finally completed on our terms, and here is why ...

It was a Friday, which is most important to my story. As with many of us, the person Dick was most fearful of upsetting was his wife. Dick's wife Sheila was quite a formidable character, and Dick had mentioned to me that he had to catch an early-evening flight to be back in New York so that he could attend Sheila's nephew's bar mitzvah the next day. When we reached the impasse, I declined to order lunch and said that I needed to speak with Dick Leahy and Tony about it privately. We retired to our room where I told Dick and Tony that we should talk about football or anything else to kill some time. After about an hour, the CBS lawyer put his head round the door and asked if we were making progress. 'Sadly not,' I replied. Half an hour later we went back in and I told Dick Asher that regretfully, we could not agree. Asher, desperate not to miss his plane, threw up his hands and conceded the point. The secretary deleted the contentious clause and we all signed off on the paperwork. Asher dashed off to get his plane and we all ordered room service on CBS's room charge.

Part of the deal obliged Dick Leahy to work for CBS as head of GTO, but there was no legal obligation for Dick to take over the running of CBS UK. And, in spite of Dick Asher's entreaties, Dick did not move over to CBS. He was not being difficult but, having had an inside taste of the politics in a big record company, he did not want to be part of it.

After Dick left CBS he went into the publishing business with Bryan Morrison, signing George Michael as a songwriter. This was in the eighties. I was not doing well and considering setting up a new company with my ex-employee David Mintz. Wham! did not have a manager and I asked Dick to arrange a meeting with them to pitch for the job. Dick sent Andrew Ridgeley to meet us. Without George Michael, I knew it was just an empty gesture, but nevertheless I appreciated the respect that he showed me in setting up the meeting. When Wham! stopped and George went on to have his brilliant solo career, Dick virtually managed him for some years. As I mentioned earlier when writing about Freddy Bienstock, he asked me to help with negotiations for a new administrator of George's catalogue, which was very flattering. Dick was a brilliant partner for me. He used to call me when I was on holiday to tell me that all was going well and there was nothing to worry about. He has retired to Spain and I wish him well.

A word about singers who are precious about their voice. Lots of singers will not record in the morning because their vocal chords have yet to wake up. Others insist on days off on tour to rest their voice. In 1987 the phenomenal Tom Jones made a record from me called 'A Boy From Nowhere'. It went to UK No. 2, his highest entry for seventeen years. Tom was doing a UK tour when the song started racing up the charts. The tour was so tight that there seemed to be no gap for Tom to record the desperately needed promotional video. Without any fuss, Tom walked off stage after his Manchester gig, went straight to the studio and recorded the song to camera in a couple of takes at about two o'clock in the morning. The next day he performed on stage at his next scheduled date. You can see Tom perform the song on YouTube, and you should. I believe that he is the greatest male singer the UK has ever produced and on 'A Boy From Nowhere' he is at his balladic best.

The song, produced by Mike Leander, was written by Mike and Eddie Seago for a stage musical called *Matador*, which I later produced on the West End stage, casting the young John Barrowman in the title role. John sang the song beautifully on stage, but he is the first to admit that Tom's version was hard to follow. Mike stuck with his old friend and writing partner, Eddie, to write the lyrics for *Matador*. Eddie had never written for theatre, his lyrics were poor and I begged Mike to drop him and let me bring in the highly acclaimed theatre lyricist Don Black, but, ever loyal, Mike would not. The reviews of the show were unkind, some particularly critical of Eddie's lyrics and I believe that the show might have had real success had Don been brought in.

Show business – everything about it is appealing.

31. GEM RECORDS – MY SWAN SONG IN THE RECORD BUSINESS

In 1979, after the sale of GTO Records to CBS, I was approached by Bob Summer – the worldwide head of RCA Records – to start a new record company to be distributed by RCA. He had once offered me the job of head of RCA UK but I had declined on the basis that it did not pay particularly well, so obviously he thought well of me. I decided to use the Gem name for the new company because it had been so lucky for me as a production company recording Bowie, Glitter and others.

I made a three-year deal under which RCA would – unusually – provide us with our overhead expenses budget as well as a generous budget for recording artists. Under my Gem deal with Bell Records I got paid a sum of money on delivery of each record. After recording costs there was little left over for overheads and the deal only worked for me because we started having hits from day one. I managed to negotiate the great deal based on my theory that record company executives were mainly concerned about the impact of a bad deal during their own tenure. With that in mind, I offered RCA an interest in the

Gem artists for ten years after the deal ended, thus enabling Bob to carry forward any loss by RCA to a time when it was reasonable to assume that he would be long gone. It was a risky deal for RCA because – with the overheads covered – there was no pressure to make profits to survive. They quite reasonably insisted that they approved any artist that we signed, and I was contractually bound to fly to New York on a regular basis to present artists to Bob for his approval. Such was the profligacy of the business at that time, I got him to agree that RCA would pay for me to fly over on Concorde, the new supersonic jet service run by BA. The fares were exorbitant, but it only took three and a half hours to New York and with the five-hour time difference, you actually arrived before you left.

At the time I had David Simone working for me as an in-house lawyer. He had been introduced to me by my brother-in-law Larry Levene. He was twenty-six years old, and was very much into the music business. He had been social secretary at his university, booking big bands. I appointed David as head of the new Gem Records. David put together a good team. He brought back ex-GTO Records employee Edward Christie as head of A&R; Clifford Gee was head of marketing; Golly Gallagher was head of promotions. Although Gem did not do well, all of these guys were talented and went on to have success within the industry. When I knew that Gem was coming to an end I encouraged David take a job as head of business affairs at Arista, where he was soon moved up to be MD. He was then head of Phonogram before moving to be chairman of MCA. He went to the USA to start UNI Records for MCA, then joined Geffen Records where he was head of A&R. He is currently a very successful manager living and working in New York and remains a close friend.

Edward Christie started Abstract Records, an independent record label dealing with the heaviest of heavy metal bands and Abstract Distribution in the States. Both companies did extremely well. He sold his interests in 2017. He lives in London with his wife Yvonne – also a clever person – who, through her glamour model agency, started the *Sun*'s Page 3 girls in 1970.

After leaving Gem, Golly did very well as an independent record plugger until he was exposed on TV for hyping records up the charts by buying multiple copies of singles. He bought from independent record retailers who reported their sales to the compilers of the singles charts. He would give the singles back to the shop owner or manager, who could then resell them and keep the cash.

Gem Records' biggest hit single was 'Born To Be Alive' by Spanish/French artist Patrick Hernandez, which made UK No. 10. We picked it up for the UK at Marsha's insistence after she and I heard it being played at Whisky À Gogo at Midem in Cannes. Claude Pellerin, a Frenchman who owned the record world, had cleverly arranged to have it played in the club, in the hope that it would help him sell it internationally – and it worked. David and Edward were not excited to put the record out as it was a Gary Glitter soundalike. Musical tastes were diversifying and moving away from the domination of wide-appeal artists that had given me success in the past. David and Edward were quite rightly looking to have Gem perceived as a record company for the future and when I insisted that we released 'Born To Be Alive', they considered it a step backwards.

When it started rapidly climbing up the charts, they forgave me. A Top 10 record is something to be proud of, but I had been so spoiled by the many No. 1s of so many previous records, that I, personally, could not get too excited.

I secured the right to release the soundtrack of *The Wanderers* – a GTO film crammed with great sixties hits. It made the album charts. After the Gem deal, I licensed it to third parties and it was a consistent seller for another twenty years or so, eventually recouping the loss I made on the film.

Looking to the future, David and Edward were impressed by Trevor Horn, a multi-instrumentalist/producer whom they signed with his band Garbo. Garbo was not a success for us, but they were right about Trevor. He called his next band The Buggles and had an instant No. 1 with 'Video Killed the Radio Star' through Island Records. Trevor also masterminded the promo video for the song, which was the first clip to be played on MTV. He went on to be one of the most important producers of the eighties.

Again, moving away from my comfort zone, we signed Samson, a stereotypically shock-rock heavy metal band put together by Paul Samson. The band's drummer, Thunderstick, wore an evil-looking leather mask over his face and played in a cage on stage. The lead singer was Bruce Dickinson, widely acclaimed as a great artist in heavy metal. We made an album called *Head On* with Samson. It briefly made the charts but was not a big seller. The band were fighting with their management, always a problem for the caught-in-the-middle record company. In all honesty our promotion department's DNA was more mainstream pop, so we did not really know how to help them.

We were contacted by Sanctuary Records, a successful company that had signed top heavy metal band Iron Maiden and desperately wanted Bruce Dickinson to take over in the band as lead singer. As a condition of releasing Bruce, David sold the Gem album to Sanctuary for more than its cost: a brilliant deal.

Gem had a couple of other minor hits but the most successful signing was the UK Subs, a punk band signed to Gem by Edward. I commissioned quirky director Julien Temple, young and up-and-coming – to make a short film about them to release as support to the main feature that my GTO Films then had on general release. The film *Punk Can Take It* was a very clever parody of wartime newsreel, portraying the punk movement as under attack from conventional society. John Snagg, a still recognisable voice of wartime news reporting, did the stylised commentary. Julien is now a respected maker of off-beat movies, and he directed *Habaneros*, a brilliant documentary on Cuba. It being a small world, the film was produced by Richard Conway, the son of great friends of ours.

UK Subs were important to Gem Records, giving us half a dozen Top 50 hits, but I had no sense of connection to them or to their music. As I have frequently mentioned before, I had a passion for songwriters. Whilst none of my writers could, or even tried to, compete with the lyrics of Cole Porter or Johnny Mercer, they wrote clever lyrics, contemporary to the day. The UK Subs' songs had lyrics like: 'Tomorrow's girl is pissing in your ear.' I rest my case. It was a UK Subs gig that decided me that it was time to go. Marsha had already opted out of the role of Manager's Dutiful Wife. In ten years of tirelessly supporting me in my work, she had developed her own career as a very successful antique dealer and was tired of schlepping to gigs. A couple of months earlier, we had gone to see Heatwave perform a sold-out concert at what was then the Hammersmith Odeon (currently the Eventim Apollo). The band's charismatic frontman Johnnie Wilder Jr – arms up, stabbing the air, was chanting 'Ooh, ooh,' to the driving beat of Rod Temperton's 'Boogie Nights'. I was up there 'Ooh-oohing' with the best of them. The packed audience leapt to their feet to join in – except one person. I looked down and there was Marsha, sitting unmoved.

I indicated with my head that she should jump up and join in the fun.

Nothing.

More 'ooh-ooing' and emphatic head-messaging from me for Marsha to jump up and have an 'ooh, ooh'. Still nothing.

On stage, Johnny worked up a sweat. The audience worked up a sweat too, particularly ripe when outstretched arms exposed sweaty armpits. As the song ended, Marsha used her head to indicate that I was to sit down next to her, which I did. She leaned over and whispered in my ear. 'Enough with the ooh-oohing. Next time take me to see Streisand.'

Then it was my time to opt out. The Subs were playing a sold-out gig at a regular punk venue and, having never seen them perform, I decided to go and enjoy their success. Picture, if you can, a seedy venue in a seedy part of north London. An audience of punks are there, many with spiky mohican hair, their pierced faces, ears (and no doubt other parts unseen) decorated with metal skulls, chains and other ornamentation that is mysterious to me. Charlie Harper, the UK Subs' charismatic leader, is on stage sneering 'Stranglehold' – one of their hits – to his adoring fans.

At Charlie's feet, in the mosh pit, more punks are body-slam-
ming each other as they pogo up and down. They show their
further appreciation by spraying family-size globules of spit over
the band, making pretty rainbow effects in the stage lighting. I, a
rictus smile on my face, am trying to pretend that I am enjoying
the show. Next to me is an unsmiling punk, his punk lady-friend
next to him, his doppelganger apart from her metal-studded
leather-clad boobs. Some of the audience are 'weekend punks',
their mohicans artfully slicked back for their day job in a bank,
but these two are the real thing.

Mr Punk, his eyes fixed on Charlie Harper, is slurping a pint
of beer, his head nodding viciously in time to the ear-bashing
mono-melody coming from the stage. Without warning, he
pukes voluminously down his punk, black leather jacket. The
vomit glides from the jacket, explodes over his punk standard
issue Doc Martens, splattering vomit on to my Gucci loafers. But
here's the killer. Mr Punk does not move. He does not acknowledge any dilemma. He does not apologise. He just carries on
drinking his beer and nodding in time to the music. My own
instinct to move away is hampered by the carpet, so filthy that
my sick-patterned Gucci shoes are sticking to it.

I should not mock punk. Charlie Harper, with an ever-changing line-up of musicians, still works. His fans, some still in
uniform, are loyal. He still sells some records and makes a
modest contribution to my catalogue.

Pioneered by my old house guest Iggy Pop, punk was part
of a social movement arising out of the anger of the disenfran-
chised youth around the world. It was a genuine influence on the
music of the day. It also influenced fashion, and the 'punk look'

frequently reappears on catwalks even to this day. Unlike the sometimes physical warfare between mods and rockers in the sixties, punks did not go out on a Saturday night looking for a fight. The fact that I have chosen to mock punk behaviour that particular Saturday night at the Camden Palace I think reflects badly on me, but reinforces that I just didn't 'get it' as I didn't 'get' heavy metal. The music did not drive mainstream rock and pop out of the market but I took my antipathy to these genres as a warning sign. Music-business executives who made their judgements based on public trends, irrespective of their personal taste, could thrive in the music business as they got older. My success in the music business came because my musical taste coincided with much of the record-buying public. Clearly the times, they were a-changin'. Rap did not start to evolve until the nineties but – had I carried on – I would have felt completely redundant.

My deal with RCA was coming to an end. I was forty-two, had lost my enthusiasm for the business and I decided there and then, in my vomit-splattered Gucci shoes, that I had reached my sell-by date. It was time for me to say 'Thank you and goodbye' to the music business.

My journey had not been without its highlights. Some artists would not have had the careers that they did without my influence. My thumbprint was on records that had sold more millions than I can count. My reputation was still such that I could call anybody in the business to get an immediate 'No' which, if you think about it, is almost as good as a 'Yes'. The reluctance of people at the top to muck you about is, I believe, a mark of your stature in any business and I felt that I was quitting when I was just about ahead.

I can't believe that it was fifty years – a *half a century* – ago that I worked with the Rolling Stones, David Bowie, The Beatles and record-makers Mickie Most, Mike Leander and Tony Macaulay. There were many other talented people who I worked with on both sides of the microphone who also put my kids through private school.

I earned a lot of money in the music business and lost a lot in the film business, with no regrets. I would possibly have done as well or even better had I stayed in my previous career, as an accountant, but I was never in music for the money. I loved what I did. I mixed with talented, exciting, vibrant people at a time in the development of popular music when London was the place to be. To some extent, we were all riding on the crest of the British Invasion that was taking over the American music charts. Part of this was because some of the most successful British bands were in fact playing music 'borrowed' from black American artists. Middle America's moms, who did not like the idea of a poster of Chuck Berry, Muddy Waters – or even the overtly sexy Elvis – on their daughters' bedroom wall, happily drove their kids to see those cute English boys with their cute haircuts and cute English accents. Those moms even liked the Rolling Stones I think because, in the privacy of their own bedrooms, they fancied Mick.

Over the past fifty years, other than mankind's determination to continue to kill each other over religious differences, the world has changed. Technology has changed the music-buying habits of the young. Fifty years ago, young people listened to their music in the privacy of their bedrooms on inferior record players. Homes had one telephone line, and mum and dad rationed teenage use. There were very few hours of TV with youth appeal and, as often as they could, teenagers disappeared from their homes to meet their friends, passing their younger siblings playing happily in the street. Kids did not get routinely mugged, stabbed or abused, and, generally speaking, their parents were rightly not concerned for their offspring's safety, even without the invisible umbilical cord of the yet-to-be-invented mobile phone.

Music is now bought – or more often pirated – and downloaded onto mobile phones and many devices called 'I' something that I would just as soon never have to learn about. You can ask your little box called Alexa to play any song that has ever been recorded, without even saying 'Please', and she will oblige. There are no record stores where kids can gather on a Saturday morning to listen to the latest hits before they buy. Kids now 'gather' on social media sites and establish firm friendships with other kids that they have never met.

In previous generations, popular music was recorded using big bands or orchestras. Many homes in the sixties still had a piano in the parlour, but it was a difficult instrument to learn, and money had to be found for lessons. You only needed a cheap guitar to play rock'n'roll and three easy-to-learn chords gave kids an extensive repertoire. I even learned them myself, taught by Mickie Most.

All over the UK, groups were formed, collars were turned up à la Presley, and the sales of Brylcreem rocketed. Thousands of kids dreamed of making their living playing music, and although most didn't, some did. Two kids called John and Paul did rather well and changed the way that the world viewed youth.

The 2i's basement cellar, where so many UK artists started their careers, has long gone, but if it were still there, like many of the pubs that used to book bands, it would now be hosting stand-up comedy, the new rock'n'roll.

The legendary Woodstock festival put on at a farm in the Catskill Mountains in 1969 was pretty much a one-off at the time. Following the example of Mr Eavis, who started the Glastonbury festival on his farm in Somerset the following year, half the farms in the UK seem now to be putting on festivals. Music fans are very well entertained at these mega-concerts by great shows, which the majority of the tens of thousands attending watch on giant screens. I am not at all critical of this. The fans have a great time and there are very few stars who do not play these events. Interestingly, most of the top attractions at these events are well-established names who have been performing live for some years.

Pop stars are now fast-tracked to fame by reality shows. Some contestants will last but most will fail, not having learned their trade schlepping around the country to badly paid gigs, crammed into a Ford Transit van. Apart from jealousy that I have no financial interest in these programmes (something that I have touched on before), the reason I particularly dislike them is that the audiences allow themselves to be manipulated to scream with delight when a contestant reaches a high note or, in some cases, any note at all. The people who vote from home are often influenced by the contestant's 'back story' – the more emotionally upsetting the better when it comes to getting votes. The owners of the shows sign every artist who might prove to be popular – as would I in their position – but I believe that these shows are bad for the business. They are unfair competition for artists who are striving for success the hard way, working for years to try to capture a following.

The major record companies, Universal, Sony and Warner Music, control about 80 per cent of the music sold in the world. Also, in my view, a bad thing. Artists can, and do, bypass the establishment and find success, but it is rare. Do I sound like an out-of-touch grumpy old man? I hope so, I worked hard for the right to be one.

I loved my time in the music business. Many years ago, Andrew Oldham adopted the slogan 'Happy to be part of the industry of human happiness' for Immediate Records. On reflection, it was a very corny sentiment but – for me – it was true. Music does bring happiness, especially when it makes you want to get up and dance. It is an integral part of our memories and, like me, I am sure that you identify certain times and events in your life with certain songs. I still get a kick out of hearing a song on the radio that might never have been exposed to the public without my involvement and, although I no longer get up and dance as well as I used to, there is definitely still a twitch in my legs.

ACKNOWLEDGEMENTS

Thank you to my family and friends, who have encouraged me to write this book for many years (probably to stop me telling them a story that I have told them many times before…)

For help with turning my sometimes hazy recollections into something tangible, I'd like to thank Clare Lockhart for her research, editing and general encouragement.

For giving their time and generously allowing me to plunder their own material, I'd like to thank and acknowledge Kevin Cann (*Any Day Now: David Bowie The London Years 1947–1974*); Peter and Leni Gillman (*Alias David Bowie*); Fred Goodman (*Allen Klein: The Man Who Bailed Out the Beatles, Made the Stones, and Transformed Rock & Roll*); and Tony Zanetta (*Stardust: The David Bowie Story*, written with Henry Edwards).

For sharing their memories with me and reminding me what a blast we had, I'd like to thank Angie Bowie, Eileen Bradley (former V.P. GTO Inc); Jon Brewer (film-maker and former Gem employee); Dana Gillespie (former Gem artist and close friend of David Bowie); Don Hunter (former Gem employee who brought in Stevie Wonder); Penny Leander (my dear departed friend Mike Leander's wife); and Anya Wilson (former Gem record plugger).

For their help with getting this book published, I'd like to thank my copyeditor Lucian Randall, John Bond and George Edgeller at whitefox Publishing, and Simon Levy who designed the cover.

I am indebted to you all...

INDEX